THE GOOD
THE NORTH
OF ENGLAND

Edited by

Alisdair Aird and Fiona Stapley

Managing Editor: Karen Fick

Associate Editor: Patrick Stapley

Editorial Assistance: Fiona Wright

EBURY PRESS

Please send reports on pubs to:

The Good Pub Guide
FREEPOST TN1569
Wadhurst
East Sussex
TN5 7BR

or feedback@goodguides.com

or visit our website:
www.thegoodpubguide.co.uk

This updated edition published in 2012 by Ebury Press, an imprint of Ebury Publishing

Material first published by Ebury Press in 2011

A Random House Group Company

The Random House Group Limited Reg. No. 954009

Addresses for companies within the Random House Group can be found at
www.randomhouse.co.uk

A CIP catalogue record for this book is available from the British Library

The Random House Group Limited supports The Forest Stewardship
Council (FSC®), the leading international forest certification organisation.
Our books carrying the FSC label are printed on FSC® certified paper. FSC
is the only forest certification scheme endorsed by the leading
environmental organisations, including Greenpeace. Our paper
procurement policy can be found at www.randomhouse.co.uk/environment

FSC
www.fsc.org
MIX
Paper from
responsible sources
FSC® C016897

To buy books by your favourite authors and register for offers visit
www.randomhouse.co.uk

Printed and bound in the UK by CPI Group (UK) Ltd, Croydon, CR0 4YY

ISBN 9780091949617

Contents

Editors' Acknowledgements   4

Introduction   5
What is a Good Pub?   7
Using the *Guide*   9

Top Pubs   15
Editors' Favourites   15
The North East & Yorkshire   18
The North West   51

Also Worth a Visit   96
The North East   96
Yorkshire   113
Cheshire   159
Cumbria   168
Greater Manchester, Lancashire & Merseyside   181

Pubs Near Motorway Junctions   206
Pubs Serving Food All Day   206

Maps   207
Report Forms   215

Editors'
Acknowledgements

We could not produce the *Guide* without the huge help we have from the many thousands of readers who report to us on the pubs they visit, often in great detail. Particular thanks to these greatly valued correspondents: Paul Humphreys, Phil and Jane Hodson, Chris and Angela Buckell, George Atkinson, Jeremy King, the Didler, Michael and Jenny Back, Tony and Wendy Hobden, Guy Vowles, N R White, LM, Phil Bryant, Alan and Eve Harding, Michael Doswell, Dennis Jenkin, Brian and Anna Marsden, Martin and Karen Wake, Michael Dandy, Gordon and Margaret Ormondroyd, John Wooll, Tracey and Stephen Groves, Ian Phillips, Ann and Colin Hunt, Joan and Michel Hooper-Immins, Roger and Donna Huggins, Phyl and Jack Street, Clive and Fran Dutson, Gerry and Rosemary Dobson, Simon and Mandy King, Martin and Pauline Jennings, Val and Alan Green, Michael Butler, Dennis Jones, Andy and Claire Barker, Pat and Tony Martin, Terry Buckland, Susan and John Douglas, David Jackman, Tony Hobden, Edward Mirzoeff, Reg Fowle, Helen Rickwood, Peter Meister, Ed and Anna Fraser, Steve Whalley, Barbarrick, Brian and Janet Ainscough, Ian Herdman, Sara Fulton and Roger Baker, Brian Glozier, John Beeken, Richard Tilbrook, David and Sue Smith, J F M and M West, Dave Braisted, Sue and Mike Todd, GSB, B and M Kendall, John Prescott, JJW, CMW, Chris Flynn, Wendy Jones, Mike Gorton, Mike and Eleanor Anderson, Mike and Mary Carter, Richard and Jean Green, John and Eleanor Holdsworth, Roy Hoing, Sheila Topham, Mrs Margo Finlay and Jörg Kasprowski, M G Hart, R K Phillips, Derek and Sylvia Stephenson, Dr and Mrs C W Thomas, Peter F Marshall, Comus and Sarah Elliott, Ian Malone, Andy and Jill Kassube, Rob and Catherine Dunster, John Pritchard, Mrs Susan Brooke, MLR, Barry and Anne, Dr and Mrs A K Clarke, Ryta Lyndley, Tony and Maggie Harwood, Dr Kevan Tucker, Tony and Jill Radnor, Christian Mole, Simon Collett-Jones, Les and Sandra Brown, Dr J Barrie Jones, Martin and Judith Tomlinson, Neil and Anita Christopher, Canon Michael Bourdeaux, Terry and Nickie Williams, Ross Balaam, Pete Flower, Hunter and Christine Wright, John and Helen Rushton, Bob and Margaret Holder, R T and J C Moggridge, Mr and Mrs P R Thomas, Giles and Annie Francis, David M Smith, Anthony Longden, Peter Crozier, Phil and Sally Gorton, Paul Rampton, Julie Harding, Chris Johnson, Tony and Gill Powell, Roger and Lesley Everett, Colin and Louise English, John and Gloria Isaacs, MP, R C Vincent, Mike Proctor, R L Borthwick, Martin Smith, Jim and Frances Gowers, Roger and Marion Brown, Margaret Dickinson, Theocsbrian, Conor McGaughey, Taff Thomas, Tim Maddison, Chris and Jeanne Downing, JCW, John Saville, Di and Mike Gillam, Nick Lawless, C and R Bromage, Charles and Pauline Stride, Ewan Shearer, Ian Barker, D and M T Ayres-Regan, Richard Fendick, Roger and Kathy Elkin, KC, MDN, Tim and Sue Halstead, Denys Gueroult, John and Joan Nash, Sue Rowland, David Lamb, Neil Kellett, Tim and Ann Newell, Bill Adie, Bruce and Sharon Eden, Stanley and Annie Matthews, Robert Lester, Andrew and Ruth Triggs, Mark, Amanda, Luke and Jake Sheard, Steven King and Barbara Cameron, Chris Evans, Ian and Helen Stafford, Robert Watt, Meg and Colin Hamilton, John and Sylvia Harrop, David Crook, Ann and Tony Bennett-Hughes, Lucien Perring and David and Gill Carrington.

Warm thanks, too, to John Holliday of Trade Wind Technology, who built and looks after our database.

Alisdair Aird and Fiona Stapley

Introduction

In this book we have combined the areas of the North East and North West of England, to create a concise guide to these much-loved and visited parts of Britain. The chapters include pubs from the vibrant cities within these counties, as well as rural ones that are to be found amongst dramatic and often idyllic countryside.

The pubs in the northern counties also boast some of the lowest prices in the country, with beer on average costing 30p a pint less than the most expensive region – London and the South East. Each county has its own unique countryside, architectural gems, as well as speciality ales, and each and every pub featured in this book also comes recommended by contented visitors.

In the North West, Manchester and Liverpool, the two great cities of Lancashire, combine grand Victorian cityscapes and striking visitor-friendly modern developments – and both have a good deal of character. The seaside resorts here have a vibrant atmosphere in season but when the long stretches of beach and dune are empty, they have a lonely charm for walkers, and the treacherous tidal sands of Morecambe Bay continue to fascinate. And the countryside is glorious with magnificent moorland and country parks. Pubs in Lancashire tend to be very good value – both for beer and for food – and publicans support the region's top-quality farm produce that they use in the strongly regional dishes.

Some of Britain's finest scenery can be found in the north-western county of Cumbria, and as the National Trust control over a quarter of the land, it means the preservation of and access to the countryside is first class. You could stay here for weeks every year of your life and never walk the same path twice – and many pubs with bedrooms have walks straight from the door. The most beautiful scenery is concentrated around the central area, especially around the towns of Ambleside and Windermere but each lake has its own character and varied landscape. Real ales and good, hearty food have always mattered to pubs here and quite a few places now brew their own beers. A roaring fire for damp walkers and meals that make the most of the top-class local produce (fell-bred lamb, Cumberland sausages and fantastic cheeses) are paramount.

Over in the North East, lively Newcastle and beautiful Durham are two of Northumbria's most popular cities. Both are loved by visitors and have lots to see and do by day or night. The visible history in the area is second to none with the awesome 73 ½ –mile, 2,000-year-old Hadrian's Wall and the Roman forts, museums and visitor centres along the way (Segedunum and Vindolanda are the best). The abundance of fine castles is pretty impressive and there are haunting ruins, extraordinary houses and gardens, a majestic coastline and stunning beaches, great sweeps of largely unspoilt upland scenery contrasting with lower landscapes and plenty of unhurried market towns. The pubs here are particularly supportive of the local breweries with their interesting beers and the food makes the best use of the wonderful fresh fish and seafood, local game and fine lamb and beef.

Just south of Durham lies Yorkshire with its many attractions: first-class walking country in magnificent landscape, appealing villages, colourful market towns, civilised and vibrant cities, preserved castles, venerable houses with lovely gardens and fantastic museums. And some of the very best pubs are almost on their doorsteps. We've always been struck by friendliness and the warmth of the welcome from the landlords and landladies in this area – and this applies to all their customers whether they are regulars or visitors passing through; it's just a natural Yorkshire trait. It's the diversity of these pubs, too, that is so appealing with places that range from simple moorland locals through bustling and lively city taverns to civilised gastro pubs and on to smart hotels with informal little bars of some character and comfortable bedrooms. It's not a surprise then that many of our national favourites are to be found in this special part of the country.

What is a Good Pub?

The entries for top pubs featured in this *Guide* have been through a two-stage sifting process. First of all, some 2,000 regular correspondents keep in touch with us about the pubs they visit, and double that number report occasionally. We also get a flow of reports sent to us at **feedback@goodguides.com**. This keeps us up-to-date about pubs included in previous editions – it's their alarm signals that warn us when a pub's standards have dropped (after a change of management, say), and it's their continuing approval that reassures us about keeping a featured top pub for another year. Very important, though, are the reports they send us on pubs we don't know at all. It's from these new discoveries that we make up a shortlist, to be considered for possible inclusion as new top pubs. The more people who report favourably on a new pub, the more likely it is to win a place on this shortlist – especially if some of the reporters belong to our hard core of about 600 trusted correspondents on whose judgement we have learned to rely. These are people who have each given us detailed comments on dozens of pubs, and shown that (when we ourselves know some of those pubs, too) their judgement is closely in line with our own.

This brings us to the acid test. Each pub, before inclusion as a featured top pub, is inspected anonymously by one of the editorial team. They have to find some special quality that would make strangers enjoy visiting it. What often marks the pub out for special attention is good value food (and that might mean anything from a well made sandwich, with good fresh ingredients at a low price, to imaginative cooking outclassing most restaurants in the area). The drinks may be out of the ordinary – maybe several hundred whiskies, remarkable wine lists, interesting ciders, or a wide range of well kept real ales possibly with some home-brewed or bottled beers from all over the world. Perhaps there's a special appeal about it as a place to stay, with good bedrooms and obliging service. Maybe it's the building itself (from centuries-old parts of monasteries to extravagant Victorian gin-palaces), or its surroundings (lovely countryside, attractive waterside, extensive well kept garden), or what's in it (charming furnishings, extraordinary collections of bric-a-brac).

Above all, though, what makes the good pub is its atmosphere – you should be able to feel at home there, and feel not just that *you're* glad you've come but that *they're* glad you've come. A good landlord or landlady makes a huge difference here – they can make or break a pub.

It follows from this that a great many ordinary locals, perfectly good in their own right, don't earn a place in the *Guide*. What makes them attractive to their regular customers (an almost clubby chumminess) may even make strangers feel rather out-of-place.

Another important point is that there's not necessarily any link between charm and luxury. A basic unspoilt village tavern, with hard seats and a flagstoned floor, may be worth travelling miles to find, while a deluxe pub-restaurant may not be worth crossing the street for.

This year, for the first time, we have asked the top pubs featured with full entries to pay a fee. This is a necessary change without which we could not cover our research and production costs, because of the way people are now using the *Guide* – with fewer buying the printed version, and more using the Internet version or the iPhone app. However, selection of the pubs for inclusion remains exactly as before. No pub can gain an entry simply by paying a fee. Only pubs which have been inspected anonymously, approved and then invited to join are included.

Using the *Guide*

THE REGIONS
We have divided this Guide into two main regions: the North East and Yorkshire, including Cleveland, County Durham, Northumberland, Tyne and Wear and, of course, Yorkshire, and the North West: Cheshire, Cumbria, Greater Manchester, Lancashire and Merseyside. The featured top pubs are listed in alphabetical order of their town or village. Other pubs worth knowing in the region are then listed county by county.

The county boundaries we use are those for the administrative counties (not the old traditional counties, which were changed back in 1976).

We list pubs in their true county, not their postal county. Occasionally, when the village itself is in one county but the pub is just over the border in the next-door county, we have used the village county, not the pub one.

STARS ★
Really outstanding pubs are awarded a star, and in a few cases two stars: these are the aristocrats among pubs. The stars do NOT signify extra luxury or specially good food – in fact, some of the pubs which appeal most distinctively and strongly of all are decidedly basic in terms of food and surroundings. The detailed description of each pub reveals its particular appeal, and this is what the stars refer to.

FOOD AWARD ⑪
Pubs where food is quite outstanding.

STAY AWARD ⇐
Pubs that are good as places to stay at (obviously you can't expect the same level of luxury at £60 a head as you'd get for £100 a head). Pubs with bedrooms are marked on the maps at the back of the book as a dot within a square.

WINE AWARD ♀
Pubs with particularly enjoyable wines by the glass – often a good choice.

BEER AWARD ◖
Pubs where the quality of the beer is quite exceptional, or pubs which keep a particularly interesting range of beers in good condition.

VALUE AWARD £
This distinguishes pubs that offer really good value food. In all the award-winning pubs, you will find an interesting choice at under £10.

RECOMMENDERS
At the end of each featured pub, we include the names of readers who have recently recommended that pub (unless they've asked us not to).

Important note: the description of the pub and the comments on it are our own and not the recommenders'; they are based on our own personal inspections and on later verification of facts with each pub.

OTHER GOOD PUBS
The second part of each regional chapter is a county-by-county descriptive listing of the other pubs that we know are worth a visit – many of them, indeed, are as good as the featured top pubs (these are identified with a star). We have inspected and

approved nearly half of these ourselves. All the others are recommended by our trusted reader-reporters. The descriptions of these other pubs, written by us, usually reflect the experience of several different people, and sometimes dozens.

It is these other good pubs which may become featured top pub entries in future editions. So do please help us know which are hot prospects for our inspection programme (and which are not!) by reporting on them. There are report forms at the back of the *Guide*, or you can email us at **feedback@goodguides.com**, or write to us at The Good Pub Guide, FREEPOST TN1569, Wadhurst, East Sussex TN5 7BR.

LOCATING PUBS

To help readers who use digital mapping systems we include a **postcode** for every pub (at the end of the directions for the top pubs and on the right for other pubs).

Pubs outside London are given a British Grid four-figure **map reference**. Where a pub is exceptionally difficult to find, we include a six-figure reference in the directions. The map number (featured top entries only) refers to the map at the back of the *Guide*.

PRICES AND OTHER FACTUAL DETAILS

The *Guide* went to press during the summer of 2011, after each pub was sent a checking sheet to confirm up-to-date food, drink and bedroom prices, and other factual information. By the summer of 2012, prices are bound to have increased, but if you find a significantly different price please let us know.

Breweries or independent chains to which pubs are 'tied' are named at the beginning of the rubric of useful information at the end of each featured top pub. That generally means the pub has to get most, if not all, of its drinks from that brewery or chain. If the brewery is not an independent one but just part of a combine, we name the combine in brackets. When the pub is tied, we have spelled out whether the landlord is a tenant, has the pub on a lease, or is a manager. Tenants and leaseholders of breweries generally have considerably greater freedom to do things their own way, and in particular are allowed to buy drinks including a beer from sources other than their tied brewery.

Free houses are pubs not tied to a brewery. In theory they can shop around but in practice many free houses have loans from the big brewers, on terms that bind them to sell those breweries' beers. So don't be too surprised to find that so-called free houses may be stocking a range of beers restricted to those from a single brewery.

Real ale is used by us to mean beer that has been maturing naturally in its cask. We do not count as real ale beer which has been pasteurised or filtered to remove its natural yeasts. If it is kept under a blanket of carbon dioxide to preserve it, we still generally mention it – as long as the pressure is too light for you to notice any extra fizz, it's hard to tell the difference. (For brevity, we use the expression 'under light blanket pressure' to cover such pubs; we do not include among them pubs where the blanket pressure is high enough to force the beer up from the cellar, as this does make it unnaturally fizzy.)

Other drinks We've also looked out particularly for pubs doing enterprising non-alcoholic drinks (including good tea or coffee), interesting spirits (especially malt whiskies), country wines, freshly squeezed juices, and good farm ciders.

Bar food usually refers to what is sold in the bar; we do not describe menus that are restricted to a separate restaurant. If we know that a pub serves sandwiches, we say so – if you don't see them mentioned, assume you can't get them. Food listed is an example of the sort of thing you'd find served in the bar on a normal day, and we try to indicate any difference we know of between lunchtime and evening.

Children If we don't mention children at all, assume that they are not welcome. All but one or two pubs allow children in their garden if they have one. 'Children welcome' means the pub has told us that it lets them in with no special restrictions. In other cases, we report exactly what arrangements pubs say they make for children. However, we have to note that in readers' experience some pubs make restrictions that they haven't told us about (children only if eating, for example). If you come across this, please let us know, so that we can clarify with the pub concerned for the next edition. The absence of any reference to children in the shorter entries for pubs also worth a visit means we don't know either way. Children's Certificates exist, but in practice children are allowed into some part of most pubs in this *Guide* (there is no legal restriction on the movement of children over 14 in any pub). Children under 16 cannot have alcoholic drinks. Children aged 16 and 17 can drink beer, wine or cider with a meal if it is bought by an adult and they are accompanied by an adult.

Dogs If the licensees of featured top pubs have told us they allow dogs in their pub or bedrooms we say so; absence of reference to dogs means dogs are not welcome. If you take a dog into a pub, you should have it on a lead. We also mention in the text any pub dogs or cats (or indeed other animals) that we've come across ourselves, or heard about from readers.

Parking If we know there is a problem with parking, we say so; otherwise assume there is a car park.

Credit cards We say if a pub does **not** accept them; some which do may put a surcharge on credit card bills, to cover charges made by the card company. We also say if we know that a pub tries to retain customers' credit cards while they are eating. This is a reprehensible practice, and if a pub tries it on you, please tell them that all banks and card companies frown on it – and please let us know the pub's name, so that we can warn readers in future editions.

Telephone numbers are given for all featured top pubs that are not ex-directory.

Opening hours are for summer; we say if we know of differences in winter, or on particular days of the week. In the country, many pubs may open rather later and close earlier than their details show (if you come across this, please let us know – with details). Pubs are allowed to stay open all day if licensed to do so. However, outside cities many pubs in England and Wales close during the afternoon. We'd be grateful to hear of any differences from the hours we quote.

Bedroom prices normally include full english breakfasts (if available), VAT and any automatic service charge. If we give just one price, it is the total price for two people sharing a double or twin-bedded room for one night. Otherwise, prices before the '/' are for single occupancy, prices after it for double. A capital B against the price means that it includes a private bathroom, a capital S a private shower. As all this coding packs in quite a lot of information, some examples may help to explain it:

£60	on its own means that's the total bill for two people sharing a twin or double room without a private bath or shower; the pub has no rooms with a private bath or shower, and a single person might have to pay that full price
£60B	means the same – but all the rooms have a private bath
£60S	means the rooms have a private shower
£60(£90B)	means rooms with private baths cost £30 extra
£35/£60(£90B)	means the same as the last example, but also shows that there are single rooms for £35, none of which has a private bathroom

If there's a choice of rooms at different prices, we normally give the cheapest. If there are seasonal price variations, we give the summer price (the highest), but during the winter you may find all sorts of cheaper rates and bargain breaks.

Meal times Bar food is commonly served from 12-2 and 7-9, at least from Monday to Saturday. If we don't give a time, assume you can get bar food at those times. However, we do spell out the times if they are significantly different. To be sure of a table, it's best to book before you go. Sunday hours vary considerably from pub to pub, so it makes sense to ring to check they are open.

Disabled access Deliberately, we do not ask pubs about this, as their answers would not give a reliable picture of how easy access is. Instead, we depend on readers' direct experience. If you are able to give us help about this, we would be particularly grateful for your reports.

SAT NAV AND ELECTRONIC ROUTE PLANNING
In conjunction with Garmin *The Good Pub Guide* is now available for your Sat Nav. Available as an SD card or download, it integrates quickly and easily into your Garmin Sat Nav and gives you access to all recommended pubs in the *Guide*. The Sat Nav guide will tell you the nearest pubs to your current location, or you can get it to track down a particular pub. Microsoft® AutoRoute™, a route-finding software package, shows the location of *Good Pub Guide* pubs on detailed maps and shows our text entries for those pubs on screen.

iPHONE AND iPAD
You can download an iPhone or iPad version of this edition from Apple's App Store. The iPhone is brilliant for us as it means users can report on a pub even while they are in it – perhaps adding a photo.

OUR WEBSITE: www.thegoodpubguide.co.uk
Our website includes every pub in this *Guide* plus many more. It has sophisticated search tools and shows the location of every pub on detailed maps.

CHANGES DURING THE YEAR – PLEASE TELL US
Changes are inevitable during the course of the year. Landlords change, and so do their policies. We hope that you will find everything just as we say but if not please let us know. You can find out how by referring to the Report Forms section at the end of the *Guide*.

Top Pubs

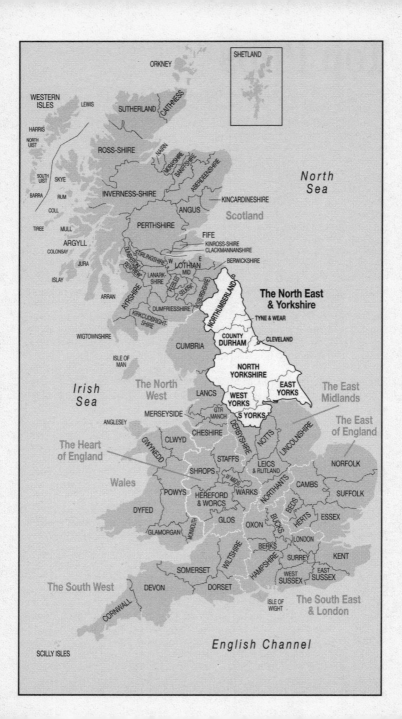

EDITORS' FAVOURITES

The top pub in the North East and Yorkshire for 2012 is the Crown at Roecliffe in **Yorkshire** (our **North East & Yorkshire Pub of the Year**: a smashing all-rounder, warm welcome from friendly family owners, fine choice of drinks and excellent food – it's also our **Yorkshire Dining Pub of the Year**). Other special pubs in this county are the Bay Horse in Burythorpe (highly enjoyable dining pub, good mix of customers), Fauconberg Arms at Coxwold (hospitable family, interesting food, huge breakfasts, pretty bedrooms), Blue Lion at East Witton (civilised dining pub with proper bar, imaginative food), Tempest Arms at Elslack (well run and bustling, generous helpings of well liked food), Horseshoe in Levisham (two jovial landlord brothers – one cooks the particularly good food – friendly atmosphere, nice bedrooms), Sandpiper in Leyburn (locals' bar, dogs welcome, delicious landlord-cooked food), Old Bridge at Ripponden (charming old pub, popular lunchtime salad carvery), and Pack Horse in Widdop (honest, traditional inn, hearty breakfasts). Also worth a visit are the Fleece in Addingham, Game Cock at Austwick, Birch Hall in Beck Hole, Carpenters Arms at Felixkirk, General Tarleton in Ferrensby, Grantley Arms in Grantley, Angel at Hetton, Blacksmiths Arms at Lastingham, Black Sheep Brewery in Masham, Dog & Gun at Oxenhope, Laurel in Robin Hood's Bay, Anvil in Sawdon and the Fat Cat in Sheffield.

Pubs that are doing well in the **North East** include the Rat at Anick (cosy all rounder), Barrasford Arms at Barrasford (delicious food, super staff and **Northumberland Dining Pub of the Year**), Feathers at Hedley on the Hill (well cooked traditional food), Rose & Crown at Romaldkirk (another terrific all-rounder) and Olde Ship at Seahouses (unchanging and stuffed with seafaring memorabilia). Other pubs worth a visit include the Red Lion in Alnmouth, Bacchus and Crown Posada which are both in Newcastle upon Tyne, Ship at Newton-by-the-Sea and the Travellers Rest at Slaley.

In the **North West**, the top pub for 2012 is the Masons Arms at Cartmel Fell in **Cumbria** (full of character, smashing food, friendly staff and special setting). Other great pubs in this county are the Hare & Hounds at Bowland Bridge (new to us this year and should do really well), Blacksmiths Arms at Broughton Mills (charming country pub, consistently good food, friendly welcome), George & Dragon at Clifton (inventive food using their estate produce), Highland Drove in Great Salkeld (popular, fair value food and cheerful welcome), Watermill at Ings (own brews plus 11 guests, reliable pubby food, lots of atmosphere), Strickland Arms in Levens (a much-loved all-rounder), Black Swan in Ravenstonedale (pubby bar in friendly, family-run hotel; super walks), Queens Head at Troutbeck (civilised relaxed atmosphere, seven real ales, imaginative food, nice bedrooms), Derby Arms at Witherslack (new to us and under the same ownership as the Strickland Arms; should do really well), and the Gate at Yanwath (**Cumbria Dining Pub of the Year**,

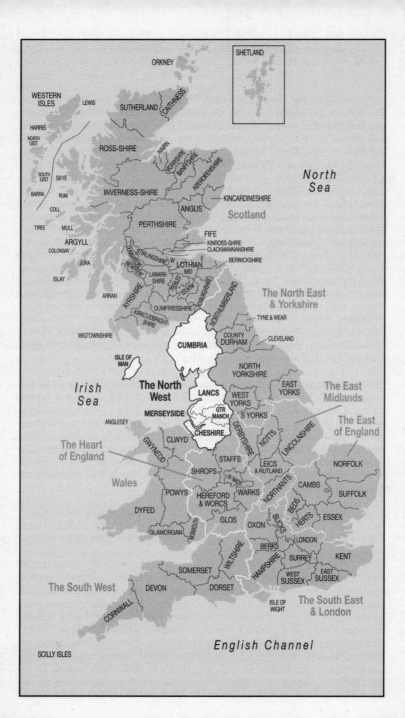

first-class food and a friendly landlord). Other pubs worth visiting include the White Hart at Bouth, Bitter End in Cockermouth, Black Bull in Coniston, Punch Bowl at Crosthwaite, Bower House in Eskdale Green, Dog & Gun at Keswick, Sun in Kirkby Lonsdale, Plough at Lupton, and Herdwick at Penruddock.

Cheshire pubs are on jolly good form. Of note are the Egerton Arms in Astbury (welcoming with good value food), the Bhurtpore in Aston (impressive range of drinks and genuine atmosphere), Pheasant at Burwardsley (enjoyable all-rounder), Albion in Chester (utterly unique), Old Harkers Arms in Chester (lively town pub), Fox & Barrel at Cotebrook (stylish with terrific food and **Cheshire Dining Pub of the Year**), Hanging Gate at Langley (snug and unchanging) and Sutton Hall at Macclesfield (great dining in a stunning building). A really tremendous batch of new entries in this county includes the Egerton Arms at Chelford (something for everyone), Swan at Kettleshulme (charming cottage with great fish menu), Davenport Arms at Marton (maintaining the best of the traditional without being stuck in the past), Plough & Flail at Mobberley (comfortable dining pub) and the Yew Tree at Spurstow (top-notch all-rounder with entertaining décor). Other pubs doing well include the White Lion in Barthomley, Farmers Arms at Huxley and the Ship in Wincle.

Two new top pubs in **Lancashire** this year are the Waddington Arms in Waddington (a jolly good all-rounder) and the Freemasons Arms at Wiswell, a contender for County Dining Pub (top-notch restaurant). But the **Lancashire Dining Pub of the Year** is the Eagle & Child in Bispham Green (effortlessly good all-rounder). Good food is also to be had at the Three Fishes in Great Mitton, Clog & Billycock at Pleasington and Highwayman at Nether Burrow (all in the same ownership and featuring good local produce). The ancient Inn at Whitewell offers luxury on all fronts. For interesting beer, try the Church Inn at Uppermill (own-brew beers and lively atmosphere) and the Philharmonic Dining Rooms in Liverpool (splendid old building). Other pubs worth a visit include the Duke of York in Grindleton, Britons Protection and Marble Arch in Manchester, Wheatsheaf in Raby, Spread Eagle at Sawley, and the Station Buffet in Stalybridge.

THE NORTH EAST & YORKSHIRE'S TOP PUBS

AMPLEFORTH Yorkshire   SE5878   Map A

White Swan

Off A170 W of Helmsley; East End; YO62 4DA

Quite a choice of seating areas in this attractive pub, attentive service, enjoyable food and real ales; seats on back terrace

As this first-class pub is close to Ampleforth College and Abbey, many of the customers are visitors and parents – but there's a warm welcome for all. It's a civilised place with a beamed lounge, cream-coloured décor, sporting prints, quite a mix of tables and chairs on the slate flooring and a double-sided woodburning stove. The more conventional beamed front bar, liked by locals, has a blazing log fire, red patterned wall seating and plenty of stools, some standing timbers and a comfortable end seating area with big soft red cushions; piped music, pool table, darts and dominoes. Black Sheep Best and Theakstons Best on handpump, good wines by the glass and ten malt whiskies. The restaurant area is more formal with plush furnishings and crisp, white linen-covered tables. There are seats and tables on the large, attractive back terrace overlooking the valley.

Good, popular food includes lunchtime sandwiches, mushroom, cream and brandy linguine, a burger with melted mozzarella and bacon, gammon and egg, and steak in ale pie, with evening choices like smoked, fresh and marinated seafood salad, slow-roasted pork ribs in a barbecue sauce, salmon with a prawn and chive sauce, and half a gressingham duckling with orange sauce. *Benchmark main dish: deep-fried haddock with mushy peas £13.30. Two-course evening meal £19.50.*

Free house ~ Licensees Mr and Mrs R Thompson ~ Real ale ~ Bar food (12-2, 6-9) ~ Restaurant ~ (01439) 788239 ~ Children welcome ~ Open 12-3, 6-11.15; midday-1am(11.15 Sun) Sat

Recommended by John and Eleanor Holdsworth, Walter and Susan Rinaldi-Butcher, Janet and Peter Race, Margaret Dickinson, Dr and Mrs R G J Telfer, Ed and Anna Fraser

 ANICK Northumberland   NY9565   Map A

Rat

Village signposted NE of A69/A695 Hexham junction; NE46 4LN

Views over North Tyne Valley from terrace and garden, refurbished bar and lounge, lots of interesting knick-knacks, half a dozen mainly local real ales and interesting bar food

All seems to be going very well at this relaxed country pub, with plenty of care and thought being put in by the hard-working and enthusiastic licensees – so much so that we've given them a new Food Award this year. The traditional bar is snug and welcoming with a coal fire in the blackened kitchen range, lots of cottagey knick-knacks from antique floral chamber-pots hanging from the beams to china and glassware on a delft shelf, and little curtained windows that allow in a soft and gentle light. A conservatory has pleasant valley views and the garden is quite charming with its dovecote, statues, pretty flower beds and North Tyne Valley views from seats on the terrace; piped music, daily papers and magazines. Half a dozen changing beers on handpump are from mostly local brewers such as Allendale, Bass, Cumberland, Geltsdale, High House Farm and Wylam. They also keep ten wines (including champagne) by the glass, a local gin and farm cider. Parking is limited, but you can park around the village green.

Using carefully sourced local meat, game and seasonal local and own-grown vegetables and fruit, the good, interesting bar food, all cooked from scratch, includes sandwiches, terrine of local game, charcuterie, fried coley with creamed samphire, lemon and capers, sausage, leek and potato cake, confit duck leg with dauphinoise potato, butternut and local cheese risotto, and popular roast rib of beef with béarnaise sauce (for two people). *Benchmark main dish: braised local beef in ale £10.95. Two-course evening meal £18.30.*

Free house ~ Licensees Phil Mason and Karen Errington ~ Real ale ~ Bar food (12-2 (3 Sun), 6-9; not Sun evening, or Mon in winter except bank holidays; sandwiches only Mon 12-6 in summer) ~ Restaurant ~ (01434) 602814 ~ Open 12-3, 6-11 Mon; 12-11 Tues-Sat (10.30 Sun)

Recommended by GNI, Eric Larkham, Pat and Stewart Gordon, Chris Clark, W K Wood, Denis Newton, Comus and Sarah Elliott

AYCLIFFE County Durham   NZ2822   Map A

County ① ♀ ◀

The Green, Aycliffe village; just off A1(M) junction 59, by A167; DL5 6LX

Friendly, well run pub with four real ales, good wines and popular, interesting food; bedrooms

More or less open-plan throughout, this popular pub is cheerily decorated with blue, green and yellow paintwork, some bright red carpeting, local art and careful lighting. The wood-floored bar has attractive solid pine dining chairs and cushioned settles around a mix of pine tables, and some high bar chairs by the counter from which genuinely friendly staff serve a beer named for the pub from Yard of Ale, three guests such as Black Sheep and Harviestoun Bitter & Twisted on handpump and several wines by the glass. The carpeted lounge has a woodburning stove in a brick fireplace with candles in brass candlesticks on either side, a second fireplace with nightlights, similar furniture to the bar and painted ceiling joists. The wood-floored restaurant is minimalist with high-backed black leather dining chairs and dark window blinds. Metal tables and chairs in front overlook the pretty village green.

Good, interesting bar food includes sandwiches, ploughman's, ham hock terrine with pineapple chutney and fried quail egg, salmon fishcake with sautéed samphire and spinach cream sauce, battered cod, garlic king prawns, haunch of venison with grilled celeriac and sweet chilli and chocolate sauce, pumpkin tortellini with sage butter, parmesan and asparagus, and well hung steak with peppercorn sauce. *Benchmark main dish: steak and ale pie £9.95. Two-course evening meal £20.00.*

Free house ~ Licensee Colette Farrell ~ Real ale ~ Bar food (12-2, 5.30-9; 12-9 Sun) ~ Restaurant ~ (01325) 312273 ~ Children welcome ~ Open 11.30-3, 5-midnight; 11.30-midnight Sun ~ Bedrooms: £49S/£69S(£89B)

Recommended by Alan Thwaite, S Bloomfield, MJVK, Dave and Jenny Hughes

You can send reports directly to us at **feedback@goodguides.com**

BARRASFORD Northumberland NY9173 Map A

Barrasford Arms 🍴

Village signposted off A6079 N of Hexham; NE48 4AA

NORTHUMBERLAND DINING PUB OF THE YEAR

Friendly proper pub with good country cooking, real ales, a bustling bar, and plenty of nearby walks; bedrooms

---

On really good form at the moment, this bustling sandstone inn is a terrific all-rounder with great food and super staff. The traditional bar plays a big part, with its genuinely local atmosphere, good log fire, old local photographs, country bric-a-brac from horsebrasses to antlers and three interesting guests such as Caledonian Deuchars IPA, Hadrian & Border Gladiator and Wylam Gold Tankard on handpump; also good value wines by the glass. Two nice dining rooms; one is carefully decorated in greys and creams, dominated by a great stone chimneybreast hung with guns and copper pans, and has wheelback chairs around half a dozen neat tables. The second, perhaps rather more restrained, has more comfortably upholstered dining chairs; piped music, darts and TV. They have well equipped bunkhouse accommodation as well as 11 proper bedrooms. The pub is on the edge of a small North Tyne village quite close to Hadrian's Wall and looks across lovely valleys to the impressive medieval Haughton Castle (not open to the public).

🍴 Cooked by the landlord and his team using carefully sourced local meats, game and fish, the enjoyable food might include twice-baked cheddar soufflé, spinach, roast pepper and ricotta pie with bean cassoulet, brioche-crumbed fillet of plaice with chunky tomato salad and garlic mayonnaise, roast chicken with cider and honey sauce, and roast loin of deer with boulangère potatoes. *Benchmark main dish: rib-eye steak with peppercorn sauce £16.00. Two-course evening meal £19.65.*

Free house ~ Licensee Tony Binks ~ Real ale ~ Bar food ~ Restaurant ~ (01434) 681237 ~ Children welcome ~ Open 12-2.30, 6-midnight; 12-midnight Sat; 12-11.30 Sun; closed Mon lunchtime ~ Bedrooms: £65B/£85B

Recommended by Bruce and Sharon Eden, W K Wood, Michael Doswell, M A Borthwick

---

BLAKEY RIDGE Yorkshire SE6799 Map A

Lion 🍺 🛏

From A171 Guisborough—Whitby follow Castleton, Hutton le Hole signposts; from A170 Kirkby Moorside—Pickering follow Keldholm, Hutton le Hole, Castleton signposts; OS Sheet 100 map reference 679996; YO62 7LQ

Extended pub in fine scenery and open all day; bedrooms

Despite this extended old pub being so remote – it's at the highest point of the North York Moors National Park – there's always a good crowd of customers. The views are stunning and there are also lots of surrounding hikes; the Coast to Coast Footpath is nearby. The beamed and rambling bars have warm open fires, a few big high-backed rustic settles around cast-iron-framed tables, lots of small dining chairs, a nice leather sofa, and stone walls hung with some old engravings and photographs of the pub under snow (it can easily get cut off in winter; eight days in the record so far). There are up to seven real ales on handpump: Black Sheep Best, Copper Dragon Golden Pippin, Greene King Old Speckled Hen, Theakstons Best, Old Peculier and XB, and Thwaites Wainwright; piped music and games machine. If you are thinking of staying, you must book well in advance. This is a regular stop-off for coach parties.

 Usefully served all day, the generous helpings of traditional bar food include lunchtime sandwiches, pâté and toast, giant yorkshire pudding with gravy, home-cooked ham and egg, beef curry, haddock in batter, half a chicken, stilton and vegetable crumble, and specials like pork fillet with a watercress and ginger cream sauce, salmon with seafood sauce, and beef wellington. *Benchmark main dish: steak and mushroom pie £10.95. Two-course evening meal £18.25.*

Free house ~ Licensee Barry Crossland ~ Real ale ~ Bar food (12-10) ~ Restaurant ~ (01751) 417320 ~ Children welcome ~ Dogs allowed in bar ~ Open 10am-11pm(midnight Sat) ~ Bedrooms: £22(£43.50B)/£76B
Recommended by Dr J Barrie Jones, WAH

BLANCHLAND County Durham NY9650 Map A

Lord Crewe Arms 🛏

B6306 S of Hexham; DH8 9SP

Ancient, historic building with some unusual features, real ales, straightforward bar food and a more elaborate restaurant menu; bedrooms

The pubbiest part of this comfortable high moorland hotel is the ancient-feeling bar that is housed in an unusual long and narrow, stone barrel-vaulted crypt. In here, plush stools on ancient flagstones are lined along a narrow drinks' shelf attached to the curving wall (which is up to eight feet thick in some places) down one side of the room, with a similar row opposite along the counter. They serve Black Sheep Best, Hadrian & Border Tyneside Blonde, Wylam and a guest on handpump and several wines by the glass; flatscreen TV, darts. The Hilyard Room has a massive 13th-c fireplace once used as a hiding place by the Jacobite Tom Forster (part of the family who had owned the building before it was sold in 1704 to the formidable Lord Crewe, Bishop of Durham). Upstairs, the Derwent Room has low beams, old settles and sepia photographs on its walls and the restaurant overlooks a lovely walled garden that was formerly the cloisters.

 Pubby bar food includes sandwiches, fish and chips, steak mince burger, seared lambs liver, bacon and gravy, gammon and chips, and mixed fish grill. *Benchmark main dish: mixed fish grill £13.95. Two-course evening meal £20.00.*

Free house ~ Licensee Mat Thomson ~ Real ale ~ Bar food (12-9) ~ Restaurant ~ (01434) 675251 ~ Children welcome ~ Dogs allowed in bar and bedrooms ~ Open 11-11; 12-10.30 Sun ~ Bedrooms: £60B/£90B
Recommended by Dr A McCormick, Comus and Sarah Elliott, M and J White, Claes Mauroy

BOROUGHBRIDGE Yorkshire SE3966 Map C

Black Bull ♀ £

St James Square; B6265, just off A1(M); YO51 9AR

Bustling town pub with real ales, several wines by the glass and traditional bar food; bedrooms

A good break from the busy A1, this is an attractive old town pub on the edge of the market square. It's said to date from the 13th c and has been looking after travellers between England and Scotland for centuries. There are lots of separate drinking and eating areas where plenty of cheerful locals drop in regularly for a pint and a chat, and the main bar area has a big stone fireplace and comfortable seats and is served through an old-fashioned hatch; there's also a cosy snug with traditional wall settles, a tap room, lounge bar and restaurant. John Smiths, Timothy Taylors Best and Theakstons XB on handpump, nine wines by the glass and 17 malt whiskies; dominoes. The two borzoi dogs are called Spot and Sadie and the two cats Kia and Mershka. The hanging baskets are lovely.

🍴 Fair value bar food includes sandwiches, chicken liver pâté, pork and chive sausages with onion gravy, a pie of the day, vegetable lasagne, beef curry and chicken pasta in a spicy tomato sauce, with more restaurant choices like pork tenderloin in a pink peppercorn and calvados sauce, chargrilled tuna loin, and venison steak with smoked bacon and blue cheese with a berry glaze. *Benchmark main dish: pie of the day £8.90. Two-course evening meal £17.50.*

Free house ~ Licensees Anthony and Jillian Burgess ~ Real ale ~ Bar food (12-2(2.30 Sun), 6-9(9.30 Fri and Sat) ~ Restaurant ~ (01423) 322413 ~ Children welcome ~ Dogs welcome ~ Folk music Sun lunchtime ~ Open 11(12 Sun)-11(midnight Fri and Sat) ~ Bedrooms: £45S/£68S

Recommended by Bob Broadhurst, the Didler, Ian and Nita Cooper, Mike and Lynn Robinson, C J Beresford-Jones

---

BRADFIELD Yorkshire   SK2290   Map C

Strines Inn 🛏

From A57 heading E of junction with A6013 (Ladybower Reservoir) take first left turn (signposted with Bradfield) then bear left; with a map can also be reached more circuitously from Strines signpost on A616 at head of Underbank Reservoir; W of Stocksbridge; S6 6JE

Surrounded by fine scenery with quite a mix of customers and traditional beer and bar food; bedrooms

---

Walkers and their well behaved dogs are made very welcome in this traditional old pub – which is just as well as it's surrounded by superb scenery on the edge of the High Peak National Park and there are fine walks and views all around. The main bar has black beams liberally decked with copper kettles and so forth, quite a menagerie of stuffed animals, homely red-plush-cushioned traditional wooden wall benches and small chairs, and a coal fire in the rather grand stone fireplace. Two other rooms to the right and left are similarly furnished. Bradfield Farmers Blonde, Jennings Cocker Hoop, and Marstons Pedigree on handpump and several wines by the glass; piped music. There are plenty of picnic-sets outside, and peacocks, geese and chickens. The bedrooms have four-poster beds and a dining table as the good breakfasts are served in your room – the front room overlooks the reservoir.

🍴 As well as seasonal game and daily fish dishes, the reasonably priced food includes sandwiches, game pâté, chilli con carne in a giant yorkshire pudding, a pie of the day, broccoli and cream cheese bake, liver and onions, and a huge mixed grill. *Benchmark main dish: steak in ale pie £9.25. Two-course evening meal £14.00.*

Free house ~ Licensee Bruce Howarth ~ Real ale ~ Bar food (12-2.30, 5.30-8.30 winter weekdays; all day in summer and on winter weekends) ~ (0114) 285 1247 ~ Children welcome ~ Dogs welcome ~ Open 10.30am-11pm; 10.30-3, 5.30-11 weekdays in winter ~ Bedrooms: £60B/£80B

Recommended by the Didler, Brian and Anna Marsden, Malcolm and Barbara Southwell, Gordon and Margaret Ormondroyd

BREARTON Yorkshire · SE3260 Map C

Malt Shovel ⑪ ♀

Village signposted off A61 N of Harrogate; HG3 3BX

Friendly, family-run dining pub with imaginative food and good choice of drinks in heavily beamed rooms; airy conservatory

The Bleiker family and their staff could not be more welcoming to all their customers – our readers enjoy their visits here very much. It's mainly a dining pub with excellent food but they do keep Black Sheep Best and Timothy Taylors Landlord and a very good wine list with 14 by the glass. The heavily beamed rooms have a warm, friendly atmosphere and radiate from the attractive linenfold oak bar counter, with painted walls and light blue skirting, an attractive mix of wooden dining chairs around tables on wood or slate floors, and some partitioning that separates several candlelit dining areas. The conservatory is light and airy with lemon trees and a piano (which is used for Sunday jazz); they also hold occasional live opera evenings. There are seats in the parasoled garden. The family are also associated with Bleiker's Smokehouse near Harrogate.

The family rear their own pigs and use top-quality local produce for the imaginative, restaurant-style food: chicken and game liver pâté with home-made toasted bread, oxtail and kidney pudding, free-range chicken marinated in lemon and home-grown thyme on spinach and rösti with beetroot crisps, their speciality smoked platter, slow-cooked pork belly and crackling with black pudding mash and cider gravy, skate wing with black butter and capers, and slices of fillet steak on a sizzling platter with oyster and mint sauce and chilli; they also have a lunchtime and early evening two- and three-course set menu. *Benchmark main dish: smoked haddock with free-range egg, wild mushroom risotto and hollandaise £12.95. Two-course evening meal £20.90.*

Free house ~ Licensee Jurg Bleiker ~ Real ale ~ Bar food (12-2(3 Sat, 4 Sun), 5.30-9.30; not Sun evening, Mon or Tues) ~ Restaurant ~ (01423) 862929 ~ Children welcome ~ Jazz pianist Sun, occasional opera evenings with dinner ~ Open 12-3, 5.30-11; 12-5 Sun; closed Sun evening, all day Mon and Tues

Recommended by Peter Hacker, Michael Butler, Emma Parr

BROUGHTON Yorkshire · SD9450 Map C

Bull ⑪ ♀

A59; BD23 3AE

Handsome, carefully refurbished inn making good use of pale oak and contemporary paintwork, good choice of drinks and enjoyable food

This handsome stone inn is a welcoming place whatever the season. In summer you can eat at the solid benches and tables on the terrace and look over the grounds of Broughton Hall, and in winter there are open log fires; you can walk through the Hall Estate's 3,000 acres of rolling countryside and parkland at any time of year. They've sensibly kept the various carefully furnished rooms separate: lots of pale oak, handsome flagstones, exposed stone walls, built-in wall seats and a mix of dining chairs around polished tables, contemporary paintwork hung with photographs of local suppliers and open log fires. Copper Dragon Scotts 1816, Dark Horse Hetton Pale Ale, and Thwaites Original on handpump, several malt whiskies and a dozen wines (including champagne) by the glass; if you are dining, they will let you bring your own wine for a £10 corkage fee per bottle.

🍽 Interesting food using carefully sourced local produce includes sandwiches, nibbles with home-made bread, rabbit faggots with courgette purée and tomato relish, local seafood platter, a pie with braised veal tails, ham shank, smoked pig's jowl, button mushrooms, yellow split peas and broccoli, chargrilled minced rump steak with dripping chips and mustard mayonnaise on a toasted muffin, and seasonal sea trout with asparagus and wild garlic mash. *Benchmark main dish: fish pie £10.75. Two-course evening meal £17.50.*

Free house ~ Licensee Leanne Richardson ~ Real ale ~ Bar food (all day) ~ (01756) 792065 ~ Children welcome ~ Dogs allowed in bar ~ Open 12-11(10.30 Sun)

Recommended by Steve Whalley, John and Eleanor Holdsworth, Karen Eliot, Stu Mac, Keith Moss, Claire Hall, G Jennings, Hilary Forrest, Margaret and Jeff Graham, Ed and Anna Fraser

BURYTHORPE Yorkshire   SE7964 Map C

Bay Horse 🍽 ♀ £

Off A64 8.5 miles NE of York ring road, via Kirkham and Westow; 5 miles S of Malton, by Welham Road; YO17 9LJ

Friendly, civilised dining pub with contemporary décor in stylish rooms, real ales, good wines and highly enjoyable food

As well as a good mix of both locals and visitors (and there's a welcome for all from the genuinely friendly staff), this well run dining pub has a lovely atmosphere and excellent food, and is surrounded by plenty of fine walks. The linked rooms are cosy, candlelit and civilised with up-to-date paintwork, stripped floorboards, a mix of chunky pine tables and elegant high-backed black or wooden dining chairs, and shelves of books. The end dining room has several attractive and amusing farmyard animal paintings, the main bar has a couple of nice old carved antique pews with interesting cushions and some ancient hunting prints, and there's a tiny end room with a sofa and open log fire and yet another red-walled room with rugs on flagstones. Tetleys, Theakstons Black Bull and Timothy Taylors Landlord on handpump and 11 good wines by the glass. On the outside terrace are some good contemporary tables and seats under parasols. The nearby Burythorpe House hotel, a former gentleman's residence, is under the same ownership.

🍽 First-rate food includes sandwiches, lunchtime choices such as garlic mushrooms on eggy bread, fish and chips with mushy peas, ham and egg and a good burger with bacon, cheese and guacamole, and evening dishes like smoked salmon rose with lemon and baby capers, risotto verde with parmesan, stir-fried beef with noodles, thai chicken curry and grilled swordfish steak with chilli and lime. The Value Award is for fair-priced lunchtime dishes. *Benchmark main dish: gressingham duck breast with raspberry sauce £14.75. Two-course evening meal £16.50.*

Free house ~ Licensee Dawn Pickering ~ Real ale ~ Bar food (12-2.30(4 Sun), 6.30-9.30 (9 Sun); not Mon) ~ Restaurant ~ (01653) 658302 ~ Children welcome ~ Dogs allowed in bar ~ Open 12-3, 6-11.30; 12-11.30 Sun; closed Mon

Recommended by Christopher Turner, Pat and Graham Williamson, C A Hall, Ed and Anna Fraser

---

Please keep sending us reports. We rely on readers for news of new discoveries, and particularly for news of changes – however slight – at the fully described pubs: **feedback@goodguides.com**, or (no stamp needed) The Good Pub Guide, FREEPOST TN1569, Wadhurst, E Sussex TN5 7BR.

CARTERWAY HEADS County Durham
NZ0452 Map A

Manor House Inn
A68 just N of B6278, near Derwent Reservoir; DH8 9LX

Handy after a walk with a simple bar and more comfortable lounge, bar food and five real ales; bedrooms

Homely and old-fashioned, this simple slate-roofed stone inn is a useful place if you've been walking around the nearby Derwent Valley and Reservoir. The straightforward locals' bar has an original boarded ceiling, pine tables, chairs and stools, old oak pews and a mahogany counter. The comfortable lounge bar (warmed by a woodburning stove) and restaurant both have picture windows that make the most of the lovely setting. Copper Dragon Golden Pippin, Greene King Old Speckled Hen and Ruddles County, Timothy Taylors Landlord and a guest beer from a brewer such as Concertina are on handpump alongside 70 malt whiskies; TV, darts, board games and piped music. There are rustic tables in the garden.

Usefully served all day, bar food includes sandwiches and wraps, sausage and mash, fish pie, pasta of the day, and daily specials such as baked vegetable pancake with cheese sauce, fried scallops with sweet chilli sauce, confit duck leg with sweet chilli noodles, peppered venison loin with red wine jus, and roast trout with chorizo. *Benchmark main dish: fish and chips £9.95. Two-course evening meal £16.60.*

Free house ~ Licensees Neil and Emma Oxley ~ Real ale ~ Bar food (12-9) ~ Restaurant ~ (01207) 255268 ~ Children welcome ~ Dogs allowed in bar and bedrooms ~ Open 11-11; 12-10.30 Sun ~ Bedrooms: £45B/£65B

Recommended by Stuart and Sarah Barrie, Eric Larkham, Michael Doswell, Comus and Sarah Elliott, Mr and Mrs M Hargrave, GSB, Henry Paulinski

CONSTABLE BURTON Yorkshire
SE1690 Map A

Wyvill Arms
A684 E of Leyburn; DL8 5LH

Well run, friendly dining pub with interesting food, a dozen wines by the glass, real ales and efficient helpful service; comfortable bedrooms

The friendly Stevens family have now run this 18th-c former farmhouse for over a decade, and this year they've added more comfortable bedrooms, which our readers enjoy very much. There's a small bar area with a mix of seating, a finely worked plaster ceiling with the Wyvill family's coat of arms and an elaborate stone fireplace with a warm winter fire. The second bar has a lower ceiling with fans, leather seating, old oak tables, various alcoves and a model train on a railway track running around the room; the reception area includes a huge leather sofa which can seat up to eight people, another carved stone fireplace and an old leaded church stained-glass window partition. Both rooms are hung with pictures of local scenes. John Smiths and Theakstons Best on handpump, a dozen wines by the glass and some rare malt whiskies; board games. There are several large wooden benches under large white parasols for outdoor dining and picnic-sets by the well. Constable Burton Gardens are opposite and worth a visit.

Using home-grown herbs and vegetables and game from the estate across the road, the highly thought-of food includes lunchtime sandwiches, ham, pork, chicken and cheese terrine with pear and apple chutney, wild mushroom risotto, parmesan pork with a tomato and herb sauce, breaded chicken suprême stuffed with mozzarella and smoked bacon on creamed leeks with stilton sauce, sea bream with potted prawns and shrimps with a lemon butter sauce, and venison on roast vegetable purée with a cranberry and cassis jus. *Benchmark main dish: fillet steak black jack (mixed herbs and spices and a red wine and smoked bacon sauce) £23.45. Two-course evening meal £20.93.*

Free house ~ Licensee Nigel Stevens ~ Real ale ~ Bar food (12-2, 5.30-9) ~ Restaurant ~ (01677) 450581 ~ Children welcome ~ Dogs allowed in bar and bedrooms ~ Open 11-3, 5.30-11; 12-3, 5.30-10.30 Sun; closed Mon (except bank holidays) ~ Bedrooms: £60B/£75B

Recommended by John and Eleanor Holdsworth, Noel Thomas, Janet and Peter Race, Walter and Susan Rinaldi-Butcher, Ed and Anna Fraser

 COXWOLD Yorkshire   SE5377 Map C

Fauconberg Arms 🍴 ♀ 🛏

Off A170 Thirsk—Helmsley, via Kilburn or Wass; easily found off A19, too; YO61 4AD

Friendly family-run inn with enjoyable generous food, a good range of drinks, and seats in the back garden; comfortable bedrooms

The extremely friendly and hospitable Rheinberg family always make their customers feel glad they came for a drink, a meal or an overnight stay in this nicely updated 17th-c inn; the breakfasts are especially good. The heavily beamed and flagstoned bar has log fires in both linked areas – one in an unusual arched fireplace in a broad low inglenook – muted contemporary colours, some attractive oak chairs by local craftsmen alongside more usual pub furnishings, nicely chosen old local photographs and other pictures, and copper implements and china. Hambleton Bitter, Theakstons Best and Wold Top Gold on handpump, a thoughtful choice of wines by the glass and 28 malt whiskies. The pub dogs, Peggy, Bramble and Phoebe, welcome other four-legged friends, if well behaved. The candlelit dining room is quietly elegant with a gently upmarket yet relaxed atmosphere. The garden behind the inn has seats and tables on the terrace and views across the fields to Byland Abbey; picnic-sets and teak benches out on the front cobbles look along this charming village's broad tree-lined verges, bright with flower tubs. This year, they've opened a shop selling home-baked bread, their own cheese and other groceries.

🍴 Cooked by the landlord and his daughters using seasonal local produce and game, the excellent food includes lunchtime sandwiches, a daily-changing terrine or pâté, black pudding with crispy, dry-cured bacon on a cucumber and red onion salad, fresh whitby cod in beer batter, ham and eggs, home-made burgers, vegetable pancakes, corn-fed chicken, prawns and mushrooms in a pernod-laced creamy sauce, daily fresh fish dishes, and pork medallions flamed in madeira with walnuts, figs and ginger. *Benchmark main dish: beer-battered fish and chips £9.75. Two-course evening meal £19.00.*

Free house ~ Licensee Simon Rheinberg ~ Real ale ~ Bar food (12-2, 6-9(10 Sat); 12-8 Sun) ~ Restaurant ~ (01347) 868214 ~ Children welcome ~ Dogs welcome ~ Open 11-3, 6-midnight; 11-midnight Sat ~ Bedrooms: £75B/£95S

Recommended by Brian and Jacky Wilson, Alan McDougall, Pete Coxon, Tony and Glenys Dyer, Peter Hacker, Michael Doswell, Janet and Peter Race

---

We accept no free drinks or meals and inspections are anonymous.

CRAYKE Yorkshire

SE5670   Map C

Durham Ox 🍴 🍷 🛏

Off B1363 at Brandsby, towards Easingwold; West Way; YO61 4TE

Friendly, well run inn, interesting décor in old-fashioned, relaxing rooms, fine drinks and smashing food; lovely views and comfortable bedrooms

A new Burns Bar with a woodburning stove, exposed brickwork and large french windows that open on to a balcony area has been created in this particularly well run inn – a favourite with quite a few of our readers. The old-fashioned lounge bar has an enormous inglenook fireplace, pictures and photographs on the dark red walls, interesting satirical carvings in the panelling (Victorian copies of medieval pew ends), polished copper and brass, and venerable tables, antique seats and settles on the flagstones. In the bottom bar is a framed illustrated account of the local history (some of it gruesome) dating back to the 12th c, and a large framed print of the original famous Durham Ox which weighed 171 stone. Black Sheep Best and Timothy Taylors Landlord on handpump, 15 wines by the glass and ten malt whiskies; piped music. There are seats in the courtyard garden, and fantastic views over the Vale of York on three sides; on the fourth side there's a charming view up the hill to the medieval church – the tale is that this is the hill up which the Grand Old Duke of York marched his men. The comfortable bedrooms are in converted farm buildings and the breakfasts are good.

Using the best seasonal, local produce and making their own bread and petits fours, the good, flavoursome food includes sandwiches, ham hock terrine with pineapple and piccalilli dressing, baked queen scallops with garlic, butter and cheese, butternut squash and sage risotto, beefburger with cheese, bacon and onion rings, sticky pork ribs with home-made spicy beans, pollack with a fricassée of clams and peas, and confit duck leg with cassoulet of toulouse sausage and pork belly. *Benchmark main dish: rib-eye steak £19.95. Two-course evening meal £20.95.*

Free house ~ Licensee Michael Ibbotson ~ Real ale ~ Bar food (12-2.30(3 Sun), 6-9.30 (8.30 Sun) ~ Restaurant ~ (01347) 821506 ~ Children welcome but must be well behaved ~ Dogs allowed in bedrooms ~ Open 11-11 ~ Bedrooms: /£100B

Recommended by Comus and Sarah Elliott, Karen Eliot, Christopher Turner, Pete Coxon, Michael Doswell, Tony and Wendy Hobden, Jeff and Wendy Williams, Peter and Anne Hollindale, Ed and Anna Fraser

CROPTON Yorkshire

SE7588   Map A

New Inn

Village signposted off A170 W of Pickering; YO18 8HH

Genuinely warm welcome in a modernised village pub with own-brew beers, traditional furnishings and brewery tours; bedrooms

By the time this edition is published, this comfortable, modernised village inn will be heading towards its 17th annual beer festival. Of course, it's their own-brewed beers that customers are here to enjoy and of the six on handpump at any one time, they might offer Blackout, Endeavour, Monkmans Slaughter, North Peaks Vicious, Two Pints and Yorkshire Warrior. They also keep a dozen malt whiskies and seven wines by the glass. The traditional village bar has wood panelling, plush seating, lots of brass and a small fire. A local artist has designed historical posters all around the downstairs conservatory that doubles as a visitor centre during busy times. The elegant restaurant has locally made furniture and paintings by local artists. Piped music, TV, games machine, darts, pool and a juke box. There's a neat terrace, a garden with a pond and a brewery shop. Brewery tours are available most days at £4.95 per person.

🍴 Generous helpings of bar food includes lunchtime sandwiches and filled ciabatta rolls, terrines, fishcakes, steak in ale pie, beer-battered cod, a trio of local sausages, and slow-braised leg of lamb with rosemary and redcurrant jus. *Benchmark main dish: steak in stout pie £9.75. Two-course evening meal £18.00.*

Own brew ~ Licensee Philip Lee ~ Real ale ~ Bar food (12-2(2.30 Sun), 6-9(8.30 Sun) ~ Restaurant ~ (01751) 417330 ~ Children welcome ~ Dogs allowed in bar and bedrooms ~ Folk festival four times a year ~ Open 11(11.30 Sun)-11(midnight Sat) ~ Bedrooms: £60B/£85B

Recommended by Tony and Wendy Hobden, Mike and Mary Strigenz, Mo and David Trudgill

DOWNHOLME Yorkshire   SE1197 Map A

Bolton Arms

Village signposted just off A6108 Leyburn—Richmond; DL11 6AE

Enjoyable food in unusual village's cosy country pub, lovely views; bedrooms

This little stone-built pub is one of the last pubs in Britain to be owned by the state – the Ministry of Defence owns the place and it's surrounded by MoD land (a largely unspoilt swathe of Swaledale); the red-walled, simple and attractive back conservatory dining room enjoys the fine views. Down a few steps, the friendly and softly lit black-beamed and carpeted bar has two smallish linked areas off the servery where they keep Black Sheep Best and Theakstons Best on handpump, eight wines by the glass at fair prices, ten malt whiskies and interesting cordials. There are comfortable plush wall banquettes, a log fire in one neat fireplace, quite a lot of gleaming brass, a few small country pictures and drinks, advertisements on pinkish rough-plastered walls. Service is friendly and efficient; piped music and dominoes. The neat garden, on the same level as the dining room (and up steps from the front), shares the same view; there are also some lower picnic-sets and benches, and quoits. The two bedrooms, sharing a bathroom, are good value.

🍴 Cooked by the landlord, the popular bar food includes sandwiches, tasty caesar salad with smoked chicken and hot crispy bacon, spinach and ricotta pancakes, steak and mushroom pie, chicken in a creamy mushroom sauce, fresh seafood pasta, lambs liver and bacon, gammon and egg, and crispy duck with an orange, ginger and honey sauce; they also offer a two- and three-course early-bird menu Monday-Thursday evenings 6-7pm and takeaway fish and chips. *Benchmark main dish: lamb kleftiko (slow-baked and marinated) £14.50. Two-course evening meal £19.00.*

Free house ~ Licensees Steve and Nicola Ross ~ Real ale ~ Bar food (not Tues lunchtime) ~ Restaurant ~ (01748) 823716 ~ Children welcome ~ Open 10.30-3, 6-midnight; closed Tues lunchtime ~ Bedrooms: £45S/£60S

Recommended by John and Sylvia Harrop, Dr D Jeary, Ed and Anna Fraser

---

Bedroom prices normally include full english breakfast, VAT and any inclusive service charge that we know of. Prices before the '/' are for single rooms, after the '/' for two people in a double or twin (B includes a private bath, S a private shower). If there is no '/', the prices are only for twin or double rooms (as far as we know there are no singles). If there is no B or S, as far as we know no rooms have private facilities.

DURHAM County Durham

NZ2742 Map A

Victoria ◀

Hallgarth Street (A177, near Dunelm House); DH1 3AS

Unchanging and neatly kept Victorian pub with royal memorabilia, cheerful locals, and well kept regional ales; bedrooms

The unspoilt layout of this welcoming 19th-c local consists of three little rooms leading off a central bar. Their typical Victorian décor takes in mahogany, etched and cut glass and mirrors, colourful William Morris wallpaper over a high panelled dado, some maroon plush seats in little booths, leatherette wall seats and long narrow drinkers' tables. There are also some handsome iron and tile fireplaces for the coal fires, photographs and articles showing a very proper pride in the pub, lots of period prints and engravings of Queen Victoria, and staffordshire figurines of her and the Prince Consort. It's been in the same friendly family for 36 years and attracts a good mix of locals and students. Big Lamp Bitter and Wylam Gold Tankard and up to three usually local guests from brewers such as Durham and York are on handpump, they've over 40 irish whiskies and cheap house wines; dominoes.

Bar food is limited to toasties. *Benchmark main dish: toasties £1.70.*

Free house ~ Licensee Michael Webster ~ Real ale ~ Bar food ~ (0191) 386 5269 ~ Children welcome ~ Dogs welcome ~ Open 11.45-3, 6-11; 12-2, 7-10.30 Sun ~ Bedrooms: £49B/£68B

Recommended by Comus and Sarah Elliott, Eric Larkham, the Didler, Phil and Sally Gorton, Dr and Mrs P Truelove, Peter Smith and Judith Brown, Peter F Marshall

EAST WITTON Yorkshire

SE1486 Map A

Blue Lion

A6108 Leyburn—Ripon; DL8 4SN

Civilised dining pub with interesting rooms, daily papers, real ales, delicious food, and courteous service; comfortable bedrooms

Although most customers are here to enjoy the excellent food or to stay overnight in the individually decorated bedrooms, this civilised but informal dining pub does have a proper small bar where drinkers and their dogs mingle quite happily with those waiting to eat. This big squarish room has high-backed antique settles and old windsor chairs on the turkey rugs and flagstones, ham-hooks in the high ceiling decorated with dried wheat, teazles and so forth, a delft shelf filled with appropriate bric-a-brac, several prints, sporting caricatures and other pictures, a log fire and daily papers. Black Sheep Best and Golden Sheep and Theakstons Best on handpump, and an impressive wine list with quite a few (plus champagne) by the glass; courteous, attentive service. Picnic-sets on the gravel outside look beyond the stone houses on the far side of the village green to Witton Fell, and there's a big, pretty back garden.

Excellent and interesting – if not cheap – food might include sandwiches, slow-braised pig's cheek with red wine sauce, black pudding and apple and parsnip purée, duck and orange parfait with sage and onion toast and piccalilli, home-made tagliatelle with pancetta, wild mushrooms, cream and truffle oil, poached fillet of smoked haddock on new potatoes topped with a poached egg, leek and mushroom sauce and gruyère, a trio of free-range herb-fed chicken (breast, thigh and drumstick) each with their own garnish, and chargrilled rib-eye steak with caramelised onion butter and duck fat potatoes. *Benchmark main dish: slow-braised beef with red wine and thyme risotto £16.95. Two-course evening meal £24.45.*

Free house ~ Licensee Paul Klein ~ Real ale ~ Bar food ~ Restaurant ~ (01969) 624273 ~ Children welcome ~ Dogs allowed in bar and bedrooms ~ Open 11-11 ~ Bedrooms: £67.50S/£94S(£109B)

Recommended by Jon Clarke, David and Sue Atkinson, Mike and Shelley Woodroffe, Brian and Janet Ainscough, Pat and Stewart Gordon, the Didler, Michael Butler, Susan and Neil McLean, Dr Kevan Tucker, Janet and Peter Race, Hunter and Christine Wright, Comus and Sarah Elliott

 ELSLACK Yorkshire   SD9249   Map C

Tempest Arms
Just off A56 Earby—Skipton; BD23 3AY

Friendly inn with three log fires in stylish rooms, six real ales, good wines and extremely popular food; bedrooms

Even when this 18th-c stone dining inn is at its busiest – which it often deservedly is – the licensees and their staff remain willing and friendly. There's a wide mix of customers coming and going from families to diners and walkers with their dogs, but everyone feels welcomed and relaxed. It's stylish but understated with plenty of character in the bar and surrounding dining areas: cushioned armchairs, built-in wall seats with comfortable cushions, stools and lots of tables and three log fires – one greets you at the entrance and divides the bar and restaurant. There's quite a bit of exposed stonework, amusing prints on the cream walls, half a dozen real ales such as Dark Horse Hetton Pale Ale, Theakstons Best, Thwaites Lancaster Bomber, Timothy Taylors Golden Best and Landlord, and a beer named for the pub on handpump, 16 wines by the glass and 25 malt whiskies. There are tables outside largely screened from the road by a raised bank. The comfortable bedrooms are in a newish purpose-built extension.

Highly enjoyable and generously served, the food includes lunchtime sandwiches, tapas-style nibbles, stir-fried baby squid with asian greens and noodles, beer-battered corned beef and black pudding fritters with curry sauce, onion and cheese pie with asparagus sauce, toad in the hole, fish pie, liver and bacon with onion and madeira gravy, and chicken breast filled with mushroom mousse on rösti potato with creamy mushroom sauce. *Benchmark main dish: slow-cooked lamb shank in a redcurrant and mint gravy £12.50. Two-course evening meal £17.25.*

Free house ~ Licensees Martin and Veronica Clarkson ~ Real ale ~ Bar food (12-2.30, 6-9(9.30 Fri and Sat); 12-7.30 Sun) ~ Restaurant ~ (01282) 842450 ~ Children welcome ~ Dogs allowed in bar and bedrooms ~ Open 11-11; 12-10.30 Sun ~ Bedrooms: £62.50B/£79.95B

Recommended by Brian and Janet Ainscough, John and Eleanor Holdsworth, Ian Malone, Pat and Tony Martin, Michael Butler, Christopher Mobbs, Janet and Peter Race, Chris Brewster, Tony and Maggie Harwood, Mrs Edna M Jones, Gordon and Margaret Ormondroyd, David and Ruth Shillitoe, Jeremy King

GRETA BRIDGE County Durham NZ0813 Map A

Morritt Arms ❪❫ ♇ 🛏

Hotel signposted off A66 W of Scotch Corner; DL12 9SE

Country house hotel with nice bar, extraordinary mural, interesting food, and attractive garden with play area; bedrooms

The walls of the Dickens bar at this striking 17th-c former coaching inn were painted in 1946 by J T Y Gilroy (better known for his Guinness advertisements) with a remarkable mural depicting a series of larger-than-life Dickensian characters. Although part of a thriving and busy hotel with weddings and the like sometimes taking place, this friendly bar right at its heart does maintain a proper pubby atmosphere. Big windsor chairs and sturdy oak settles cluster around traditional cast-iron-framed tables, large windows look out on the extensive lawn and there are warm open fires. Friendly knowledgeable staff serve Thwaites Major Morritt (brewed for the pub) and Timothy Taylors Landlord from handpumps, alongside 19 wines by the glass from an extensive list; piped music. The attractively laid-out garden has some seating and teak tables in a pretty side area looking along to the graceful old bridge by the stately gates to Rokeby Park; there's also a play area for children.

🍴 Good tasty food includes sandwiches, fried lambs liver with garlic mash and thyme gravy, battered cod, lasagne, vegetable ratatouille in a filo basket, pork and leek sausages, grilled pork loin steak with creamy mushroom sauce, and chicken caesar salad. *Benchmark main dish: home-made burger £9.50. Two-course evening meal £14.00.*

Free house ~ Licensees Peter Phillips and Barbara Johnson ~ Real ale ~ Bar food (12-3, 6-9) ~ Restaurant ~ (01833) 627232 ~ Children welcome ~ Dogs allowed in bar and bedrooms ~ Open 11-11; 12-10.30 Sun ~ Bedrooms: £85S(£90B)/£110B

Recommended by Maurice Ricketts, Comus and Sarah Elliott, Jerry Brown, Barry Collett, Dr and Mrs R G J Telfer

GRINTON Yorkshire SE0498 Map A

Bridge Inn ◖ 🛏

B6270 W of Richmond; DL11 6HH

Bustling pub with traditional, comfortable bars, log fires, several real ales and malt whiskies, and tasty bar food; neat bedrooms

This former coaching inn, in a pretty Swaledale village, is popular with walkers and their dogs – which is appropriate since there are plenty of good, surrounding walks. There are bow-window seats and a pair of stripped traditional settles among more usual pub seats, all well cushioned, a good log fire, Jennings Cumberland and Cocker Hoop and guests such as Brakspears Oxford Gold and Ringwood Best on handpump, several wines by the glass and 25 malt whiskies. On the right, a few steps take you down into a room with darts, a well lit pool table and ring the bull. On the left, past leather armchairs and a sofa by a second log fire (and a glass chess set) is an extensive two-part dining room. The décor is in mint-green and shades of brown, with a modicum of fishing memorabilia. The bedrooms are neat and simple, and breakfasts are good. There are picnic-sets outside and the inn is right opposite a lovely church known as the Cathedral of the Dales.

🍴 Using local produce where possible, the well liked food includes sandwiches, black pudding with bacon, onion and mushrooms in a creamy mustard sauce on a herb croûton, leek, wild mushroom and parmesan risotto, steak in ale pie, free-range chicken filled with cheese, wrapped in bacon with a cranberry and wine sauce, moroccan lamb casserole, and salmon steak with a gruyère and parsley crust on vegetable stew. *Benchmark main dish: fish and chips £9.25. Two-course evening meal £16.00.*

Jennings (Marstons) ~ Lease Andrew Atkin ~ Real ale ~ Bar food (all day) ~ Restaurant ~ (01748) 884224 ~ Children welcome ~ Dogs allowed in bar and bedrooms ~ Open 12-midnight(1am Sat) ~ Bedrooms: £50B/£80B

Recommended by David Thornton, JJW, CMW, Sandie and Andrew Geddes

 HALIFAX Yorkshire   SE1027   Map C

Shibden Mill 🍴 ☐ 🍺

Off A58 into Kell Lane at Stump Cross Inn, near A6036 junction; keep on, pub signposted from Kell Lane on left; HX3 7UL

Tucked-away 300-year-old mill with cosy rambling bar, five real ales and inventive bar food; comfortable bedrooms

This 17th-c restored mill comes as a nice surprise – tucked away as it is at the bottom of a peaceful wooded valley. There's a good, bustling atmosphere and a happy mix of both locals and visitors who are here to enjoy the first-class food and well equipped, individually decorated bedrooms. The rambling, friendly bar has cosy side areas with banquettes heaped with cushions and rugs, there are well spaced nice old tables and chairs, and the candles in elegant iron holders give a feeling of real intimacy; also, old hunting prints, country landscapes and so forth, and a couple of big log fires. Little Valley Hebdens Wheat and Withens IPA, Moorhouses Premier Bitter, and a couple of guest beers on handpump, and 16 wines by the glass from a wide list. There's also an upstairs restaurant; piped music and TV. Outside on the attractive heated terrace, there are plenty of seats and tables, and the building is prettily floodlit at night.

 Highly thought-of and interesting, the food might include sandwiches, potted ham hock and foie gras with piccalilli, slow-cooked rabbit with confit onions and a coddled duck egg, beetroot and red wine risotto with apple and blue cheese salad, beer-battered haddock with dripping chips, chorizo-stuffed free-range pork belly with smoked paprika cream, and braised wild bass with crispy potato and cauliflower, pickled fennel, cumin and a hazelnut and peppercorn sauce. *Benchmark main dish: confit duck leg £16.95. Two-course evening meal £22.20.*

Free house ~ Licensee Glen Pearson ~ Real ale ~ Bar food (12-2, 6-9.30; 12-7.30 Sun) ~ Restaurant ~ (01422) 365840 ~ Children welcome ~ Dogs allowed in bar and bedrooms ~ Open 12-2.30, 5.30-11; 12-11(10.30 Sun) Sat ~ Bedrooms: £81B/£100B

Recommended by Michael Butler, Ian Malone, Peter Burton, Derek and Sylvia Stephenson

HALTWHISTLE Northumberland   NY7166   Map A

Milecastle Inn £

Military Road; B6318 NE – OS Sheet 86 map reference 715660; NE49 9NN

Close to Hadrian's Wall and some wild scenery, with cosy little rooms warmed by winter log fires; fine views and a walled garden

This useful place is just 500 metres from Hadrian's Wall and some of its most celebrated sites. It's open all day in summer when it makes a perfect stop for liquid refreshments, and in winter you can have a pleasant warm-up by the two log fires. The snug little rooms of the beamed bar are decorated with brasses, horsey and local landscape prints and attractive fresh flowers; at lunchtime, the small comfortable restaurant is used as an overflow. Big Lamp Prince Bishop and a couple of guests are on handpump and they stock several malt whiskies. There are tables and benches in the pleasantly sheltered big walled garden, with a dovecote and rather stunning views; two self-catering cottages and a large car park.

Straightforward bar food includes sandwiches, potato skins with garlic dip, game pâté, prawn cocktail, battered haddock, scampi, lasagne, vegetable curry, venison in red wine and Guinness, various pies and steaks. *Benchmark main dish: wild boar and duckling pie £9.75. Two-course evening meal £14.50.*

Free house ~ Licensees Clare and Kevin Hind ~ Real ale ~ Bar food (12-8.45(8.30 Sun); 12-2.30, 6-8.30 in winter) ~ (01434) 321372 ~ Children welcome ~ Dogs welcome ~ Open 12-10.30(11 Sat); 12-3, 6-10 in winter

Recommended by Bruce and Sharon Eden, Sheena W Makin, Maurice and Gill McMahon, Mr and Mrs John Taylor, Clive Watkin, Jean and Douglas Troup

HARTSHEAD Yorkshire   SE1822 Map C

Gray Ox ⊗ ⊤

3.5 miles from M62 junction 25; A644 towards Dewsbury, left on to A62, next left on to B6119, then first left on to Fall Lane; left into Hartshead Lane; pub on right; WF15 8AL

Attractive dining pub with cosy beamed bars, inventive cooking, real ales, several wines by the glass, and fine views

At its most pubby at lunchtime, this is an attractive stone-built dining pub that's handy for the M62. The main bar has beams and flagstones, bentwood chairs, leather stools around stripped-pine tables and a roaring log fire. Comfortable carpeted dining areas with bold paintwork and leather dining chairs around polished tables lead off; the hunting-theme wallpaper is interesting and unusual. Jennings Cumberland, Cocker Hoop, Sneck Lifter and a changing guest on handpump, 14 wines by the glass and two champagnes; piped music. There are picnic-sets outside, and fine views through the latticed pub windows across the Calder Valley to the distant outskirts of Huddersfield – the lights are pretty at night.

Using local, seasonal produce, the good, modern food at lunchtime includes sandwiches, hot smoked salmon and dill risotto topped with a poached egg, beer-battered haddock and spicy lamb with coriander and coconut milk, with more pricey evening dishes like duck liver and foie gras parfait with apricot chutney, pork fillet wrapped in smoked pancetta, blue cheese croquettes, fennel and apple salad and cider cream sauce, and goan fish curry with king prawns and cashew nuts; they also offer a good value two- and three-course set menu (Monday-Friday lunchtimes and from 6-7pm). *Benchmark main dish: special fish pie £9.95. Two-course evening meal £20.20.*

Banks's (Marstons) ~ Lease Bernadette McCarron ~ Real ale ~ Bar food (12-2, 6-9 (9.30 Sat); 12-7 Sun) ~ (01274) 872845 ~ Children welcome ~ Open 12-3, 6-midnight; 12-midnight Sat; 12-11 Sun

Recommended by Dr Kevan Tucker, DC, Gordon and Margaret Ormondroyd, Carl Rahn Griffith, Tim and Sue Halstead, Sam and Christine Kilburn, Jeremy King

---

Half pints: by law, a pub should not charge more for half a pint than half the price of a full pint, unless it shows that half-pint price on its price list.

HAYDON BRIDGE Northumberland   NY8364   Map A

General Havelock

A69 Corbridge—Haltwhistle; NE47 6ER

Bustling, chatty riverside dining pub with local beers and some interesting food

The attractively lit L-shaped bar at this homely terrace house is imaginatively decorated in shades of green. It's at its best in the back part with a stripped-pine chest of drawers topped with bric-a-brac, colourful cushions on long pine benches and a sturdy stripped settle, interestingly shaped mahogany-topped tables and good wildlife photographs. They serve Allendale Curlew's Return and a local guest such as Geltsdale Cold Fell or Houston Killellan on handpump, ten wines by the glass and a choice of apple juices; board games and boules. Both the stripped-stone barn dining room and the terrace enjoy fine South Tyne river views and it's just a short, pretty stroll downstream from Haydon Bridge itself.

Cooked by the landlord (who makes his own bread and ice-cream) using local produce, the well liked bar food includes lunchtime baguettes, cullen skink, ham hock terrine with warm pease pudding and mustard sauce, sautéed scallops on black pudding and cauliflower purée, chicken caesar salad, pork belly stuffed with prunes on asparagus, calves liver with pancetta and chive gravy, and fish of the day. *Benchmark main dish: duck breast on apple mash with gravy £14.00. Two-course evening meal £20.00.*

Free house ~ Licensees Gary and Joanna Thompson ~ Real ale ~ Bar food (not Sun evening) ~ Restaurant ~ (01434) 684376 ~ Children welcome ~ Dogs allowed in bar ~ Open 12-3, 7-midnight; 12-5, 7.30-10.30 Sun; closed Mon

Recommended by Bruce and Sharon Eden, Comus and Sarah Elliott, James Thompson, Mrs L Wells, Andy and Jill Kassube, Helen and Brian Edgeley, Alan Sutton

HEATH Yorkshire   SE3520   Map C

Kings Arms  £

Village signposted from A655 Wakefield—Normanton – or, more directly, turn off to the left opposite the Horse & Groom; WF1 5SL

Old-fashioned gaslit pub in interesting location with dark-panelled original bar, up to 11 real ales and well liked bar food; seats outside

Now owned by Ossett and with a new landlady, this remains an old-fashioned pub – still making the most of the village green setting opposite. The original bar has gas lighting which adds a lot to the atmosphere, a fire burning in the old black range (with a long row of smoothing irons on the mantelpiece), plain elm stools, oak settles built into the walls, and dark panelling. A more comfortable extension has carefully preserved the original style, down to good wood-pegged oak panelling (two embossed with royal arms) and a high shelf of plates; there are also two other small flagstoned rooms and a conservatory that opens on to the garden. Ossett Silver King, Yorkshire Blonde and a beer named for the pub from Ossett, as well as Fullers London Pride and five guest beers on handpump. There are some sunny benches facing the green (which is surrounded by 19th-c stone merchants' houses), picnic-sets on a side lawn and a nice walled garden.

Bar food now includes sandwiches, thai salmon fishcakes, a poached duck egg with asparagus and bacon soldiers, pea and home-grown mint risotto, chicken with bacon, cheese and barbecue sauce, giant battered haddock, and lambs liver with crispy parma ham. *Benchmark main dish: beef in ale pie £9.95. Two-course evening meal £14.95.*

Ossett ~ Manager Angela Cromack ~ Real ale ~ Bar food (12-2, 6-9; 12-9 Fri and Sat; 12-5 Sun; not Sun evening) ~ Restaurant ~ (01924) 377527 ~ Children allowed away from main lounge ~ Dogs allowed in bar ~ Open 12-11(midnight Sat); may open 12-3, 5-11 weekdays in winter

Recommended by the Didler, Pat and Tony Martin

HEDLEY ON THE HILL Northumberland   NZ0759   Map A

Feathers ❦ ♀ ◖

Village signposted from New Ridley, which is signposted from B6309 N of Consett; OS Sheet 88 map reference 078592; NE43 7SW

Imaginative food, interesting beers from small breweries, and friendly welcome in quaint tavern

Although most tables at this thoughtfully run hilltop tavern are laid for dining, its three neat beamed bars do still at least look properly pubby with their open fires, stripped stonework, solid furniture, including settles, and old black and white photographs of local places and farm and country workers. Friendly knowledgable staff serve four ales from a different local brewer each time a barrel is changed; maybe Jarrow, Mordue Workie Ticket, Wylam Gold Tankard and a guest such as Orkney Red MacGregor from handpumps, as well as farm ciders, 28 wines by the glass, 34 malt whiskies and several bourbons. They hold a beer and food festival at Easter with over two dozen real ales, a barrel race on Easter Monday and other traditional events; darts and dominoes. Picnic-sets in front are a nice place to sit and watch the world drift by.

Leaning towards traditional british cooking and using home-butchered game from local shoots, beef from rare breeds and home-baked bread (and listing their carefully chosen suppliers on the daily-changing menu), the imaginative food might include ploughman's, lobster and crayfish cocktail, charcuterie, roe deer merguez sausages with couscous and harissa, battered haddock and chips, mushroom risotto, pigeon pie, lamb shank with dauphinoise potatoes and braised red cabbage, and saddle of rabbit stuffed with black pudding with cream cider sauce. *Benchmark main dish: pot-roast beef £12.00. Two-course evening meal £19.80.*

Free house ~ Licensees Rhian Cradock and Helen Greer ~ Real ale ~ Bar food (12-2(2.30 Sun), 6-8.30 not Mon or first two weeks in Jan) ~ (01661) 843607 ~ Children welcome ~ Folk music first Sun of month ~ Open 12-11(10.30 Sun); closed Mon lunchtime except bank holidays

Recommended by David and Cathrine Whiting, Eric Larkham, James Thompson, Mike and Lynn Robinson, John Coatsworth, Lawrence Pearse, Andy and Jill Kassube, Peter and Eleanor Kenyon, Graham Oddey, Dr and Mrs P Truelove, GSB, Comus and Sarah Elliott

LEDSHAM Yorkshire   SE4529   Map C

Chequers ◖

1.5 miles from A1(M) junction 42: follow Leeds signs, then Ledsham signposted; Claypit Lane; LS25 5LP

Friendly village pub, handy for the A1, with hands-on landlord, log fires in several beamed rooms, real ales and interesting food; pretty back terrace

Although many customers come to this well-run 16th-c stone inn to enjoy the interesting food, the friendly hands-on landlord also keeps five real ales on handpump. There are several small, individually decorated rooms with low beams, lots of cosy alcoves, toby jugs and all sorts of knick-knacks on the walls and ceilings, and log fires. From the old-fashioned little central panelled-in servery, they offer beers from breweries such as Brown Cow, John Smith, Theakston and Timothy Taylor; good, attentive service. A sheltered two-level terrace behind the house has tables among roses and the hanging baskets and flowers are very pretty. RSPB Fairburn Ings reserve is close by. This is a lovely village and the pub is handy for the A1.

As well as some pubby choices like sandwiches, corned-beef hash, pork, leek and apple sausages and gammon with a duck egg and sweetcorn rösti, the more pricey, restaurant-style food might include a tian of smoked fish with a honey and mustard dressing, king scallops with pea purée, crispy pancetta and truffle oil, butternut squash and pine nut risotto, halibut fillet with potted shrimps and parsley butter, and venison loin with black pudding, smoked bacon and red cabbage; side dishes are extra. *Benchmark main dish: steak in mushroom pie £10.85. Two-course evening meal £23.45.*

Free house ~ Licensee Chris Wraith ~ Real ale ~ Bar food (12-9 Mon-Sat; not Sun) ~ Restaurant ~ (01977) 683135 ~ Well behaved children allowed ~ Dogs allowed in bar ~ Open 11-11; closed Sun

Recommended by Christine Vallely, MJVK, Neil Whitehead, Victoria Anderson, Pat and Stewart Gordon, Sam and Christine Kilburn, Terry and Nickie Williams, Andy and Jill Kassube, the Didler, GSB, Jeff and Wendy Williams, Grahame Brooks, Gerard Dyson, Paul Cooper

LEVISHAM Yorkshire   SE8390   Map A

Horseshoe 🍴 ⇐
Off A169 N of Pickering; YO18 7NL

Friendly village pub run by two brothers; neat rooms, real ales, very good food, and seats on the village green; bedrooms

Our readers very much enjoy their visits to this friendly, traditional pub, well run by two jovial brothers; they also have warm praise for the smart, comfortable bedrooms – some of which have fine views. The bars have beams, smart blue banquettes, wheelback and captain's chairs around a variety of tables on the polished wooden floors, vibrant landscapes by a local artist on the walls, and a log fire in the stone fireplace; an adjoining snug has a woodburning stove, comfortable leather sofas and old photographs of the pub and the village. Black Sheep and a guest such as Cropton Endeavour Ale or Yorkshire Moors Bitter on handpump, home-made elderflower cordial, 20 malt whiskies and a farm cider; board games and piped music. There are seats on the attractive green, more in the back garden, and fine surrounding walks.

Using their own chicken and goose eggs and cooked by one of the landlords, the particularly good, attractively presented food includes sandwiches, grilled black pudding with sautéed potatoes and apple sauce, wild mushroom risotto, whitby haddock with home-made chips, duck breast on sweet potato mash with a red wine and port sauce, and specials such as seafood platter, and venison suet pudding with sloe gin gravy. *Benchmark main dish: pork belly with thyme mash and cider gravy £11.95. Two-course evening meal £17.75.*

Free house ~ Licensees Toby and Charles Wood ~ Real ale ~ Bar food (12-2, 6-8.30) ~ (01751) 460240 ~ Children welcome but bedrooms not ideal for them ~ Dogs welcome ~ Open 11-11 ~ Bedrooms: $40/$80S

Recommended by Ann and Tony Bennett-Hughes, Andy Lickfold, Nick Dalby, P G Wooler,
Michael Goodden, Ed and Anna Fraser

LEYBURN Yorkshire   SE1190   Map A

Sandpiper 🍴 ♀ 🛏

Just off Market Place; DL8 5AT

**Emphasis on appealing food though cosy bar for drinkers in 17th-c
cottage, real ales, and amazing choice of whiskies; bedrooms**

This is a first-class pub with a warm welcome for all – and several
readers were delighted that their dogs were allowed to sit in front of
the fire in the snug; this cosy room is liked by locals for a drink and a chat,
which keeps the atmosphere relaxed and informal. Another little bar has a
couple of black beams in the low ceiling, wooden or cushioned built-in
wall seats around a few tables, and the back room up three steps has
attractive Dales photographs; get here early to be sure of a seat. Down by
the nice linenfold panelled bar counter, there are stuffed sandpipers, more
photographs and a woodburning stove in the stone fireplace; to the left is
the attractive restaurant, with fresh flowers and dark wooden tables and
chairs on floorboards. Black Sheep Golden and a beer from Copper
Dragon or Daleside on handpump, up to 100 malt whiskies and a decent
wine list with several by the glass; piped music. In good weather, you can
enjoy a drink on the front terrace among the lovely hanging baskets and
flowering climbers. The boutique-style bedrooms are comfortable.

🍴 Cooked by the landlord, who also makes his own bread and ice-creams, the
excellent, imaginative food might include lunchtime sandwiches and specials
like smoked haddock and potato omelette, beer-battered fish and chips, and a rib
burger with thin fries, as well as pigeon, blood orange and walnut salad, ham hock
and chicken terrine with home-made piccalilli, double-baked vintage cheese soufflé,
moroccan-style chicken with lemon and coriander couscous, and fish, crayfish and
fennel pasta. *Benchmark main dish: pressed local lamb with creamed leeks and
garlic £15.75. Two-course evening meal £21.80.*

Free house ~ Licensee Jonathan Harrison ~ Real ale ~ Bar food (12-2.30, 6.30-9(9.30 Fri
and Sat); not Mon or winter Tues) ~ Restaurant ~ (01969) 622206 ~ Children welcome ~
Dogs allowed in bar and bedrooms ~ Open 11.30-3, 6.30-11(10.30 Sun); closed Mon and
some winter Tues ~ Bedrooms: £75S(£80B)/£85S(£90B)

*Recommended by Gordon Briggs, Pat and Graham Williamson, Sandie and Andrew Geddes,
John and Eleanor Holdsworth*

LONG PRESTON Yorkshire   SD8358   Map C

Maypole 🍺 🛏

A65 Settle—Skipton; BD23 4PH

**A good base for walkers with friendly staff, a bustling atmosphere, well
liked pubby food, and a fair choice of real ales**

This comfortingly traditional village pub usefully offers food all day and
makes a good base for walking in the Dales; the bedrooms are quiet
and clean. Mr and Mrs Palmer have been at the helm here for over
25 years and there's a list of landlords dating back to 1695 on the butter-
coloured walls of the bar. This carpeted two-room bar also has good solid
pub furnishings – red leather wall seats, heavy carved wall settles and
plush red-topped bar stools around cast-iron-framed pub tables with
unusual inset leather tops on the red patterned carpet, and plenty of local

photographs. There's a separate dining room. Moorhouses Premier Bitter, Timothy Taylors Landlord and a couple of guests like Goose Eye Barm Pot Bitter and Moorhouses Pendle Witches Brew on handpump, ten wines by the glass, Weston's cider and a dozen malt whiskies. The left-hand tap room has darts, dominoes, and TV for important sporting events. On a back terrace, there are a couple of picnic-sets under an ornamental cherry tree, with more tables under umbrellas on another terrace (which has outdoor heaters).

Tasty bar food includes sandwiches, chicken liver pâté with plum chutney, cheese and spinach or meaty lasagne, various salads, ham and eggs, battered haddock with mushy peas, sausages with mash and onion gravy, braised lamb shank with mint, and daily specials. *Benchmark main dish: steak in ale pie £9.95. Two-course evening meal £15.50.*

Enterprise ~ Lease Robert Palmer ~ Real ale ~ Bar food (12-9(9.30 Fri and Sat)) ~ Restaurant ~ (01729) 840219 ~ Children welcome ~ Dogs allowed in bar and bedrooms ~ Quiz first Weds night of month; live mike evening quarterly ~ Open 12-11(12.30 Sat) ~ Bedrooms: £42S/£75B

Recommended by Mrs Judith Kirkham, Dudley and Moira Cockroft, Clive Flynn, Gerard Dyson, Dr Ann Henderson

LOW CATTON Yorkshire   SE7053 Map C

Gold Cup

Village signposted with High Catton off A166 in Stamford Bridge or A1079 at Kexby Bridge; YO41 1EA

Friendly, pleasant pub with attractive bars, real ales, decent food, seats in garden, and ponies in paddock

At weekends, this spacious white-rendered house usefully serves food all day and is just the place to head for after a walk. It's run by a helpful and informative landlord and the beamed bars have a country feel with coach lights on the rustic-looking walls, smart tables and chairs on the stripped wooden floors, an open fire at one end opposite the woodburning stove, and quite a few pictures. The restaurant has solid wooden pews and tables (said to be made from a single oak tree) and pleasant views of the surrounding fields. Theakstons Best and maybe a guest beer on handpump; piped music and pool. The garden has a grassed area for children and the back paddock houses Candy the horse and Polly the shetland pony. They have fishing rights on the adjoining River Derwent.

As well as lunchtime sandwiches (not Sunday), the reasonably priced food using some home-grown produce includes creamed stilton mushrooms, chicken liver pâté with onion marmalade, three-egg omelette, beer-battered cod, spicy cajun chicken with a mint and yoghurt dip, salmon and prawn pie, and venison steak in red wine gravy. *Benchmark main dish: braised lamb shank in port and redcurrant gravy £13.50. Two-course evening meal £15.50.*

Free house ~ Licensees Pat and Ray Hales ~ Real ale ~ Bar food (12-2.30, 6-9; all day weekends; not Mon lunchtime) ~ Restaurant ~ (01759) 371354 ~ Children welcome ~ Dogs allowed in bar ~ Open 12-2.30, 6-11; 12-11(10.30 Sun) Sat; closed Mon lunchtime

Recommended by Pat and Graham Williamson, Gerard Dyson, Pete Coxon, Peter and Anne Hollindale

> The price we give for a two-course evening meal in the featured top pub entries is the mean (average of cheapest and most expensive) price of a starter and a main course – no drinks.

LUND Yorkshire

SE9748 Map D

Wellington 🍴 🍷

Off B1248 SW of Driffield; YO25 9TE

Busy, smart pub with plenty of space in several rooms, real ales, helpfully noted wine list, and interesting changing food

Smart and neatly kept, this bustling village pub is run by friendly people. The cosy Farmers Bar has a good mix of both drinkers and diners, beams, a quirky fireplace, well polished wooden banquettes and square tables and gold-framed pictures and corner lamps on the walls. Off to one side is a plainer, no less smart, flagstoned room with a wine theme. At the other end of the bar, a york-stoned walkway leads to a room with a display of the village's Britain in Bloom awards. There's also a restaurant and a bistro dining area with another open log fire. The main bar in the evening is a haven for drinkers only: Black Sheep Ruddy Ram, John Smiths, Timothy Taylors Landlord and a guest like York Yorkshire Terrier on handpump, a good wine list with a helpfully labelled choice by the glass and 25 malt whiskies. Piped music, board games and TV. There are some benches in a small, pretty back courtyard.

 Good, interesting food includes sandwiches, pressed ham hock terrine with a quail's egg and pineapple piccalilli, pigeon, apple and raspberry salad with raspberry gin dressing, aubergine, chickpea and green olive tagine with toasted almond couscous, chicken breast with gnocchi carbonara, sautéed leeks and truffle oil, grilled wild bass fillets with crab and samphire risotto and crab bisque, and loin of venison, haunch cobbler, fondant potato and braised red cabbage. *Benchmark main dish: beef and mushroom suet pudding £16.10. Two-course evening meal £23.30.*

Free house ~ Licensees Russell Jeffery and Sarah Jeffery ~ Real ale ~ Bar food (not Sun evening or Mon lunchtime) ~ Restaurant (Tues-Sat evenings) ~ (01377) 217294 ~ Children welcome ~ Open 12-3, 6.30-midnight; 12-midnight Sun; closed Mon lunch
Recommended by Roger and Ann King, Adrian Johnson, Pat and Stewart Gordon, Gerard Dyson

MOULTON Yorkshire

NZ2303 Map A

Black Bull 🍴 🍷

Just E of A1, 1 mile E of Scotch Corner; DL10 6QJ

Character bar in civilised dining pub, interesting lunchtime bar food (more elaborate restaurant menu, strong on fish), and smart dining areas (one is a Pullman dining car)

Decidedly civilised, this is strictly a dining pub but it does have a bar with a lot of proper character. There's a huge winter log fire, an antique panelled oak settle and an old elm housekeeper's chair, built-in red cushioned black settles and pews around cast-iron tables, silver-plated turkish coffee pots and copper cooking utensils hanging from black beams, and fresh flowers. There's also a Fish Bar (first come, first served as no bookings are taken), an airy conservatory with a massive grapevine and antique train company signs on the walls, a traditional restaurant with nooks and crannies leading off it, and the elegant *Brighton Belle* dining car. Eight wines by the glass (including champagne) and 50 malt whiskies. There are some seats outside in the central court. The pub is handy for the A1.

At lunchtime, the very good bar food includes sandwiches, chicken and ham terrine with onion jam, smoked haddock and spring onion risotto with a soft poached egg, cheddar and spinach soufflé, local sausages with mustard mash and crispy onions, minute steak with crispy onion rings and chips, and seafood mixed grill with sauce antiboise (tomatoes, olives, coriander, cress, shallots and garlic). *Benchmark main dish: dover sole with black butter £28.50. Two-course evening meal £24.50.*

Free house ~ Licensee Mr Barker ~ Bar food (12-2.30(2 Sat), 6-9.30(10 Fri and Sat); 12-4 Sun; not Sun evening) ~ Restaurant (evening) ~ (01325) 377289 ~ Children over 12 welcome ~ Open 12-2.30(2 Sat, 4 Sun), 6-11; closed Sun evening

Recommended by GNI, Pat and Stewart Gordon, Chris Flynn, Wendy Jones, Derek Thomas

 NUNNINGTON Yorkshire   SE6679 Map C

Royal Oak

Church Street; at back of village, which is signposted from A170 and B1257; YO62 5US

Friendly staff and good food in reliable, neat pub, lots to look at in beamed bar, winter open fires, and real ales

Standards are as high as ever at this well run and attractive little pub. The neatly kept bar has high black beams strung with earthenware flagons, copper jugs and lots of antique keys, one of the walls is stripped back to the bare stone to display a fine collection of antique farm tools, and there are open fires; also, carefully chosen furniture such as kitchen and country dining chairs and a long pew around the sturdy tables on the turkey carpet. The dining area is linked to the bar by a double-sided wood-burning stove. Black Sheep Ale and Wold Top Wolds Way on handpump, ten wines by the glass and several malt whiskies; piped music. There are seats on the terrace. Nunnington Hall (National Trust) is a ten-minute walk away.

Using game from the local estate and other local produce, the enjoyable food includes sandwiches, smoked salmon mousseline with cucumber and dill pickle, black pudding with parmentier potatoes, quail's egg and roasted garlic toast, mixed wild mushroom stroganoff, pork medallions in a cider, cream and apple sauce, chicken breast stuffed with stilton and wrapped in Italian ham, and specials like roast cod with garlic king prawns and pheasant or rabbit casserole. *Benchmark main dish: steak pie £11.50. Two-course evening meal £18.90.*

Free house ~ Licensee Anita Hilton ~ Real ale ~ Bar food (not Mon – except bank holiday lunchtimes) ~ Restaurant ~ (01439) 748271 ~ Children welcome ~ Dogs welcome ~ Open 11.45(12 weekends)-2.30, 6.30(7 Sun)-11; closed Mon (except bank holiday lunchtimes)

Recommended by Neil Whitehead, Victoria Anderson, Nick Dalby, John and Eleanor Holdsworth, Michael Butler, Gerard Dyson

 OLDSTEAD Yorkshire   SE5380 Map C

Black Swan

Main Street; YO61 4BL

16th-c restaurant-with-rooms in remote countryside with first-class food, real ales, several wines by the glass and friendly staff; comfortable bedrooms

Of course, much emphasis is placed on the excellent food in this 16th-c restaurant-with-rooms but they do have a proper bar with real ales and you can be sure of a friendly welcome. This bar has beams and flagstones, furniture by 'Mousey' Thompson, window seats with soft cushions and pretty valley views, an open log fire, Black Sheep Best and Copper Dragon Best on handpump, 13 wines by the glass and several malt whiskies; courteous, attentive staff. The back dining rooms are comfortable and attractive. At the front of the building are some picnic-sets under parasols beneath the cherry trees. The well equipped ground floor bedrooms have their own terrace and breakfasts are highly thought of. There are plenty of fine surrounding walks in the glorious National Park countryside. Please note that the bedroom price includes dinner for two.

At lunchtime, the imaginative, beautifully presented food includes sandwiches, ham hock ballottine with cider jelly and apples, beer-battered haddock with pea purée, home-made sausages with mash and buttered greens, and a french-style rib of beef stew, with more pricey evening choices such as hand-dived king scallops with sweetcorn, chorizo and tortilla chips, confit and cured wild sea trout niçoise, slow-braised belly and soy-glazed pig's cheek with a pork and vegetable spring roll and pak choi, and gressingham duck breast with duck confit potatoes, braised chicory, french onion purée and sherry vinegar jus; they also offer a two- and three-course set lunch menu. *Two-course evening meal £33.00.*

Free house ~ Licensee Tom Banks ~ Real ale ~ Bar food (12-2(2.30 Sun), 6-9; not Mon-Weds lunchtimes) ~ Restaurant ~ (01347) 868387 ~ Children welcome but must be over 10 in bedrooms ~ Open 12-3, 6-10.30(11 Sat); closed Mon-Weds lunchtimes; two weeks in Jan ~ Bedrooms: /£210S

Recommended by Jill and Julian Tasker, Dr Ian S Morley, John and Verna Aspinall

PICKERING Yorkshire

SE7984 Map A

White Swan 🍴 ⢕ 🛏

Market Place, just off A170; YO18 7AA

Relaxed little bar in civilised coaching inn with several smart lounges, an attractive restaurant, real ales, an excellent wine list and first-class food; lovely bedrooms

At the heart of this smart and civilised old coaching inn is a small bar with a friendly welcome. The atmosphere is relaxed and there are sofas and a few tables, wood panelling, a log fire, Black Sheep Best and Copper Dragon Golden Pippin on handpump, 14 wines by the glass from an extensive list that includes fine old St Emilions and pudding wines, and 20 malt whiskies. Opposite, a bare-boards room with a few more tables has another fire in a handsome art nouveau iron fireplace, a big bow window and pear prints on its plum-coloured walls. The restaurant has flagstones, yet another open fire, comfortable settles and gothic screens, and the residents' lounge is in a converted beamed barn. The old coach entry to the car park is very narrow. Luxurious bedrooms and delicious breakfasts.

Excellent food at lunchtime might include sandwiches, venison carpaccio with redcurrant jelly, green vegetable risotto with white truffle oil, and whitby fish and chips, with evening choices like potted crab and celeriac remoulade, free-range chicken with parmentier potatoes, wild mushrooms, crisp ham and bread sauce, and grilled sea bream with aioli, skinny chips and watercress salad. *Benchmark main dish: slow-cooked gloucester old spot belly pork with crackling, mustard mash and apple sauce £17.50. Two-course evening meal £24.90.*

Free house ~ Licensees Marion and Victor Buchanan ~ Real ale ~ Bar food ~ Restaurant ~ (01751) 472288 ~ Children welcome ~ Dogs allowed in bar and bedrooms ~ Open 10am-11pm; 11am-10.30pm Sun ~ Bedrooms: £115B/£150B

Recommended by Marian and Andrew Ruston, Janet and Peter Race, Peter Burton

RIPLEY Yorkshire

SE2860 Map C

Boars Head ♀ ◀ ⇌

Off A61 Harrogate—Ripon; HG3 3AY

Smart coaching inn with friendly bar/bistro, several real ales, an excellent wine list, good food and helpful service; comfortable bedrooms

The bar in this welcoming old coaching inn has been refurbished this year and the restaurant is now more of a brasserie. This bar/bistro now has a nice mix of dining chairs around various wooden tables, warm yellow walls hung with golf clubs, cricket bats and jolly little drawings of cricketers or huntsmen, a boar's head (part of the family coat of arms), an interesting religious carving, and Black Sheep Best, Daleside Pride of England, Hambleton White Boar and Theakston Best on handpump; also, 20 wines by the glass and several malt whiskies. Some of the furnishings in the hotel came from the attic of next-door Ripley Castle, where the Ingilbys have lived for over 650 years. A pleasant little garden has plenty of tables.

Using their own kitchen garden produce (within Ripley Castle), the food includes lunchtime open sandwiches, morecambe bay potted shrimps, wild mushroom stroganoff, sausages of the day with spring onion mash and onion gravy, an open pie of beef, mushrooms and Guinness, braised lamb shank with glazed root vegetables, kilnsey trout with lemon and caper butter, and Estate venison with rösti and jus. *Benchmark main dish: honey-roast belly pork with black pudding mash and glazed apples £14.95. Two-course evening meal £20.45.*

Free house ~ Licensee Sir Thomas Ingilby ~ Real ale ~ Bar food (12-2, 6.30-9.30; 12-9 Sun) ~ Restaurant ~ (01423) 771888 ~ Children welcome ~ Dogs allowed in bedrooms ~ Open 11-11; 12-10.30 Sun; 11-3, 5-11 weekdays in winter ~ Bedrooms: £105B/£125B

Recommended by Adrian and Dawn Collinge, Jeremy King, the Didler, Susan and Nigel Brookes, Janet and Peter Race, Pete Coxon

RIPPONDEN Yorkshire

SE0419 Map C

Old Bridge ♀ ◀

From A58, best approach is Elland Road (opposite the Golden Lion), park opposite the church in pub's car park and walk back over ancient hump-back bridge; HX6 4DF

Pleasant old pub by medieval bridge with relaxed communicating rooms, half a dozen real ales, quite a few wines by the glass, lots of whiskies, and well liked food

This is a charming 14th-c pub by a beautiful medieval pack-horse bridge over the little River Ryburn, and there are seats in the garden overlooking the water. Inside, the three communicating rooms, each on a slightly different level, all have a relaxed, friendly atmosphere. Oak settles are built into the window recesses of the thick stone walls, and there are antique oak tables, rush-seated chairs, a few well chosen pictures and prints, and a big woodburning stove. The fine range of real ales on handpump might include Timothy Taylors Best, Dark Mild, Golden Best and Landlord and a couple of guests such as Empire Royal Scot and York First Light; also, quite a few foreign bottled beers, a dozen wines by the glass and 30 malt whiskies. If you have trouble finding the pub (there is no traditional pub sign outside), just head for the church.

On weekday lunchtimes, bar food only includes sandwiches and soup or the popular help-yourself salad carvery (rare roast beef, virginia ham, home-made scotch eggs and so forth); at weekends and in the evening (not Sunday evening), there might potted salmon and shrimps with lemon and capers, steak in ale pie, mediterranean vegetable and goats cheese wraps, crispy belly pork with pak choi and oriental sauce, and corn-fed chicken with tomato, red pepper and butter bean stew. *Benchmark main dish: smoked haddock and spinach pancakes £9.25. Two-course evening meal £17.25.*

Free house ~ Licensees Tim and Lindsay Eaton Walker ~ Real ale ~ Bar food (12-2(2.30 Sat), 6.30-9.30; not Sun evening) ~ (01422) 822595 ~ Children allowed until 8pm but must be seated away from bar ~ Open 12-3, 5.30-11; 12-11(10.30 Sun) Fri and Sat

Recommended by Roger and Anne Newbury, Tony Hill

ROECLIFFE Yorkshire SE3765 Map C

Crown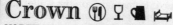

NORTH EAST & YORKSHIRE PUB OF THE YEAR

Off A168 just W of Boroughbridge; handy for A1(M) junction 48; YO51 9LY

YORKSHIRE DINING PUB OF THE YEAR

Smartly updated and attractively placed pub with a civilised bar, excellent enterprising food and a fine choice of drinks; lovely bedrooms

Going from strength to strength under the hard-working and friendly Mainey family, this well run place is extremely popular with our readers. Of course, much emphasis is placed on the top-class food but they do keep Black Sheep Ale, Ilkley Mary Jane, Theakstons Best and Timothy Taylors Landlord on handpump, 20 wines by the glass and home-made lemonade. The bar has a contemporary colour scheme of dark reds and near-whites with attractive prints carefully grouped and lit; one area has chunky pine tables on flagstones and another part, with a log fire, has dark tables on plaid carpet. For meals, you have a choice between a small candlelit olive-green bistro with nice tables, a longcase clock and one or two paintings and a more formal restaurant; at weekends, it's wise to book ahead. The country-style bedrooms are highly thought-of. The pub faces the village green.

They make their own goats cheese, bread, jams and chutneys, home-smoke their fish and use only small local suppliers and game from local estates for the first-class, imaginative food which might include lunchtime sandwiches, delicious whitby crab soup, smoked salmon terrine with ricotta and dill with a spiced cucumber and lemon salad, a proper steak and mushroom pie, pink trout fillets with a king prawn, basil and roast red pepper piperade, leek and lemon grass risotto with spiced cauliflower fritters, free-range chicken with a wild mushroom and tarragon mousse, and 24-day-hung rib-eye steak with pepper sauce and aioli. *Benchmark main dish: fish pie £12.95. Two-course evening meal £23.00.*

Free house ~ Licensee Karl Mainey ~ Real ale ~ Bar food (12-2.30, 6-9.30; 12-7 Sun) ~ Restaurant ~ (01423) 322300 ~ Children welcome ~ Dogs allowed in bar ~ Open 12-4, 5-11; 12-10 Sun ~ Bedrooms: £82B/£97B

Recommended by Les and Sandra Brown, Michael and Maggie Betton, Michael Doswell, Hunter and Christine Wright, Peter Hacker

---

'Children welcome' means the pub says it lets children inside without any special restriction. If it allows them in, but to restricted areas such as an eating area or family room, we specify this. Places with separate restaurants often let children use them, and hotels usually let them into public areas such as lounges. Some pubs impose an evening time limit — let us know if you find one earlier than 9pm.

ROMALDKIRK County Durham   NY9922 Map A

Rose & Crown ★ 🍴 🍷 🛏

Just off B6277; DL12 9EB

A civilised base for the area, with accomplished cooking, attentive service, and a fine choice of drinks; lovely bedrooms

Firmly rooted in quite a special league, this handsome 18th-c country coaching inn is run with keen attention to detail, resulting in a charming environment, fabulous service, superbly cooked food (you do need to book) and a first-class place to stay. The cosily traditional beamed bar has lots of brass and copper, old-fashioned seats facing a warming log fire, a Jacobean oak settle, a grandfather clock, and gin traps, old farm tools and black and white pictures of Romaldkirk on the walls. Allendale, Black Sheep and Theakstons are on handpump alongside 14 wines by the glass, organic fruit juices and pressed vegetable juices. The smart brasserie-style Crown Room (bar food is served in here, too) has large cartoons of french waiters, big old wine bottles and high-backed dining chairs. The hall has farm tools, wine maps and other interesting prints, along with a photograph (taken by a customer) of the Hale Bopp comet over the interesting old village church. There's also an oak-panelled restaurant. Pleasantly positioned tables outside look out over the village green with its original stocks and water pump. The extraordinary Bowes Museum and High Force waterfall are close by and the owners can provide their own in-house guide to days out in the area, and a *Walking in Teesdale* book.

As well as making their own ice-creams, jams, chutneys and marmalade, using only seasonal local produce (they list their suppliers on the menu) and eggs from their own hens (whose names are on a board in the brasserie), the imaginative bar food might include baked smoked salmon soufflé with tomato fondue and chive cream, linguine with butternut and pumpkin seed pesto, fish and chips with mushy peas, steak, kidney and mushroom pie, bass fillets with pea and prawn risotto, pancetta and chive cream, and fried pigeon with carrot and parsnip rösti and mushrooms. *Benchmark main dish: steak, kidney, mushroom and ale pie £13.95. Two-course evening meal £22.65.*

Free house ~ Licensees Christopher and Alison Davy ~ Real ale ~ Bar food (12-1.45, 6.30-9.30) ~ Restaurant ~ (01833) 650213 ~ Children welcome, must be over 6 in restaurant ~ Dogs allowed in bar and bedrooms ~ Open 11(12 Sun)-11 ~ Bedrooms: £95B/£135S(£170B)

Recommended by Roxanne Chamberlain, John Coatsworth, Mike and Sue Loseby, Lesley and Peter Barrett, Richard Cole, Peter and Josie Fawcett

SANDHUTTON Yorkshire   SE3882 Map A

Kings Arms 🍺

A167, 1 mile N of A61 Thirsk—Ripon; YO7 4RW

Good chef/landlord in cheerful and appealing pub with friendly service, good food and beer, and comfortable furnishings; bedrooms

A cosy new dining extension has been added to this interestingly furnished village pub and they now have a shop selling their own ready meals as well as cheese, chutneys and local produce. The bustling bar has an unusual circular woodburner in one corner, a high central table with four equally high stools, high-backed brown leather-seated dining chairs around light pine tables, a couple of cushioned wicker armchairs, some attractive modern bar stools, and photographs of the pub in years gone by; a shelf has odd knick-knacks such as fish jaws and a bubble-gum machine, there are various pub games, and a TV. Black Sheep Best, Hambleton Stud and White Boar and John Smiths on handpump, several wines by the glass and efficient, friendly service. The two connecting dining rooms have similar furnishings to the bar (though there's also a nice big table with smart high-backed dining chairs), arty flower photographs on the cream walls and a shelf above the small woodburning stove with more knick-knacks and some candles.

Cooked by the landlord using local produce, the good, interesting bar food includes lunchtime choices such as sandwiches, chilli con carne, generous beer-battered cod and chips and game or cottage pie, as well as queenie scallops with sautéed black pudding and pea purée, chicken liver pâté with plum chutney, wild mushroom tagliatelle with parmesan crisps, pork chops with caramelised stuffed apple and proper gravy, monkfish with a compote of peppers with caramelised olives and rocket pesto, and rack of lamb with spinach, feta and pomegranate seeds. *Benchmark main dish: salmon, cod and prawn fishcake with sweet chilli dressing £10.50. Two-course evening meal £20.25.*

Free house ~ Licensees Raymond and Alexander Boynton ~ Real ale ~ Bar food (12-2.30, 5.30-9; 12-5 Sun; not Sun evening) ~ Restaurant ~ (01845) 587887 ~ Children welcome ~ Open 11-11 ~ Bedrooms: £45S/£70S

Recommended by Michael Doswell, John and Eleanor Holdsworth, Mike and Lynn Robinson

SAWLEY Yorkshire   SE2467   Map C

Sawley Arms ♀

Village signposted off B6265 W of Ripon; HG4 3EQ

Old-fashioned dining pub with good restauranty food, decent house wines and comfortable furnishings in small rooms; pretty garden

Ultra-civilised in a decorous sort of way, this is a spotlessly kept dining pub with cheerful, friendly staff and good restaurant-style food – though locals do pop in for a chat and a drink (mainly in the evening). The small turkey-carpeted rooms have log fires and comfortable furniture ranging from small soft-cushioned armed dining chairs and sofas, to the wing armchairs down a couple of steps in a side snug; maybe daily papers and magazines to read, and quiet piped music. There's also a conservatory; good house wines. In fine weather you can sit in the pretty garden where the flowering tubs and baskets are lovely; they have two stone cottages in the grounds for rent. Fountains Abbey (the most extensive of the great monastic remains – floodlit on late summer Friday and Saturday evenings, with a choir on the Saturday) is not far away.

As well as selling home-made chutneys, relishes, pickles and biscuits, there's a 'take and bake' menu, too. In-house, the highly thought-of food includes lunchtime sandwiches, duck liver and orange pâté with port jelly, toasted brie with candied walnut and pear salad, their famous pies (steak, vegetarian, chicken and game), pork and apricot cassoulet, plaice mornay with duchesse potatoes, and rump of local lamb with bubble and squeak mash and red wine and rosemary gravy. *Benchmark main dish: various pies £10.95. Two-course evening meal £19.45.*

Free house ~ Licensee Mrs June Hawes ~ Bar food ~ Restaurant ~ (01765) 620642 ~ Well behaved children in conservatory but phone beforehand ~ Open 11.30-3, 6-11; closed Mon evenings in winter ~ Bedrooms: £50B/£85B

Recommended by Janet and Peter Race, Alan Thwaite, Ian and Nita Cooper, R J Cowley

SEAHOUSES Northumberland   NU2232   Map A

Olde Ship ★ ◀ £ ⇔
Just off B1340, towards harbour; NE68 7RD

Lots of atmosphere and maritime memorabilia in bustling little hotel; views across harbour to Farne Islands; bedrooms

This unchanging homely little hotel has been run by the same friendly family for over 100 years. Popular with locals, the snugly old-fashioned bar is packed with a rich assemblage of nautical bits and pieces. Even the floor is scrubbed ship's decking. Besides lots of other shiny brass fittings, ship's instruments and equipment, and a knotted anchor made by local fishermen, there are sea pictures and model ships, including fine ones of the North Sunderland Lifeboat, and Seahouses' lifeboat the *Grace Darling*. There's also a model of the *Forfarshire*, the paddle steamer that local heroine Grace Darling went to rescue in 1838 (you can read more of the story in the pub), and even the ship's nameboard. If it's working, an anemometer takes wind speed readings from the top of the chimney. It's all gently lit by stained-glass sea picture windows, lantern lights and a winter open fire. Simple furnishings include built in leatherette pews round one end, and stools and cast-iron tables. Black Sheep Best, Courage Directors, Greene King Old Speckled Hen and Ruddles and Hadrian & Border Farne Island Pale are on handpump and they've a good wine list and quite a few malt whiskies; piped music and TV. The battlemented side terrace (you'll find fishing memorabilia out here, too) and one window in the sun lounge look out across the harbour to the Farne Islands, and if you find yourself here as dusk falls, the light of the Longstones lighthouse shining across the fading evening sky is a charming sight. It's not really suitable for children, though there is a little family room, and along with walkers, they are welcome on the terrace. You can book boat trips to the Farne Islands Bird Sanctuary at the harbour, and there are bracing coastal walks, particularly to Bamburgh, Grace Darling's birthplace.

A short choice of reasonably priced bar food includes sandwiches, ploughman's, mushroom and cashew nut pâté, scampi, gammon and egg, steak and ale pie, crab salad, and chicken and mushroom casserole. *Benchmark main dish: fish chowder £11.50. Two-course evening meal £15.60.*

Free house ~ Licensees Judith Glen and David Swan ~ Real ale ~ Bar food (no evening food mid-Dec to mid-Jan) ~ Restaurant ~ (01665) 720200 ~ Children in louge and dining room and must be over 10 if staying ~ Open 11(12 Sun)-11 ~ Bedrooms: £59S/£130B

Recommended by Emma Harris, George Cowie, Frances Gosnell, John and Angie Millar, Andy and Jill Kassube, Mike and Sue Loseby, Comus and Sarah Elliott, the Didler, Dave and Shirley Shaw, P Dawn, Lawrence Pearse, Simon Watkins, J F M and M West, Pat and Graham Williamson, Colin and Louise English, Graham Oddey, Andrew Todd, D Crook

STANNERSBURN Northumberland   NY7286   Map A

Pheasant £ ⇔

Kielder Water road signposted off B6320 in Bellingham; NE48 1DD

Friendly village local close to Kielder Water with quite a mix of customers, and homely bar food; streamside garden; bedrooms

The comfortable low-beamed lounge at this warmly traditional inn has ranks of old local photographs on stripped stone and panelling, dark wood pubby tables and chairs on red patterned carpets and upholstered stools ranged along the counter. A separate public bar is simpler and opens into a further cosy seating area with beams and panelling; piped music. The friendly licensees and courteous staff serve Black Isle Red Kite, Timothy Taylors Landlord and Wylam Rocket on handpump and 40 malt whiskies. The pub is in a restful valley amid quiet forests, not far from Kielder Water, with picnic-sets in its streamside garden and a pony paddock behind. More reports please.

🍴 Good bar food includes farmhouse pâté, sweet marinated herring, ploughman's, steak and kidney or game and mushroom pie, dressed crab, cream cheese and broccoli bake, and roast lamb with rosemary and redcurrant sauce. *Benchmark main dish: roast lamb £10.95. Two-course evening meal £15.00.*

Free house ~ Licensees Walter and Robin Kershaw ~ Real ale ~ Bar food (12-2.30, 6(6.30 in winter)-8.30) ~ Restaurant ~ (01434) 240382 ~ Children welcome ~ Dogs allowed in bedrooms ~ Open 12-3, 6(6.30 Sun)-12; closed Mon and Tues Nov-Mar ~ Bedrooms: £55S/£90S

Recommended by Dave Braisted, Claes Mauroy

 THORNTON WATLASS Yorkshire   SE2385   Map A

Buck 🍴 🛏

Village signposted off B6268 Bedale—Masham; HG4 4AH

Honest village pub with five real ales, traditional bars, well liked food, and popular Sunday jazz

Very much the heart of the local community – but with a warm welcome for visitors as well – this friendly village pub has now been run by the long-serving licensees for 25 years. The pleasantly traditional bar on the right has upholstered old-fashioned wall settles on the carpet, a fine mahogany bar counter, a high shelf packed with ancient bottles, several mounted fox masks and brushes, and a brick fireplace. The Long Room (which overlooks the cricket green) has large prints of old Thornton Watlass cricket teams, signed bats, cricket balls and so forth. Barngates Mothbag, Black Sheep Best, Theakstons Best and Black Bull and Walls Gun Dog Bitter on handpump, a few wines by the glass and over 40 interesting malt whiskies; darts and board games. The sheltered garden has an equipped children's play area and summer barbecues, and they have their own cricket team; quoits.

🍴 Popular bar food, using local produce, includes sandwiches, chicken liver parfait with red onion marmalade, rarebit with home-made pear chutney, a choice of omelette, lasagne, beer-battered fish and chips, spinach and ricotta pasta, and specials like potato pancake with smoked salmon and chive crème fraîche, and a mild chicken curry with almonds, sultanas and banana cream. *Benchmark main dish: steak in ale pie £9.95. Two-course evening meal £17.95.*

Free house ~ Licensees Michael and Margaret Fox ~ Real ale ~ Bar food (12-2(3 Sun), 6.30-9.15(9 Sun) ~ Restaurant ~ (01677) 422461 ~ Children welcome ~ Dogs allowed in bedrooms ~ Trad jazz Sun lunchtimes ~ Open 11-11(midnight Sat) ~ Bedrooms: £55(£65S)/£80(£90B)

Recommended by Stuart and Sarah Barrie, Richard Gibbs

If a service charge is mentioned prominently on a menu or accommodation terms, you must pay it if service was satisfactory. If service is really bad, you are legally entitled to refuse to pay some or all of the service charge as compensation for not getting the service you might reasonably have expected.

WARK Northumberland   NY8676   Map A

Battlesteads 🍺 ⇌

B6320 N of Hexham; NE48 3LS

Good local ales, fair value interesting food, and a relaxed atmosphere; comfortable bedrooms

An enjoyable all-rounder, this popular stone hotel still manages to convey a relaxed unhurried atmosphere. The nicely restored carpeted bar has a woodburning stove with a traditional oak surround, low beams, comfortable seats including some comfy deep leather sofas and easy chairs, and old *Punch* country life cartoons on the terracotta walls above its dark dado. Four good changing local ales such as Black Sheep Best, Durham Magus and a couple of guests from brewers such as Hadrian & Border and Wylam are on handpumps on the heavily carved dark oak bar counter. This leads through to the restaurant and spacious conservatory; good coffee, cheerful service, piped music and TV. There are tables on a terrace in the walled garden. Disabled access to some of the ground-floor bedrooms and they are licensed to hold civil marriages.

Using home-grown vegetables and other local produce, the good value bar food includes lunchtime sandwiches, ham hock terrine with pickle, potted shrimp and crab, venison carpaccio with hot and sour beetroot, cajun spiced chicken with sweet chilli sauce, cod and chips with mushy peas, mushroom and halloumi stack, and rib-eye steak with peppercorn sauce. *Benchmark main dish: home-made venison burger £8.75. Two-course evening meal £18.80.*

Free house ~ Licensees Richard and Dee Slade ~ Real ale ~ Bar food (12-3, 6.30-9) ~ Restaurant ~ (01434) 230209 ~ Children welcome ~ Dogs allowed in bar ~ Open 11-11 ~ Bedrooms: £60S/£105B

Recommended by David Heath, S D and J L Cooke, David and Christine Merritt, Kay and Mark Denison, Helen and Brian Edgeley, Bruce and Sharon Eden, Kevin Appleby, Michael Doswell

WASS Yorkshire   SE5579   Map C

Wombwell Arms ⇌

Back road W of Ampleforth; or follow brown tourist-attraction sign for Byland Abbey off A170 Thirsk—Helmsley; YO61 4BE

Consistently enjoyable village pub with friendly atmosphere, good mix of locals and visitors, interesting bar food and real ales; bedrooms

Handy for Byland Abbey, this bustling pub is in a pretty village below the Hambleton Hills. The two bars are neatly kept with plenty of simple character, pine farmhouse chairs and tables, some exposed stone walls, and log fires; the walls of the Poacher's Bar are hung with brewery memorabilia. From the panelled bar counter, the friendly staff serve Theakstons Best, Timothy Taylors Landlord and York Yorkshire Terrier on handpump, nine wines by the glass (quite a few from Mrs Walker's South Africa) and several malt whiskies; darts. The two restaurants are incorporated into a 17th-c former granary and there are seats outside.

Using the best local produce, the well thought-of food includes sandwiches, pigeon with mushroom sauce bruschetta, smoked salmon and scrambled eggs, pork and apple sausages, beer-battered haddock, vegetarian open lasagne, bobotie (a south african fruity mince curry), chicken with a creamy leek, bacon and stilton sauce, and specials like mini smoked trout cakes with lemon and caper sauce, and beef stroganoff. *Benchmark main dish: steak pie £11.15. Two-course evening meal £19.00.*

Free house ~ Licensees Ian and Eunice Walker ~ Real ale ~ Bar food (12-2(2.30 Sat), 6.30-9(9.30 Fri and Sat); 12-7.30 Sun) ~ Restaurant ~ (01347) 868280 ~ Children welcome ~ Dogs allowed in bar ~ Folk music second Thurs of month ~ Open 12-3, 6-11; 12-11 Sat; 12-10.30 Sun ~ Bedrooms: £55S/£75S

Recommended by Janet and Peter Race, Val Carter, Edward Leetham, WW, Margaret Dickinson, Mr and Mrs D G Hallows, Michael Doswell

 WATH IN NIDDERDALE Yorkshire   SE1467   Map C

Sportsmans Arms ⏐Ψ ♀ ⇋
Nidderdale road off B6265 in Pateley Bridge; village and pub signposted over hump-back bridge on right after a couple of miles; HG3 5PP

Beautifully placed restaurant-with-rooms plus welcoming bar, real ales and super choice of other drinks, and imaginative food; comfortable bedrooms

As well as being a special place to stay in lovely, comfortable bedrooms, this civilised restaurant-with-rooms has now been run by the charming Mr Carter for well over 30 years – and the atmosphere is friendly and relaxed. Of course, much emphasis is placed on the exceptional food but there is a welcoming bar with an open fire and Black Sheep Best and Timothy Taylors Best on handpump – and locals do still pop in for a pint and a chat. There's a very sensible and extensive wine list with 20 by the glass (including champagne), over 40 malt whiskies, several russian vodkas and Thatcher's cider; maybe quiet piped music. Benches and tables outside and seats in the pretty garden; croquet. As well as their own fishing on the River Nidd, this is an ideal spot for walkers, hikers and ornithologists, and there are plenty of country houses, gardens and cities to explore.

Using butchers who breed their own animals, trout from the next village, game shot under a mile away and fish and shellfish delivered six times a week, the first-class food might include lunchtime sandwiches, king scallops with minted pea purée and grilled pancetta, home-cured gravadlax with crème fraîche and their own quail eggs, chicken stuffed with wensleydale cheese and ham with a tarragon and mushroom sauce, best end of nidderdale lamb with creamed cabbage, roasted garlic and cherry vine tomatoes, gressingham duck with cherries, oranges and preserved lemons, and venison on aubergine chutney with home-made plum jam. *Benchmark main dish: line-caught bass with roast asparagus and béarnaise sauce £13.50. Two-course evening meal £22.00.*

Free house ~ Licensee Ray Carter ~ Real ale ~ Bar food ~ Restaurant ~ (01423) 711306 ~ Children welcome ~ Dogs allowed in bar ~ Open 12-2.30, 6.30-11 ~ Bedrooms: £70B/£120B

Recommended by Janet and Peter Race, Jill and Julian Tasker, Stephen Woad, Keith Moss, Malcolm and Pauline Pellatt, David and Jenny Reed, Derek Thomas, Bruce and Sharon Eden, R and S Bentley

 WELDON BRIDGE Northumberland   NZ1398   Map A

Anglers Arms ⇋
B6344, just off A697; village signposted with Rothbury off A1 N of Morpeth; NE65 8AX

Large helpings of food in appealing bar or converted railway dining car, real ales, and a friendly welcome; fishing on River Coquet; bedrooms

Although emphasis at this sizeable but warmly welcoming place is on the comfortable bedrooms and enjoyable food, the whole thing is nicely rounded out by a traditional turkey-carpeted bar tucked into its heart. This bustling bar is divided into two parts: cream walls on the right and oak panelling and some shiny black beams hung with copper pans on the left, with four constantly changing real ales from brewers such as Adnams, Courage, Greene King and Timothy Taylor on handpump, and around 30 malt whiskies and decent wines. There's also a grandfather clock and sofa by the coal fire, staffordshire cats and other antique ornaments on its mantelpiece, old fishing and other country prints, a profusion of fishing memorabilia and some taxidermy. Some of the tables are lower than you'd expect for eating, but their chairs have short legs to match – different and rather engaging; piped music. The restaurant is in a former railway dining car with crisp white linen and a red carpet. There are tables in the attractive garden which has a good play area that includes an assault course. The pub is beside a bridge over the River Coquet and they have rights to fishing along a mile of the riverbank.

Generously served bar food includes sandwiches, chicken liver pâté, ploughman's, goats cheese and pea risotto, pork belly with apple compote and black pudding, cod and chips, and king prawns with peppers in garlic sauce. *Benchmark main dish: cod and chips £10.95. Two-course evening meal £15.00.*

Enterprise ~ Lease John Young ~ Real ale ~ Bar food (12-9.30) ~ Restaurant ~ (01665) 570271 ~ Dogs allowed in bedrooms ~ Open 11-11; 12-10.30 Sun ~ Bedrooms: £49.50S/£90S

Recommended by Jenny and Peter Lowater, Dennis Jones, Ann and Tony Bennett-Hughes, Colin McKerrow, Dr Peter D Smart, Jean and Douglas Troup

WIDDOP Yorkshire   SD9531   Map C

Pack Horse ◀ £
THE GOOD PUB GUIDE
The Ridge; from A646 on W side of Hebden Bridge, turn off at Heptonstall signpost (as it's a sharp turn, coming out of Hebden Bridge road signs direct you around a turning circle), then follow Slack and Widdop signposts; can also be reached from Nelson and Colne, on high, pretty road; OS Sheet 103 map reference 952317; HX7 7AT

Friendly pub high up on the moors and liked by walkers for generous, tasty food, five real ales and lots of malt whiskies; bedrooms

Our readers very much enjoy their visits to this isolated, traditional inn, and if staying overnight, the breakfasts are particularly good. The bar has welcoming winter fires, window seats cut into the partly panelled stripped-stone walls that take in the moorland view, sturdy furnishings and horsey mementoes. Black Sheep Best, Copper Dragon Golden Pippin, Thwaites Bitter and a changing guest on handpump, around 130 single malt whiskies and some irish ones as well, and ten wines by the glass. The friendly golden retrievers are called Padge and Purdey and the alsatian, Holly. There are seats outside and pretty summer hanging baskets. As well as the comfortable bedrooms, they also offer a smart self-catering apartment.

Bedroom prices normally include full english breakfast, VAT and any inclusive service charge that we know of. Prices before the '/' are for single rooms; after the '/' are for two people in a double or twin (B includes a private bath, S means there's a private shower).

❚❚ Honest food at sensible prices includes sandwiches, pâté, garlic mushrooms, large burgers, black pudding and bacon on mash, pheasant and mushroom pie, lasagne, vegetable bake, gammon and eggs, and daily specials. *Benchmark main dish: rack of lamb £13.00. Two-course evening meal £15.00.*

Free house ~ Licensee Andrew Hollinrake ~ Real ale ~ Bar food (all day Sun; not Mon or weekday lunchtimes Oct-Easter) ~ (01422) 842803 ~ Children in eating area of bar until 8pm ~ Dogs allowed in bar ~ Open 12-3, 7-11; 12-11 Sun; closed Mon and weekday lunchtimes Oct-Easter ~ Bedrooms: £43S/£48S(£69B)

Recommended by Ian and Nita Cooper, Simon Le Fort, Geoff Boswell, Martin Smith

THE NORTH WEST'S TOP PUBS

 ALDFORD Cheshire   SJ4259   Map C

Grosvenor Arms ★ ❚❶ ❢ ◀

B5130 Chester—Wrexham; CH3 6HJ

Spacious place with buoyantly chatty atmosphere, impressive range of drinks, well balanced sensibly imaginative menu, good service; lovely big terrace and gardens

Although part of a small chain, this substantial building still retains plenty of individuality, and friendly staff engender a welcoming atmosphere. Spacious cream-painted areas are sectioned by big knocked-through arches with a variety of wood, quarry tile, flagstone and black and white tiled floor finishes – some richly coloured turkey rugs look well against these natural materials. Good solid pieces of traditional furniture, plenty of interesting pictures and attractive lighting keep it all intimate enough. A big panelled library room has tall bookshelves lining one wall, and a handsomely boarded floor; good selection of board games. Lovely on summer evenings, the airy terracotta-floored conservatory has lots of gigantic low-hanging flowering baskets and chunky pale wood garden furniture. This opens out to a large elegant suntrap terrace, and a neat lawn with picnic-sets, young trees and a characterful old tractor. Attentive staff dispense a very wide array of drinks from a fine-looking bar counter, including 20 wines by the glass, an impressive range of over 80 whiskies, distinctive soft drinks such as peach and elderflower cordial and Willington Fruit Farm pressed apple juice, as well as five real ales including Brunning & Price Original (brewed for them by Phoenix) and Deuchars IPA and guests such as Moorhouses Pride of Pendle and Red Willow Headless; more reports please.

❚❶ Food here is very good. The well balanced changing menu includes something to please most tastes. As well as sandwiches, there might be chicken, mushroom and tarragon risotto, moroccan spiced lamb with sweet potato and chickpea salad with honey-roasted plum and yoghurt dressing, aubergine, spinach and lentil lasagne with feta and pepper salad, pork and chorizo meatballs with pasta and tomato sauce, battered haddock and chips, and roast duck breast with root vegetable casserole and bacon and puy lentils. *Benchmark main dish: shoulder of lamb with red wine and thyme gravy £16.75. Two-course evening meal £18.95.*

Brunning & Price ~ Manager Tracey Owen ~ Real ale ~ Bar food (12-9.30(9 Sun)) ~ (01244) 620228 ~ Children welcome ~ Dogs allowed in bar ~ Open 11.30-11; 12-10.30 Sun
Recommended by Clive Watkin, Phil and Gill Wass, John Andrew

AMBLESIDE Cumbria   NY3704   Map B

Golden Rule

Smithy Brow; follow Kirkstone Pass signpost from A591 on N side of town;
LA22 9AS

Simple town local with a cosy, relaxed atmosphere, and real ales

This is very much an honest, unchanging Lakeland local where all are
welcomed. The bar area has built-in wall seats around cast-iron-
framed tables (one with a local map set into its top), horsebrasses on the
black beams, assorted pictures on the walls, a welcoming winter fire and
a relaxed atmosphere. Robinsons Crusoe, Cumbria Way, Dark Mild, Dizzy
Blonde, Double Hop and Hartleys XB on handpump. A brass measuring
rule hangs above the bar (hence the pub's name). There's also a back
room with TV (not much used), a left-hand room with darts and a games
machine, and a further room, down a couple of steps on the right, with
lots of seating. The backyard has benches and a covered heated area, and
the window boxes are especially colourful. There's no car park.

There might be scotch eggs and pies but they tend to run out fast, so don't
assume you'll be able to get something to eat.

Robinsons ~ Tenant John Lockley ~ Real ale ~ No credit cards ~ (015394) 32257 ~
Children welcome away from bar and must leave by 9pm ~ Dogs welcome ~ Open 11am-
midnight
Recommended by David and Sue Atkinson, Dr and Mrs A K Clarke, Chris Johnson, John Prescott

 ASTBURY Cheshire   SJ8461   Map C

Egerton Arms £

Village signposted off A34 S of Congleton; CW12 4RQ

**Cheery village pub with straightforward bar food, large garden, and
nice bedrooms**

With its long-standing staff and friendly caring landlord, this partly
16th-c farmhouse has a particularly welcoming atmosphere.
Rambling around the bar, its pubby cream-painted rooms are decorated
with the odd piece of armour and shelves of books. In summer, dried
flowers replace the fire in the big fireplace. Mementoes of the Sandow
Brothers who performed as 'the World's Strongest Youths' are particularly
interesting as one of them was the landlady's father; piped music, TV.
Four Robinsons ales are on handpump, in addition to Pimms (served hot
in winter), a dozen wines by the glass and a range of malt whiskies. Well
placed tables outside enjoy pleasant views of the church, and a play area
has a wooden fort. Despite the large car park you might struggle for a
place Sunday lunchtime; handy for Little Moreton Hall (National Trust).

As well as sandwiches, bar food might include mango and brie parcels, tempura
prawns with lemon and lime mayonnaise, mini vegetable samosas with pear
chutney, battered cod, chilli, grilled salmon with tarragon butter, macaroni cheese
with roasted red peppers, and meatballs in bolognese sauce with pasta; good value
lunchtime OAP specials. *Benchmark main dish: braised steak in ale £9.00. Two-
course evening meal £14.00.*

Robinsons ~ Tenants Alan and Grace Smith ~ Real ale ~ Bar food (11.30-2, 6-9; 12-8 Sun)
~ Restaurant ~ (01260) 273946 ~ Children welcome ~ Open 11.30-11(10.30 Sun) ~
Bedrooms: £50S/£70B
Recommended by David Rutter, Joan and Tony Walker, John Branston, Brian and Janet Ainscough,
Christopher Mobbs, Brian and Anna Marsden, Mike Proctor

ASTON Cheshire   SJ6146   Map C

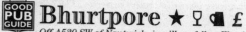

Bhurtpore ★ ♀ ◖ £

Off A530 SW of Nantwich; in village follow Wrenbury signpost; CW5 8DQ

Fantastic range of drinks (especially real ales) and tasty curries in a warm-hearted pub with some unusual artefacts; big garden

Tables in the comfortable public bar at this well cared for place are reserved for drinkers and, with the terrific range of drinks here, including 11 real ales, they are put to good use. They usually run through over 1,000 superbly kept real ales a year, sourced from an enterprising range of national brewers such as Acorn, Copper Dragon, Monty, Phoenix, Salopian, Slater, Titanic and Wincle. They also stock dozens of unusual bottled beers and fruit beers, a great many bottled ciders and perries, over 100 different whiskies, carefully selected soft drinks and a good wine list; summer beer festival. The pub is named to commemorate the siege of Bhurtpore (a town in India) during which local landowner Sir Stapleton Cotton (later Viscount Combermere) was commander in chief. The connection with India also explains some of the exotic artefacts in the carpeted lounge bar – look out especially for the sunglasses-wearing turbaned statue behind the counter; also good local period photographs and some attractive furniture; board games, pool, TV and games machine. Cheery staff usually cope superbly with the busy weekends.

The enjoyably varied menu includes sandwiches, toasted panini, smoked haddock pancake with cheese and leek sauce, sausage ring with sweet potato mash, battered haddock, chips and mushy peas, grilled duck breast on red cabbage with plum sauce, steak, kidney and ale pie, grilled goats cheese salad, and a range of curries. *Benchmark main dish: chicken and spinach balti £9.50. Two-course evening meal £16.00.*

Free house ~ Licensee Simon George ~ Real ale ~ Bar food (12-2, 7-9; 12-9.30 Sat (9 Sun)) ~ Restaurant ~ (01270) 780917 ~ Children welcome till 8.30pm ~ Dogs allowed in bar ~ Open 12-2.30, 6.30-11.30; 12-(11 Sun) midnight Fri and Sat

Recommended by Dr D J and Mrs S C Walker, the Didler, Mr and Mrs P R Thomas, Tony Hobden, Brian and Anna Marsden, Mike Proctor, Dave Webster, Sue Holland, Gill and Keith Croxton, Dennis Jones, Joe Hoyles

BASHALL EAVES Lancashire   SD6943   Map C

Red Pump ◖

NW of Clitheroe, off B6478 or B6243; BB7 3DA

Cosy bar, good food in more contemporary dining rooms and regional beers in a beautifully placed country inn; bedrooms

This rewarding 18th-c pub is in lovely country where the River Hodder carves a course beneath Longridge Fell just south of the moors of the Forest of Bowland. There are splendid views from the terraced gardens and bedrooms, and residents can fish in the nearby river. As well as two pleasantly up-to-date dining rooms, there's a traditional, cosy central bar with bookshelves, cushioned settles and a log fire; board games. The choice of regional ales on handpump includes beers from Black Sheep and Moorhouses with a couple of guests from brewers such as Tirril; 11 wines by the glass and a good range of malt whiskies.

Using locally sourced meat, game from local shoots, and herbs from their own garden, robust country food might include smoked goats cheese tart and seared pigeon breast, ox cheek pie, linguine salsa verde, and blackcurrant sponge with liquorice ice-cream; good value Sunday lunch and perhaps a good value two-course weekday lunchtime menu. *Benchmark main dish: rabbit casserole £13.95. Two-course evening meal £18.00.*

Free house ~ Licensees Jonathan and Martina Myerscough ~ Real ale ~ Bar food (12-2, 6-9(7 Sun)) ~ Restaurant ~ (01254) 826227 ~ Open 12-2(3 Sat), 6-11; 12-9 Sun; closed Mon (except bank holidays), Tues in winter, two weeks in Jan ~ Bedrooms: £65S/£95B

Recommended by Steve Whalley, Margaret Dickinson, John and Eleanor Holdsworth

  BASSENTHWAITE Cumbria NY2332 Map B

Sun

Off A591 N of Keswick; CA12 4QP

Bustling old pub with good views, real ales, and changing bar food

A new sun terrace with café screens and parasols has been added to this white-rendered slate house and there are fine views of the fells and Skiddaw. Inside, the rambling bar has been refurbished but there are still low 17th-c black oak beams, two good stone fireplaces with big winter log fires and built-in wall seats and plush stools around heavy wooden tables – these are on a first come first served basis, but you can reserve a table in the new cosy dining room. Jennings Bitter, Cumberland Ale, Golden Host, Sneck Lifter and a guest on handpump and several wines by the glass. The pub is handy for osprey viewing at Dodd Wood and the village is charming.

Well liked food includes sandwiches, creamy garlic mushrooms, chicken liver, Guinness and stilton pâté with a plum and apple chutney, battered cod and chips, lasagne, liver and bacon, pork steak in a brandy, peppercorn sauce, seafood pasta, and chicken breast stuffed with cumberland sausage and wrapped in bacon. *Benchmark main dish: steak in ale pie £9.15. Two-course evening meal £16.00.*

Jennings (Marstons) ~ Lease Mike and Susan Arnold ~ Real ale ~ Bar food (6-8.45 weekdays; 12-2, 6-8.45 weekends) ~ (017687) 76439 ~ Children welcome if dining with adults but must leave by 9pm ~ Dogs welcome ~ Open 4-11(11.30 Fri); 12-11 Sat and Sun; closed weekday lunchtimes

Recommended by Adrian Johnson, Tina and David Woods-Taylor, G Jennings, Geoff and Linda Payne, Howard Bowen, Andy and Alice Jordan

 BASSENTHWAITE LAKE Cumbria NY1930 Map B

Pheasant ★

Follow Pheasant Inn sign at N end of dual carriageway stretch of A66 by Bassenthwaite Lake; CA13 9YE

Charming, old-fashioned bar in smart hotel with enjoyable bar food, and a fine range of drinks; comfortable bedrooms

Civilised and rather smart, this is a very well run hotel – so of course most customers are here to stay overnight in the comfortable bedrooms and to enjoy the particularly good food. But it's the surprisingly pubby and old-fashioned bar that many of our readers enjoy dropping into for a quiet pint or informal lunch. There are mellow polished walls, cushioned oak settles, rush-seat chairs and library seats, hunting prints and photographs, and Bass, Coniston Bluebird and Cumberland Corby Ale on handpump served by friendly, knowledgeable staff; also, 14 good wines by the glass, over 60 malt whiskies and several gins and vodkas. There's a front bistro, a formal back restaurant overlooking the garden and several comfortable lounges with log fires, beautiful flower arrangements, fine parquet flooring, antiques and plants. There are seats in the garden, attractive woodland surroundings and plenty of walks in all directions.

Interesting if not particularly cheap, the lunchtime bar food (sharing the same menu as the bistro which also serves evening food) includes sandwiches, potted shrimps with toasted crumpets, twice-baked cheese soufflé with mustard cress and pistachio vinaigrette, smoked haddock and chive risotto with a poached egg, fish and chips, fricassée of lemon and garlic chicken with lyonnaise potatoes, stout-braised beef, and daily specials. *Benchmark main dish: braised beef £14.00. Two-course evening meal £20.00.*

Free house ~ Licensee Matthew Wylie ~ Real ale ~ Bar food (12-2, 6-9) ~ Restaurant ~ (017687) 76234 ~ Children over 8 only ~ Dogs welcome ~ Open 11-2.30, 5-11; 12-2.30, 6-10.30 Sun ~ Bedrooms: £85B/£160B

Recommended by Adrian Johnson, Noel Grundy, Sylvia and Tony Birbeck, Henry Midwinter, Pat and Stewart Gordon, J F M and M West, Howard Bowen, Jane and Alan Bush

BICKLEY MOSS Cheshire   SJ5550 Map C

Cholmondeley Arms ♀

Cholmondeley; A49 5.5 miles N of Whitchurch; the owners would like us to list them under Cholmondeley village, but as this is rarely located on maps we have mentioned the nearest village which appears more often; SY14 8HN

Imaginatively converted high-ceilinged schoolhouse with decent range of real ale and wines, well presented food, and a sizeable garden

By the time this edition is published there will have been some changes and refurbishment here. It's a clever schoolhouse conversion (handily placed for Cholmondeley Castle Gardens), is thoroughly good fun and makes a memorable setting for a meal or a drink. The cross-shaped lofty bar, high gothic windows, huge old radiators and old school desks on a gantry above the bar are all testament to its former identity. Well used chairs in all shapes and forms – some upholstered, some bentwood, some with ladderbacks and some with wheelbacks – are set in groups round an equally eclectic mix of tables, all on comfy carpets. There's a stag's head over one of the side arches, an open fire and lots of Victorian portraits and military pictures on colourwashed walls; piped music and board games. Salopian Shropshire Gold and Weetwood Eastgate, and a couple of guests from brewers such as Brakspears and Slaters, are served from a pine-clad bar, alongside around ten interesting and reasonably priced wines by the glass (listed on a blackboard), and a growing selection of whiskies. There are seats outside on the sizeable lawn and more in front overlooking the quiet road.

Readers very much enjoy the food here. As well as sandwiches there might be rabbit and ham hock terrine, oxtail and horseradish croquette, steak and kidney pie, chilli, roast cod loin with saffron sabayon and chorizo mash, moroccan goat stew with roast red pepper and herb couscous, and pork belly stuffed with pear and hazelnuts. *Benchmark main dish: steak and kidney pie £9.95. Two-course evening meal £16.90.*

Free house ~ Licensee Paul Dimelow ~ Real ale ~ Bar food (12-9.30) ~ (01829) 720300 ~ Children welcome ~ Dogs welcome ~ Open 11-11(10.30 Sun) ~ Bedrooms: £55B/£80B

Recommended by J S Burn, Alan and Eve Harding, R L Borthwick, P J and R D Greaves

Stars after the name of a pub show exceptional character and appeal. They don't mean extra comfort. And they are nothing to do with food quality, for which there's a separate knife-and-fork symbol. Even quite a basic pub can win stars, if it's individual enough.

BISPHAM GREEN Lancashire   SD4813   Map C

Eagle & Child 🍴 ♀ ◀

Maltkiln Lane (Parbold—Croston road, off B5246); L40 3SG

LANCASHIRE DINING PUB OF THE YEAR

Successful all-rounder with antiques in stylishly simple interior, great food, interesting range of beers, appealing rustic garden

Hitting the nail on the head with unfussy effortless charm, this country pub is largely open-plan and discerningly furnished with a lovely mix of small old oak chairs, an attractive oak coffer, several handsomely carved antique oak settles (the finest apparently made partly from a 16th-c wedding bed-head), old hunting prints and engravings, and low hop-draped beams. There are red walls and coir matting up a step and oriental rugs on ancient flagstones in front of the fine old stone fireplace and counter; the pub's dogs are called Betty and Doris. Friendly young staff serve Thwaites Original alongside five guests from brewers such as Coniston, Phoenix, Prospect, Slaters and Southport, as well as Saxon farm cider, decent wines and around 25 malt whiskies. They hold a popular beer festival over the first May bank holiday weekend. The spacious gently rustic garden has a well tended but unconventional bowling green, and beyond this, a wild area that is home to crested newts and moorhens. Selling interesting wines and pottery, the shop housed in the handsome side barn includes a proper butcher and a deli.

 There's quite an emphasis on the well cooked food (you need to book). As well as a good choice of wraps and ciabattas, there might be black pudding, potato and bacon salad, moules marinière, game salad, sausage and mash, thai-style vegetable curry, crayfish and lemon risotto, seared bass with saffron and vanilla tiger prawns, chicken breast with green peppercorn and brandy cream sauce, and braised oxtail with red wine sauce. *Benchmark main dish: steak and ale pie £10.00. Two-course evening meal £19.00.*

Free house ~ Licensee David Anderson ~ Real ale ~ Bar food (12-2, 5.30-8.30(9 Fri, Sat); 12-8.30 Sun) ~ (01257) 462297 ~ Children welcome away from bar ~ Dogs welcome ~ Open 12-3, 5.30-11; 12-11 Sat; 12-10.30 Sun

Recommended by Peter Heaton, Mike Tucker, Adrian and Dawn Collinge, Dr Clive Elphick, Yvonne and Mike Meadley, John and Helen Rushton, Ann and Tony Bennett-Hughes, Maurice and Gill McMahon, Jack Clark, Ed and Anna Fraser

BOWLAND BRIDGE Cumbria   SD4189   Map B

Hare & Hounds ♀ 🛏

Signed from A5074; LA11 6NN

17th-c inn in quiet spot with a friendly, cheerful landlady, real ales, popular food, and fine views; comfortable bedrooms

Now in the capable and friendly hands of the former management of the Strickland Arms at Levens, this attractive 17th-c coaching inn is getting high praise from our readers. There's a little bar with a log fire, daily papers to read and high chairs by the wooden counter where they serve Hare of the Dog (brewed especially for them by Tirril) and guests from Kirkby Lonsdale and Ulverston on handpump, a farm cider from half a mile away, and around a dozen wines by the glass. Leading off here are other rooms appealingly furnished with a happy mix of interesting dining chairs around all sorts of tables on the black slate or old pine-boarded floors, lots of prints on painted or stripped-stone walls, a candlelit moroccan-style lantern in a fireplace with neatly stacked logs to one side, and a relaxed atmosphere; piped music and board games. The bedrooms are comfortable and the breakfasts are first class. There are teak tables and chairs under parasols on the front terrace, with more seats in the spacious side garden and fine valley views. The inn is by the bridge itself in a quiet hamlet in the Winster Valley and Lake Windermere is just ten minutes away.

Using seasonal local produce, the very good food at lunchtime includes sandwiches, chicken liver pâté with date and orange chutney, home-made burger topped with a garlic field mushroom and cheese, and beer-battered haddock, with evening choices such as a smoked salmon parcel with crab and lemon mayonnaise, a seasonal vegetarian risotto, chicken stuffed with goats cheese, wrapped in bacon with a sweet chilli and tomato sauce, and lamb cutlets with a red wine, rosemary and mint jus. *Benchmark main dish: steak in ale pie £11.25. Two-course evening meal £17.20.*

Free house ~ Licensee Kerry Parsons ~ Real ale ~ Bar food (12-9(8.30 Sun); 12-2, 6-9 in winter) ~ (015395) 68333 ~ Children welcome ~ Dogs welcome ~ Live music during May bank holiday beer festival ~ Open 12-11(10.30 Sun) ~ Bedrooms: /£75B

Recommended by V and E A Bolton, Michael Doswell

BROUGHTON MILLS Cumbria   SD2190   Map B

Blacksmiths Arms ▯▯

Off A593 N of Broughton-in-Furness; LA20 6AX

Friendly little pub with imaginative food, local beers and open fires; fine surrounding walks

Going from strength to strength, this is a bustling pub run by warmly friendly licensees. It's tucked away in a little hamlet in peaceful countryside – just the place to relax after a day on the fells. There are four little bars that are simply but attractively decorated with straightforward chairs and tables on ancient slate floors and warm log fires. Barngates Cracker Ale, Dent Golden Fleece and Hawkshead Bitter on handpump, nine wines by the glass and summer farm cider; darts, cards and cribbage. The hanging baskets and tubs of flowers in front of the building are pretty in summer.

You must book a table in advance to enjoy the consistently good food which at lunchtime includes nibbles and sandwiches, ham hock and pigeon terrine with a fried egg, pineapple chutney and an apple, crackling and pea shoot salad, beer-battered hake with home-made chips, cumberland sausage with black pudding and an oxtail and red wine gravy, and creamy cheese, broccoli and sun-dried tomato tartlet with a pesto-dressed salad; evening extras such as chargrilled lime and coriander chicken with a carrot, beetroot and chickpea salad, and honey and lemon roasted duck breast with confit leg pie and madeira jus. *Benchmark main dish: slow-roasted lamb shoulder in mint and honey £13.55. Two-course evening meal £18.35.*

Free house ~ Licensees Mike and Sophie Lane ~ Real ale ~ Bar food (12-2, 6-9; not Mon) ~ Restaurant ~ (01229) 716824 ~ Children welcome ~ Dogs welcome ~ Open 12-11(5-11 Mon); 12-10.30 Sun; 12-2.30, 5-11 Tues-Fri in winter; closed Mon lunchtime

Recommended by Veronica Gwynn, Tina and David Woods-Taylor, John Luckes, E Ling, Michael Butler, the Didler, JES, Rosemary and Mike Fielder

---

Half pints: by law, a pub should not charge more for half a pint than half the price of a full pint, unless it shows that half-pint price on its price list.

BUNBURY Cheshire   SJ5658 Map C

Dysart Arms

Bowes Gate Road; village signposted off A51 NW of Nantwich; and from A49 S of Tarporley – coming this way, coming in on northernmost village access road, bear left in village centre; CW6 9PH

Civilised chatty dining pub attractively filled with good furniture in thoughtfully laid-out rooms; very enjoyable food, lovely garden with pretty views

Although very much opened up, the rooms at this comfortable country pub still retain a cottagey feel and an easy-going sociable atmosphere. Neatly kept, they ramble gently around the pleasantly lit central bar. Cream walls keep it all light, clean and airy, with deep venetian red ceilings adding cosiness, and each room (some with good winter fires) is nicely furnished with an appealing variety of well spaced sturdy wooden tables and chairs, a couple of tall filled bookcases and just the right amount of carefully chosen bric-a-brac, properly lit pictures and plants. Flooring ranges from red and black tiles, to stripped boards and some carpet. Service is efficient and friendly. Phoenix Brunning & Price Original, Weetwood and two or three guests from brewers such as Copper Dragon, Phoenix and Wooden Hand are on handpump alongside a good selection of 17 wines by the glass from a list of about 70, and just over 20 malts. Sturdy wooden tables on the terrace and picnic-sets on the lawn in the neatly kept slightly elevated garden are lovely in summer, with views of the splendid church at the end of this pretty village, and the distant Peckforton Hills beyond.

From a changing menu, food is tasty, just imaginative enough, attractively presented and fairly priced. As well as sandwiches, there might be fried scallops with carrot and cumin purée and crisp parma ham, crab linguine with ginger, red chilli and coriander, moroccan spiced lamb rump with apricot and date salad and chickpea cakes, coq au vin, home-made burger, and fried venison rump with venison faggot and juniper jus. *Benchmark main dish: battered haddock and chips £11.95. Two-course evening meal £18.60.*

Brunning & Price ~ Manager Greg Williams ~ Real ale ~ Bar food (12-9.30(9 Sun)) ~ Restaurant ~ (01829) 260183 ~ Children welcome ~ Dogs allowed in bar ~ Open 11.30-11; 12-10.30 Sun

Recommended by John Cook, Peter Webb, Gerry and Rosemary Dobson, Clive Watkin, Sian Davies, Dr and Mrs Michael Smith, Dave Webster, Sue Holland, Mark Delap

BURLEYDAM Cheshire   SJ6042 Map C

Combermere Arms

A525 Whitchurch—Audlem; SY13 4AT

Roomy and attractive beamed pub successfully mixing a good drinking side with imaginative all-day food; rear and front garden

Décor and furnishings at this spreading pub take in a bric-a-brac-style mix of wooden chairs at dark wood tables, rugs on wood (some old and some new oak) or stone floors, frame-to-frame prints on cream walls, deep red ceilings, panelling and open fires. Friendly staff extend an equally nice welcome to drinkers and diners, with both aspects of the business seeming to do well here. Alongside Greene King Speckled Hen, Phoenix Brunning & Price Original and Weetwood Cheshire Cat, three or four guests might be from brewers such as Adnams, Acorn and Copper Dragon. They also stock around 100 whiskies and a dozen wines by the glass from an extensive list; a few board games. Outside there are good solid wood tables in a pretty, well tended garden; more reports please.

🍴 As well as interesting sandwiches and ploughman's, the enjoyable daily-changing menu might include ham hock and apricot terrine, sticky chilli and sesame seed chicken with noodle salad, cauliflower, chickpea and almond tagine with apricot and date couscous, steak, mushroom and ale pie, steamed hake fillet with crushed lemon and dill potato cake, and roast duck breast with sherry leeks, caramelised apple pastry and calvados gravy. *Benchmark main dish: steak burger £10.95. Two-course evening meal £18.00.*

Brunning & Price ~ Manager Lisa Hares ~ Real ale ~ Bar food (12-9.30; 12-10 Thurs-Sat; 12-9 Sun) ~ (01948) 871223 ~ Children welcome ~ Dogs allowed in bar ~ Open 12-11(10.30 Sun)

Recommended by R T and J C Moggridge

BURWARDSLEY Cheshire   SJ5256   Map C

Pheasant ★ 🍴 ♀

Higher Burwardsley; signposted from Tattenhall (which itself is signposted off A41 S of Chester) and from Harthill (reached by turning off A534 Nantwich—Holt at the Copper Mine); follow pub's signpost on up hill from Post Office; OS Sheet 117 map reference 523566; CH3 9PF

Fantastic views, local beer and good range of enjoyable food at this roomily fresh conversion of an old heavily beamed inn; open all day

This 17th-c sandstone and half-timbered pub is a terrific all-rounder (great food, beer and a lovely place to stay), benefiting too from its idyllic elevated position. It enjoys stunning views right across the Cheshire plains from nice hardwood furniture on the terrace – on a clear day their telescope sees as far as the pier head and cathedrals in Liverpool. Divided into separate areas and almost circling the bar, the beamed interior (great views from here too), quite airy and modern feeling in parts, has wooden floors, well spaced furniture, including comfy leather armchairs and some nice old chairs. They like to say that the see-through fireplace houses the largest log fire in the county. Local Weetwood Best and Cheshire Cat and Eastgate are served alongside a guest such as Mallard Spittin' Feathers, as well as local farm cider and apple juice; quiet piped music, daily newspapers. This is a great stop if you are walking the scenic Sandstone Trail along the Peckforton Hills.

🍴 Besides sandwiches (served until 6pm), the changing menu might include king prawns with lemon grass, chilli, coriander and samphire, seared scallops with caper, radish and chorizo salad and cannellini bean purée, home-made steak burger, mushroom and goats cheese feuilletée, thai green chicken curry, roast duck breast with braised gem lettuce and mushrooms, steak and mushroom pie, and well hung rib-eye steak. *Benchmark main dish: beer-battered haddock £12.50. Two-course evening meal £19.50.*

Free house ~ Licensee Andrew Nelson ~ Real ale ~ Bar food (12-3, 6-9.30 Mon, 12-9.30 Tues-Thurs, 12-10 Fri, Sat; 12-8.30 Sun) ~ (01829) 770434 ~ Children welcome ~ Dogs welcome ~ Open 12-11(10.30 Sun) ~ Bedrooms: £70B/£90B

Recommended by Val Carter, Maurice and Gill McMahon, Gerry and Rosemary Dobson, Pat and Graham Williamson, Bruce and Sharon Eden, Dave Webster, Sue Holland, Jonny Kershaw

---

The price we give for a two-course evening meal in the featured top pub entries is the mean (average of cheapest and most expensive) price of a starter and a main course – no drinks.

CARTMEL FELL Cumbria   SD4189   Map B

Masons Arms
NORTH WEST PUB OF THE YEAR

Strawberry Bank, a few miles S of Windermere between A592 and A5074; perhaps the simplest way of finding the pub is to go uphill W from Bowland Bridge (which is signposted off A5074) towards Newby Bridge and keep right then left at the staggered crossroads – it's then on your right, below Gummer's How; OS Sheet 97 map reference 413895; LA11 6NW

Stunning views, beamed bar with plenty of character, good food and real ales plus many foreign bottled beers; self-catering cottages and flats

Rustic benches and tables on the heated terrace here take in the stunning views down over the Winster Valley to the woods below Whitbarrow Scar; it really is an idyllic spot. The pub itself is a favourite with many of our readers and the main bar has plenty of character, with low black beams in the bowed ceiling, and country chairs and plain wooden tables on polished flagstones. A small lounge has oak tables and settles to match its fine Jacobean panelling, there's a plain little room beyond the serving counter with pictures and a fire in an open range, a family room with an old-parlourish atmosphere and an upstairs dining room; piped music, board games and TV. Cumbrian Dickie Doodle, Hawkshead Bitter and Windermere Pale, Thwaites Wainwright and Winster Valley Old School on handpump, quite a few foreign bottled beers, 13 wines by the glass and a dozen malt whiskies; service is friendly and prompt. The stylish and comfortable self-catering cottages and apartments also have fine views.

As well as offering light breakfasts and afternoon snacks, the choice of excellent food might include interesting lunchtime sandwiches, wraps, melts and toasted ciabattas, sticky ribs, black pudding stack with home-made brown sauce, a trio of sausages (wild boar and apple, venison and cranberry, duck and chilli) with red wine and roast onion gravy, steak burger topped with cheese and cajun-spiced onion rings with thin fries and chilli jam, vegetarian shepherd's pie, and specials like chicken breast wrapped in smoked bacon on asparagus and spinach with a creamy white wine sauce, and cheese-topped fish pie. *Benchmark main dish: slow-cooked lamb in rich braising gravy with dauphinoise potatoes £16.95. Two-course evening meal £19.00.*

Individual Inns ~ Managers John and Diane Taylor ~ Real ale ~ Bar food (12-2.30, 6-9 (some afternoon snacks, too); all day weekends; light breakfasts 10am-midday) ~ Restaurant ~ (015395) 68486 ~ Children welcome ~ Dogs allowed in bar ~ Open 11.30-11; 12-10.30 Sun

Recommended by D M Heath, Tina and David Woods-Taylor, Nick Lawless, Brian Dawes, Bill Adie, G Jennings, Alison Ball, Ian Walton, Pat and Stewart Gordon, Mike Gorton, Andy and Jill Kassube, John and Hilary Penny, M G Hames, Mr and Mrs P R Thomas, Val Leonard

CHELFORD Cheshire   SJ8175   Map C

Egerton Arms
A537 Macclesfield—Knutsford; SK11 9BB

Well organised and welcoming, with something for everyone including food all day

This former Chef & Brewer is really flourishing since its liberation. It's quite a big place, but nicely broken up, with an appealingly varied mix of tables and chairs, including some attractive wicker dining chairs, carved settles and a wooden porter's chair by a grandfather clock. The long bar serves well kept ales from handpump such as Copper Dragon Golden Pippin, Red River Headless Dog, Tatton Best and Wells & Youngs Bombardier, and the staff are cheerful and helpful, making for a good relaxed atmosphere in the rambling dark-beamed bar. At one end a few steps take you down into a super little raftered games area, with tempting very squashy sofas and antique farm-animal prints on stripped-brick walls, as well as pool, darts, games machines and sports TV; piped music. An outside deck has canopied picnic-sets, with more on the grass by a toddlers' play area. There's a warm welcome for both dogs and children.

Besides sandwiches, good value cream teas and a bargain moules frites night on Wednesdays, enjoyable quickly served food here includes brandy and herb pâté, ploughman's, scampi, sweet potato, chickpea and aubergine saag, cod and chips, a good pie of the day such as steak and kidney, pizzas, burgers, grills, and a popular Sunday lunch. *Benchmark main dish: liver, bacon and sausages in gravy £8.95. Two-course evening meal £15.00.*

Free house ~ Licensees Jeremy and Anne Hague ~ Real ale ~ Bar food (12-9) ~ (01625) 861366 ~ Children welcome ~ Dogs allowed in bar ~ Open 12-11(10.30 Sun)
Recommended by Roger and Anne Newbury, John Wooll, Dr D J and Mrs S C Walker

CHESTER Cheshire   SJ4066 Map C

Albion ★ ◖ £
Albion Street; CH1 1RQ

Strongly traditional pub with comfortable Edwardian décor and captivating World War I memorabilia; pubby food and good drinks

The homely interior of this peaceful Victorian pub is entirely dedicated to the Great War of 1914-18; most unusually it's also the officially listed site of four war memorials to soldiers from the Cheshire Regiment. It's been run by the same friendly sincere licensees for over 40 years and there's something inimitably genuine about its lovely old-fashioned atmosphere. Throughout its tranquil rooms you'll find an absorbing collection of World War I memorabilia, from big engravings of men leaving for war, and similarly moving prints of wounded veterans, to flags, advertisements and so on. The post-Edwardian décor is appealingly muted, with dark floral William Morris wallpaper (designed on the first day of World War I), a cast-iron fireplace, appropriate lamps, leatherette and hoop-backed chairs and cast-iron-framed tables. You might even be lucky enough to hear the vintage 1928 Steck pianola being played; there's an attractive side dining room too. Service is friendly, though groups of race-goers are discouraged (opening times may be limited during meets), and they don't like people rushing in just before closing time. A good range of drinks includes Adnams and a couple of guests from brewers such as Hook Norton and Titanic on handpump, new world wines, fresh orange juice, organic bottled cider and fruit juice, over 25 malt whiskies and a good selection of rums and gins. Dog owners can request a water bowl and cold sausage for their pets. Bedrooms are small but comfortable and furnished in keeping with the pub's style (free parking for residents and a bottle of house wine if dining).

Even the trench rations are in period, and served in such generous helpings that they don't offer starters: boiled gammon and pease pudding with parsley sauce, corned beef hash with picked red cabbage, liver, bacon and onions with cider sauce, haggis, tatties and vegetables, and filled staffordshire oatcakes. *Benchmark main dish: lambs liver and bacon in red cider gravy £9.00.*

Punch ~ Lease Michael Edward Mercer ~ Real ale ~ Bar food (12-13.50(2.20 Sat),
5-7.50(8.20 Sat); not Sun evening) ~ Restaurant ~ No credit cards ~ (01244) 340345 ~
Dogs allowed in bar ~ Open 12-3(3.30 Sat), 5(6 Sat)-11; closed Sun evening ~ Bedrooms:
£70B/£85B

*Recommended by Mrs M Smith, Alan and Eve Harding, Martin and Sue Radcliffe, Philip and
Jan Medcalf, Roger and Anne Newbury, Keith Sale, Dennis Jones, Kim Mackay, Mary Mackay,
the Didler, J S Burn, Barry Collett, Maurice and Gill McMahon, Joe Green, Mike and
Eleanor Anderson, Paul Humphreys*

CHESTER Cheshire   SJ4166   Map C

Mill ◖ £

Milton Street; CH1 3NF

**Big hotel with a huge range of real ales, good value food and cheery
service in sizeable bar**

We've included this modern hotel for its impressive range of a dozen
real ales. Cornmill (brewed for them by Phoenix), Mill Premium
(brewed for them by Coach House), Copper Dragon Golden Pippin and
Weetwood Best are kept alongside guests from brewers such as Marstons,
RCH and Whim; also a dozen wines by the glass, two farm ciders and 20
malt whiskies. Converted from an old mill, the building straddles either
side of the Shropshire Union Canal, with a glassed-in bridge connecting
its two halves. The very neatly kept bar has stripped light wood flooring
throughout, marble-topped tables, some exposed brickwork and
supporting pillars, and local photographs and cigarette cards framed on
cream-papered walls. One comfortable area is reminiscent of a bar on a
cruise liner. Service here is very friendly and you'll find a real mix of
customers; quiet piped music and unobtrusively placed big-screen sports
TV. Readers say the bedrooms are comfortable and make a handy base for
exploring the city.

Very reasonably priced pubby food includes sandwiches, ciabattas, garlic bread
and enjoyable hot dishes such as curry and rice, scampi, fish and chips, and
their popular steak and ale pie. *Benchmark main dish: steak and ale pie £6.50. Two-
course evening meal £8.75.*

Free house ~ Licensees Gary and Gordon Vickers ~ Real ale ~ Bar food (11.30-11; 12-10
Sun) ~ Restaurant ~ (01244) 350035 ~ Children welcome ~ Open 10am-midnight ~
Bedrooms: £73B/£95B

Recommended by Dennis Jones, Joe Green, Dave Webster, Sue Holland

---

CHESTER Cheshire   SJ4166   Map C

Old Harkers Arms ♀ ◖

*Russell Street, down steps off City Road where it crosses canal – under Mike
Melody antiques; CH3 5AL*

**Well run spacious canalside building with lively atmosphere, great range
of drinks (including lots of changing real ales), and good tasty food**

The Shropshire Union Canal flows just feet away from the tall windows
of this high-ceilinged early Victorian warehouse. Huge brick pillars
cleverly divide the big airy interior into user-friendly spaces, and cheery
staff spread a happy bustle. Mixed dark wood furniture is well grouped on
stripped-wood floors, walls are covered with frame-to-frame old prints,
and the usual Brunning & Price wall of bookshelves is to be found above
a leather banquette at one end. Attractive lamps add cosiness, and the bar

counter is apparently constructed from salvaged doors; selection of board games. You'll find a very wide range of drinks taking in around nine real ales on handpump including Phoenix Brunning & Price, Flowers Original and Weetwood Cheshire Cat, and half a dozen regularly changing guests from brewers such as Phoenix, Salopian and Titanic, more than 100 malt whiskies, 50 well described wines (with around half of them by the glass), eight or so farmhouse ciders and local apple juice.

🍴 As well as a good range of interesting sandwiches, nicely presented carefully sourced bar food – a good balance of homely dishes and more imaginative ones – might include ploughman's, mushroom and cheshire blue on walnut and raisin toast, crispy duck salad with spiced plum dressing, smoked fish and cider pie, beef, ale and stilton pudding, cauliflower, chickpea, sweet potato and apricot tagine with apricot couscous, battered haddock, and rump steak with tarragon butter. *Benchmark main dish: steak burger £10.95. Two-course evening meal £17.60.*

Brunning & Price ~ Manager Paul Jeffery ~ Real ale ~ Bar food (12-9.30) ~ (01244) 344525 ~ Dogs welcome ~ Open 11.30-11; 12-10.30 Sun

Recommended by Bruce and Sharon Eden, Dennis Jones, Charles and Pauline Stride, Simon J Barber, Clive Watkin, the Didler, Joe Green, Roger and Anne Newbury, Dave Webster, Sue Holland, Dr Kevan Tucker, Paul Humphreys

CLIFTON Cumbria   NY5326 Map B

George & Dragon 🍴 🍷 🛏
A6; near M6 junction 40; CA10 2ER

18th-c former coaching inn with attractive bars and sizeable restaurant, local ales, well chosen wines, imaginative food, and seats outside; smart bedrooms

Cyclists, walkers with their dogs and families are all made welcome in this carefully restored 18th-c coaching inn. There's a relaxed reception room with leather chairs around a low table in front of an open fire, bright rugs on flagstones, a table in a private nook to one side of the reception desk (just right for a group of six) and a comfortable bed for Porter, the patterdale terrier. Through some wrought-iron gates is the main bar area with more cheerful rugs on flagstones, assorted wooden farmhouse chairs and tables, grey panelling topped with yellow-painted walls, photographs of the Lowther Estate and of the family with hunting dogs, various sheep and fell pictures and some high bar stools by the panelled bar counter. Hawkshead Bitter, Lancaster Amber and a guest such as Cumberland Corby Blonde on handpump and 15 wines by the glass from a well chosen list. A further room with another open fire is similarly furnished. The sizeable restaurant to the left of the entrance is made up of four open-plan rooms: plenty of old pews and church chairs around tables set for dining, a woodburning stove, and a contemporary open kitchen. Outside, there are tables on the decoratively paved front entrance, with more in a high-walled enclosed courtyard, and a herb garden.

🍴 Using rare-breed meat, vegetables and fruit and roe and red deer – all from the Lowther Estate of which this pub is part – the inventive food might include lunchtime sandwiches, popular twice-baked cheese soufflé, wild rabbit hash with a fried duck egg, wild mushroom and wild garlic risotto, shorthorn beefburger with triple-cooked potatoes, beer-battered fish of the day, parmesan-crusted chicken with marinated tomato and basil aioli, and specials such as wild boar carpaccio with pear and truffle oil, and wild trout with baby fennel, almonds and hollandaise. *Benchmark main dish: venison medallions with a wild mushroom cream and mash £19.95. Two-course evening meal £19.95.*

Free house ~ Licensee Paul McKinnon ~ Real ale ~ Bar food (12-2.30, 6-9) ~ Restaurant ~ (01768) 865381 ~ Children welcome ~ Dogs allowed in bar and bedrooms ~ Open 11-midnight ~ Bedrooms: £70S/£90S

Recommended by Michael Doswell, Mr and Mrs Ian King, Richard J Holloway, V and E A Bolton, David Heath, Rosemary and Mike Fielder

 COCKERMOUTH Cumbria   NY1230 Map B

1761

Market Place; CA13 9NH

Civilised and welcoming retreat with good drinks and interesting snacks – good value

Behind the shop-front windows of the handsome old building, this friendly place is laid out well for a comfortable chat, or a companionable game – they have lots of board games, and dominoes, cribbage, shove-ha'penny and bar skittles. Good value wines by the glass and foreign beers such as Erdinger and Liefmans Cuvée Brut join well kept Thwaites Bitter and a couple of guests from local breweries such as Barngates, Dent, Loweswater and Hesket Newmarket on handpump. There are two woodburning stoves (one in the back family room, which has some attractive ancient stripped brick), and the young owners are enthusiastic and welcoming. With slate flagstones by the bar counter on the left, bare boards on the right, and the polychrome tiles of a former corridor floor dividing the two, there are comfortably cushioned window seats, a couple of high-backed wing settles and other pleasing furnishings including some high tables. Big Lakeland landscape photographs show well against the colour scheme of pastel pinkish-beige and dark red; unobtrusive piped music. The back courtyard, below lawn and flowers sloping up to the church, has a couple of teak tables. Dogs must be kept on a lead.

Enjoyable light snacks at attractive prices might include watermelon with feta, potato wedges with various dips, garlic or chilli prawns, and local cheeses or smoked meats. *Benchmark main dish: tapas-style dishes £3.00.*

Free house ~ Licensee Nicola and Phil Sloan ~ Real ale ~ Bar food (available during serving times) ~ (01900) 829282 ~ Children welcome ~ Dogs allowed in bar ~ Open 3-11(11.30 Fri and Sat); closed lunchtimes

Recommended by Pam and John Smith

COTEBROOK Cheshire   SJ5765 Map C

Fox & Barrel 🍴

A49 NE of Tarporley; CW6 9DZ

CHESHIRE DINING PUB OF THE YEAR

Pretty white cottage with stylishly airy décor and an enterprising menu

Much enjoyed by readers, this warmly welcoming place is run with attention to detail and attracts both drinkers and diners alike. The tiled bar is dominated by a big log fireplace and has stools along its counter. A bigger uncluttered dining area has attractive rugs and an eclectic mix of period tables on polished oak floorboards, with extensive wall panelling hung with framed old prints. Outside is plentiful seating on a terrace and in the garden, which contains old fruit trees and a tractor. Real ales include Caledonian Deuchars IPA, Weetwood Eastgate and a couple of guests such as Morlands Original and Weetwood Cheshire Cat; good array of wines, with 20 by the glass.

🍴 As well as sandwiches and ploughman's, the changing menu might include roast tomato soup with pesto, venison faggot with celeriac mash and shallot sauce, scallop, pork belly and black pudding salad with caper dressing, seared salmon with chorizo, mussel and smoked haddock stew, chickpea and aubergine moussaka, mushroom and black truffle gnocchi with madeira butter sauce, cottage pie, and battered haddock and chips. *Benchmark main dish: beer-battered haddock £12.45. Two-course evening meal £19.30.*

Free house ~ Licensee Gary Kidd ~ Real ale ~ Bar food (12-9.30(9 Sun)) ~ (01829) 760529 ~ Children welcome but no pushchairs ~ Dogs allowed in bar ~ Open 12-11(10.30 Sun)

Recommended by Bruce and Sharon Eden, Lionel Townsend, Hilary Forrest, David A Hammond, Andy and Jill Kassube

EATON Cheshire   SJ8765   Map C

Plough 🛏

A536 Congleton—Macclesfield; CW12 2NH

Neat and cosy village pub with up to four interesting beers, bar food, views from big attractive garden; good bedrooms

Friendly and welcoming, this tidy red-brick 17th-c pub has a fairly traditional feel. The carefully converted bar has plenty of beams and exposed brickwork, a couple of snug little alcoves, comfortable armchairs and cushioned wooden wall seats on red patterned carpets, long red curtains, leaded windows and a big stone fireplace. Service is attentive and readers have been given highchairs and a little table with crayons and paper for children. Beers include Flowers Original and Hydes Bitter (very reasonably priced) and a couple of guests from local Congleton and Macclesfield, and a decent wine list offers ten by the glass; piped music and occasional TV. Moved here piece by piece from its original home in Wales, the heavily raftered barn at the back makes a striking restaurant. Being not far from the fringes of the Peak District, you get good views of its nearby hills from the big tree-filled garden which has picnic-sets on the lawn and a covered decked terrace with outdoor heaters. The appealingly designed bedrooms are in a converted stable block.

🍴 It's advisable to book if you are eating. Food includes lunchtime sandwiches, as well as prawns in garlic butter, steak and kidney pudding, thai green curry, aubergine bake, well hung aberdeen angus steaks, and some interesting daily specials and unusual meats such as springbok and kangaroo; three-course Sunday lunch. *Benchmark main dish: fish and chips £11.00. Two-course evening meal £16.50.*

Free house ~ Licensee Mujdat Karatas ~ Real ale ~ Bar food (12-2.30; 6-9.30; 12-9.30 (8 Sun) Fri, Sat) ~ Restaurant ~ (01260) 280207 ~ Children welcome ~ Dogs allowed in bedrooms ~ Open 11am-midnight(1am Sat, 11 Sun) ~ Bedrooms: £60B/£75B

Recommended by Rob and Catherine Dunster, Mike Proctor

Please tell us if the décor, atmosphere, food or drink at a pub is different from our description. We rely on readers' reports to keep us up to date: **feedback@goodguides.com**, or (no stamp needed) The Good Pub Guide, FREEPOST TN1569, Wadhurst, E Sussex TN5 7BR.

ELTERWATER Cumbria   NY3204 Map B

Britannia

Off B5343; LA22 9HP

Extremely popular inn surrounded by wonderful walks and scenery; up to six real ales and well liked food; bedrooms

As this very busy pub is so well placed in the heart of the Lake District, close to Langdale and the central lakes and with tracks over the fells to Grasmere and Easedale Tarn – it's a welcome haven for hungry and thirsty walkers. The atmosphere is old-fashioned and the little front bar has beams and a couple of window seats that look across to Elterwater itself through the trees. The small back bar is traditionally furnished: thick slate walls, winter coal fires, oak benches, settles, windsor chairs and a big old rocking chair. Coniston Bluebird, Thwaites Wainwright and guests such as Coniston Oatmeal Stout, Dent Aviator and Hesket Newmarket Catbells Pale Ale on handpump, and quite a few malt whiskies. The lounge is comfortable and there's a hall and dining room. Plenty of seats outside, and summer morris and step garland dancers.

Under the new licensee, the generous helpings of popular food (you must book in advance or you might be disappointed) include filled rolls, pâté with port sauce, burgers with cheese and red onion marmalade, cumberland sausage with mash and onion gravy, mushroom stroganoff, steak and mushroom in ale pie, and beer-battered fresh haddock with tartare sauce. *Benchmark main dish: lamb henry (in mint and honey) £12.50. Two-course evening meal £17.50.*

Free house ~ Licensee Andrew Parker ~ Real ale ~ Bar food (12–5.30, 6.30–9) ~ Restaurant ~ (015394) 37210 ~ Children welcome ~ Dogs allowed in bar and bedrooms ~ Open 10am–11pm ~ Bedrooms: £60S/£90S

Recommended by David and Sue Atkinson, Tina and David Woods-Taylor, Mr and Mrs J Hilton, Alison Ball, Ian Walton, G Jennings, Mrs Pam Mattinson, J Woodgate, John and Helen Rushton, Michael Doswell, Ewan and Moira McCall, Julia and Richard Tredgett, Richard Scrase, Mr and Mrs Richard Osborne, Steve and Sue Griffiths

GREAT MITTON Lancashire   SD7139 Map C

Three Fishes

Mitton Road (B6246, off A59 NW of Whalley); BB7 9PQ

Stylish modern revamp, tremendous attention to detail, excellent regional food with a contemporary twist, interesting drinks

Despite its size, this imaginatively converted and well laid-out pub has plenty of intimate corners; the areas closest to the bar are elegantly traditional with a couple of big stone fireplaces, rugs on polished floors and upholstered stools. Then there's a series of individually furnished and painted rooms with exposed stone walls, careful spotlighting and wooden slatted blinds, ending with another impressive fireplace. Staff are young and friendly and there's a good chatty atmosphere. The long bar counter (with elaborate floral displays) serves Bowland Hen Harrier, Lancaster Bomber and Wainwright, a dozen wines by the glass and unusual soft drinks such as locally made sarsaparilla and dandelion and burdock. Overlooking the Ribble Valley, the garden and terrace have tables and perhaps their own summer menu. You write your name on a blackboard when you arrive and they find you when a table becomes free – the system works surprisingly well.

🍴 Food products are carefully sourced from small local suppliers, many of whom are pictured in black and white photographs on the walls, and located on a map on the back of the menu – the beef particularly is exclusive to here. As well as imaginative lunchtime sandwiches, there might be dishes such as beech and juniper smoked salmon, baked whitebait, smoked pig's jowl, good lancashire hotpot, curd cheese and onion pie, slow-cooked saddleback pork with garlic mash and gravy, and scampi and crispy squid with chips. You may need to order side dishes with some main courses; limited afternoon snack menu. *Benchmark main dish: fish pie £10.75. Two-course evening meal £16.50.*

Free house ~ Licensee Andy Morris ~ Real ale ~ Bar food (12-8.30(9 Fri, Sat); 12-8 Sun) ~ (01254) 826888 ~ Children welcome ~ Dogs welcome ~ Open 12-11(10.30 Sun)

Recommended by Steve Whalley, Maurice and Gill McMahon, Hilary Forrest, Dr Kevan Tucker, John and Sylvia Harrop, Ed and Anna Fraser

GREAT SALKELD Cumbria   NY5536   Map A

Highland Drove 🍴 £

B6412, off A686 NE of Penrith; CA11 9NA

Bustling place with a cheerful mix of customers, good food in several dining areas, fair choice of drinks, and fine views from the upstairs verandah; bedrooms

Our readers enjoy this well run, neatly kept pub very much and feel it's a smashing all-rounder. The chatty main bar has sandstone flooring, stone walls, cushioned wheelback chairs around a mix of tables and an open fire in a raised stone fireplace. The downstairs eating area has more cushioned dining chairs around wooden tables on the pale wooden floorboards, stone walls and ceiling joists and a two-way fire in a raised stone fireplace that separates this room from the coffee lounge with its comfortable leather chairs and sofas. There's also an upstairs restaurant. Best to book to be sure of a table. Theakstons Black Bull and a couple of guests such as Brains Milkwood and John Smiths on handpump, several wines by the glass and 30 malt whiskies. Piped music, juke box, darts, pool and dominoes. The lovely views over the Eden Valley and the Pennines are best enjoyed from seats on the upstairs verandah. There are more seats on the back terrace.

🍴 As well as lunchtime baguettes (not Sunday), the well presented food might include black pudding and apple fritter on sweet potato and parsnip purée with wholegrain mustard sauce, smoked salmon parcel filled with prawn and dill mousse, a sharing charcuterie or fishy plate, herby pancakes stuffed with vegetables in a creamy white wine sauce, tray-baked steak in ale pie, chicken and oyster mushroom fricassée in puffy pastry with a baby onion and tarragon cream sauce, and slow-roasted pork belly on cheddar and chive mash with an apple, honey and mustard sauce. The Value Award is for the more pubby dishes. *Benchmark main dish: fillet of Nile perch in a red thai curry sauce with lemon grass and coconut rice £13.95. Two-course evening meal £17.50.*

Free house ~ Licensees Donald and Paul Newton ~ Real ale ~ Bar food (not Mon lunchtime) ~ Restaurant ~ (01768) 898349 ~ Children welcome ~ Dogs allowed in bar ~ Open 12-3, 6-11; 12-midnight Sat; closed Mon lunchtime ~ Bedrooms: £42.50S/£75S

Recommended by Richard J Holloway, Dr Kevan Tucker, Chris and Jo Parsons, Maurice and Gill McMahon, Dave Braisted, Richard and Stephanie Foskett, Rosemary and Mike Fielder, John and Hazel Hayward

INGS Cumbria   SD4498   Map B

Watermill

Just off A591 E of Windermere; LA8 9PY

Busy, cleverly converted pub with fantastic range of real ales including own brews, and well liked food; bedrooms

With a genuinely friendly welcome, good hearty food, their own-brewed ales and comfortable bedrooms (some are bigger than others), it's not surprising that this well run inn is so popular; it's best to book a table in advance if you wish to eat. The building has plenty of character and is cleverly converted from a wood mill and joiner's shop and the bars have a lively atmosphere, a happy mix of chairs, padded benches and solid oak tables, bar counters made from old church wood, open fires, and interesting photographs and amusing cartoons by a local artist. The spacious lounge bar, in much the same traditional style as the other rooms, has rocking chairs and a big open fire. As well as their own brewed Watermill A Bit'er Ruff and Wruff Night, Collie Wobbles, Dogth Vadar and Isle of Dogs, they keep up to 11 other beers on handpump: Blackbeck Belle, Coniston Bluebird, Cumbrian Legendary Grasmoor Dark Ale, Hawkshead Bitter, Keswick Thirst Ascent, Kirkby Lonsdale Tiffin Gold, Theakstons Old Peculier and Ulverston Another Fine Mess. Also, scrumpy cider, a huge choice of foreign bottled beers and 40 malt whiskies; darts and board games. Seats in the gardens and lots to do nearby. Dogs may get free biscuits and water.

Using their own reared beef, the highly thought-of pubby food includes lunchtime sandwiches and baked french bread pizzas, chicken, ham hock and leek terrine, mushroom or beef stroganoff, cottage pie, venison sausage with mash and onion gravy, gammon with a free-range egg and pineapple, beer-battered fresh haddock, and lamb casserole. *Benchmark main dish: beef in ale pie £10.50. Two-course evening meal £15.00.*

Own brew ~ Licensee Brian Coulthwaite ~ Real ale ~ Bar food (12-9) ~ (01539) 821309 ~ Children welcome ~ Dogs allowed in bar and bedrooms ~ Storytelling first Tues evening of month ~ Open 11.30-11(10.30 Sun) ~ Bedrooms: £43S/£79S

Recommended by Margaret and Jeff Graham, John Clancy, Mr and Mrs Maurice Thompson, Martin Smith, Steve Whalley, A N Bance, Alison Ball, Ian Walton, Mike Gorton, Mr and Mrs Ian King, John and Helen Rushton, Chris Johnson, DC, Maurice and Gill McMahon, the Didler, Mike and Sue Loseby, Joe Green, V and E A Bolton, Jane Speed, Paul Hartley, Rosemary and Mike Fielder, Andy and Jill Kassube, Adam Brownhill, Colin Woodward

KETTLESHULME Cheshire   SJ9879   Map C

Swan

B5470 Macclesfield—Chapel-en-le-Frith, a mile W of Whaley Bridge; SK23 7QU

Charming 16th-c cottagey pub with enjoyable food (especially fish), good beer, and an attractive garden

This pretty white wisteria-clad cottage under its heavy stone roof lives up to its promise inside: snug rooms, latticed windows, very low dark beams hung with big copper jugs and kettles, timbered walls, antique coaching and other prints and maps, ancient oak settles on the turkey carpet, log fires. They have well kept Marstons on handpump with a couple of guest beers such as Bass and Tatton Hoppy Birthday; service is polite and efficient. The front terrace has teak tables, a second two-level terrace has further tables and steamer benches under cocktail parasols, and there's a sizeable streamside garden.

🍴 The chef/landlord knows the Fleetwood fishing skippers well enough to order his supplies by email before the boats dock, and the fish is so popular here that it's wise to book. There's plenty of choice beyond that, including a fine Sunday lunch and good value bar snacks from sandwiches up. There might be langoustines in garlic butter, oysters, peppered lamb kidneys with green peppercorn and brandy cream, warm smoked duck with cranberry, greek rabbit stew, hot thai chicken, seafood risotto, roast hake with brown shrimps in spiced butter, mushroom risotto, veal T-bone steak, and well hung rib-eye with beef gravy. *Benchmark main dish: fish and chips £11.50. Two-course evening meal £26.70.*

Free house ~ Licensee Robert Cloughley ~ Real ale ~ Bar food (12-2, 6.30-8.30 Tues; 12-9 Weds-Sat; 12-4 Sun; not Mon) ~ (01663) 732943 ~ Children welcome ~ Dogs welcome ~ Open 5-11 Mon; 12-3, 5-11 Tues; 12-11 Weds-Sat; 12-8.30 Sun; closed Mon lunchtime

Recommended by David Heath, Phil and Helen Holt

 LACH DENNIS Cheshire   SJ7072   Map C

Duke of Portland 🍴 ▼ ◗

Holmes Chapel Road (B5082, off A556 SE of Northwich); CW9 7SY

Good food in stylish upscale dining pub which nurtures the beer side

The carefully prepared food tends to be the main draw at this civilised pub, but you are equally welcome to sink into one of their comfortable leather sofas to enjoy a relaxing drink. The bar area is decorated in calm beige, grey and creams, with square leather pouffes opposite sofas, chunky low tables on neutral carpets and nicely framed prints above its panelled dado. Friendly young staff behind its handsomely carved counter serve five ales from handpump, including Brakspear Oxford Gold, Jennings Cocker Hoop, Marstons Pedigree, Ringwood Best and a guest such as Jennings Cumberland. The interesting changing choice of about ten wines by the glass is fairly priced; daily papers. The main dining room, with its lofty ceiling, sturdy balustrades and big pictures, gives quite a sense of occasion, but keeps a fairly relaxed feel – perhaps because of the friendly mixture of styles in the comfortable dining chairs on its floorboards; piped music. Outside, a neat terrace has picnic-sets among modernist planters and lovely countryside views. This is the sister to the Belle Epoque in Knutsford.

🍴 They take great care over sourcing really good ingredients from named local suppliers, and take pride in their meats and cheeses; even the chips come in for admiration and are cooked in beef dripping, and bread is home-baked. Dishes might include mushroom and chive pancake, curried cauliflower risotto cakes, olive, lemon and parsley polenta cake with goats cheese fritter and basil pesto, lemon and thyme roasted chicken breast and wings with tapenade and mayonnaise, steak burger, and lamb rump with baby greek salad and dauphinoise potatoes. *Benchmark main dish: beef & Guinness pie £11.95. Two-course evening meal £18.20.*

Marstons ~ Lease Matthew Mooney ~ Real ale ~ Bar food (12-2.30, 5.30-9.30; 12-9.30 Fri, Sat; 12-8 Sun) ~ Restaurant ~ (01606) 46264 ~ Children welcome ~ Dogs allowed in bar ~ Sausage and jazz last Thurs of month ~ Open 12-3, 5-11; 12-11 Sat; 12-10.30 Sun

Recommended by Paul and Margaret Baker, Dr and Mrs A K Clarke, Ran, Ian Mayland

---

Anyone claiming to arrange or prevent inclusion of a pub in the *Guide* is a fraud.
Pubs are included only if recommended by genuine readers and if our own anonymous inspection confirms that they are suitable.

LANGDALE Cumbria

NY2806 Map B

Old Dungeon Ghyll ■ £

B5343; LA22 9JY

Straightforward place in a lovely position with real ales and fine walks; bedrooms

Even on sodden, chilly days there's always a boisterous atmosphere and plenty of fell walkers and climbers in this straightforward local; the fell setting is pretty dramatic. The whole feel of the place is basic but cosy and there's no need to remove boots or muddy trousers – you can sit on seats in old cattle stalls by the big warming fire and enjoy the fine choice of up to eight real ales on handpump: Dent Porter, Jennings Cumberland, Theakston Old Peculier, Yates Best Bitter and IPA and changing guests. Also, around 20 malt whiskies and Weston's Old Rosie cider; darts. It may get lively on a Saturday night (there's a popular National Trust campsite opposite).

Decent helpings of traditional food include lunchtime sandwiches, soup with home-made bread, a changing pâté, cumberland sausage with apple sauce and onion gravy, a pie of the day, vegetable goulash, beer-battered fish, and half a roasted chicken. *Benchmark main dish: chilli con carne £9.50. Two-course evening meal £14.75.*

Free house ~ Licensee Neil Walmsley ~ Real ale ~ Bar food (12-2, 6-9) ~ Restaurant ~ (015394) 37272 ~ Children welcome ~ Dogs allowed in bar and bedrooms ~ Open 11-11(10.30 Sun) ~ Bedrooms: £51/£102(£112S)

Recommended by Tim Maddison, Mike Gorton, John and Helen Rushton, the Didler, Mr and Mrs Maurice Thompson

LANGLEY Cheshire

SJ9569 Map C

Hanging Gate ♀

Meg Lane, Higher Sutton; follow Langley signpost from A54 beside Fourways Motel, and that road passes the pub; from Macclesfield, heading S from centre on A523 turn left into Byrons Lane at Langley, Wincle signpost; in Sutton (0.5 miles after going under canal bridge, ie before Langley) fork right at Church House Inn, following Wildboarclough signpost, then 2 miles later turning sharp right at steep hairpin bend; OS Sheet 118 map reference 952696; SK11 0NG

Remotely set old place with fires in traditional cosy rooms, lovely views from airy extension and terrace

Unchanging over the years and well worth a detour, this low-beamed old drovers' pub (first licensed in 1621 but built earlier) is tucked on to the side of a hill high up in the Peak District. Its terrace, traditional pubby little rooms and airy dining room command panoramic views over a patchwork of valley pastures to distant moors and the tall Sutton Common transmitter. Still in their original layout, the three cosy little low-beamed rooms are simply furnished. The tiny little snug bar, at its pubbiest at lunchtime, has a welcoming log fire in a big brick fireplace, just one single table, plain chairs and cushioned wall seats, a few old pub pictures and seasonal photographs on its creamy walls. Beers are served in here and include well kept Hydes Original, Jekylls Gold and Over A Barrel and a guest such as Greene King Old Speckled Hen on handpump; also quite a few malt whiskies and ten wines by the glass. The second room, with just a section of bar counter in the corner, has five tables, and there's a third appealing little oak-beamed blue room; piped music, board games, dominoes, books. It does get busy so it's best to book at weekends. Walkers are made to feel welcome with tap water and there's a dog bowl outside.

🍴 As well as good sandwiches and ploughman's made with home-baked bread, tasty enjoyable bar food might include black pudding, home-made burger with stilton, ham, pâté and cheese platter, rabbit, ham and leek pie, lamb hotpot, vegetable burger, fish and chips, roast wild boar with plums, and well hung rib-eye steak. *Benchmark main dish: steak and ale pie £14.00. Two-course evening meal £20.00.*

Hydes ~ Tenants Ian and Luda Rottenbury ~ Real ale ~ Bar food (12-2, 6-9; 12-4, 6-8 Sun) ~ Restaurant ~ (01260) 252238 ~ Children welcome ~ Dogs welcome ~ Open 11-3, 5.30-11; 11-11 Sat; 10am-10pm Sun

Recommended by the Didler, Mr & Mrs N Hall, Dr John and Mrs Shirley Minns, Bob Broadhurst, N R White

LEVENS Cumbria   SD4987   Map B

Strickland Arms 🍷 🍺

4 miles from M6 junction 36, via A590; just off A590, by Sizergh Castle gates; LA8 8DZ

Friendly, open-plan pub with much enjoyed food, local ales, and a fine setting; seats outside

This extremely popular dining pub, owned by the National Trust, is in a fine spot by the entrance to Sizergh Castle. It's largely open-plan with a light and airy feel, and the bar on the right has oriental rugs on the flagstones, a log fire, Thwaites Lancaster Bomber and Wainwright and guests like Cumbrian Legendary Loweswater Pale Ale, Hesket Newmarket Scafell Blonde and Tirril Old Faithful on handpump, several malt whiskies and nine wines by the glass. On the left are polished boards and another log fire, and throughout there's a nice mix of sturdy country furniture, candles on tables, hunting scenes and other old prints on the walls, heavy fabric for the curtains and some staffordshire china ornaments; it's best to book ahead if you want to eat downstairs but there is a further dining room upstairs. Piped music and board games. The flagstoned front terrace has plenty of seats. The castle, a lovely partly medieval house with beautiful gardens, is open in the afternoon (not Friday or Saturday) from April to October. They have disabled access and facilities.

🍴 Using Estate beef and other local produce, the high-quality food includes filled baguettes, smoked salmon and dill mousse, home-potted morecambe bay shrimps, chicken casserole with smoked paprika, cranberry, mushroom and blue cheese tart, steak, button mushroom and red wine pie, lamb hotpot with pickled red cabbage, and specials such as king prawns in sweet chilli sauce, and partridge stuffed with apricot and pork, wrapped in bacon with a hazelnut and rosemary sauce; they also offer a very good value two-course weekday lunch menu. *Benchmark main dish: beer-battered fish and chips £11.50. Two-course evening meal £17.70.*

Free house ~ Licensee Martin Ainscough ~ Real ale ~ Bar food (12-2(2.30 Sat), 6-9; all day Sun and bank holidays) ~ (015395) 61010 ~ Children welcome ~ Dogs welcome ~ Open 11.30-11; 12-10.30 Sun; 11.30-3, 5.30-11 weekdays in winter

Recommended by Margaret and Jeff Graham, Michael Doswell, Pat and Stewart Gordon, Michael Butler, John and Sylvia Harrop, Mike Gorton, Maurice and Gill McMahon, V and E A Bolton, Mrs M B Gregg, David A Hammond, Dr and Mrs R G J Telfer, Malcolm and Pauline Pellatt, Dr Kevan Tucker, Mr and Mrs Maurice Thompson, Jack Clark, David and Sue Atkinson, Mr and Mrs P R Thomas, David Hartley

LITTLE LANGDALE Cumbria

NY3103 Map B

Three Shires

From A593 3 miles W of Ambleside take small road signposted The Langdales,
Wrynose Pass; then bear left at first fork; LA22 9NZ

**Friendly inn with valley views from seats on the terrace, enjoyable food
and several local real ales; comfortable bedrooms**

This year there have been some smart new changes to this well
managed, popular inn – run by the same friendly family for 29 years.
The front restaurant has been refurbished and now has chunky leather
dining chairs around solid tables on the new wooden flooring, fresh
flowers, and wine bottle prints on the dark red walls. The new snug leads
off here, with country-kitchen chairs and tables on slate floor tiles, blue
wall banquettes and the same dark red walls; there's now much more
room for walkers at lunchtime. The comfortably extended back bar still
has a mix of green Lakeland stone and homely red patterned wallpaper
(which works rather well), stripped timbers and a beam-and-joist stripped
ceiling, antique oak carved settles, country-kitchen chairs and stools on
its big dark slate flagstones, and Lakeland photographs. Barngates Cat
Nap, Coniston Old Man, Hawkshead Bitter, Jennings Cumberland, and
Whitehaven Ennerdale Blonde on handpump, over 50 malt whiskies and a
decent wine list; darts and board games. There are lovely views from
seats on the terrace over the valley to the partly wooded hills below and
more seats on a neat lawn behind the car park, backed by a small oak
wood. The award-winning summer hanging baskets are very pretty. The
three shires are the historical counties of Cumberland, Westmorland and
Lancashire, which meet at the top of the nearby Wrynose Pass.

Enjoyable food includes lunchtime sandwiches, mixed game and white pudding
terrine with home-made chutney, cumberland sausages, beef in ale pie, leek,
mushroom and smoked parmesan risotto, pork loin steak with herb mash, crispy
pork belly and a lemon and sage cream sauce, organic salmon and garlic king
prawns on wilted chard and sunblush tomatoes, and venison loin steak with a swede
fondant, wild mushrooms and bordelaise sauce. *Benchmark main dish: slow-braised
lamb shank £14.95. Two-course evening meal £18.45.*

Free house ~ Licensee Ian Stephenson ~ Real ale ~ Bar food (12-2, 6-9) ~ Restaurant ~
(015394) 37215 ~ Children welcome ~ Dogs allowed in bar ~ Open 11-10.30(11 Fri and
Sat); 12-10.30 Sun ~ Bedrooms: /£100B

*Recommended by Tina and David Woods-Taylor, Mr and Mrs Maurice Thompson, Val Carter,
John and Helen Rushton, Barry Collett, Ewan and Moira McCall, Ann Balmforth*

LIVERPOOL Merseyside

SJ3589 Map C

Philharmonic Dining Rooms ★ £

36 Hope Street; corner of Hardman Street; L1 9BX

**Beautifully preserved Victorian pub with superb period interior, ten real
ales, and sensibly priced food**

One reader told to us that 'superlatives cannot overrate' this
spectacularly ornate Victorian former club that positively drips with
period details. Its centrepiece is a mosaic-faced serving counter, from
which heavily carved and polished mahogany partitions radiate under the
intricately plasterworked high ceiling. The echoing main hall boasts
stained glass depicting Boer War heroes Baden-Powell and Lord Roberts,
rich panelling, a huge mosaic floor, and copper panels of musicians in an

alcove above the fireplace. More stained glass in one of the little lounges declares 'Music is the universal language of mankind' and backs this up with illustrations of musical instruments. Two side rooms are called Brahms and Liszt, and there are two plushly comfortable sitting rooms. However, this is no museum piece and it can be very busy with ten handpumps as testament to a high turnover. As well as Cains Finest Bitter and Jennings Cumberland, up to eight changing guest ales might be from brewers such as Adnams, Caledonian Deuchars, Kelham Island and Sharps, and several malt whiskies; quiz machine, fruit machine and piped music. Don't miss the original 1890s Adamant gents' lavatory (all pink marble and mosaics); ladies are allowed a look if they ask first.

Reasonably priced food (available in the bar or in the table-service grand lounge dining room) includes pork and sage terrine, calamari, sandwiches, a range of recommended pies (including steak in ale), chicken and chorizo salad, sausage and mash, and rump steak. *Benchmark main dish: fish and chips £7.95. Two-course evening meal £12.20.*

Mitchells & Butlers ~ Manager Emma Mason ~ Real ale ~ Bar food (11-10) ~ Restaurant ~ (0151) 707 2837 ~ Children welcome until 7pm ~ Open 11am-midnight

Recommended by Ben Williams, Tony and Wendy Hobden, Eric Larkham, Rob and Catherine Dunster, Andy Lickfold, the Didler, Edward Mirzoeff, David Crook, Andrew Bosi, Ed and Anna Fraser

LONGRIDGE Lancashire   SD6038   Map C

Derby Arms ♀

Chipping Road, Thornley; 1.5 miles N of Longridge on back road to Chipping; PR3 2NB

Welcoming, traditional country pub with hunting and fishing paraphernalia (and menu to match), and very decent wine list

This convivial old stone-built country pub has been run by the same charming family for nearly thirty years. Among hunting and fishing bric-a-brac in the main bar, old photographs commemorate notable catches and there's some nicely mounted bait above the comfortable red plush seats, together with a stuffed pheasant that seems to be flying in through the wall. To the right a smaller room has sporting trophies and mementoes, and a regimental tie collection; piped music and darts. The gents' has dozens of riddles on the wall – you can buy a sheet of them in the bar and the money goes to charity. Along with a particularly good range of wines, including several by the glass and half bottles, you'll find Black Sheep and a guest such as Moorhouses Pride of Pendle on handpump. A few tables out in front, and another two behind the car park, have fine views across to the Forest of Bowland, and there's a boules piste. The licensees put on lots of themed evenings – such as jazz, flamenco, cabaret, and game dinners.

They do lots of seasonal game here – maybe pheasant, hare, rabbit, partridge, woodcock, rabbit and mallard, as well as fresh fish and seafood. Other enjoyable food might include sandwiches, ploughman's, steak and kidney pudding, well hung steak, and home-baked fruit pies. *Benchmark main dish: roast duck £14.95. Two-course evening meal £15.00.*

Punch ~ Lease Will and Carole Walne ~ Real ale ~ Bar food (12-2.15, 6-9.30; 12-9.30 Sat, Sun) ~ Restaurant ~ (01772) 782623 ~ Children welcome ~ Open 12-3.30, 6-12; 12-12 Sat, Sun

Recommended by Margaret Dickinson, Maurice and Gill McMahon, Andy and Jill Kassube, Ed and Anna Fraser

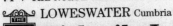

LOWESWATER Cumbria   NY1421 Map B

Kirkstile Inn ♣ ⇔

From B5289 follow signs to Loweswater Lake; OS Sheet 89 map reference 140210; CA13 0RU

Popular inn in lovely spot with busy bar, own-brewed beers and tasty bar food; bedrooms

As this country inn is between Loweswater and Crummock Water and has stunning views of the surrounding peaks and soaring fells, it's nearly always pretty packed out; you must book in advance to be sure of a table. The bustling main bar is low-beamed and carpeted with a friendly atmosphere, comfortably cushioned small settles and pews, partly stripped-stone walls, and a roaring log fire; there's a slate shove-ha'penny board. As well as their own-brewed Cumbrian Legendary Loweswater Gold, Grasmoor Dark Ale and Melbreak Bitter, they keep a guest like Yates Bitter on handpump; several wines by the glass. The fine view can be enjoyed from picnic-sets on the lawn, from the very attractive covered verandah in front of the building and from the bow windows in one of the rooms off the bar. There are marvellous surrounding walks of all levels, and maybe red squirrels in the garden.

Well liked food includes lunchtime sandwiches and wraps, haggis and black pudding balls with whisky and onion marmalade, chicken, leek and chorizo pudding with brandy and black pepper sauce, meaty or spinach, ricotta, feta and roast vegetable lasagne, steak in ale pie, and moroccan-style salmon with a spicy tomato sauce. *Benchmark main dish: slow-cooked lamb shoulder £13.50. Two-course evening meal £15.75.*

Own brew ~ Licensee Roger Humphreys ~ Real ale ~ Bar food (12-2, 6-9) ~ Restaurant ~ (01900) 85219 ~ Children welcome ~ Dogs allowed in bar and bedrooms ~ Open 11-11 ~ Bedrooms: £62.50B/£97B

Recommended by JDM, KM, Roger and Kathy Elkin, Sylvia and Tony Birbeck, Val Carter, Geoff and Linda Payne, Simon Watkins, Alison Ball, Ian Walton, Chris Clark, Comus and Sarah Elliott, Maurice and Gill McMahon, the Didler, Mike and Sue Loseby, Adrian Johnson, John Wooll, Peter Smith and Judith Brown, Richard and Tanya Smith

LYTHAM Lancashire   SD3627 Map C

Taps ♣ £

A584 S of Blackpool; Henry Street – in centre, one street in from West Beach; FY8 5LE

Thriving seaside pub with down-to-earth atmosphere, spirited landlord, eight real ales, and straightforward lunchtime snacks; open all day

The Taps Best served here is brewed exclusively for this bustling town pub by Titanic and is served alongside Greene King IPA and an impressive choice of six ever-changing guests – you can see them lined up in the view-in cellar; also country wines and a farm cider. With a good mix of customers, the Victorian-style bare-boarded bar has a sociable unassuming feel, plenty of stained-glass decoration in the windows, depictions of fish and gulls reflecting the pub's proximity to the beach (it's a couple of minutes' walk away), captain's chairs in bays around the sides, open fires, and a coal-effect gas fire between two built-in bookcases at one end. The landlord is a rugby fan and displays his expanding collection of rugby memorabilia, old photographs and portraits of rugby stars on the walls; TV, shove-ha'penny, dominoes, quiz machine and fruit machine. There are a few seats and a heated canopied area outside. Parking is difficult near the pub so it's probably best to park at the West Beach car park on the seafront (free on Sunday) and walk.

🍴 A handful of cheap bar snacks includes sandwiches, soup, hot roast sandwich, filled baked potatoes, burgers, chilli and curry. *Benchmark main dish: soup and roast sandwich £4.95.*

Greene King ~ Manager Ian Rigg ~ Real ale ~ Bar food (12-2, not Sun) ~ No credit cards ~ (01253) 736226 ~ Children welcome till 7.30pm ~ Dogs welcome ~ Open 11-11 (midnight Fri, Sat)

Recommended by G Jennings, Steve Whalley, the Didler

MACCLESFIELD Cheshire   SJ9271   Map C

Sutton Hall 🍴 ◀

Leaving Macclesfield southwards on A523, turn left into Byrons Lane signposted Langley, Wincle, then just before canal viaduct fork right into Bullocks Lane; OS Sheet 118 map reference 925715; SK11 0HE

Historic building set in attractive grounds; fine range of drinks and good food

You can't help but have the feeling of a special occasion at this rather splendid 16th-c manor house. The original hall that forms the heart of the building is beautifully impressive, particularly in its entrance space. Quite a series of delightful bar and dining areas, some divided by tall oak timbers have plenty of character with antique squared oak panelling, warmly coloured rugs on broad flagstones, boarded and tiled floors, frame-to-frame pictures and a raised open fire – all very Brunning & Price. Kind efficient staff serve five real ales including Flowers Original, Phoenix Brunning & Price Original, Wincle Lord Lucan and three guests from brewers such as Adnams, Storm and Titanic, plus several wines by the glass. The atmosphere has just enough formality, with bubbly staff and an enjoyable mix of customers from dog walkers up keeping it nicely relaxed. Pleasant gardens have good solid wood tables on terraces surrounded by a tree-sheltered lawn.

🍴 Bar food includes imaginative sandwiches, interestingly turned-out pub staples like ploughman's and beer-battered haddock, and more imaginative dishes such as salt fish pâté with baby capers and crisp poached egg, pigeon breast with madeira braised cabbage, roast pork belly with celeriac and pear gratin and mustard gravy, hake fillet poached in cockle broth with saffron potatoes, roast beetroot risotto with goats cheese and watercress, and rump steak with watercress and horseradish butter. *Benchmark main dish: beer-battered cod and chips £11.95. Two-course evening meal £21.00.*

Brunning & Price ~ Manager Syd Foster ~ Real ale ~ Bar food (12-10(9.30 Sun)) ~ (01260) 253211 ~ Children welcome ~ Dogs allowed in bar ~ Open 11.30-11; 12-10.30 Sun

Recommended by Bruce and Sharon Eden, Michael Butler, Maurice and Gill McMahon, Andy and Claire Barker, Dave Webster, Sue Holland, Brian and Anna Marsden

---

If a pub tries to make you leave a credit card behind the bar, be on your guard. The credit card firms and banks that issue them condemn this practice. After all, the publican who asks you to do this is in effect saying: 'I don't trust you'. Have you any more reason to trust his staff? If your card is used fraudulently while you have let it be kept out of your sight, the card company could say you've been negligent yourself – and refuse to make good your losses. So say that they can 'swipe' your card instead, but must hand it back to you. Please let us know if a pub does try to keep your card.

MARTON Cheshire   SJ8568 Map C

Davenport Arms ◀

A34 N of Congleton; SK11 9HF

Handsome former 18th-c farmhouse with welcoming bar, comfortable restaurant, good food and drink, and good-sized sheltered garden

Two linked front bar rooms, with a third leading off on the left, have a good traditional feel, with their woodburning stove, ticking clock, comfortably cushioned wall settles, wing armchairs and other hand-picked furnishings on the patterned carpet, old prints on the cream walls, and colourful jugs hanging from sturdy beams. You can eat anywhere here (or just have a drink or coffee), and there are more formal dining areas behind, pleasantly light and airy; piped music. They have well kept Courage Directors, Theakstons Black Bull and a couple of guests such as Wentworth Hunt the Shunt and Wincle Waller on handpump, and staff are friendly and helpful. Outside is a terrace with metal garden furniture, a fairy-lit arbour, and a timber shelter, with well spaced picnic-sets and a set of swings in the garden beyond, and a substantial separate play area. For many years they have held one of Cheshire's major gooseberry shows here, on the first Saturday in August, and the 14th-c timbered church is well worth a look. They take caravans here but you must book.

Bar food includes filled baguettes, chicken caesar salad, parmesan breaded chicken, curry of the day, pork tenderloin wrapped in parma ham with black pudding bread and butter pudding with calvados cream sauce, mushroom ratatouille with melted brie, salmon fillet with salsa of cucumber, tomato and red onion, and steak in ale pie. *Benchmark main dish: fish and chips £12.50. Two-course evening meal £15.00.*

Free house ~ Licensees Ron Dalton and Sara Griffith ~ Real ale ~ Bar food (12-2.30, 6-9; 12-9 Sat; 12-8 Sun; not Mon) ~ Restaurant ~ (01260) 224269 ~ Children welcome ~ Dogs allowed in bar ~ Open 12-3, 6-11; 12-11 Fri-Sun; closed Mon lunchtime except bank holidays

Recommended by John Wooll, Pam and John Smith

MOBBERLEY Cheshire   SJ8179 Map C

Plough & Flail ♀

Off B5085 Knutsford—Alderley Edge; at E end of village turn into Moss Lane, then left into Paddock Hill Lane (look out for small green signs to pub); WA16 7DB

Extensive family country dining pub, comfortable and well run, with enjoyable food, and plenty of outside tables

Such a spacious place comes as something of a surprise, as it's tucked away down narrow lanes. It's well laid out, with chunky cushioned dining chairs around sturdy stripped tables in the softly lit main area around the bar, which has low rustic beams, flagstones, and feels nicely up-to-date with its plain cream walls and bare panelled dado. Near the entrance, a handsomely floored side area has low sofas with scatter cushions, and sports TV. At the far end is a smaller second dining room, comfortable, light and airy, and a further conservatory dining room. They have a good choice of wines by the glass, and two guest beers such as Courage and Storm Bosley Cloud on handpump; attentive cheerful service, well reproduced nostalgic piped music. There are lots of teak tables out on heated flagstoned terraces at each end of the pub, with picnic-sets on neat lawns around the car park, and a robust play area.

Besides pubby favourites such as burgers and steaks, good more unusual but still pleasantly unpretentious food runs from light dishes such as fried pigeon breast with black pudding and pancetta on a croûton to massive sustenance for Cheshire horsemen such as a slow-cooked lamb shoulder plus a chop in mint jelly with red wine jus. *Benchmark main dish: battered haddock with marrowfat peas £12.75. Two-course evening meal £19.00.*

Deckers Hospitality Group ~ Manager Jose Lourenco ~ Real ale ~ Bar food (12-2.30, 6-9.30(10 Fri, Sat); 12-8 Sun) ~ (01565) 873537 ~ Children welcome ~ Open 12-11 (10.30 Sun)

Recommended by W K Wood, Helen Cobb

MOBBERLEY Cheshire   SJ7879   Map C

Roebuck ♀

Mill Lane; down hill from sharp bend on B5085 at E edge of 30mph limit; WA16 7HX

Stylishly simple country interior, warm welcome and very helpful service, good food, good wine list, courtyard and garden

Old tiled and boarded floors at this discerningly laid out airy place carry a comfortable mix of country furnishings, from cushioned long wood pews (rescued from a welsh chapel) to scrubbed pine farmhouse tables and a mix of old chairs. The wine list (well over a dozen by the glass) is short but well chosen and very reasonably priced, and beers are Black Sheep, Tetleys, Timothy Taylors Landlord and a guest from local Storm; piped music. Outside you'll find picnic sets on a cobbled courtyard, metal café furniture on a wooden deck, and picnic-sets in an enclosed well manicured beer garden.

 Food is thoughtfully prepared and features traditional dishes with an appealing twist. As well as a short snack menu (they call it british tapas) and upmarket sandwiches (not evenings), dishes might include pigeon and roast shallot puff pastry pie with watercress and spinach purée, crab cakes with grilled chilli marinated prawns with tomato and coriander salsa, battered fish with mushy peas, provençale style fish stew with saffron potatoes and crisp air-dried ham, roast chicken breast with pea mousse, chorizo purée and mushroom tart, and ewe cheese and onion tart with rocket leaves, artichoke hearts, almonds and scorched cherry tomatoes. *Benchmark main dish: fish and chips £10.95. Two-course evening meal £18.60.*

Free house ~ Licensee Melissa Kanaris ~ Real ale ~ Bar food (12-2.30, 5-9, Sat 12-9.30; 12-8 Sun) ~ (01565) 873322 ~ Children welcome ~ Open 12-11(10.30 Sun)

Recommended by Neil and Karen Dignan, Mrs P J Carroll, Dr and Mrs A K Clarke, P J and R D Greaves, Hilary Forrest, John and Helen Rushton, Peter Webb

MUNGRISDALE Cumbria   NY3630   Map A

Mill Inn

Off A66 Penrith—Keswick, 1 mile W of A5091 Ullswater turn-off; CA11 0XR

Bustling pub in fine setting with marvellous surrounding walks, real ales, home-cooked bar food and seats in garden; bedrooms

With the Glenderamakin river flowing below and the Blencathra Fell above, this 17th-c Lakeland inn is in a striking spot; there are lots of surrounding walks. The neatly kept bar has a wooden counter with an old millstone built into it, traditional dark wooden furnishings, hunting pictures on the walls, an open log fire in the stone fireplace and

Robinsons Cumbria Way, Dizzy Blonde, Hartleys XB and a guest beer on handpump; there's a separate dining room and an upstairs residents' lounge. Darts, winter pool, bar billiards and dominoes. There are seats in the garden.

🍴 Tasty bar food includes lunchtime sandwiches, chicken liver pâté, italian-style prawns, cumberland sausages with onion gravy, a changing vegetarian dish, steak in ale pie, haddock mornay, and duck breast with honey and port. *Benchmark main dish: slow-cooked lamb shoulder £12.95. Two-course evening meal £14.95.*

Robinsons ~ Tenant Andrew Teasdale ~ Real ale ~ Bar food (12-2, 6-9; all day weekends) ~ Restaurant ~ (017687) 79632 ~ Children welcome ~ Dogs allowed in bar and bedrooms ~ Open 10am-1am(midnight Sun) ~ Bedrooms: £47.50S/£75S

Recommended by Noel Grundy, Dave Braisted, Geoff and Linda Payne, Comus and Sarah Elliott, James Morrell, J Buckby, John and Angie Millar

NEAR SAWREY Cumbria   SD3795 Map B

Tower Bank Arms 🍺

B5285 towards the Windermere ferry; LA22 0LF

Backing on to Beatrix Potter's farm, with well kept real ales, tasty bar food, and a friendly welcome; nice bedrooms

Our readers very much enjoy their visits to this friendly, well run inn, and staying overnight has come in for particularly warm praise this year; smashing breakfasts, too. The low-beamed main bar has plenty of rustic charm, seats on the rough slate floor, game and fowl pictures, a grandfather clock, a log fire and fresh flowers; there's also a separate restaurant. The three real ales on handpump and two tapped from the cask come from breweries like Barngates, Cumbrian Legendary, Hawkshead, Ulverston and Yates; several wines by the glass and a good choice of soft drinks; board games. There are pleasant views of the wooded Claife Heights from seats in the garden. It does get pretty crowded during the school holidays – especially in the summer. Many illustrations in the Beatrix Potter books can be traced back to their origins in this village – including the pub, which features in *The Tale of Jemima Puddleduck.*

🍴 Using locally sourced produce, the generous helpings of well liked food include lunchtime sandwiches, moules marinière, cumberland sausage with a rich onion gravy, vegetable wellington, beer-battered haddock, chicken breast stuffed with mozzarella, cherry tomatoes and basil, wrapped in air-dried ham with a tomato sauce, and slow-braised lamb shoulder with a mint and rosemary jus. *Benchmark main dish: beef in ale stew £11.50. Two-course evening meal £16.75.*

Free house ~ Licensee Anthony Hutton ~ Real ale ~ Bar food (12-2, 6-9(8 Sun, winter Mon-Thurs and bank holidays) ~ Restaurant ~ (015394) 36334 ~ Children welcome ~ Dogs allowed in bar and bedrooms ~ Open 11.30-11; 12-10.30 Sun; 11.30-2.30, 5.30-10.30 (11 weekends) weekdays in winter ~ Bedrooms: /£90S

Recommended by Michael Doswell, Adrian Johnson, Margaret Dickinson, Jayne Inman, Dave Braisted, David and Ruth Hollands

---

'Children welcome' means the pub says it lets children inside without any special restriction. If it allows them in, but to restricted areas such as an eating area or family room, we specify this. Places with separate restaurants often let children use them, and hotels usually let them into public areas such as lounges. Some pubs impose an evening time limit – let us know if you find one earlier than 9pm.

NETHER ALDERLEY Cheshire SJ8576 Map C

Wizard 🍽

Bradford Lane; SK10 4UE

Bustling dining pub on National Trust land with interesting food, real ales, a friendly welcome and relaxed atmosphere

Of course, most customers come to this well run dining pub to enjoy the particularly good food – but you will be made just as welcome if it's only a pint or a cup of coffee that you want. It's just a few minutes from Alderley Edge, a dramatic red sandstone escarpment with fine views and woodland walks, and there are seats and tables in the pub's sizeable back garden that are just right for a relaxing lunch afterwards. Inside, the various rooms are connected by open doorways and cleverly done up in a mix of modern rustic and traditional styles: beams and open fires, a happy mix of antique dining chairs (some prettily cushioned) and settles around all sorts of tables, rugs on pale wooden floorboards, prints and paintings on contemporary paintwork and items ranging from a grandfather clock to staffordshire dogs and modern lampshades; lovely fresh flowers and plants dotted about. Thwaites Wainwright and a guest from Storm on handpump, and several wines by the glass served by helpful, friendly staff.

🍴 Using locally sourced produce, the highly thought-of food includes spiced smoked haddock and shallot pie, beetroot cured smoked salmon with lime jelly and horseradish cream, ploughman's, fish plate, smoked eel, rocket and pea risotto, sausage, cheese mash and onion gravy, crispy pork belly with puy lentils and black pudding, seared chicken breast with chorizo, moroccan couscous salad and orange and cinnamon dressing, roast squash with chillies and pine nuts and tagliatelle with crème fraîche, lamb steak with mint butter, and steaks. *Benchmark main dish: steak and ale pie £12.50. Two-course evening meal £21.00.*

Free house ~ Licensee Dominic Gottelier ~ Real ale ~ Bar food (12-2, 7-9; 12-10 Sat, 12-7 Sun) ~ (01625) 584000 ~ Children welcome ~ Dogs welcome ~ Open 12-2, 5.30-11; 12-11 Sat; 12-10 Sun

Recommended by Richard Gibbs

NETHER BURROW Lancashire SD6175 Map C

Highwayman 🍽 🍷

A683 S of Kirkby Lonsdale; LA6 2RJ

Substantial and skilfully refurbished old stone house with country interior serving carefully sourced food; lovely gardens

Black and white wall prints and placemats show the characterful local farmers and producers (a map on the menu even locates these 'regional food heroes') that supply ingredients to this friendly and inviting pub. Although large, the stylishly simple flagstoned 17th-c interior is nicely divided into intimate corners, with a couple of big log fires and informal wooden furnishings. French windows open to a big terrace and lovely gardens. Local Thwaites Original and Lancaster Bomber and Wainwright are served on handpump, alongside good wines by the glass, just over a dozen whiskies and a particularly good range of soft drinks. They don't take bookings at the weekend (except for groups of six or more), but write your name on a blackboard when you arrive, and they'll find you when a table is free. Service is busy, welcoming and efficient.

🍴 As well as bar nibbles, imaginative sandwiches, ploughman's and some traditional lancastrian dishes, the menu might include ploughman's, scotch quail eggs with chicken and mushroom watercress mayonnaise and pickled white cabbage, warm salad of wood pigeon and black pudding and local bacon with cumberland sauce, scampi, twice-baked chestnut mushroom soufflé with mushroom crisp and mushroom cappuccino, battered haddock, devilled chicken breast, shepherd's pie, and well hung rump steak; they do just snacks in the afternoon; Sunday roasts. *Benchmark main dish: lancashire hotpot £10.50. Two-course evening meal £16.50.*

Thwaites ~ Lease Andy Morris and Craig Bancroft ~ Real ale ~ Bar food (12-8.30(9 Fri, Sat; 8 Sun)) ~ (01254) 826888 ~ Children welcome ~ Dogs allowed in bar ~ Open 12-11 (10.30 Sun)

Recommended by Noel Thomas, Liz Bell, Paul and Penny Dawson, Maurice and Gill McMahon, Karen Eliot, Brian and Janet Ainscough

PEOVER HEATH Cheshire   SJ7973 Map C

Dog 🍺

Off A50 N of Holmes Chapel at the Whipping Stocks, keep on past Parkgate into Wellbank Lane; OS Sheet 118 map reference 794735; note that this village is called Peover Heath on the OS map and shown under that name on many road maps, but the pub is often listed under Over Peover instead; WA16 8UP

Homely pub with interesting range of beers and generously served food; bedrooms

What makes this unpretentious pub special is that it has a genuine local atmosphere, with its areas set aside for a drink, regular clientele, games room and very friendly welcome. Gently old fashioned and comfortably cottagey, the neatly kept bar has tied-back floral curtains at little windows, a curved cushioned banquette built into a bay window and mostly traditional dark wheelbacks arranged on a patterned carpet. A coal fire, copper pieces and pot plants add to the homely feel. The games room has darts, pool, a games machine, dominoes, board games and TV; piped music. Hydes (very good value at £2.30 a pint) and two beers from Weetwood are on handpump. They also have a good range of malt whiskies and wines by the glass. Friendly efficient staff cope well when it's busy. There are picnic-sets beneath colourful hanging baskets on the peaceful lane, and more out in a pretty back garden. It's a pleasant walk from here to the Jodrell Bank Centre and Arboretum.

🍴 As well as sandwiches, bar food might include fried squid and king prawns in garlic butter with coriander and watercress salad, confit of duck terrine with plum chutney and toasted brioche, steak and ale pie, braised lamb shank on roast garlic mash with rosemary pan gravy, fish pie, grilled tuna steak with soy, ginger and chilli sauce, and baby stuffed aubergine with tomato and basil sauce. *Benchmark main dish: cod and chips with mushy peas £12.50. Two-course evening meal £17.60.*

Free house ~ Licensee Steven Wrigley ~ Real ale ~ Bar food (12-2.30, 6-9; 12-8.30 Sun) ~ Restaurant ~ (01625) 861421 ~ Children welcome ~ Dogs allowed in bar ~ Open 11.30-3, 4.30-11.30; 11.30-midnight Sat; 12-11.30 Sun ~ Bedrooms: £60B/£80B

Recommended by John Cook, Sylvia and Tony Birbeck, S Bloomfield, Gerry and Rosemary Dobson, Brian and Janet Ainscough, Brian and Anna Marsden

---

If you have to cancel a reservation for a bedroom or restaurant, please telephone or write to warn them. You may lose your deposit if you've paid one.

PLEASINGTON Lancashire

SD6528   Map C

Clog & Billycock

Village signposted off A677 Preston New Road on W edge of Blackburn; Billinge End Road; BB2 6QB

Carefully sourced local food in appealingly modernised stone-built village pub

Rumour has it that the name of this skilfully refurbished and extended village pub comes from the preferred attire of a former landlord. Light and airy with flagstoned floors and pale grey walls, in places it has the feel of an upmarket barn conversion. A cosier room has high-backed settles and a fireplace at the end. The whole pub is packed with light wooden tables, and although you may find them all full on arrival, such is the size of the place that you probably won't have to wait long in the little bar area for one to come free. The sheer volume of satisfied customers ensures a good, chatty atmosphere and service is polite and helpful. Drinks include well kept Thwaites Bomber and Original and Wainwright and a good choice of wines. There are some tables outside, beside a small garden.

Dishes here tend to be traditionally british, and the menu identifies many of their suppliers, some of whom can also be seen in photographs on the walls. Particularly good food includes well filled sandwiches, twice-baked cheese soufflé, cauliflower fritters with curried mayonnaise, fish pie, slow-cooked pork belly with garlic mash, cheese and onion pie, lancashire hotpot, and well hung steak. There's a snack menu during the afternoon. *Benchmark main dish: fish pie £10.75. Two-course evening meal £16.50.*

Thwaites ~ Lease Andy Morris and Craig Bancroft ~ Real ale ~ Bar food (12-9 (8.30 Sun)) ~ (01254) 201163 ~ Children welcome ~ Dogs allowed in bar ~ Open 12-11(10.30 Sun)
Recommended by RJH, Karen Eliot, Steve Whalley, W K Wood, Alex Blyth, Ed and Anna Fraser

PLUMLEY Cheshire

SJ7075   Map C

Smoker

2.5 miles from M6 junction 19: A556 towards Northwich and Chester; WA16 0TY

Spotless comfortable lounges and a breakfast menu; handy for M6

Tucked in among the military prints you'll find a rather delightful Edwardian print of a hunt meeting outside this neatly kept 400-year-old thatched coaching inn. It shows how little it has changed over the years. Popular with an older set, its three connecting rooms have dark panelling, open fires in impressive period fireplaces, deep sofas, other comfortable seats and settles, and a sweet collection of copper kettles; piped music. Particularly kind staff serve five Robinsons beers from handpumps and they've a good choice of wines and whiskies. The sizeable garden has roses, flower beds and a children's play area.

Breakfast is served till midday, followed by sandwiches, potted shrimps, tempura king prawns, black pudding fritter with crispy pancetta and poached egg, fishcakes with lemon mayonnaise, red thai chicken curry, lamb marinated with mint and herbs, fried lambs liver with fried onions and crispy pancetta, and fried salmon and scallops with chilli and ginger. *Benchmark main dish: steak braised in red wine with mushrooms £10.95. Two-course evening meal £18.00.*

Robinsons ~ Tenants John and Diana Bailey ~ Real ale ~ Bar food (10-2.15, 6-9.15; 10-9 Sun) ~ Restaurant ~ (01565) 722338 ~ Children welcome away from bar ~ Open 10-3, 6-11; 10am-10.30pm Sun

Recommended by Peter Webb, John and Helen Rushton, David and Sue Atkinson, Clive Watkin, Gordon and Margaret Ormondroyd, Lesley and Peter Barrett, Andy Dolan

RAVENSTONEDALE Cumbria NY7203 Map A

Black Swan 🍴 🛏

Just off A685 SW of Kirkby Stephen; CA17 4NG

Bustling hotel with thriving bar, several real ales, enjoyable food, and good surrounding walks; bedrooms

This smart, family-run Victorian hotel is a fine place for a break when crossing from North Yorkshire to Cumbria – though you may want to stay overnight in the comfortable bedrooms; it's in a charming peaceful village and surrounded by lots of good walks (the inn has leaflets describing the walks and their lengths). There's a friendly atmosphere and plenty of original period features and the thriving U-shaped bar has stripped-stone walls, plush bar stools by the bar counter, a comfortable green button-back banquette, various dining chairs and little plush stools around a mix of tables, and fresh flowers. Black Sheep Ale and Bitter, John Smiths, and three changing guests from Hesket Newmarket or Tirril on handpump, eight wines by the glass, 25 malt whiskies and a good choice of fruit juices and pressés; piped music, TV, darts, board games, and newspapers and magazines to read. Service is genuinely friendly and helpful. There are picnic-sets in the tree-sheltered streamside garden over the road; they also run the village store with outside café seating.

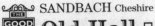Using seasonal, local produce, the highly thought-of food might include sandwiches, various nibbles, terrine of smoked trout, mackerel and salmon with horseradish and home-made bread, black pudding in a creamy pepper sauce with sautéed apple and crispy bacon, beer-battered fresh haddock, tasty chicken or vegetable curry, slow-cooked beef in Guinness, and specials like scallops with a butternut squash purée and crispy pancetta, and lamb cutlets on a mushroom and potato rösti with parsnip crisps and madeira syrup. *Benchmark main dish: slow-roasted pork belly £12.95. Two-course evening meal £16.75.*

Free house ~ Licensees Louise and Alan Dinnes ~ Real ale ~ Bar food (12-2, 6-9 but some sort of food all day) ~ Restaurant ~ (015396) 23204 ~ Children welcome ~ Dogs allowed in bar and bedrooms ~ Live music monthly (phone to check) ~ Open 8am-midnight(1am Sat) ~ Bedrooms: £50B/£75B

Recommended by Noel Thomas, David Heath, Liz Bell, Lesley and Peter Barrett, Dr Kevan Tucker, Andy and Jill Kassube, C Cooper

SANDBACH Cheshire SJ7560 Map C

Old Hall ♀ 🍴

1.2 miles from M6 junction 17: A534 into town, then right into High Street; CW11 1AL

Stunning mid-17th-c hall house with wonderful original features, plenty of drinking and dining space, interesting décor, six real ales, imaginative food, and seats outside

Opened just as we went to press, this is a magnificent Grade I listed manor house with wonderful timbering and fine carved gable-ends. Brunning & Price spent two years restoring the abandoned building which

English Heritage had on their 'buildings at risk' register as category A. There are many lovely original features – particularly in the room to the left of the entrance hall which is much as it has been for centuries with a Jacobean fireplace, oak panelling and priest's hole. This leads into the Oak Room with standing timbers creating two dining rooms – heavy beams, oak flooring and reclaimed panelling. Other rooms in the original building have more hefty beams and oak boards and there are three open fires and a woodburning stove; the cosy snugs are carpeted. The newly built Garden Room is big and bright with reclaimed quarry tiling and exposed A-frame oak timbering and opens onto the suntrap back terrace with teak tables and chairs among flowering tubs. Throughout, the walls are covered with countless interesting prints, there's a happy mix of antique dining chairs and tables of all sizes, and plenty of rugs, bookcases and plants. From the handsome bar counter they serve a beer named for them from Phoenix, Beartown Kodiak Gold, Storm Silk of Amnesia, Thornbridge Kipling, Three Tuns XXX, and Wincle Sir Philip on handpump, 15 good wines by the glass and 40 malt whiskies. There are picnic-sets in front of the building by rose bushes and clipped box hedging.

Enjoyable food includes sandwiches, avocado, crème fraîche and chilli panna cotta with black olive tapenade, potted salmon, smoked mackerel and trout with pickled vegetables, pork sausages with red wine and onion gravy, sweet potato, red pepper and dolcelatte filo pie with spinach and fennel salad, malaysian chicken curry, fish pie, and rose veal with sage, spinach and lemon tagliatelle. *Benchmark main dish: braised lamb shoulder with crushed potatoes and tarragon £16.95. Two-course evening meal £17.75.*

Brunning & Price ~ Manager Chris Button ~ Real ale ~ Bar food (12-10(9.30 Sun) ~ (01270) 758170 ~ Children welcome ~ Dogs allowed in bar ~ Open 11.30-11; 12-10.30 Sun
Recommended by Richard Gibbs

SPURSTOW Cheshire   SJ5657   Map C

 Yew Tree ★ ★ (🍴) ⏍ 🍺

Off A49 S of Tarporley; follow Bunbury 1, Haughton 2 signpost into Long Lane; CW6 9RD

Great place, a top-notch all-rounder with a good deal of individuality and plenty of bounce

Giant bees swarming on the bar ceiling sum up the thriving bustle of this cheerful pub, and other witty decorative touches include panels of most unexpected wallpaper – hugely magnified hunting print, or tartans in variety. It's all been kept nicely simple, though, with terracotta tiles or bare boards, uncluttered pale grey or off-white paintwork, and a log fire in the raised fireplace. The island bar has well kept and sensibly priced ales such as Acorn Blonde, Adnams, Merlins Gold, Moorhouses Black Cat and Stonehouse Station on handpump, a beer of the month (on our visit Gorlovka, a mind-blasting bottle-conditioned Imperial Stout from Barnsley), a local cider, and a good range of wines by the glass from an interesting bin ends list of about 50. The informal service is quick even when they are busy. A more dining-oriented area spreads off, sharing the same feeling of relaxed bonhomie (our favourite table there was the one snugged into a stable-stall-style alcove of stripped wood). A terrace outside has teak tables, with more on the grass beside it.

A quickly changing menu might include duck and pistachio terrine, crab tian with lemon and chervil mayonnaise, seared bass fillet with saffron mash, asparagus and dill sabayon and duck breast with dauphinoise potatoes, oyster mushroom and pepper sauce; they also do sausage and mash, fish and chips or a vegetarian dish, with a pint or a glass of wine, for £10. *Benchmark main dish: fish pie £11.95. Two-course evening meal £19.00.*

Free house ~ Licensees Jon and Lindsay Cox ~ Real ale ~ Bar food (12-2.30, 6-9.30 (10 Fri); 12-10 Sat; 12-8 Sun) ~ (01829) 260274 ~ Well behaved children welcome ~ Dogs allowed in bar ~ Open 12-11(10.30 Sun)

Recommended by Alun Jones

STAVELEY Cumbria   SD4797   Map B

Eagle & Child 🍺 ⇌

Kendal Road; just off A591 Windermere—Kendal; LA8 9LP

Welcoming inn with warming log fires, a good range of local beers and enjoyable food; bedrooms

With comfortable bedrooms and hearty breakfasts, this little inn is just right as a base for those exploring the area; there are plenty of surrounding walks (the pub is on the Dales Way). There's a welcoming fire under an impressive mantelbeam, a friendly, bustling atmosphere, and a roughly L-shaped flagstoned main area with plenty of separate parts to sit in, furnished with pews, banquettes, bow window seats and high-backed dining chairs around polished dark tables. Also, police truncheons and walking sticks, some nice photographs and interesting prints, a few farm tools, a delft shelf of bric-a-brac and another log fire. The five real ales on handpump come from breweries such as Caledonian Deuchars IPA, Coniston Bluebird, Cumbrian Legendary Grasmoor Dark Ale, Hawkshead Bitter and Yates Bitter on handpump, several wines by the glass, 30 malt whiskies and farm cider; piped music and board games. An upstairs barn-theme dining room (with its own bar for functions and so forth) doubles as a breakfast room. There are picnic-sets under cocktail parasols in a sheltered garden by the River Kent, with more on a good-sized back terrace and a second garden behind.

Fair value, generous helpings of tasty food include sandwiches, chicken and port pâté, Guinness pancakes filled with bacon and cheese, vegetarian shepherd's pie, local cumberland sausages with red wine and caramelised onion gravy, steak in ale pie, chicken wrapped in smoked bacon with barbecue sauce and a cheese topping, and changing fresh fish dishes. *Benchmark main dish: cumberland hotpot £9.95. Two-course evening meal £16.95.*

Free house ~ Licensees Richard and Denise Coleman ~ Real ale ~ Bar food (12-2.30, 6-9) ~ Restaurant ~ (01539) 821320 ~ Children welcome ~ Dogs allowed in bar ~ Open 12-2.30, 6-9 ~ Bedrooms: £50S/£70S

Recommended by Chris Evans, Bob Broadhurst, Dennis Jones, Ann and Tony Bennett-Hughes, the Didler, Joe Green, Dr Kevan Tucker, John and Helen Rushton, Steve and Sue Griffiths

---

TALKIN Cumbria   NY5457   Map A

Blacksmiths Arms ⚑ ⇌

Village signposted from B6413 S of Brampton; CA8 1LE

Neatly kept and welcoming with tasty bar food, several real ales, and good surrounding walks; bedrooms

Run by genuinely friendly licensees, this former blacksmith's has plenty of walks from the door or just a short drive away; it's a quiet and comfortable place to stay. There are several neatly kept, traditionally furnished rooms and the warm lounge on the right has a log fire, upholstered banquettes and wheelback chairs around dark wooden tables on the patterned red carpeting, and country prints and other pictures on the walls. The restaurant is to the left, there's a long lounge opposite the bar, and another room up a couple of steps at the back. Cumberland Corby Ale, Geltsdale Brampton Bitter and Cold Fell and Yates Bitter on handpump, 20 wines by the glass and 30 malt whiskies; piped music, darts and board games. There are a couple of picnic-sets outside the front door with more in the back garden.

Reliable, pubby food includes lunchtime sandwiches, creamy garlic mushrooms, vegetable curry, lasagne, sweet and sour chicken, beer-battered haddock, beef stroganoff, and specials like black pudding topped with wholegrain mustard, bacon and cheese sauce, liver, bacon and onion casserole, and duck breast in a port and plum sauce. *Benchmark main dish: steak and kidney pie £8.25. Two-course evening meal £16.50.*

Free house ~ Licensees Donald and Anne Jackson ~ Real ale ~ Bar food (12-2, 6-9) ~ Restaurant ~ (016977) 3452 ~ Children welcome ~ Open 12-3, 6-11 ~ Bedrooms: £50S/£70S

Recommended by Dr and Mrs Leach, Maurice and Gill McMahon, Dr Peter D Smart, David and Katharine Cooke

TARPORLEY Cheshire

SJ5562 Map C

Rising Sun £

High Street; village signposted off A51 Nantwich—Chester; CW6 0DX

Friendly, bustling and quaint, with pubby food

Run by the same family for over 25 years, this brick-fronted old place is charmingly friendly and down-to-earth. The low-ceilinged characterful interior is prettily furnished with eye-catching old seats and tables, including creaky 19th-c mahogany and oak settles and features an attractively blacked iron kitchen range. Sporting and other old-fashioned prints decorate the walls. Accommodating staff serve Robinsons Dizzy Blonde, Unicorn and a seasonal ale from handpumps. There are one or two seats and a TV for sporting events in a tiny side bar; piped music. More reports please.

A good range of reasonably priced bar food includes dim sum, smoked fish platter, spicy chicken wings, lots of pies, poached chicken breast with leek and stilton sauce, fruity beef curry, spinach pancake, rack of lamb, and a good range of steaks. *Benchmark main dish: fish and chips £7.10. Two-course evening meal £13.50.*

Robinsons ~ Tenant Alec Robertson ~ Real ale ~ Bar food (12-2, 7-9; 12-9 Sat, Sun) ~ Restaurant (evening) ~ (01829) 732423 ~ Children welcome away from public bar ~ Open 11.30-3, 5.30-11; 11.30-11 Sat; 12-10.30 Sun

Recommended by the Didler, Alistair Stanier, P J and R D Greaves, Don Bryan

THRELKELD Cumbria

NY3225 Map B

Horse & Farrier £

A66 Penrith—Keswick; CA12 4SQ

Well run 17th-c fell-foot dining pub with good food and drinks; bedrooms

Even if you are a bedraggled walker or cyclist, you can be sure of a warm welcome in this attractive 17th-c inn. The neat, mainly carpeted bar has sturdy farmhouse and other nice tables, seats from comfortably padded ones to pubby chairs and from stools to bigger housekeeper's chairs and wall settles, country pictures on its white walls, one or two stripped beams and some flagstones; several open fires. Jennings Bitter, Cocker Hoop, Cumberland and Sneck Lifter on handpump and several wines by the glass; friendly, efficient service. The partly stripped-stone restaurant is smart and more formal, with quite close-set tables. There are a few picnic-sets outside. If you plan to stay, the rooms in the inn itself are the best bet. The views towards Helvellyn range are stunning and there are walks straight from the door. Good disabled access and facilities.

Good value bar food (which is what our Value Award is for) includes lunchtime sandwiches, a curry of the day, steak and kidney pie, mediterranean vegetable lasagne, and gammon with fresh pineapple with more elaborate (and pricey) restaurant choices such as chicken breast stuffed with gruyère and wrapped in bacon on fennel risotto and a mushroom, garlic and creamy white wine sauce, and slow-roasted belly pork on grain mustard mash and an apple, sage and spring onion sauce; they also offer breakfasts to non-residents and afternoon tea. *Benchmark main dish: slow-braised lamb shoulder £14.35. Two-course evening meal £19.00.*

Jennings (Marstons) ~ Lease Ian Court ~ Real ale ~ Bar food (12-9) ~ Restaurant ~ (017687) 79688 ~ Children welcome ~ Dogs allowed in bar and bedrooms ~ Open 7.30am-midnight ~ Bedrooms: £50B/£80B

Recommended by Tina and David Woods-Taylor, Geoff and Linda Payne, Dominic McGonigal, Maurice and Gill McMahon, James Morrell, Phil Bryant, Adele Summers, Alan Black

TIRRIL Cumbria   NY5026 Map A

Queens Head
B5320, not far from M6 junction 40; CA10 2JF

18th-c Lakeland pub with several bars, real ales, speciality pies, and seats outside; bedrooms

The oldest parts of the main bar in this busy old inn have low beams, black panelling, original flagstones and floorboards, and there are nice little tables and chairs on either side of the inglenook fireplace (always lit in winter). Another bar to the right of the door has pews and chairs around sizeable tables on the wooden floor and candles in the fireplace, and the back locals' bar has heavy beams and a pool table; there are two dining rooms as well. Robinsons Dizzy Blonde, Hatters, Old Stockport and Unicorn on handpump and several wines by the glass. At the front of the building are some picnic-sets, with modern chairs and tables under covering on the back terrace. They also run the village shop. The pub is very close to a number of interesting places, such as Dalemain House at Dacre, and is just 2.5 miles from Ullswater.

As well as lunchtime sandwiches and popular pies made by their sister company, the Pie Mill, the bar food might include chicken liver pâté with cumberland sauce, creamy garlic mushrooms and crispy bacon, a curry of the day, roasted mediterranean vegetable lasagne, local cumberland sausage, salmon fillet with parsley butter, and chicken breast with a mushroom, fresh tarragon, white wine and cream sauce. *Benchmark main dish: home-made pies £8.95.*

Robinsons ~ Tenants Margaret and Jim Hodge ~ Bar food (12-2.30, 5.30-8.30) ~ Restaurant ~ (01768) 863219 ~ Children welcome ~ Dogs allowed in bar and bedrooms ~ Open 12-11; 12-10.30 Sun ~ Bedrooms: /£70B

Recommended by Richard Gibbs

TORVER Cumbria

SD2894 Map A

Church House 🍴 ♀

A593/A5084 S of Coniston; LA21 8AZ

Rambling coaching inn with bustling bar, interesting food, five real ales, and seats in a neat garden with fine views; bedrooms

Just a short walk from Coniston Lake and in the shadow of Coniston Old Man, this rambling 14th-c coaching house has seats in a big garden with splendid hill views. Inside, the bar has a pubby atmosphere, heavy beams, built-in wall seats and stools around plain tables on the slate flooring, a fine log fire in a sizeable stone fireplace, bits and pieces of Lakeland bric-a-brac and a bar made from polished wooden barrels. Barngates Tag Lag, Copper Dragon Golden Pippin, Cumbrian Legendary Loweswater Gold, Hawkshead Lakeland Gold, and a guest beer on handpump, several wines by the glass and quite a few malt whiskies; friendly staff. There's also a comfortable lounge and a separate yellow-walled dining room; the jack russell terrier, Molly, loves catching beer mats. As well as bedrooms, they have hard standing for six caravans.

🍴 Using local produce, the changing food might include sandwiches, chicken liver parfait with red onion marmalade, seared scallops and crispy pork belly with a celeriac and apple purée, red wine and star anise dressing and spring onion oil, lentil, mushroom and aubergine lasagne, steamed steak and kidney in ale pudding, beer-battered haddock, and a proper cassoulet. *Benchmark main dish: cumbrian hotpot £13.75. Two-course evening meal £19.30.*

Enterprise ~ Lease Mike and Mandy Beaty ~ Real ale ~ Bar food (12-3, 6-9) ~ Restaurant ~ (015394) 41282 ~ Children welcome ~ Dogs allowed in bar and bedrooms ~ Open 12-12 ~ Bedrooms: £45S/£70S

Recommended by Dennis Jones, John and Hilary Penny, JCW, Jon Quirk

TROUTBECK Cumbria

NY4103 Map B

Queens Head 🍴 ♀ 🍺 🛏

A592 N of Windermere; LA23 1PW

Civilised inn with several rambling rooms, interesting food, quite a few real ales, and friendly staff; comfortable bedrooms

Right at the heart of Lakeland, this is a gently upmarket and extended old coaching inn with a lot of character. It's a fine place to stay, they keep seven real ales and the food is extremely good. The big rambling, original U-shaped bar has a very nice mix of old cushioned settles and mate's chairs around some sizeable tables, beams and flagstones and a log fire in the raised stone fireplace with horse harness and so forth on either side of it; there's also a coal fire, some trumpets, cornets and saxophones on one wall with country pictures on others, stuffed pheasants in a big glass case, and a stag's head with a tie around his neck. A massive Elizabethan four-poster bed is the basis of the finely carved counter where they serve Robinsons Cumbrian Way, Dizzy Blonde, Double Hop, Hannibals Nectar, Hartleys XB, Old Tom and Unicorn on handpump and eight wines by the glass. Other dining rooms are decorated similarly to the main bar, with oak beams and stone walls, settles along big tables, and one has an open fire; piped music. Seats outside have a fine view over the Troutbeck Valley to Applethwaite Moors. The highly thought-of bedrooms are in the inn itself or in the carefully transformed barn opposite.

🍴 Imaginative – if not particularly cheap – food includes nibbles, filled baguettes (up until 6pm), a trio of pork (pressed and potted ham hock with apple and calvados purée), roasted confit of honeyed belly pork and szechuan-style pork parcel with satay sauce), home-made black pudding with sautéed scallops, a drizzle of mustard sauce and topped with crispy streaky smoked bacon, moules thai-style or marinière, sausages of the day with crispy onion rings and home-made gravy, venison and Guinness cottage pie with a red berry compote, and bobotie (a delicious south african dish). *Benchmark main dish: creamy fish pie with tempura green beans and home-made tartare sauce £13.95. Two-course evening meal £21.45.*

Robinsons ~ Lease Ian and Anette Dutton ~ Real ale ~ Bar food (12-9(10 Fri and Sat)) ~ Restaurant ~ (015394) 32174 ~ Children welcome ~ Dogs allowed in bar ~ Open 10am-midnight ~ Bedrooms: /£120B

Recommended by Peter and Josie Fawcett, Martin Smith, Hugh Roberts, Adrian Johnson, Lesley and Peter Barrett

TUNSTALL Lancashire   SD6073   Map C

Lunesdale Arms 🍴 �

A683 S of Kirkby Lonsdale; LA6 2QN

Civilised pub with emphasis on good imaginative food; separate area with traditional games

The light and airy opened-up interior of this bustling dining pub has bare boards and a lively acoustic that gives it a cheery buzz. A white-walled area has a good mix of stripped dining tables and blue sofas facing each other across a low table (with daily papers) by a woodburning stove in a solid stone fireplace. Another area has pews and armchairs (some of the big unframed oil paintings are for sale) and to one end, an airy games section with pool, table football, board games and TV. A snugger little flagstoned back part has another woodburning stove. Black Sheep and a couple of local guests from brewers such as Brysons are on handpump alongside a farm cider; table football. The church in this Lune Valley village has Brontë associations.

🍴 Real care goes into the food here which is prepared using locally sourced ingredients and home-grown herbs and vegetables. They make their own bread and have their own blend of coffee. The seasonally changing menu might include shallot tart with goats cheese, mezze to share, tiger prawn and smoked salmon salad with dill and chervil dressing, steak and kidney pie, pork loin chop on crushed carrot and celeriac with sausage stuffing, battered haddock, ginger sponge with poached rhubarb and orange crème brûlée. *Benchmark main dish: burger and chips £11.00. Two-course evening meal £15.50.*

Free house ~ Licensee Emma Gillibrand ~ Real ale ~ Bar food (12-2(2.30 Sat, Sun, bank holidays), 6-9) ~ (01524) 274203 ~ Children welcome ~ Dogs welcome ~ Pianist some Thurs evenings ~ Open 11-3.30, 6-midnight; closed Mon except bank holidays

Recommended by Mr and Mrs D Mackenzie, Malcolm and Pauline Pellatt, Dr Kevan Tucker

---

If a pub tries to make you leave a credit card behind the bar, be on your guard. The credit card firms and banks that issue them condemn this practice. After all, the publican who asks you to do this is in effect saying: 'I don't trust you'. Have you any more reason to trust his staff? If your card is used fraudulently while you have let it be kept out of your sight, the card company could say you've been negligent yourself – and refuse to make good your losses. So say that they can 'swipe' your card instead, but must hand it back to you. Please let us know if a pub does try to keep your card.

 ULVERSTON Cumbria   SD3177 Map C

Bay Horse ♀ ⇱

Canal Foot signposted off A590 and then you wend your way past the huge Glaxo factory; LA12 9EL

Civilised waterside hotel with lunchtime bar food, three real ales and a fine choice of wines; smart bedrooms

Lunchtime is when this civilised hotel – on the water's edge of the Leven Estuary – is at its most informal. The bar has a relaxed atmosphere despite its smart furnishings: attractive wooden armchairs, some pale green plush built-in wall banquettes, glossy hardwood traditional tables, blue plates on a delft shelf, a huge stone horse's head, and black beams and props with lots of horsebrasses. Magazines are dotted about, there's an open fire in the handsomely marbled grey slate fireplace and decently reproduced piped music; board games. Jennings Cross Buttocks, Cumberland and Golden Host on handpump, 16 by the glass (including champagne and prosecco) from a carefully chosen and interesting wine list and several malt whiskies. The conservatory restaurant has fine views over Morecambe Bay (as do the bedrooms) and there are some seats out on the terrace.

Good lunchtime bar food includes interesting sandwiches, chicken liver pâté with cranberry and ginger purée, chilli prawns on a sweet and sour sauce, pasta with leeks, basil and asparagus in a light cream sauce, lambs liver with black and white puddings on a madeira sauce, poached smoked haddock on a mushroom and onion pâté and a wine and herb sauce, smoked pork cutlet on an apple and stilton cream, and steak and kidney pie. *Benchmark main dish: home-made corned beef £18.00. Two-course evening meal £25.00.*

Free house ~ Licensee Robert Lyons ~ Real ale ~ Bar food (12-3(2 Mon, 4 weekends); one evening restaurant sitting 7.30-8pm; no bar food evenings) ~ Restaurant ~ (01229) 583972 ~ Children welcome but must be over 9 in bedrooms or in evening ~ Dogs allowed in bar and bedrooms ~ Open 11-11; 12-10.30 Sun ~ Bedrooms: $80B/$120B

Recommended by John and Sylvia Harrop, Henry Midwinter, V and E A Bolton, Peter Salmon

 UPPERMILL Lancashire   SD0006 Map C

Church Inn ◖ £

From the main street (A607), look out for the sign for Saddleworth Church, and turn off up this steep narrow lane – keep on up! OL3 6LW

Lively good value community pub with big range of own-brew beers, lots of pets, and good food; children very welcome

The burgeoning menagerie of animals at this enjoyably quirky pub, high up on the moors, and with fine views down the valley includes rabbits, chickens, dogs, ducks, geese, alpacas, horses, 14 peacocks in the next-door field and some cats resident in an adjacent barn. The big unspoilt L-shaped main bar has high beams and some stripped stone, settles, pews, a good individual mix of chairs, and lots of attractive prints and staffordshire and other china on a high delft shelf, jugs, brasses and so forth; TV (only when there's sport on) and unobtrusive piped music; the conservatory opens on to a terrace. The horse-collar on the wall is worn by the winner of their annual gurning (face-pulling) championship which is held during the lively traditional Rush Cart Festival, which is usually over the August bank holiday. Local bellringers arrive on Wednesdays to practise with a set of handbells that are kept here, while anyone is invited to join the morris dancers who meet here on Thursdays. When the spring water levels aren't high enough for brewing, they bring in guest beers such as Black Sheep and Hydes Jekylls Gold. At other times, you might find up to 11 of their own-brew Saddleworth beers, starting at just £1.70 a pint. Some of the seasonal ones (look out for Ruebens, Ayrtons, Robyns and Indya) are named after the licensee's children, only appearing around their birthdays; dark lager on tap, too. Children and dogs are made to feel very welcome.

Very reasonably priced bar food includes soup, sandwiches, steak and ale pie, jumbo cod, a range of pies, and mixed grill. *Benchmark main dish: cod and chips £9.75. Two-course evening meal £11.80.*

Own brew ~ Licensee Christine Taylor ~ Real ale ~ Bar food (12-2.30, 5.30-9; 12-9 Sat, Sun and bank holidays) ~ Restaurant ~ (01457) 820902 ~ Children welcome ~ Dogs allowed in bar ~ Open 12-12(1am Sat)

Recommended by Ben Williams, the Didler, John Fiander, Roger and Lesley Everett, Bob Broadhurst

WADDINGTON Lancashire   SD7243   Map C

Lower Buck £

Edisford Road; BB7 3HU

Hospitable village pub with reasonably priced, tasty food; five real ales

Readers enjoy the gently relaxing atmosphere at this pretty 18th-c village pub which is handily placed for walks in the Ribble Valley. It's split into several little neatly kept cream-painted bars and dining rooms, each with a warming coal fire and good solid wood furnishings on new wood floors. Staff and other customers are chatty and welcoming; darts and pool; two dining rooms. The friendly landlord keeps a range of five ales, usually Bowland Hen Harrier, Moorhouses Premier and guests such as Bowland Sky Dancer, over a dozen malts and several wines by the glass. There are picnic-sets out on cobbles at the front and in the sunny back garden.

Using meat reared at a farm in nearby Longridge and vegetables grown in Longridge too, the reasonably priced tasty food includes lunchtime sandwiches and ploughman's, duck breast terrine, potted morecambe bay shrimps, lancashire cheese and onion pie, lancashire hotpot, fish and chips, and grilled chicken breast marinated in garlic, lemon and herbs with garlic mayonnaise. *Benchmark main dish: steak and mushroom pie £10.25. Two-course evening meal £15.90.*

Free house ~ Licensee Andrew Warburton ~ Real ale ~ Bar food (12-2.30, 6-9; 12-9 Sat, Sun and bank holidays) ~ (01200) 423342 ~ Children welcome ~ Dogs welcome ~ Open 11(12 Sun)-11(midnight Sat)

Recommended by Roger and Donna Huggins, Lucien Perring, Ed and Anna Fraser

WADDINGTON Lancashire   SD7243   Map C

Waddington Arms ★ ♀ ◀ 🛏

Clitheroe Road (B6478 N of Clitheroe); BB7 3HP

Classic *Guide* pub, good all round, with plenty of character, cheerful landlord, good value bedrooms – and open all day

This lovely place has four linked rooms, the one on the left is snuggest in winter, with its blazing woodburning stove in a monumental fireplace putting real warmth into the ancient flagstones. There's plenty to look at in the various low-beamed rooms, from antique prints through an

interesting series of vintage motor-racing posters to the contemporary
Laurie Williamson prints over on the right – and some intriguing
wallpaper (an enlarged 19th-c sporting print here, leather-bound books
there). The furniture too gives the feeling that it's all been carefully
chosen and thought through, with some fine antique oak settles as well as
chunky stripped-pine tables. They have a good choice of wines by the
glass, an ale Moorhouses brew for them (The Waddy), and other well kept
ales on handpump such as Goose Eye and Grays Best; the helpful and
welcoming landlord ensures a friendly easy-going atmosphere. Wicker
chairs on a sunny flagstoned front terrace look across to this attractive
village's church (it's just on the edge of the Forest of Bowland, too), and
there are more tables on a two-level back terrace, with picnic-sets on a
neat tree-sheltered lawn.

Besides generous sandwiches, enjoyable country cooking here includes light
dishes such as nourishing soups, duck confit or black pudding and poached egg,
as well as robust main courses like sausage and mash, steak and ale pie, fried bass
with spring vegetables, hotpot, and steaks. *Benchmark main dish: lancashire hotpot
£10.95. Two-course evening meal £16.50.*

Free house ~ Real ale ~ Bar food (12-2, 7-9.30; 12-9.30 Sat, Sun) ~ (01200) 423262 ~
Children welcome ~ Dogs allowed in bar ~ Open 11-12 ~ Bedrooms: /£65B

Recommended by Philip and Helen Temperley, Steve Whalley

WHEATLEY LANE Lancashire   SD8338   Map C

Sparrowhawk

*Wheatley Lane Road; towards E end of village road which runs N of and
parallel to A6068; one way of reaching it is to follow Fence, Newchurch 1¼ signpost,
then turn off at Barrowford ¾ signpost; BB12 9QG*

Comfortably civilised pub, with well prepared food and five real ales

Smart young waitresses work their way through the attractively laid out
areas of this imposing black and white pub. The interior has quite a
1930s feel with its quirky domed stained-glass skylight, parquet flooring,
oak panelling, leather tub chairs and red floor tiles; daily papers. The
cushioned leatherette bar counter (cheerful with fresh flowers) serves
Bass, Greene King IPA, Thwaites Original, a couple of guests such as
Bank Top Flat Cap and Pavillion on handpump, draught Fransizkaner
wheat beer and good wines by the glass. TV, piped music and board
games. Heavy wood tables out on a spacious and attractive front terrace
with pretty flower beds and a water feature have good views to the moors
beyond Nelson and Colne.

Good fresh bar food includes sandwiches, ploughman's, smoked haddock tart
with poached egg, salmon fishcake with grilled king prawn and tomato and
coriander salsa, steak, ale and mushroom pie, steak burger, crab linguine, duck
pasty with apple and currant chutney, baked rump of lamb with minted pea pudding
and braised lentils, and pork fillet wrapped in prosciutto with brandy soaked prunes
and truffle mash. *Benchmark main dish: fish and chips £11.95. Two-course evening
meal £20.00.*

Mitchells & Butlers ~ Lease Neil Morley ~ Real ale ~ Bar food (12-2.30, 5-9; 12-9.30 Sat;
12-8 Sun) ~ (01282) 603034 ~ Children welcome ~ Dogs allowed in bar ~ Open
12-11(midnight Sat, 10.30 Sun)

*Recommended by Dr Kevan Tucker, Roger and Donna Huggins, Steve Whalley, Ann and
Tony Bennett-Hughes*

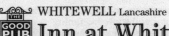

WHITEWELL Lancashire SD6546 Map C

Inn at Whitewell ★ ⏥ ⇱

Most easily reached by B6246 from Whalley; road through Dunsop Bridge from B6478 is also good; BB7 3AT

Elegant manor house hotel with smartly pubby atmosphere, good bar food, and luxury bedrooms

This ancient upmarket inn is a stylish place to stay, dine or just enjoy a drink. Handsome old wood furnishings, including antique settles, oak gateleg tables and sonorous clocks, are set off beautifully against powder blue walls that are neatly hung with big attractive prints. The pubby main bar has roaring log fires in attractive stone fireplaces and heavy curtains on sturdy wooden rails; one area has a selection of newspapers and magazines, local maps and guide books; there's a piano for anyone who wants to play and even an art gallery; board games. Early evening sees a cheerful bustle which later settles to a more tranquil and relaxing atmosphere. Drinks include a good wine list of around 230 wines with 16 by the glass (there is a good wine shop in the reception area), organic ginger beer, lemonade and fruit juices and up to five real ales on handpump that might be from Bowland, Copper Dragon, Moorhouses and Timothy Taylor. Staff are courteous and friendly. The building is nicely positioned in a super setting deep among the hills and moors that rise to the high points of the Forest of Bowland and has delightful views from the riverside bar and adjacent terrace. They own several miles of trout, salmon and sea-trout fishing on the Hodder, and can arrange shooting and make up a picnic hamper.

Besides lunchtime sandwiches, well presented bar food might include spicy fried squid, duck terrine with poached pear and apple jelly, fish and chips, roast chicken breast with sage and onion stuffing and smoked bacon and onion jus, cheese and onion pie, and grilled salmon fillet with basil and olive mash and ratatouille; they also have a separate dining room menu. *Benchmark main dish: fish pie £10.72. Two-course evening meal £21.00.*

Free house ~ Licensee Charles Bowman ~ Real ale ~ Bar food (12-2, 7.30-9.30) ~ Restaurant ~ (01200) 448222 ~ Children welcome ~ Dogs allowed in bar and bedrooms ~ Open 11-midnight ~ Bedrooms: £85B/£115B

Recommended by Noel Thomas, Steve Whalley, Mark Sowery, Dr Clive Elphick, Yvonne and Mike Meadley, Roger and Donna Huggins, David Heath, John Taylor

WINSTER Cumbria SD4193 Map B

Brown Horse 🍴 ⏥ 🍺 ⇱

A5074 S of Windermere; LA23 3NR

Welcoming bar, smart restaurant, a friendly, informal atmosphere, first-class food, own-brewed real ales, good wines, and seats outside; comfortable bedrooms

This charming inn now has its own microbrewery up and running, Winster Valley, which produces Best and Old School, and they keep guests such as Kirkby Lonsdale Tiffin Gold and Lytham Lowther on handpump; also, a dozen wines by the glass, ten malt whiskies and raspberry lemonade and elderflower pressé. There's a chatty, bustling atmosphere in the bar which has beams and some half-panelling, stools and a mix of wooden chairs around pubby tables (each with a light candle), a woodburning stove in a little stone fireplace, and high bar chairs by the counter. The restaurant has a relaxed, informal atmosphere, high-backed leather dining chairs around attractive light and dark wood tables, more candles and fresh flowers. Piped music, TV, darts and board games. There's a front terrace with solid tables and chairs, and a side garden with views of the Winster Valley. Our readers enjoy staying here very much.

Using their own Estate-reared and own-grown produce, the excellent food might include sandwiches, home tea-smoked mackerel with horseradish cream, home-smoked salmon and prawn fishcake with a soft poached egg and watercress mayonnaise, tomato and olive tagliatelle, pheasant and apricot sausages with red wine jus, trout from Ullswater with almond beurre blanc, corn-fed chicken with bacon and a light poultry cream, and 21-day-hung rib-eye steak with dripping-cooked chips and a creamed peppercorn reduction; they offer a good value two- and three-course set lunch menu. *Benchmark main dish: pheasant breast with bacon, black pudding and cranberry sauce £14.95. Two-course evening meal £20.25.*

Free house ~ Licensees Karen and Steve Edmondson ~ Real ale ~ Bar food (12-2, 6-9) ~ Restaurant ~ (015394) 43443 ~ Children welcome ~ Dogs allowed in bar ~ Open 11-11 ~ Bedrooms: £65S/£97S

Recommended by Tina and David Woods-Taylor, Peter Webb, Walter and Susan Rinaldi-Butcher, Henry Midwinter, Michael Doswell, Alison Ball, Ian Walton, Malcolm and Pauline Pellatt, Brian and Janet Ainscough, Jane and Alan Bush, Peter Smith and Judith Brown

WISWELL Lancashire   SD7437   Map C

Freemasons Arms ★ ⑪ ♀ ◨

Village signposted off A671 and A59 NE of Whalley; pub on Vicarage Fold, a gravelled pedestrian passage between Pendleton Road and Old Back Lane in village centre (don't expect to park very close); BB7 9DF

Top-drawer dining pub, a place for a special treat

Best thought-of as a good civilised restaurant, this does have the look and comfortingly informal feel of an upmarket pub – not to mention the thoroughly pubby plus point of its well kept local ales on handpump, such as Bank Top Golden Legacy, Moorhouses Pride of Pendle and Tirril Nameless, as well as the racks of well chosen wine bottles behind its tempting bar counter (there's an excellent choice by the glass). Three rooms open together, with lots of mainly sporting antique prints on the cream or pastel walls, rugs on polished flagstones, carved oak settles and an attractive variety of chairs around handsome stripped or salvaged candlelit tables (all beautifully laid), and open fires, with a woodburning stove on the right. There are more rooms upstairs, including a comfortable one that's popular for pre-meal drinks, or their good coffee afterwards. Service by neatly uniformed young staff is meticulous and courteous. Teak seats for the candlelit tables under an extendable awning on the quiet flagstoned front terrace have not only infra-red heaters, but also plaid rugs to wrap around you.

Besides lunchtime sandwiches (try the dry-aged sirloin), dishes we or readers have particularly enjoyed here include beef bourguignon, pork belly rissoles, bream done with shrimps from Morecambe Bay, and an outstanding banana soufflé with toffee ice-cream; best value is the two- or three-course lunch, with around three choices for each course. *Benchmark main dish: tandoori monkfish with pork nuggets and scratchings and sweet potato £21.95. Two-course evening meal £33.60.*

Free house ~ Licensee Steven Smith ~ Real ale ~ Bar food (12-2.30, 5.30-9(6-9.30 Fri, Sat); 12-7.30 Sun; not Mon) ~ (01254) 822218 ~ Dogs allowed in bar ~ Open 12-2.30, 5.30-midnight; 12-midnight Sat; 12-11 Sun; closed first two weeks in Jan

Recommended by Margaret Dickinson, Nick White, Steve Whalley, W K Wood

WITHERSLACK Cumbria   SD4482   Map A

Derby Arms 🍴 🍺 🛏

Just off A590; LA11 6RH

Bustling country inn with six real ales, good wines, excellent food and a friendly welcome; reasonably priced bedrooms

Handy for Levens Hall with its topiary garden and for Sizergh Castle (NT), this stylish country inn is a fine place for an interesting meal, a drink and a chat (they keep up to half a dozen real ales) or to stay overnight in the comfortable bedrooms. The main bar has lots of sporting prints on pale grey walls, elegant old dining chairs and tables on large rugs over floorboards, some hops over the bar counter, and an open fire. A larger room to the right is similarly furnished (with the addition of some cushioned pews), and has lots of political cartoons and local castle prints, a cumbrian scene over another open fire and alcoves in the back wall full of nice Bristol blue glass, ornate plates and staffordshire dogs and figurines; the large windows do lighten up the rooms, helped by evening candles in brass candlesticks. There are two further rooms – one with dark red walls, a red velvet sofa, more sporting prints and a handsome mirror over the fireplace. Barngates Cat Nap, Hawkshead Bitter, Lytham Blonde, Thwaites Lancaster Bomber and Wainwright, and a beer named for the pub brewed for them by Cumbrian Legendary and several wines by the glass. The atmosphere is friendly and relaxed, and the staff are helpful and courteous. They have plans for the garden.

Very good food includes sandwiches (the sandwich and soup deal is smashing value), duck and chicken liver pâté with home-made fruit chutney, grilled black pudding on a crispy pancetta and goats cheese salad with a grain mustard dressing, butternut squash and sage risotto, steak in ale pie, organic beefburger on a toasted muffin with cream lancashire cheese, a bacon skewer, onion rings and their own tomato relish, and a trio of sausages with red onion marmalade and cider gravy. *Benchmark main dish: beer-battered fish and chips £12.65. Two-course evening meal £17.45.*

Free house ~ Licensee Sue Luxton ~ Real ale ~ Bar food (12-2(2.30 Sat), 6-9; 12-8.30 Sun) ~ Restaurant ~ (015395) 52207 ~ Children welcome ~ Dogs welcome ~ Open 12-3, 5.30-11; 12-12 Fri and Sat; 12-10.30 Sun ~ Bedrooms: /£65S

Recommended by Sarah Priday, Jack Clark, Michael Doswell

YANWATH Cumbria   NY5128   Map B

Gate Inn 🍴 ♟

2.25 miles from M6 junction 40; A66 towards Brough, then right on A6, right on B5320, then follow village signpost; CA10 2LF

CUMBRIA DINING PUB OF THE YEAR

Emphasis on imaginative food but with local beers and thoughtful wines, a pubby atmosphere and warm welcome from the helpful staff

Handy for Ullswater and a civilised break from the M6, this is an immaculately kept 17th-c dining pub, much loved by our readers. There's a cosy bar of charming antiquity with country pine and dark wood furniture, lots of brasses on the beams, church candles on all the tables and a good log fire in the attractive stone inglenook. Friendly, courteous staff serve real ales on handpump from breweries such as Cumbrian Legendary, Hesket Newmarket and Tirril, and they keep around a dozen good wines by the glass, quite a few malt whiskies and maybe Weston's cider. Two restaurant areas have oak floors, panelled oak walls and heavy beams; piped music. There are seats on the terrace and in the garden. They have a self-catering cottage to let.

Using top quality local produce, free-range and organic where possible, the excellent food at lunchtime includes sandwiches, seafood ceviche, a platter of smoked meats, fish, cheese and home-baked bread with chutney and pickles, squash, rosemary and pine nut risotto, and venison burger with plum chutney, with evening choices such as steamed mussels with creamed leeks and scrumpy cider, braised belly of saddleback pork stuffed with apricots and spinach forcemeat with a sweet potato purée and coriander and lemon couscous, and wild bass fillet with sunblush tomato and black olive potatoes. *Benchmark main dish: herdwick mutton loin with home-made black pudding and a berry sauce £18.95. Two-course evening meal £22.00.*

Free house ~ Licensee Matt Edwards ~ Real ale ~ Bar food (12-2.30, 6-9) ~ Restaurant ~ (01768) 862386 ~ Children welcome ~ Dogs allowed in bar ~ Open 12-11

Recommended by Richard J Holloway, John and Eleanor Holdsworth, Chris and Jo Parsons, Mr and Mrs Maurice Thompson, Michael Doswell, J S Burn, Neil and Karen Dignan, Maurice and Gill McMahon, V and E A Bolton, Terry Davis, Michael and Maggie Betton, Gordon and Margaret Ormondroyd, Rosemary and Mike Fielder, Dave Snowden, Andy Orton, Pat and Stewart Gordon, Dr and Mrs T E Hothersall

ALSO WORTH A VISIT IN THE NORTH EAST

Besides the region's top pubs, we recommend the following. Do tell us
what you think of them: **feedback@goodguides.com**

ALLENDALE NY8355   NE47 9BD
Kings Head
Market Place (B6295)

Refurbished early 18th-c former coaching inn, popular with locals, with four real ales,
good selection of wines and soft drinks, decent food served by friendly staff, glowing coal
fire, newspapers; children welcome, bedrooms, open all day. *Recommended by JJW, CMW,
John Coatsworth, Brett Jones, Comus and Sarah Elliott*

ALNMOUTH NU2511   NE66 2RA
Hope & Anchor
Northumberland Street

Old pub with cheery bar and long beamed dining room, well kept Hadrian & Border Farne
Island Pale and Northumberland Sheepdog, hearty home-made food, china and brass,
local art for sale; children and dogs welcome, quietly appealing coastal village, attractive
beaches and good coastal walks, seven bedrooms, open all day. *Recommended by John Beeken*

ALNMOUTH NU2410   NE66 2RJ
☆ ## Red Lion
Northumberland Street

Welcoming 18th-c coaching inn, relaxed and unpretentious, with good choice of
traditional food from good crab sandwiches to popular reasonably priced Sun lunch,
cheerful efficient staff, well kept ales such as Black Sheep, Hadrian & Border,
Northumberland and Wylam, mainly New World wines by the glass, attractive bistro-style
dining room, log fire in cosy panelled locals' bar; dogs welcome, neat garden by alley with
raised deck looking over Aln estuary, comfortable bedrooms, open all day (till 8pm Sun).
*Recommended by Comus and Sarah Elliott, Celia Minoughan, Michael Doswell, Ann and Tony Bennett-
Hughes, John Beeken and others*

ALNMOUTH NU2410   NE66 2RA
Sun
Northumberland Street

Comfortable banquettes in long low-beamed bar with open fire and woodburner at either
end, carpet or bare-boards, decorations made from driftwood, friendly chatty staff, good
value food including interesting sandwiches, Black Sheep and Mordue, good coffee, small
contemporary dining area; piped music; attractive seaside village. *Recommended by Colin and
Louise English*

ALNWICK NU1813   NE66 1PN
Blackmores
Bondgate Without

Smart contemporary pub/boutique hotel in Victorian stone building, well kept Black
Sheep and Caledonian Deuchars IPA in lively front bar, several wines by the glass,
consistently good food all day from snacky things up in bar, bistro or upstairs restaurant,
attentive service; pleasant street-side raised terrace, 13 bedrooms. *Recommended by
Jenny and Peter Lowater, Comus and Sarah Elliott, Michael Doswell, Richard and Stephanie Foskett,
Rosemary and Mike Fielder and others*

We include some hotels with a good bar that offers facilities comparable to those of a pub.

ALNWICK NU1813
NE66 1UY

John Bull
Howick Street

Popular chatty drinkers' pub, essentially front room of early 19th-c terraced house, four changing ales, real cider, bottled belgian beers and over 100 malt whiskies; closed weekday lunchtime. *Recommended by the Didler*

AMBLE NU2604
NE65 0LD

Wellwood Arms
High Street

Recently refurbished dining pub with pleasant welcoming staff, enjoyable food from traditional things up including set menu choices, well selected wines, separate nicely laid-out restaurant area with own bar. *Recommended by Dr Peter D Smart*

BACKWORTH NZ3072
NE27 0FG

Pavilion
Hotspur North

Brightly modern Fitzgeralds pub (opened 2008), good food and service, four ales including Black Sheep and Consett; children welcome, disabled facilities, terrace tables, open all day. *Recommended by the Dutchman*

BAMBURGH NU1834
NE69 7BW

Castle
Front Street

Clean comfortably old-fashioned pub with friendly landlord and staff, well kept ales such as Black Sheep and Mordue, decent house wines, winter mulled wine, standard modestly priced food all day including good kippers from Craster, recently expanded dining area to cope with summer visitors, open fires; big courtyard, garden. *Recommended by Lawrence Pearse, Comus and Sarah Elliott*

BAMBURGH NU1734
NE69 7BS

Mizen Head
Lucker Road

Refurbished hotel with light airy bar, open fire, enjoyable locally sourced food, ales such as Black Sheep, good house wines, friendly staff; children and dogs welcome, nice bedrooms. *Recommended by Penny and Peter Keevil, Comus and Sarah Elliott*

BAMBURGH NU1834
NE69 7BP

☆ Victoria
Front Street

Substantial Victorian hotel with sofas, squashy leather chairs and high stools in mildly contemporary partly divided bar, chunky tables and chairs in dining room, good food all day from sandwiches up, two real ales from Black Sheep and/or Mordue, good wines by the glass, young children's playroom; lovely setting, comfortable bedrooms, open all day. *Recommended by Colin and Louise English*

BARDON MILL NY7566
NE47 7AN

Twice Brewed
Military Road (B6318 NE of Hexham)

Large busy inn well placed for fell-walkers and major Wall sites, six ales including local microbrews and two for the pub by Yates, 50 rums, 20 malts, reasonably priced wines, good value hearty pub food from baguettes up, quick friendly staff, local photographs and art for sale; quiet piped music, no dogs; children welcome, picnic-sets in back garden, 14 bedrooms, open all day. *Recommended by Dave Braisted, Pete Coxon, Peter Dearing*

BARNINGHAM NZ0810
DL11 7DW
Milbank Arms
On main road into village from Newsham

Cosy little one-room village local, simple and unspoilt with welcoming landlord (in same family for 70 years), no bar counter or kitchen, drinks brought from the cellar. *Recommended by C Elliott*

BEADNELL NU2229
NE67 5AY
Beadnell Towers
The Wynding, off B1340

Large slightly old-fashioned pub/hotel with unusual mix of furnishings, good food including local game and fish, well kept ales such as Hadrian & Border Farne Island, reasonably priced wines by the glass, nice coffee, pleasant obliging service; can get more touristy in summer; seats outside, bedrooms. *Recommended by DHV, Comus and Sarah Elliott, Michael Doswell*

BEADNELL NU2229
NE67 5AX
Craster Arms
The Wynding

Popular pubby food and blackboard specials including local fish, well kept Black Sheep and Mordue, good choice of wines by the glass, friendly efficient staff, roomy neatly kept old building with modern fittings, red banquettes, patterned carpets, stripped-brick and stone walls, pictures for sale, nice local atmosphere; children welcome, enclosed gardens, open all day. *Recommended by DHV, Michael Doswell*

BEAMISH NZ2154
DH9 0YB
Beamish Hall
NE of Stanley, off A6076

Converted stone-built stables in courtyard at back of hotel, popular and family friendly (can get crowded), five or six good beers from own microbrewery, decent choice of food all day, uniformed staff; plenty of seats outside. *Recommended by Peter Smith and Judith Brown, GSB, Mr and Mrs Maurice Thompson, Rob Weeks*

BEAMISH NZ2153
DH9 0QH
☆ ## Beamish Mary
Off A693 signed No Place and Cooperative Villas, S of museum

Friendly down-to-earth former pit village inn under new management, eight well kept mainly local ales (May beer festival), farm cider, good home-made pubby food at bargain prices, coal fires, two bars with 1960s-feel mix of furnishings, bric-a-brac, 1920s/30s memorabilia and Aga with pots and pans, regular live music in converted stables; sports TV; children allowed until evening, updated bedrooms. *Recommended by Peter Smith and Judith Brown*

BELSAY NZ1277
NE20 0DN
Highlander
A696 S of village

Roomy country dining pub with enjoyable food from lunchtime baguettes up, good friendly service, Black Sheep and Caledonian Deuchars IPA, comfortable raised side area with nice plain wood tables and high-backed banquettes, plenty of nooks and corners for character, good log fires, plainer locals' bar; unobtrusive piped music; open all day. *Recommended by Guy and Caroline Howard*

BERWICK-UPON-TWEED NT9952
TD15 1ES
Barrels
Bridge Street

Small friendly pub with interesting collection of pop memorabilia and other bric-a-brac, eccentric furniture including dentist's chair in bare-boards bar, red banquettes in back room, five well kept changing ales, foreign bottled beers, live music (Fri) and DJs (Sat) in basement bar, good quality piped music; open all day, may be closed weekday lunchtimes in winter. *Recommended by Dave and Shirley Shaw*

☆ **BERWICK-UPON-TWEED** NT9952   TD15 1AB

Foxtons
Hide Hill

More chatty and comfortable two-level wine bar than pub, with wide choice of good imaginative food at reasonable prices, prompt friendly service, good range of wines, whiskies and coffees, real ales such as Caledonian, a local cider, lively side bistro; busy, so worth booking evenings, open all day, closed Sun. *Recommended by John and Sylvia Harrop, M Mossman*

BERWICK-UPON-TWEED NT9952   TD15 1BG

Leaping Salmon
Golden Square

Wetherspoons in late 18th-c former school, very reasonably priced beer and usual food choices; modern conservatory extension. *Recommended by Ian Phillips*

BIRTLEY NZ2856   DH3 1RE

Mill House
Blackfell, via A1231 slip road off southbound A1

Extensively refurbished dining pub with enjoyable food all day including bargain two-course lunches, oyster bar and tapas too, compact bar area, changing real ale, nice wines by the glass, dining room with olde-barn décor, alcoved eating areas and conservatory, friendly staff. *Recommended by Dave and Jenny Hughes, Deb Dawson*

BISHOPTON NZ3621   TS21 1HE

Talbot
The Green

Busy village dining pub with wide choice of good food from light dishes up, good value set lunch too, modern bar with smart dining areas either side, three real ales and several wines by the glass, friendly efficient uniformed staff. *Recommended by Ed and Anna Fraser*

BLYTH NZ2779   NE24 4HF

Three Horseshoes
Just off A189, W of town

Isolated and much-extended building (dates from 1780) perched above dual carriageway, various rooms off central bar (some with view to coast), front conservatory, good value food (all day Fri-Sun) from sandwiches up, wide choice of well kept ales, efficient friendly service from uniformed staff; children welcome, outside play area, tree house, open all day. *Recommended by GSB*

BOULMER NU2614   NE66 3BP

Fishing Boat
Beach View

Worth knowing for its position, with conservatory dining room and decking overlooking sea; light and airy inside with interesting nautical memorabilia, good value food, real ales such as Black Sheep and Tetleys; dogs welcome. *Recommended by John Beeken, Richard Pearson*

CARLBURY NZ2115   DL2 3SJ

Carlbury Arms
Just off A67 just E of Piercebridge

Welcoming dining pub locally popular for good choice of reasonably priced food, well kept Black Sheep and Jennings Cumberland, good wine choice, pine tables on wood floors. *Recommended by Pat and Stewart Gordon*

CASTLE EDEN NZ4237   TS27 4SD
Castle Eden Inn
B1281 S of Peterlee

Refurbished dining pub with enjoyable fairly priced local food, ales such as Black Sheep, Caledonian Deuchars IPA and Timothy Taylors Landlord. *Recommended by Andy Maher, JHBS*

CATTON NY8257   NE47 9QS
☆ Crown
B6295

Cosy 19th-c pub under new management (same owners as the Rat at Anick), four or five well kept changing local ales, maybe a farm cider, very good locally sourced food from daily changing menu, stripped stone, big log fire, warm friendly atmosphere, dining extension; children welcome, no dogs at food times, pretty beer garden, lovely walks, open all day except Mon afternoon. *Recommended by Michael Doswell, Comus and Sarah Elliott, S Jackson, B Thompson, Philip Huddleston*

CORBRIDGE NY9964   NE45 5LA
☆ Angel
Main Street

Imposing white coaching inn at end of broad street facing handsome bridge over Tyne; sizeable modernised main bar, plain light wood chairs and tables, just a few prints on pastel walls, big-screen TV, carpeted lounge bar also with modern feel, strongly patterned wallpaper, tall metal-framed café-bar seats and leather bucket chairs, up to six real ales, a dozen wines by the glass, 30 malt whiskies, Weston's cider, well liked bar food; separate lounge with oak panelling, big stone fireplace, sofa and button-back wing armchairs, daily papers, smart raftered restaurant with stripped masonry and local art; piped music; children welcome, seats in front on cobbles below wall sundial, bedrooms, open all day. *Recommended by Eric Larkham, Michael Doswell, Mike and Lynn Robinson, Andy and Jill Kassube, Pete Coxon, Clive Watkin and others*

CORBRIDGE NY9864   NE45 5AT
☆ Black Bull
Middle Street

Rambling linked old rooms, reasonably priced food all day from sandwiches and light lunches up, good friendly service, Black Sheep and Greene King ales, good attractively priced wine choice, roaring fire, neat comfortable seating including traditional settles on flagstones in softly lit low-ceilinged core; open all day. *Recommended by Comus and Sarah Elliott*

CORBRIDGE NY9863   NE45 5AY
Dyvels
Station Road

Refurbished traditional stone inn, friendly and well run, with good value pub food from duck egg sandwiches up, well kept ales such as Black Sheep, Mordue and Shepherd Neame, decent wines by the glass; children welcome, picnic-sets on side terrace and lawn, three bedrooms, open all day. *Recommended by Andy and Jill Kassube, Comus and Sarah Elliott*

CORBRIDGE NY9868   NE45 5QB
☆ Errington Arms
About 3 miles N of town; B6318, on A68 roundabout

18th-c stone-built roadside pub by Hadrian's Wall, good mix of diners and walkers, beamed bars with pine panelling, stone and burgundy walls, mix of chairs around pine tables on strip-wood flooring, log fire and woodburner, well liked home-made food, Jennings and Wylam ales, friendly staff; piped music; children welcome, tables out in front, closed Sun evening, Mon. *Recommended by David and Sue Smith, Comus and Sarah Elliott, David and Katharine Cooke, Andy and Jill Kassube*

☆ **Fox & Hounds**
COTHERSTONE NZ0119
DL12 9PF
B6277

18th-c inn with simple beamed bar, log fire, various alcoves and recesses, local photographs and country pictures, Black Sheep and a guest, malt whiskies from smaller distilleries, generous food using local ingredients, efficient friendly service, restaurant, african grey parrot called Reva; children welcome if eating, seats on terrace, quoits, bedrooms, pretty spot overlooking village green, good nearby walks. *Recommended by GNI, Guy Morgan, Chris and Jo Parsons, Ian Herdman, SGN Bennett, Jerry Brown and others*

☆ **Snowy Owl**
CRAMLINGTON NZ2373
NE23 8AU
Just off A1/A19 junction via A1068; Blagdon Lane

Large Vintage Inn, relaxed and comfortable, with reasonable prices, good choice of well-liked food all day including popular Sun lunch, friendly efficient young staff, beers such as Black Sheep, Jennings Cumberland and Timothy Taylors Landlord, nice wines, beams, flagstones, stripped stone and terracotta paintwork, soft lighting and an interesting mix of furnishings and decorations, daily papers; may be piped music; disabled access, bedrooms in adjoining Innkeepers Lodge, open all day. *Recommended by Guy and Caroline Howard, Dr Peter D Smart, Comus and Sarah Elliott*

☆ **Jolly Fisherman**
CRASTER NU2519
NE66 3TR
Off B1339, NE of Alnwick

Simple local in great spot, long a favourite for its lovely sea and coast views from picture window and grass behind, and for its good value crab sandwiches, crab soup and locally smoked seafood; this makes up for the take-us-as-you-find-us style, which can verge on scruffiness (not to everyone's taste); ales such as Black Sheep or Mordue, good cider, local art for sale, games area with pool; children and dogs welcome, smokehouse opposite, open all day in summer. *Recommended by Penny and Peter Keevil, Christine and Malcolm Ingram, John and Sylvia Harrop, the Didler, Ann and Tony Bennett-Hughes and others*

No Twenty 2
DARLINGTON NZ2814
DL3 7RG
Coniscliffe Road

Long bistro-feel Victorian pub with high ceiling, bare boards and exposed brickwork, up to 22 beers on handpump including own Village ales (brewed by Hambleton), draught continentals, decent lunchtime food in compact panelled back room, good friendly service; open all day, closed Sun. *Recommended by Mark Brittain, Julian Pigg, Peter Abbott*

☆ **Dipton Mill Inn**
DIPTONMILL NY9261
NE46 1YA
S of Hexham; off B6306 at Slaley

Small two-roomed pub tucked away in little hamlet, five good own-brewed Hexhamshire beers, Weston's cider, lots of wines by the glass, 20 malt whiskies, neatly kept snug bar, dark ply panelling, low ceilings, red furnishings, two open fires, good homely food and prompt friendly service; no credit cards; children welcome, seats in sunken crazy-paved terrace by restored mill stream or in attractively planted garden with aviary, nice walk through woods along little valley; Hexham racecourse nearby, closed Sun evening.
Recommended by Eric Larkham, the Didler, Lawrence Pearse, GSB, Claes Mauroy and others

Colpitts
DURHAM NZ2642
DH1 4EG
Colpitts Terrace/Hawthorn Terrace

Comfortable two-bar traditional backstreet pub, friendly landlady and locals, cheap well kept Sam Smiths, open fires and original Victorian fittings, back pool room; seats in yard, open all day. *Recommended by the Didler, Phil and Sally Gorton, Mr and Mrs Maurice Thompson*

DURHAM NZ2742   DH1 3AW
Court
Court Lane

Comfortable town pub with good hearty home-made food all day from sandwiches to steaks and late-evening bargains, real ales such as Bass, Marstons Pedigree and Mordue, friendly helpful staff, extensive stripped-brick eating area, no mobile phones; bustling in term-time with students and teachers, piped music; seats outside, open all day.
Recommended by Eric Larkham, Mike and Lynn Robinson, P and D Carpenter

DURHAM NZ2742   DH1 3HN
☆ Dun Cow
Old Elvet

Unchanging backstreet pub in pretty 16th-c black-and-white timbered cottage, cheerful licensees, tiny chatty front bar with wall benches, corridor to long narrow back lounge with banquettes, machines etc (can be packed with students), particularly well kept Camerons and other ales such as Black Sheep and Caledonian Deuchars IPA, good value basic lunchtime snacks, decent coffee; piped music; children welcome, open all day except Sun in winter. *Recommended by Eric Larkham, the Didler, Phil and Sally Gorton*

DURHAM NZ2642   DH1 4PS
Old Elm Tree
Crossgate

Comfortable friendly pub on steep hill across from castle, two-room main bar and small lounge, four well kept local ales (occasional beer festivals), reasonably priced home-made food, open fires, folk and quiz nights; dogs welcome, small back terrace. *Recommended by Phil and Sally Gorton, Mr and Mrs Maurice Thompson*

DURHAM NZ2742   DH1 3NU
Shakespeare
Saddler Street

Unchanging pub with signed actor photographs in busy basic front bar, charming panelled snug and neatly refurbished back room, well kept Caledonian Deuchars IPA, Fullers London Pride and two guests, simple cheap bar snacks, friendly staff, pub and board games; children (till 6pm) and dogs welcome, convenient for castle, cathedral and river, open all day. *Recommended by the Didler, Eric Larkham*

DURHAM NZ2742   DH1 3AG
Swan & Three Cygnets
Elvet Bridge

Refurbished Victorian pub in good bridge-end spot high above river, city views from big windows and picnic-sets out on terrace, bargain lunchtime food and Sam Smiths OB, helpful personable young staff; open all day. *Recommended by the Didler, Phil and Sally Gorton, Peter Smith and Judith Brown*

EGLINGHAM NU1019   NE66 2TX
Tankerville Arms
B6346 Alnwick—Wooler

Traditional pub with contemporary touches, cosy friendly atmosphere, beams, bare boards, some stripped stone, banquettes, warm fires, well kept local ales like Hadrian & Border and Wylam, nice wines, good imaginative food from changing menu, raftered split-level restaurant; children welcome, nice views from garden, three bedrooms, attractive village. *Recommended by Comus and Sarah Elliott, John and Sylvia Harrop*

Virtually all pubs in the *Good Pub Guide* sell wine by the glass. We mention wines
if they are a cut above the average.

ELWICK NZ4532   TS27 3EF
McOrville
0.25 miles off A19 W of Hartlepool

Open-plan dining pub with good blackboard food, Black Sheep and a changing ale, carved panelling, slippers provided for walkers. *Recommended by JHBS*

ELWICK NZ4533   TS27 3EF
Spotted Cow
0.25 miles off A19 W of Hartlepool

18th-c two-bar pub facing village green, three real ales, good food (not Sun evening), lounge and dining room, Weds quiz night. *Recommended by JHBS*

EMBLETON NU2322   NE66 3UY
Greys
Stanley Terrace, off W T Stead Road, turn at the Blue Bell

Carpeted main front bar with pubby furniture, more lived-in part with old photographs and cuttings, cottagey back dining room, open fires, well priced home-made food from sandwiches and pizzas to good specials including local fish, four well kept changing local ales, afternoon teas; small walled back garden, raised decking with village views. *Recommended by Andy and Jill Kassube, Michael Doswell*

FALSTONE NY7287   NE48 1AA
Blackcock
E of Yarrow and Kielder Water

Cosy, clean and friendly 17th-c inn, homely bar with beams and open fires, well kept ales such as Camerons, High House Farm and their own cheap Blackcock, bottled beers, Webster's cider, 50 malt whiskies, lunchtime bar food, evening restaurant with good vegetarian choice, pool room; quiet juke box; children allowed, dogs very welcome (own menu), garden with covered smokers' area, six bedrooms, handy for Kielder Water, open all day weekends, closed winter weekday lunchtimes (all day Weds). *Recommended by Alan Sutton*

FRAMWELLGATE MOOR NZ2644   DH1 5EE
Tap & Spile
Front Street; B6532 just N of Durham

Thriving two-bar pub with fine range of well kept changing local ales, farm ciders, good friendly staff, warm and comfortable atmosphere, pub and board games; children welcome. *Recommended by Jeff Brunton*

GATESHEAD NZ2559   NE9 6JA
Aletaster
Durham Road (A167), Low Fell

Great range of real ales and friendly helpful staff, traditional pub, Newcastle United memorabilia; TV. *Recommended by Mike Gerrard*

GATESHEAD NZ2563   NE8 2AN
Central
Half Moon Lane

Large multi-room pub recently renovated by the Head of Steam chain, good choice of changing ales, lots of bottled beers, real ciders, low-priced food including themed evenings, roof terrace, live music; open all day (till 1am Fri, Sat). *Recommended by Eric Larkham, Peter Smith and Judith Brown*

Half pints: by law, a pub should not charge more for half a pint than half the price of a full pint, unless it shows that half-pint price on its price list.

GREAT WHITTINGTON NZ0070   NE19 2HP

☆ Queens Head

Village signed off A68 and B6018 N of Corbridge

Handsome golden-stone pub with dark leather chairs around sturdy tables, one or two good pictures on stripped-stone or grey/green walls, soft lighting, Caledonian Deuchars IPA, Hadrian & Border and Jennings, several malt whiskies, nice hunting mural above old fireplace in long narrow bar, much emphasis on popular food (not Sun evening) in tartan-carpeted dining areas with modern furnishings, friendly efficient staff; piped music; children and dogs welcome, picnic-sets under parasols on little front lawn, open all day Fri-Sun. *Recommended by GSB, Michael Doswell, Graham Oddey, John Prescott*

HART NZ4634   TS27 3AW

White Hart

Just off A179 W of Hartlepool; Front Street

Interesting nautical-theme pub with old ship's figurehead outside, fires in both bars, food from landlady-chef, two changing real ales; open all day (closed Mon afternoon). *Recommended by JHBS*

HARTLEPOOL NZ5132   TS24 7ED

Rat Race

Hartlepool Station

Former station newsagents, one small room (no bar), four well kept changing ales, real cider and perry, you can bring your own food, newspapers; open all day Sat till 8pm, closed Sun and four hours either side of home football matches. *Recommended by Arthur Pickering, JHBS*

HAWTHORN NZ4145   SR7 8SD

Stapylton Arms

Off B1432 S of A19 Murton exit

Chatty carpeted bar with old local photographs, enjoyable food from sandwiches to steaks and Sun roasts, one well kept changing ale, friendly service; dogs welcome, nice wooded walk to sea (joins Durham Coastal Path). *Recommended by JHBS*

HIGH HESLEDEN NZ4538   TS27 4QD

Ship

Off A19 via B1281

Half a dozen good value changing ales from the region, log fire, sailing ship models including a big one hanging with lanterns from boarded ceiling, landlady cooks enjoyable bar food and some interesting restaurant dishes; yacht and shipping views from car park, six bedrooms in new block, closed Mon. *Recommended by JHBS*

HOLY ISLAND NU1241   TD15 2RX

Crown & Anchor

Causeway passable only at low tide, check times: (01289) 330733

Comfortably unpretentious pub/restaurant, enjoyable food from shortish menu including good fish and chips, Wells & Youngs Bombardier and Caledonian Deuchars IPA, welcoming helpful staff, compact bar, roomy modern back dining room; dogs welcome, enclosed garden with picnic-sets, bedrooms. *Recommended by Mr and Mrs D J Nash, Dr A McCormick, Jean and Douglas Troup*

HURWORTH-ON-TEES NZ2814   DL2 2AQ

Bay Horse

Church Row

Welcoming dining pub with top-notch imaginative food, quite pricey but they offer a fixed-price lunch menu, children's choices too, three real ales, smiling efficient young staff, sizeable bar with good open fire, restaurant; seats on back terrace and in well tended walled garden beyond, charming village by River Tees. *Recommended by Peter Thompson, Michael Doswell, Jill and Julian Tasker*

LANGDON BECK NY8531
Langdon Beck Hotel
DL12 0XP
B6277 Middleton—Alston

Isolated unpretentious inn with two cosy bars and spacious lounge, well placed for walks and Pennine Way, Black Sheep, Jarrow and a guest ale (late May beer festival), good choice of enjoyable generous food including good local teesdale beef and lamb, decent coffee, helpful friendly staff; garden with wonderful fell views, bedrooms, open all day, closed Mon winter. *Recommended by Roxanne Chamberlain, Mr and Mrs Maurice Thompson, M and J White, John H Smith*

LEAMSIDE NZ3147
Three Horseshoes
DH4 6QQ
Pit House Lane

Popular welcoming pub with enjoyable food all day including bargain two-course lunch, five changing ales, good wine and whisky choice, bright airy dining room. *Recommended by David Hughes, Tim Skelton*

☆ LESBURY NU2311
Coach
NE66 3PP
B1339

Welcoming attractively refurbished stone pub at heart of pretty village, Black Sheep and Mordue, generous helpings of well liked food all day (till 7pm Sun), good service, pubby tables and stools in tartan-carpeted low-beamed bar, small left-hand area with sofas and armchairs, compact dining room with high-backed cane and leather dining chairs around light wood tables, yet another seating area with woodburner; piped music; TV; no small children after 7.30pm, rustic furniture under parasols on neat terrace, tubs and hanging baskets, handy for Alnwick Castle Gardens, open all day, but closed Sun evening Oct-March. *Recommended by Michael Doswell, P A Rowe, Dr Peter D Smart, Comus and Sarah Elliott and others*

LONGHORSLEY NZ1597
Linden Tree
NE65 8XF
N of Longhorsley on A697

Former granary behind country house conference hotel in extensive grounds; comfortable bar and light conservatory restaurant, enjoyable food, Greene King ales, good wines by the glass, efficient uniformed staff; children welcome, terrace tables, bedrooms in main hotel, golf course, open all day from 9.30am. *Recommended by Comus and Sarah Elliott*

LONGHORSLEY NZ1494
Shoulder of Mutton
NE65 8SY
East Road; A697 N of Morpeth

Comfortable bar and restaurant, welcoming landlady, good choice of generous home-made food including some imaginative dishes, Courage Directors, Caledonian Deuchars IPA and Everards Tiger, good selection of other drinks, Tues quiz night; piped music; children welcome, tables outside. *Recommended by JJW, CMW, Robert Wivell*

MIDDLESTONE NZ2531
Ship
DL14 8AB
Low Road

Half a dozen well kept interesting ales including local ones, welcoming licensees and bustling friendly atmosphere, standard good value pub food, oak boards and nice fire, May beer festival and lots of other events including Thurs quiz, darts; piped music; good view from roof terrace, closed till 4pm Mon-Thurs, otherwise open all day. *Recommended by Mr and Mrs Maurice Thompson, Andrew Quinn*

Though we don't usually mention it in the text, most pubs now provide coffee or tea - so it's always worth asking.

MILFIELD NT9333 NE71 6JD
Red Lion
Main Road (A697 Wooler—Cornhill)

Welcoming 17th-c former coaching inn with good sensibly priced food (may be local game) from chef/landlord, well kept Black Sheep and Wylam, organic wine, good service; pretty garden by car park at back. *Recommended by Comus and Sarah Elliott, Michael Doswell, M Mossman*

NETHERTON NT9807 NE65 7HD
Star
Off B6341 at Thropton, or A697 via Whittingham

Simple unchanging village local under charming long-serving landlady (licence has been in her family since 1917), welcoming regulars, Camerons Strongarm tapped from cellar casks and served from hatch in small entrance lobby, large high-ceilinged room with wall benches, many original features; no food, music, children or dogs; closed lunchtime, open from 7pm, closed Mon, Thurs. *Recommended by Eric Larkham, the Didler*

NEW YORK NZ3269 NE29 8DZ
☆ Shiremoor Farm
Middle Engine Lane; at W end of New York A191 bypass turn S into Norham Road, then first right (pub signed)

Incredibly busy dining pub – the transformation of derelict agricultural buildings with several well divided spacious areas, beams and joists (the conical rafters of former gin-gan in one part), broad flagstones, several kelims, a mix of interesting and comfortable furniture, farm tools, shields and swords, country pictures, wide range of customers of all ages, bar quieter and more civilised, Mordue and Timothy Taylors, good wines by the glass, enjoyable popular food all day, efficient service even when busy; picnic-sets on heated terrace. *Recommended by Lawrence Pearse, Sheena W Makin, Mike and Lynn Robinson, GSB*

NEWBURN NZ1665 NE15 8ND
☆ Keelman
Grange Road: follow Riverside Country Park brown signs off A6085

Converted 19th-c pumping station, eight well kept/priced Big Lamp beers from on-site brewery, relaxed atmosphere and good mix of customers, high-ceilinged airy bar with lofty arched windows and well spaced tables and chairs, upper gallery with more seats, modern all-glass conservatory dining area, straightforward food; piped music; children welcome, plenty of tables on spacious terraces among flower tubs and baskets, good play area, bedrooms, open all day. *Recommended by David and Sue Smith, Stuart and Sarah Barrie, Eric Larkham, GSB, Joe Green*

NEWCASTLE UPON TYNE NZ2464 NE1 6BX
☆ Bacchus
High Bridge E, between Pilgrim Street and Grey Street

Smart, spacious and comfortable with ocean liner look, ship and shipbuilding photographs, good lunchtime food from sandwiches and panini through pubby things to some interesting specials, Sun roasts, keen prices, great choice of well kept changing ales, plenty of bottled imports, farm cider, decent coffee, relaxed civilised atmosphere (but busy on match days), pleasant staff; disabled facilities, handy for Theatre Royal, open all day. *Recommended by Eric Larkham, Michael Doswell, Peter Smith and Judith Brown, Henry Paulinski, Derek Wason and others*

NEWCASTLE UPON TYNE NZ2464 NE1 4AG
Bodega
Westgate Road

Majestic Edwardian drinking hall next to Tyne Theatre, Big Lamp Prince Bishop, Durham Magus and six interesting guests, farm cider, friendly service, colourful walls and ceiling, bare boards, snug front cubicles, spacious back area with two magnificent stained-glass cupolas; piped music, machines, big-screen TV, very busy on Newcastle United match days; open all day. *Recommended by Eric Larkham, Jeremy King*

NEWCASTLE UPON TYNE NZ2563

NE1 1RQ

☆ **Bridge Hotel**

Castle Square, next to high-level bridge

Big cheery well divided high-ceilinged bar around servery with replica slatted snob screens, well kept changing ales, farm cider, friendly staff, bargain generous lunchtime food (not Sat), Sun afternoon teas, magnificent fireplace, great river and bridge views from raised back area; sports TV, piped music, games machines, live music upstairs including long-standing Mon folk club; flagstoned back terrace overlooking part of old town wall, open all day. *Recommended by Eric Larkham, James Thompson, Andy Lickfold, the Didler, Graham Oddey and others*

NEWCASTLE UPON TYNE NZ2464

NE1 5HL

Centurion

Central Station, Neville Street

Glorious high-ceilinged Victorian décor with tilework and columns in former first-class waiting room, well restored with comfortable leather seats giving club-like feel, Black Sheep and local ales such as Allendale and Jarrow, farm cider, friendly staff; piped music, unobtrusive sports TV; useful deli next door. *Recommended by Mike and Eleanor Anderson, Eric Larkham, Mike and Lynn Robinson, Tony and Wendy Hobden*

NEWCASTLE UPON TYNE NZ2664

NE1 2PQ

☆ **Cluny**

Lime Street

Trendy bar/café in interesting 19th-c mill/warehouse, striking setting below Metro bridge, good value home-made food all day from massive sandwiches up, cheerful staff, up to eight well kept ales including Banks's and Big Lamp, exotic beers and rums, sofas in comfortable raised area with daily papers and local art magazines, back gallery with artwork from studios in same complex; piped music, good live music nightly; children welcome till 7pm, picnic-sets out on green, open all day. *Recommended by Alex and Claire Pearse, Eric Larkham, James Thompson, Mike and Lynn Robinson*

NEWCASTLE UPON TYNE NZ2563

NE1 3JE

☆ **Crown Posada**

The Side; off Dean Street, between and below the two high central bridges (A6125 and A6127)

Popular unchanging city-centre pub with grand architecture, long narrow room with elaborate coffered ceiling, stained glass in counter screens, line of gilt mirrors each with tulip lamp on curly brass mount (matching the great ceiling candelabra), long built-in green leather wall seat flanked by narrow tables, fat low-level heating pipes, old working record player in wooden cabinet, six well kept ales, lunchtime sandwiches, helpful staff and good mix of regular customers (packed at peak times); piped music; only a stroll to castle, open all day, but closed Sun lunchtime. *Recommended by Mike and Eleanor Anderson, Eric Larkham, James Thompson, Myke and Nicky Crombleholme, the Didler, P Dawn and others*

NEWCASTLE UPON TYNE NZ2664

NE6 1LD

Cumberland Arms

Byker Buildings

Friendly unspoilt traditional local, seven particularly well kept mainly local ales (straight from the cask if you wish) including a house beer from Wylam, eight farm ciders, beer/cider festivals, good value pubby food all day, obliging staff; live music or other events most nights (regular ukulele band), tables out overlooking Ouseburn Valley, four bedrooms, closed Mon lunchtime otherwise open all day. *Recommended by Eric Larkham, Mike and Lynn Robinson, the Didler*

All *Guide* inspections are anonymous. Anyone claiming to be a *Good Pub Guide* inspector is a fraud. Please let us know.

NEWCASTLE UPON TYNE NZ2470   NE3 5EH

Falcons Nest

Rotary Way, Gosforth – handy for racecourse

Roomy Vintage Inn with comfortably olde-worlde linked rooms, good value food, pleasant staff, good choice of wines by the glass, well kept Black Sheep and Timothy Taylors Landlord; open all day, bedrooms in adjacent Innkeepers Lodge. *Recommended by Dr Peter D Smart*

NEWCASTLE UPON TYNE NZ2664   NE6 1AP

Free Trade

St Lawrence Road, off Walker Road (A186)

Splendidly basic proper pub with outstanding views up river from big windows, terrace tables and seats on grass, real ales such as High House, Jarrow and Mordue, good sandwiches, warmly friendly atmosphere, real fire, original Formica tables; steps down to back room and lavatories; open all day. *Recommended by Eric Larkham*

NEWCASTLE UPON TYNE NZ2464   NE1 5SE

Newcastle Arms

St Andrew's Street

Open-plan drinkers' pub on fringe of Chinatown, Caledonian Deuchars IPA and five quickly changing guests including a porter or stout, farm ciders and perries, beer festivals, friendly staff, interesting old local photographs; piped music, big-screen sports TV, can get very busy especially on match days; open all day. *Recommended by Eric Larkham, Mr and Mrs Maurice Thompson, Ab Hamed*

NEWTON NZ0364   NE43 7UL

Duke of Wellington

Off A69 E of Corbridge

Extensively refurbished old stone inn in attractive farming hamlet, good interesting well presented food, real ales, large open L-shaped bar/dining area, comfortable mix of modern and traditional furnishings, sofas and armchairs in one corner, woodburner, daily papers, darts; dogs welcome in bar area, back terrace, seven bedrooms. *Recommended by Mourveen Scott, W K Wood, Graham Oddey*

NEWTON ON THE MOOR NU1705   NE65 9JY

☆ Cook & Barker Arms

Village signed from A1 Alnwick—Felton

Nicely traditional stone-built country inn, beamed bar with stripped-stone and partly panelled walls, broad-seated settles around oak-topped tables, horsebrasses, coal fires, Black Sheep, Timothy Taylors and a guest beer, extensive wine list, popular food using own-farm meat (early-bird deal midweek evenings), friendly helpful staff, separate restaurant with french windows opening on to terrace; piped music, TV; children welcome, comfortable bedrooms, open all day. *Recommended by J A Snell, Bruce and Sharon Eden, John and Angie Millar, P A Rowe, Jenny and Peter Lowater, John and Sylvia Harrop and others*

NEWTON-BY-THE-SEA NU2424   NE66 3EL

☆ Ship

Village signed off B1339 N of Alnwick

In charming square of fishermen's cottages by green sloping to sandy beach, plainly furnished but cosy bare-boards bar, nautical charts on dark pink walls, simple room on left with beams, hop bines, bright modern pictures on stripped-stone walls and woodburner in stone fireplace, own-brewed ales, real cider and tasty bar food (good crab sandwiches), live folk, blues and jazz; no credit cards, can get very busy; children and dogs welcome, seats among flowering pots on edge of square and picnic-sets on green, no nearby parking (unless disabled), open all day in summer, phone for winter hours (01665) 576262. *Recommended by Penny and Peter Keevil, James Thompson, Andy and Jill Kassube, Mike and Sue Loseby, Comus and Sarah Elliott, the Didler and others*

NORTH SHIELDS NZ3568
Magnesia Bank
Camden Street
NE30 1NH

Lively well run pub in former bank, Caledonian Deuchars IPA, Durham Magus, Theakstons Old Peculier and guests, good value pubby food, friendly staff, bare boards, cherry walls and green button-back banquettes, regular live music; children welcome, open all day. *Recommended by Michael Doswell*

PONTELAND NZ1771
Badger
Street Houses; A696 SE, by garden centre
NE20 9BT

Vintage Inn with relaxing rooms and alcoves, old furnishings and olde-worlde décor, good log fire, five well kept beers such as Black Sheep, Leeds and Timothy Taylors, decent range of wines by the glass, standard food all day, prompt friendly service; piped music; children welcome. *Recommended by Dr Peter D Smart*

PONTELAND NZ1773
Blackbird
North Road
NE20 9UH

Imposing recently refurbished old pub opposite church, stylish open-plan interior with mix of furniture including striped tub chairs and button-backed banquettes, unframed prints, skilful lighting, good imaginative food attracting attention, nice lunchtime sandwiches too, including rare roast beef. *Recommended by Michael Doswell, Peter and Eleanor Kenyon*

RENNINGTON NU2118
☆ Horseshoes
B1340
NE66 3RS

Comfortable family-run flagstoned pub with nice local feel (may be horses in car park), well kept ales such as Hadrian & Border and John Smiths, good value generous food including two-course lunch deals, good local fish and meat, decent wines by the glass, friendly efficient unrushed service, simple neat bar with woodburner, spotless compact restaurant; children welcome, tables outside, attractive quiet village near coast, closed Mon. *Recommended by Guy and Caroline Howard, Mike and Lynn Robinson, Dr Peter D Smart*

RENNINGTON NU2118
☆ Masons Arms
Stamford Cott; B1340 N
NE66 3RX

Comfortably carpeted beamed bar with neat pubby furniture, well kept ales such as Black Sheep, Hadrian & Border, High House Farm and Northumberland, good malt whisky range, enjoyable straightforward food, smiling relaxed service, brassware, flintlock pistols etc, woodburner between bar and family room; tables on lavender-edged roadside terrace, more picnic-sets behind, comfortable bedrooms in former stables block. *Recommended by George Cowie, Frances Gosnell, Michael Butler, the Dutchman, Ann and Tony Bennett-Hughes, John Beeken*

ROOKHOPE NY9342
Rookhope Inn
Off A689 W of Stanhope
DL13 2BG

Friendly old inn on coast-to-coast bike route, real ales such as Black Sheep and Timothy Taylors Landlord, enjoyable home-made food from fresh sandwiches to good Sun roasts, black beams and open fires, small dining room; sports TV; seats outside, spectacular views, five bedrooms. *Recommended by Andy and Jill Kassube, Claes Mauroy*

The letters and figures after the name of each town are its Ordnance Survey map reference. 'Using the *Guide*' explains how it helps you find a pub, in road atlases or on large-scale maps as well as in our own maps.

SEATON NZ3950   SR7 0LP
Seaton Lane Inn
Seaton Lane

Contemporary roadside bar/restaurant/hotel, popular with locals, good choice of
enjoyable food (all day) from sandwiches and pub favourites up including two-course set
menu, well kept Mordue, Theakstons and Wells & Youngs, lounge and restaurant on split
levels, attentive staff; 18 bedrooms. *Recommended by Mr and Mrs Maurice Thompson, Barry Moses,
Mike and Lynn Robinson*

SEDGEFIELD NZ3528   TS21 3AT
Dun Cow
Front Street

Popular refurbished village inn with low-beamed bar, back tap room and dining room,
above-average food including good Sun roast, cheerful efficient staff, well kept ales such
as Black Sheep and Camerons; children welcome, reasonably priced comfortable
bedrooms, good breakfast. *Recommended by John and Sylvia Harrop, Andy Cole*

SHINCLIFFE NZ2940   DH1 2NU
☆ Seven Stars
High Street N (A177 S of Durham)

Comfortable old-fashioned 18th-c village inn, varied choice of good food from pub
favourites to gently upmarket dishes, good value set menus, four well kept ales including
Black Sheep, coal fire and plenty of atmosphere in lounge bar, candlelit panelled dining
room, caring service from licensees; children in eating areas, dogs in bar, some picnic-sets
outside, eight bedrooms, open all day. *Recommended by Bruce and Sharon Eden, Richard and
Stephanie Foskett, Tim Tomlinson*

SLALEY NY9658   NE46 1TT
☆ Travellers Rest
B6306 S of Hexham (and N of village)

Attractive and busy stone-built country pub, spaciously opened up, with farmhouse-style
décor, beams, flagstones and polished wood floors, huge fireplace, comfortable high-
backed settles forming discrete areas, friendly uniformed staff, popular fairly standard
food (not Sun evening) in bar and appealingly up-to-date dining room, good children's
menu, basic sandwiches, friendly staff, real ales such as Allendale, Black Sheep and
Wylam, limited wines by the glass; dogs welcome, tables outside with well equipped
adventure play area on grass behind, three good value bedrooms, open all day.
Recommended by Mr and Mrs Maurice Thompson, GSB

SOUTH SHIELDS NZ3666   NE33 4PG
Maltings
Claypath Road

Former dairy now home to Jarrow brewery, their full range and guest ales from upstairs
bar (showpiece staircase); open all day, no food Fri-Sun evenings. *Recommended by
Eric Larkham*

SOUTH SHIELDS NZ3767   NE33 2LD
Sand Dancer
Sea Road

Great location on beach, with views from raised terrace, decent well priced food including
fresh fish and lobster tank, rustic décor, friendly staff and good atmosphere. *Recommended
by John Coatsworth*

Most pubs with any outside space now have some kind of smokers' shelter. There are
regulations about these – for instance, they have to be substantially open to the outside air.
The best have heating and lighting and are really quite comfortable.

STAMFORDHAM NZ0772   NE18 0PB
Bay Horse
Off B6309

Refurbished beamed and stone-built pub at end of green in attractive village, good fresh food from new owners (both chefs) with emphasis on local produce, well kept ales, bare-boards bar area with woodburner, restaurant; bedrooms. *Recommended by Michael Doswell*

STANNINGTON NZ2179   NE61 6EL
☆ Ridley Arms
Village signed off A1 S of Morpeth

Attractive extended 18th-c stone pub with several linked rooms, each with slightly different mood and style, proper front bar with stools along counter, Black Sheep, Caledonian, Derwent and Jarrow, beamed dining areas with comfortable bucket armchairs around dark tables on bare boards or carpet, cartoons and portraits on cream, panelled or stripped-stone walls, bar food (not Sun evening) from sandwiches up (mixed reports lately); piped music, fruit machine; children welcome, good disabled access, front picnic-sets by road, more on back terrace, open all day. *Recommended by Michael Doswell, Dr Peter D Smart, Eric Larkham, GSB, Comus and Sarah Elliott and others*

WARDEN NY9166   NE46 4SQ
Boatside
0.5 miles N of A69

Cheerful attractively modernised old stone-built pub with enjoyable pubby food, well kept ales and good friendly service; children and muddy walkers welcome, small neat enclosed garden, attractive spot by Tyne bridge, bedrooms in adjoining cottages. *Recommended by Angela*

WARENFORD NU1429   NE70 7HY
White Swan
Off A1 S of Belford

Simply decorated friendly bar with changing ales such as Adnams and Black Sheep, steps down to cosy restaurant with good imaginative food including prettily presented puddings, good value set lunch, efficient helpful service, warm fires; dogs welcome. *Recommended by Mr J V Nelson, Mr and Mrs J P Syner, Michael Doswell*

WARKWORTH NU2406   NE65 0UL
Hermitage
Castle Street

Rambling local (former coaching inn) doing tasty home-made food (all day Mon-Sat) such as rabbit pie, Jennings ales, friendly staff, quaint décor with old range for heating, small upstairs restaurant; piped music; children welcome, benches out in front, attractive setting, five bedrooms. *Recommended by Ann and Tony Bennett-Hughes*

WARKWORTH NU2406   NE65 0UR
Masons Arms
Dial Place

Welcoming village pub in shadow of castle, enjoyable food including daily specials and Sun carvery, local beers, friendly staff, Tues quiz night; dogs and children welcome, disabled facilities, back flagstoned courtyard, appealing village not far from sea, open all day. *Recommended by Guy and Caroline Howard, Clive Flynn*

WEST BOLDON NZ3460   NE36 0PZ
Red Lion
Redcar Terrace

Bow-widowed and flower-decked family-run pub, hop-strung beamed bar with open fire, ales such as Mordue Workie Ticket from ornate wood counter, separate snug and conservatory dining room, good choice of well priced pubby food; seats out on back decking, open all day. *Recommended by Roger and Donna Huggins*

WHITLEY BAY NZ3473   NE26 1UE
Briar Dene
The Links

Smart brightly decorated two-room pub, fine sea-view spot, with up to eight interesting changing ales, good value pubby food from sandwiches up, friendly efficient staff; children welcome, seats outside, open all day. *Recommended by Eric Larkham, Dr Peter D Smart, Henry Paulinski, Guy and Caroline Howard*

WIDDRINGTON NZ2596   NE61 5DY
Widdrington Inn
Off A1068 S of Amble

Open-plan busy family pub, comfortably carpeted and popular for good value fresh food all day, good friendly staff, beers including John Smiths, reasonably priced wines by the glass; open all day. *Recommended by Jean and Douglas Troup*

WOLVISTON NZ4525   TS22 5JX
Ship
High Street

Gabled red-brick Victorian pub in centre of bypassed village, open-plan multi-level carpeted bar, bargain food, changing real ales from northern breweries, quiz nights; garden. *Recommended by JHBS*

WOOLER NT9928   NE71 6AD
Tankerville Arms
A697 N

Pleasant hotel bar in modernised early 17th-c coaching inn, relaxed and friendly, with reasonably priced food including local meat and fish, ales such as Hadrian & Border, good wines by the glass, small restaurant and larger airy one overlooking nice garden, big log fire; disabled facilities, 16 bedrooms, good local walks. *Recommended by Comus and Sarah Elliott, Dr Peter D Smart*

WYLAM NZ1164   NE41 8HR
☆ ## Boathouse

Station Road, handy for Newcastle—Carlisle rail line; across Tyne from village (and Stephenson's birthplace)

Thriving convivial pub with splendid ale range including local Wylam, keen prices, good choice of malt whiskies, bargain weekend lunches, polite helpful young staff, open stove in bright low-beamed bar, dining room; children and dogs welcome, seats outside, close to station and river, open all day. *Recommended by Mr and Mrs Maurice Thompson, Eric Larkham, the Didler*

ALSO WORTH A VISIT IN YORKSHIRE

Besides the region's top pubs, we recommend the following. Do tell us
what you think of them: **feedback@goodguides.com**

ABERFORD SE4337   LS25 3AA
Swan
Best to use A642 junction to leave A1; Main Street N

Busy dining pub (may have to wait for a table), vast choice of good generous food from
sandwiches to bargain carvery, lots of black timber, prints, pistols, cutlasses and stuffed
animals, well kept Black Sheep and Tetleys, generous glasses of wine, good friendly
uniformed service, upstairs evening restaurant; children welcome, tables outside.
Recommended by Pete Coxon, Ed and Anna Fraser

ADDINGHAM SE0749   LS29 0LY
☆ Fleece
Main Street

Comfortable two-level pub, nice farmhouse-style eating area with good value home-made
food from hearty sandwiches (home-baked bread) to interesting blackboard choices using
good local ingredients (some from own back allotment), popular all-day Sun roasts,
friendly service, well kept Yorkshire ales, good choice of wines by the glass, low ceilings,
flagstones and log fire, plain tap room with darts and dominoes, quiz nights Tues, trad
jazz Weds; very busy weekends (worth booking then); children and dogs welcome, lots of
picnic-sets on front terrace, open all day. *Recommended by Gordon and Margaret Ormondroyd,
Jeremy King, John and Sylvia Harrop, Tina and David Woods-Taylor, Peter and Judy Frost and others*

ALDBOROUGH SE4166   YO51 9ER
Ship
Off B6265 just S of Boroughbridge, close to A1

Attractive 14th-c beamed village dining pub, enjoyable food and good service, Greene
King, John Smiths and Theakstons, some old-fashioned seats around cast-iron-framed
tables, lots of copper and brass, inglenook fire, restaurant; a few picnic-sets outside,
handy for Roman remains and museum, bedrooms, open all day Sun, closed Mon
lunchtime. *Recommended by Susan Davey, NS Orr*

APPLETON-LE-MOORS SE7388   YO62 6TF
☆ Moors
N of A170, just under 1.5 miles E of Kirkby Moorside

Traditional stone-built village pub, beamed bar with built-in high-backed settle next to
old kitchen fireplace, plenty of other seating, some sparse decorations (a few copper
pans, earthenware mugs, country ironwork), Black Sheep and Timothy Taylors, tasty bar
food (all day Sun), darts; piped music; children and dogs welcome, tables in lovely walled
garden with quiet country views, walks to Rosedale Abbey or Hartoft End, paths to
Hutton-le-Hole, Cropton and Sinnington, bedrooms, open all day. *Recommended by Greta and
Christopher Wells, Ann and Tony Bennett-Hughes, Ed and Anna Fraser*

APPLETREEWICK SE0560   BD23 6DA
☆ Craven Arms
Off B6160 Burnsall—Bolton Abbey

Character creeper-covered 17th-c beamed pub, comfortably down-to-earth settles and
rugs on flagstones, oak panelling, fire in old range, good friendly service, up to eight well
kept ales, good choice of wines by the glass, home-made food from baguettes up, small
dining room and splendid thatched and raftered barn extension with gallery; children,
dogs and boots welcome (plenty of surrounding walks), nice country views from front
picnic-sets, more seats in back garden, open all day Weds-Sun. *Recommended by WW, John and
Eleanor Holdsworth, Dr Kevan Tucker*

APPLETREEWICK SE0560   BD23 6DA
New Inn
W end of main village

Unpretentious warmly welcoming country local with lovely views, six well kept ales including Black Sheep and Daleside, good choice of continental bottled beers, generous tasty home cooking, distinctive décor, interesting old local photographs; children and dogs welcome, three garden areas, good walking, five bedrooms and nearby camping, open all day. *Recommended by Dr Kevan Tucker, John and Helen Rushton*

ARTHINGTON SE2644   LS21 1NL
Wharfedale
A659 E of Otley (Arthington Lane)

Good value food from sandwiches and pub staples to popular Sun lunch, four ales including Black Sheep and Copper Dragon, several wines by the glass, efficient friendly service, spacious open-plan bar, lots of dark wood and some intimate alcoves, separate restaurant in long, beamed room; disabled facilities, big garden with terrace, three bedrooms, open all day. *Recommended by Richard Meek, Jeremy King*

ASENBY SE3975   YO7 3QL
☆ Crab & Lobster
Dishforth Road; village signed off A168 – handy for A1

Most emphasis on civilised hotel and restaurant side, but has rambling L-shaped bar with Copper Dragon and Theakstons, interesting jumble of seats from antique high-backed settles through sofas to rather theatrical corner seats, mix of tables too and a jungle of bric-a-brac, especially good (not cheap) food in smart main restaurant and dining pavilion (big tropical plants), live jazz Sun lunchtime; well behaved children allowed, seats on mediterranean-style terrace, opulent bedrooms in surrounding house with seven acres of gardens and 180-metre golf hole, open all day till midnight. *Recommended by Janet and Peter Race, Jon Clarke, Comus and Sarah Elliott, Dr D Jeary, Dr and Mrs R G J Telfer and others*

ASKRIGG SD9491   DL8 3HQ
☆ Kings Arms
Signed from A684 Leyburn—Sedbergh in Bainbridge

Great log fire in former coaching inn's flagstoned high-ceilinged main bar, traditional furnishings and décor, well kept ales such as Black Sheep, John Smiths and Theakstons, decent wines by the glass, good choice of malts, enjoyable food from sandwiches up, friendly staff, restaurant with inglenook, barrel-vaulted former beer cellar; piped music; children and dogs welcome, pleasant courtyard, bedrooms run separately as part of Holiday Property Bond complex behind, open all day weekends. *Recommended by Eric Ruff, Gordon and Margaret Ormondroyd*

ASKWITH SD1648   LS21 2JQ
Black Horse
Off A65

Biggish stone-built open-plan family pub in lovely spot (superb Wharfedale views from dining conservatory and good terrace), well kept Timothy Taylors Landlord, wide choice of enjoyable home-made food including Sun carvery, good service, woodburner; children welcome. *Recommended by Gordon and Margaret Ormondroyd, Robert Wivell*

AUSTWICK SD7668   LA2 8BB
☆ Game Cock
Just off A65 Settle—Kirkby Lonsdale

Quaint civilised place in a pretty spot below Three Peaks, good log fire in old-fashioned beamed bare-boards back bar, cheerful efficient staff and friendly locals, good choice of well kept ales, winter mulled wine, nice coffee, most space devoted to the food side, with good fairly priced choice from french chef/landlord including evening special offers, pizzas and children's meals as well, two dining rooms and modern front conservatory-type extension; walkers and dogs welcome, tables out in front with play area, three neat bedrooms, open all day Sun. *Recommended by Michael Lamm, Peter Fryer, David Heath, Martin Smith, John and Verna Aspinall*

AYSGARTH SE0088 DL8 3AD
George & Dragon
Just off A684

Welcoming 17th-c posting inn with emphasis on good varied food from sandwiches up, two big dining areas, small beamed and panelled bar with log fire, well kept Black Sheep Bitter, Theakstons Best and a beer brewed for the pub, good choice of wines by the glass; may be piped music; children welcome, nice paved garden, lovely scenery and walks, handy for Aysgarth Falls, seven bedrooms, open all day. *Recommended by Mr and Mrs Maurice Thompson, Keith Moss*

BAILDON SE1538 BD17 6AB
Junction
Baildon Road

Wedge-shaped traditional local with three linked rooms, friendly atmosphere, well kept Dark Star and changing microbrews, home-made weekday lunchtime food, live music and sing-alongs Sun evening, pool; open all day. *Recommended by the Didler, Andy Barker*

BARKISLAND SE0419 HX4 0DJ
Fleece
B6113 towards Ripponden

18th-c beamed moorland pub smartened up under new landlord, two rooms laid out for the enjoyable reasonably priced food including a set menu, good service, well kept Black Sheep, stripped stone, woodburner and open fire, mezzanine, brightly painted children's room with games; Pennine views from first-floor terrace and garden, bedrooms, handy for M62. *Recommended by Gordon and Margaret Ormondroyd*

BARMBY ON THE MARSH SE6828 DN14 7HT
Kings Head
High Street

Early 19th-c refurbished and extended beamed village pub, enjoyable locally sourced home-made food with some interesting choices, four ales including Black Sheep, good service, large restaurant, deli; children welcome, disabled facilities, open all day weekends, closed Mon and Tues lunchtimes. *Recommended by Ross Gibbins, Michael Butler*

BECK HOLE NZ8202 YO22 5LE
☆ ### Birch Hall
Off A169 SW of Whitby, from top of Sleights Moor

Tiny pub-cum-village-shop in stunning surroundings, two unchanging rooms (shop sells postcards, sweets and ice-creams), simple furnishings – built-in cushioned wall seats, wooden tables (one with 136 pennies embedded in the top), flagstones or composition flooring, unusual items like french breakfast cereal boxes, tube of toothpaste priced 1/3d and model train running around head-height shelf; Durham, Wentworth and a guest, bar snacks including local pies and cakes (lovely beer cake), exceptionally friendly service, dominoes and quoits; no credit cards; children in small family room, dogs welcome, old painting of river valley outside and benches, steps up to steeply terraced side garden, self-catering cottage, good walks – one along disused railway, open all day in summer, closed Mon evening in winter, all day Tues Nov-Mar. *Recommended by Comus and Sarah Elliott, the Didler, Kevin Thomas, Nina Randall, Matt and Vikki Wharton*

'Children welcome' means the pub says it lets children inside without any special restriction; some may impose an evening time limit earlier than 9pm – please tell us if you find this.

BEDALE SE2688   DL8 1ED
Old Black Swan
Market Place

Attractive façade, welcoming efficient staff, good choice of generously served straightforward food, well kept ales including Theakstons Old Peculier, log fire, darts, pool; sports TV; children welcome, disabled facilities, small back terrace, Tues market, open all day. *Recommended by Janet and Peter Race, Mike Horgan, Di Wright*

BEVERLEY TA0339   HU17 8BH
Dog & Duck
Ladygate

Cheerful popular two-bar local handy for playhouse and Sat market, good home-made lunchtime food using local produce from sandwiches to bargain Sun lunch, OAP deals too, well kept Caledonian Deuchars IPA, Copper Dragon, John Smiths and guests, good value wines, several malts, helpful friendly staff, coal fires; piped music, TV for racing, games machine; cheap basic courtyard bedrooms up iron stairs. *Recommended by the Didler, Mike and Lynn Robinson*

BEVERLEY TA0339   HU17 8BN
White Horse
Hengate, off North Bar

Carefully preserved Victorian interior with basic little rooms huddled around central bar, brown leatherette seats (high-backed settles in one little snug) and plain chairs and benches on bare boards, antique cartoons and sentimental engravings, gaslit chandelier, open fires, games room, upstairs family room, bargain Sam Smiths and guest beers, basic food; children till 7pm, open all day. *Recommended by the Didler, Huw Jones*

BEVERLEY TA0239   HU17 8EN
Woolpack
Westwood Road, W of centre

Small welcoming pub with no pretensions in a pair of 19th-c cottages, sound traditional food and well kept ales such as Jennings, cosy snug, real fires, simple furnishings, brasses, teapots, prints and maps; no nearby parking; open all day weekends, closed lunchtimes Mon and Tues. *Recommended by Pat and Graham Williamson*

BILBROUGH SE5346   YO23 3PH
Three Hares
Off A64 York—Tadcaster

Smart neatly kept village dining pub with enjoyable good value food all day, Sun roasts, well kept real ale, good choice of wines by the glass, leather sofas and log fire. *Recommended by Marlene and Jim Godfrey*

BIRSTALL SE2126   WF17 9HE
Black Bull
Kirkgate, off A652; head down hill towards church

Medieval stone-built pub opposite part-Saxon church, dark panelling and low beams in a long row of five small linked rooms, traditional décor complete with stag's head, low-priced home-made food including bargain OAP menu, John Smiths, upstairs former courtroom (now a function room, but they may give you a guided tour); children welcome. *Recommended by Michael Butler, John and Eleanor Holdsworth*

BLUBBERHOUSES SE1755   LS21 2NZ
Hopper Lane
A65 Skipton—Harrogate

Fully refurbished Inns of Yorkshire pub/hotel, enjoyable reasonably priced food; garden, bedrooms. *Recommended by John and Eleanor Holdsworth*

BOLSTERSTONE SK2796   S36 3ZB
Castle Inn
Off A616

Stone-built local in small hilltop conservation-area village, spectacular surroundings by
Ewden Valley at edge of Peak District National Park, great views from picnic-sets outside;
open-plan but with distinct areas including tap room and restaurant, well kept Black
Sheep, Caledonian Deuchars IPA and Marstons Pedigree, enjoyable good value basic food,
unofficial HQ of award-winning male voice choir. *Recommended by Michael Butler*

BRADFIELD SK2692   S6 6LG
Old Horns
High Bradfield

Friendly old stone-built pub with comfortable divided L-shaped bar, lots of pictures, good
value generous home-made pub food, efficient service, real ales including Thwaites and
continental beers on tap; children welcome, picnic-sets and play area outside, hill village
with stunning views, interesting church, good walks. *Recommended by Roger and Pauline Pearce*

BRADFORD SE1528   BD12 0HP
Chapel House
Chapel House Buildings, Low Moor

Busy stone-built beamed pub in pretty setting opposite church, plenty of atmosphere in
L-shaped bare-boards bar, open fires, well kept Greene King, traditional food, helpful
friendly staff, restaurant; open all day. *Recommended by Clive Flynn*

BRADFORD SE1533   BD7 1JE
Fighting Cock
Preston Street (off B6145)

Busy bare-boards alehouse by industrial estate, great choice of well kept changing ales,
foreign draught and bottled beers, farm ciders, lively atmosphere, all-day doorstep
sandwiches and good simple lunchtime hot dishes (not Sun), may be free bread and
dripping on the bar, low prices, coal fires; open all day. *Recommended by the Didler, Barbarrick*

BRADFORD SE1533   BD1 3AA
New Beehive
Westgate

Robustly old-fashioned Edwardian inn with several rooms including good pool room, wide
range of changing ales, gas lighting, candles and coal fires, friendly atmosphere and
welcoming staff; basement music nights; nice back courtyard, bedrooms, open all day (till
2am Fri, Sat). *Recommended by the Didler*

BRAMHAM SE4242   LS23 6QA
Swan
Just off A1 2 miles N of A64

Civilised and unspoilt three-room country local with engaging long-serving landlady, good
mix of customers, well kept Black Sheep, Hambleton and Leeds Pale. *Recommended by
Les and Sandra Brown*

BURN SE5928   YO8 8LJ
☆ ## Wheatsheaf
Main Road (A19 Selby—Doncaster)

Welcoming busy mock-Tudor roadside pub, comfortable seats and tables in partly divided
open-plan bar with masses to look at – gleaming copper kettles, black dagging shears,
polished buffalo horns, cases of model vans and lorries, decorative mugs above one bow-
window seat, open log fire with drying rack above, John Smiths, Timothy Taylors and
guests, 20 malt whiskies, good value straightforward food (not Sun-Weds evenings), roasts
only on Sun; pool table, games machine, TV and may be unobtrusive piped music; children

and dogs welcome, picnic-sets on heated terrace in small back garden, open all day till midnight. *Recommended by Rob and Catherine Dunster, Terry and Nickie Williams, Lawrence R Cotter, Barbarrick, Lesley and Peter Barrett, Bob and Tanya Ekers*

BURNSALL SE0361 BD23 6BU
Red Lion
B6160 S of Grassington

Family-run 16th-c inn in lovely spot by the River Wharfe, looking across village green to Burnsall Fell, tables out on front cobbles and on big back terrace; attractively panelled, sturdily furnished front dining rooms with log fire, more basic back public bar, good imaginative food (all day weekends), well kept ales such as Copper Dragon and Timothy Taylors, nice wines, efficient friendly service, conservatory; children welcome, comfortable bedrooms (dogs allowed in some and in bar), fishing permits available, open all day. *Recommended by Robert Wivell, John and Helen Rushton, Michael Butler*

BURTON LEONARD SE3263 HG3 3SG
☆ Hare & Hounds
Off A61 Ripon—Harrogate, handy for A1(M) exit 48

Civilised and welcoming country dining pub, good popular food from sandwiches up including Sun roasts, well kept ales such as Black Sheep and Timothy Taylors from long counter, good coffee, large carpeted main area divided by log fire, traditional furnishings, bright little side room; children in eating areas, pretty back garden. *Recommended by James and Melanie Blades, Peter Hacker, Phil and Gill Wass*

CALDER GROVE SE3017 WF4 3DL
British Oak
A639 towards Denby Dale from M1 junction 39

Popular for good value quickly served food (all day), well kept ales such as Marstons and Tetleys, regular quiz and karaoke nights; children welcome, garden with good play area, heated smokers' shelter, less than a mile from the M1. *Recommended by Dave Braisted*

CARLTON NZ5004 TS9 7DJ
Blackwell Ox
Just off A172 SW of Stokesley

Three linked rooms off big central bar, thai landlady and helpful friendly staff, standard pub and good thai food including weekday lunchtime deals, lots of dark wood, blazing log fire; children welcome, garden with play area, bedrooms, picturesque village location, handy for Coast to Coast and Cleveland Way walkers. *Recommended by WW, Graham Denison*

CARLTON HUSTHWAITE SE4976 YO7 2BW
Carlton Bore
Butt Lane

Cosy modernised beamed dining pub, good food from traditional favourites to interesting restaurant dishes including seasonal game, everything home-made from bread to ice-cream, good value set lunch (Mon-Sat), well kept ales including local Hambleton, nice wines, capable cheerful service, country tables and chairs with colourful cushions, lots of odds and ends including four stuffed boars' heads; garden picnic-sets. *Recommended by Peter Thompson, Michael Doswell, Ed and Anna Fraser*

CARTHORPE SE3083 DL8 2LG
☆ Fox & Hounds
Village signed from A1 N of Ripon, via B6285

Welcoming neatly kept dining pub with emphasis on good well presented food, attractive high-raftered restaurant with lots of farm and smithy tools, Black Sheep and Worthington in L-shaped bar with two log fires, plush seating, plates on stripped beams and evocative Victorian photographs of Whitby, some theatrical memorabilia in corridors; piped classical music; children welcome, handy for the A1, closed Mon and first week in Jan. *Recommended by P A Rowe, Jon Clarke, Peter and Eleanor Kenyon, Walter and Susan Rinaldi-Butcher, Janet and Peter Race*

CHAPEL HADDLESEY SE5826   YO8 8QQ
Jug
Quite handy for M62 junction 34; off A19 towards Selby

Small three-room village local with enjoyable reasonably priced home-made food from traditional things up, children's meals and weekday early-bird deal (5-7pm), four changing ales, carpets and comfortable banquettes, restaurant; TV; garden with play equipment, open all day weekends. *Recommended by Matthew Teft*

CHAPEL LE DALE SD7477   LA6 3AR
 ## Hill Inn
B5655 Ingleton—Hawes, 3 miles N of Ingleton

Former farmhouse with fantastic views to Ingleborough and Whernside, a haven for weary walkers (wonderful remote surrounding walks); relaxed, chatty atmosphere, beams, log fires, straightforward furniture on stripped wooden floors, nice pictures, bare-stone recesses, Black Sheep, Dent and Theakstons, enjoyable bar food, separate dining room and well worn-in sun lounge; children welcome, dogs in bar, bedrooms, open all day Sat, closed Mon except bank holidays. *Recommended by Brian and Anna Marsden*

CLIFTON SE1622   HD6 4HJ
☆ ## Black Horse
Westgate/Coalpit Lane; signed off Brighouse Road from M62 junction 25

Friendly 17th-c inn/restaurant, pleasant décor, front dining rooms with good generous food from lunchtime snacks up, can be pricey but good value set meals, efficient uniformed service, back bar area with beam-and-plank ceiling and open fire, well kept Timothy Taylors Landlord and a house beer brewed by Brass Monkey, decent wines; nice courtyard area, 21 comfortable bedrooms, pleasant village, open all day. *Recommended by Michael Butler, John and Eleanor Holdsworth, Tim and Sue Halstead*

COLEY SE1226   HX3 7SD
Brown Horse
Lane Ends, Denholme Gate Road (A644 Brighouse—Keighley, a mile N of Hipperholme)

Attractive and comfortable with open fires in three bustling rooms, popular good value traditional food (restaurant booking advised evenings/weekends), Greene King, Timothy Taylors and Tetleys, decent house wines, good service, lots of bric-a-brac on ceilings and walls, small back conservatory overlooking garden; open all day. *Recommended by John and Eleanor Holdsworth, Clive Flynn*

COLTON SE5444   LS24 8EP
 ## Old Sun
Off A64 York—Tadcaster

Some accomplished and inventive cooking at this 18th-c beamed dining pub, also traditional pub dishes and set deals (food till 7pm Sun, not Mon lunchtime), good wine list with ten by the glass, well kept Black Sheep and Cropton ales, competent service, several linked low-ceilinged rooms (tables a little close in some), log fires, cookery demonstrations, deli; children welcome, front terrace and decking, new bedrooms in separate building. *Recommended by David and Sue Smith, Tim and Sue Halstead, Ian Prince*

CONEYTHORPE SE3958   HG5 0RY
☆ ## Tiger
E of Knaresborough

Pretty dining pub on the green of a charming village, friendly efficient staff, enjoyable wholesome home-made food sensibly priced including Sun carvery, well kept local ales, straightforward open-plan décor in linked areas around bar and adjoining dining room. *Recommended by WW, Pat and Graham Williamson, Les and Sandra Brown, Peter Hardisty, Ed and Anna Fraser*

CRAY SD9479   BD23 5JB
☆ White Lion
B6160 N of Kettlewell

Highest Wharfedale pub in lovely countryside and popular with walkers; welcoming licensees, simple bar with open fire and flagstones, enjoyable well priced food including filled yorkshire puddings and good local trout, Copper Dragon, John Smiths and Timothy Taylors Landlord, back room, original bull 'ook game; children and dogs welcome, picnic-sets above quiet steep lane or you can sit on flat limestone slabs in the shallow stream opposite, bedrooms. *Recommended by Walter and Susan Rinaldi-Butcher, the Didler, Michael Lamm, David M Potts, Lawrence Pearse, Dr Kevan Tucker and others*

DACRE BANKS SE1961   HG3 4EN
☆ Royal Oak
B6451 S of Pateley Bridge

Popular solidly comfortable 18th-c pub with Nidderdale views, traditional food done very well, attentive friendly staff, well kept Boddingtons, Rudgate and Theakstons, good wine choice, beams and panelling, log-fire dining room, games room with darts, dominoes and pool; TV, piped music; children in eating areas, terrace tables, informal back garden, three character bedrooms, good breakfast. *Recommended by Robert Wivell, Angus and Carol Johnson*

DEWSBURY SE2622   WF12 7SW
Huntsman
Walker Cottages, Chidswell Lane, Shaw Cross – pub signed

Cosy low-beamed converted cottages alongside urban-fringe farm, lots of agricultural bric-a-brac, blazing log fire, small front extension, long-serving landlord and friendly locals, well kept Chidswell (brewed for them), Timothy Taylors Landlord and guests, decent home-made food (not lunchtimes Sun, Mon or evenings except Thurs, Fri). *Recommended by Michael Butler, the Didler*

DEWSBURY SE2420   WF12 9BD
Leggers
Robinsons Boat Yard, Savile Town Wharf, Mill Street E (SE of B6409)

Good value basic hayloft conversion by Calder & Hebble Navigation marina, low-beamed upstairs bar, well kept Everards Tiger and five guests, bottled belgian beers, farm cider and perry, straightforward food, real fire, friendly staff, daily papers, brewery and pub memorabilia, pool; picnic-sets outside, boat trips, open all day. *Recommended by Eric Ruff, the Didler*

DEWSBURY SE2321   WF13 2RP
Shepherds Boy
Huddersfield Road, Ravensthorpe

Four-room pub with interesting ales and good range of foreign lagers, bottled beers and wines, bargain generous basic lunchtime food; open all day. *Recommended by the Didler*

DEWSBURY SE2421   WF13 1HF
☆ West Riding Licensed Refreshment Rooms
Station, Wellington Road

Convivial three-room early Victorian station bar, eight well kept changing ales such as Acorn, Anglo Dutch, Fernandes and Timothy Taylors, foreign bottled beers and farm ciders, bargain generous lunchtime food on scrubbed tables, popular pie night Tues, curry night Weds and steak night Thurs, good weekend breakfast too, friendly staff, daily papers, coal fire, lots of steam memorabilia including paintings by local artists, impressive juke box, jazz nights; children in two end rooms, disabled access, open all day. *Recommended by Andy Lickfold, Andy and Jill Kassube, the Didler, Joe Green*

DONCASTER SE5702   DN1 3AH
Corner Pin
St Sepulchre Gate West, Cleveland Street

Plushly refurbished beamed lounge with old local pub prints, welsh dresser and china, John Smiths and interesting guests kept well (beer festivals), good value traditional food from fine hot sandwiches to Sun roasts, friendly landlady, cheery bar with darts, games machine and TV; open all day. *Recommended by the Didler*

DONCASTER SK6299   DN4 7PB
Hare & Tortoise
Parrots Corner, Bawtry Road, Bessacarr (A638)

Popular Vintage Inn all-day dining pub, their standard well priced food, Adnams Broadside, Black Sheep and Everards Tiger, friendly attentive young staff, several small rooms off central bar, log fire; piped music. *Recommended by Stephen Woad, Kay and Alistair Butler and others*

DONCASTER SE5703   DN1 1SF
Plough
West Laith Gate, by Frenchgate shopping centre

Small old-fashioned local with friendly long-serving licensees and chatty regulars, Acorn Barnsley Bitter, Bass and guests, bustling front room with darts, dominoes and sports TV, old town maps, quieter back lounge; tiny central courtyard, open all day (Sun afternoon break). *Recommended by Tim Mountain, the Didler*

DONCASTER SE5703   DN1 1SF
Tut 'n' Shive
West Laith Gate

Well kept ales such as Black Sheep, Batemans, Brewsters and Greene King, farm cider, bargain food all day, small raised carpeted area, eccentric décor (even old doors pressed into service as wall/ceiling coverings), flagstones lots of pump clips, dim lighting; good juke box, pinball, games machines, big-screen sports TV, music nights; open all day. *Recommended by the Didler*

DORE SK3081   S17 3AB
Dore Moor Inn
A625 Sheffield—Castleton

Extended well cared for Vintage Inn (built 1816) on edge of the Peak District, extensive choice of reasonably priced tasty food, good range of wines by the glass, ales such as Black Sheep, Marstons Pedigree and Timothy Taylors Landlord, pleasant young staff, comfortably appointed with superb central log fires; tables outside, views over Sheffield. *Recommended by Jo Rees, Margaret and Jeff Graham*

EASINGWOLD SE5270   YO61 3AD
☆
George
Market Place

Neat, bright and airy, market town hotel (former 18th-c coaching inn), quiet corners even when busy, helpful cheerful service, well kept Black Sheep, Moorhouses and a guest, enjoyable food in bar and restaurant, beams, horsebrasses and warm log fires, slightly old-fashioned feel and popular with older customers; pleasant bedrooms, good breakfast. *Recommended by Pete Coxon, Ian and Helen Stafford, Tony and Wendy Hobden, Michael Butler, Janet and Peter Race, Ed and Anna Fraser*

EAST WITTON SE1487   DL8 4SQ
☆
Cover Bridge Inn
A6108 out towards Middleham

Cosy 16th-c flagstoned country local with friendly accommodating landlord and staff, good choice of well kept Yorkshire ales, enjoyable generous pub food, sensible prices, small restaurant, roaring fires; children and dogs welcome, riverside garden, three bedrooms, open all day. *Recommended by Mr and Mrs Maurice Thompson, the Didler, Simon Le Fort, Jon Forster, Ed and Anna Fraser*

EGTON NZ8006   YO21 1TZ
Wheatsheaf
Village centre

Village pub of real character, interesting paintings and prints in simple main bar, good choice of enjoyable well presented food, charming service, Black Sheep, Timothy Taylors Landlord and a guest, several wines by the glass, restaurant; bedrooms, open all day weekends, closed Mon. *Recommended by Peter Dearing*

EGTON BRIDGE NZ8005   YO21 1XE
☆ Horseshoe
Village signed off A171 W of Whitby

Attractively placed 18th-c inn with open fire, high-backed built-in winged settles, wall seats and spindleback chairs, a big stuffed trout (caught nearby in 1913), Black Sheep, John Smiths and three guests, good home-made bar food, friendly service; piped music; children welcome, dogs in bar, seats on quiet terrace in attractive mature garden, redecorated bedrooms, open all day weekends. *Recommended by Pat and Stewart Gordon, Chris and Jeanne Downing, Peter Burton, Matt and Vikki Wharton*

EGTON BRIDGE NZ8005   YO21 1UX
☆ Postgate
Village signed off A171 W of Whitby

Moorland village pub doing good imaginative fairly priced food, friendly staff, well kept Black Sheep and a guest, traditional quarry-tiled panelled bar with beams, panelled dado and coal fire in an antique range, elegant restaurant; children and dogs welcome, garden picnic-sets, three nice bedrooms. *Recommended by Dr and Mrs R G J Telfer*

ELLERBY NZ7914   TS13 5LP
Ellerby Hotel
Just off A174 Whitby Road; Ryeland Lane

Small friendly well looked after hotel with good pub atmosphere, enjoyable nicely presented traditional food from lunchtime sandwiches up, well kept ales including Theakstons, log fire, restaurant; comfortable reasonably priced bedrooms, good breakfast. *Recommended by C A Hall*

FADMOOR SE6789   YO62 7HY
☆ Plough
Village signed off A170 in or just W of Kirkbymoorside

This village-green dining pub was closed and for sale as we went to press. *Recommended by John Hume, Marlene and Jim Godfrey, Stanley and Annie Matthews, Stephen Woad, Pat and Stewart Gordon*

FELIXKIRK SE4684   YO7 2DP
☆ Carpenters Arms
Village signed off A170 E of Thirsk

Dining pub now under same ownership as the good Durham Ox at Crayke; refurbished opened-up interior with beams and stone-floors, deep-red walls, log fires and woodburner, good food including early evening deal (not Sat) in bar and restaurant, extensive wine list with good choice by the glass, Black Sheep and Timothy Taylors Landlord, bright attentive service, some live acoustic music Weds; terrace and garden, open all day weekends. *Recommended by Robert Wivell, Ed and Anna Fraser*

All *Guide* inspections are anonymous. Anyone claiming to be a *Good Pub Guide* inspector is a fraud. Please let us know.

FERRENSBY SE3660   HG5 0PZ

☆ **General Tarleton**

A655 N of Knaresborough

Smart civilised atmosphere and more restaurant-with-rooms than pub, excellent modern cooking including good value early evening set deal, good attentive service (framed pictures of staff on walls), Black Sheep and Timothy Taylors, nice wines by the glass from good list, beamed bar area divided up by brick pillars, dark brown leather dining chairs around wooden tables, more formal restaurant with exposed stonework; children welcome, covered courtyard and pleasant tree-lined garden, white-painted or plain wood furniture under blue parasols, comfortable contemporary bedrooms, good breakfast. *Recommended by Jon Clarke, G Jennings, David Thornton, Janet and Peter Race, Richard and Mary Bailey, Pat and Graham Williamson and others*

FINGHALL SE1889   DL8 5ND

☆ **Queens Head**

Off A684 E of Leyburn

Welcoming comfortable dining pub, log fires either end of tidy low-beamed bar, settles making stalls around big tables, Black Sheep, Greene King, John Smiths and Theakstons, wide choice of good food from traditional things up, extended back Wensleydale-view dining room; children and dogs welcome, disabled facilities, back garden with decking sharing same view, three bedrooms. *Recommended by Karen Sharman, Ed and Anna Fraser*

FIXBY SE1119   HD2 2EA

Nags Head

New Hey Road, by M62 junction 24 south side, past Hilton

Fairly large chain dining pub, attractive outside and comfortable in, four well kept ales, decent well priced food including carvery, good friendly service, linked areas with wood and slate floors; garden tables, bedrooms in adjoining Premier Inn. *Recommended by John and Eleanor Holdsworth, Gordon and Margaret Ormondroyd*

FLAXTON SE6762   YO60 7RJ

Blacksmiths Arms

Off A64

Small welcoming traditional pub on attractive village green, enjoyable home-made food, well kept Black Sheep, Timothy Taylors, Theakstons and York, good friendly service, carpeted L-shaped bar and restaurant, open fire; seats out at front and behind, three bedrooms, closed Sun evening, Mon, lunchtimes Tues-Sat. *Recommended by David and Ruth Hollands, Roger and Anne Newbury*

FLOCKTON SE2314   WF4 4DW

Sun

Off A642 Wakefield—Huddersfield at Blacksmiths Arms

Nicely refurbished old beamed pub with open fires in bar and dining area, enjoyable reasonably priced food from shortish menu, real ales, prompt efficient service; children welcome, garden tables with lovely views, open all day. *Recommended by Michael Butler, John and Eleanor Holdsworth*

GIGGLESWICK SD8164   BD24 0BE

☆ **Black Horse**

Church Street

Very hospitable father and son landlords in prettily set 17th-c village pub, spotless cosy bar with horsey bric-a-brac and gleaming brasses, coal-effect fire, reasonably priced hearty food, well kept Timothy Taylors, Tetleys and guests, intimate dining room, good service, piano (often played); no dogs; children till 9pm, heated back terrace, smokers' shelter, three good value comfortable bedrooms, good breakfast, open all day weekends. *Recommended by the Didler, Dudley and Moira Cockroft, Tony and Maggie Harwood, Trevor Spalding*

GIGGLESWICK SD8164   BD24 0EB
Craven Arms
Just off A65, opposite station

Modern refurbishment and interesting well presented food including meat from licensee's organic farm (good vegetarian options too), moderate prices, well kept ales such as Black Sheep, Copper Dragon and Tetleys, attentive friendly service, restaurant; suntrap garden, seven bedrooms, closed Mon. *Recommended by Peter and Liz Smalley, John and Susan Miln, Tony and Maggie Harwood*

GIGGLESWICK SD8164   BD24 0BA
Harts Head
Belle Hill

Cheerful bustling village inn, well kept ales such as Black Sheep, public bar (dogs welcome) with dominoes, good choice of enjoyable reasonably priced food in restaurant, folk music night first Fri of month; Sky TV; outside smokers' area, bedrooms. *Recommended by Tony and Maggie Harwood*

GILLAMOOR SE6890   YO62 7HX
☆ Royal Oak
Off A170 in Kirkbymoorside

Stone-built 18th-c dining pub with interesting food at fair prices, friendly staff, ales such as Black Sheep and Copper Dragon, reasonably priced wines, roomy bar with heavy dark beams, log fires in two tall stone fireplaces (one with old kitchen range), overspill dining room (dogs allowed here); children welcome, eight comfortable modern bedrooms, good breakfast, attractive village handy for Barnsdale Moor walks. *Recommended by Stanley and Annie Matthews, WAH, C A Hall, Ed and Anna Fraser*

GILLING EAST SE6176   YO62 4JH
☆ Fairfax Arms
Main Street (B1363)

Attractive refurbished stone-built country inn under same management as the good White Swan at Ampleforth, enjoyable traditional food with some upmarket twists, well kept Black Sheep and Tetleys, good wine choice, friendly staff, beams and log fires, restaurant; piped music; children welcome, dogs outside only, disabled access, streamside front lawn, pleasant village with castle and miniature steam railway, 11 bedrooms, good breakfast, open all day weekends. *Recommended by WW, Michael Butler*

GOLCAR SE0815   HD7 4JR
Golcar Lily
Slades Road, Bolster Moor

Unusual building (former Co-op and manager's house) with fine Colne Valley views, small carpeted bar area with comfortable pink wall seats and stools, swagged curtains, good value food here and in big restaurant leading off (special diets catered for), Tetleys and two guests from brick-faced bar, decent wines; Sun quiz night; open all day weekends. *Recommended by John and Eleanor Holdsworth*

GRANTLEY SE2369   HG4 3PJ
☆ Grantley Arms
Off B6265 W of Ripon

Attractive, popular and well run 17th-c stone-built dining pub in quiet Dales village, beams and big open fire, good freshly made food from traditional things to enterprising well presented restaurant dishes, set menus available too, attentive friendly service, good wines and well kept beers, linen-clothed tables in carpeted restaurant, quiz supper (last Sun of month); soft piped music; terrace with lovely country views. *Recommended by Janet and Peter Race, John and Eleanor Holdsworth, Grahame Brooks, Ed and Anna Fraser*

GRASSINGTON SE0064   BD23 5AD

☆ **Devonshire**
The Square

Small handsome reliably run hotel, good window seats and tables outside overlooking
sloping village square, decent food from sandwiches up, three real ales, interesting
pictures and ornaments, beams and open fires, pleasant family room, big restaurant;
comfortable bedrooms, open all day Sun. *Recommended by Janet and Peter Race, Dr Kevan Tucker,*
B and M Kendall

GRASSINGTON SE0064   BD23 5AA

Foresters Arms
Main Street

Comfortable opened-up old coaching inn with friendly bustling atmosphere, good
generous well priced food, good choice of ales including Black Sheep and Timothy Taylors,
cheerful efficient service, log fires, dining room off on right, pool and sports TV on left,
popular Mon quiz; children welcome, outside tables, 14 affordable bedrooms, good
walking country, open all day. *Recommended by Linda Carter, Dudley and Moira Cockroft, the Didler,*
Michael Lamm, Dr Kevan Tucker, B and M Kendall

GREAT HABTON SE7576   YO17 6TU

☆ **Grapes**
Corner of Habton Lane and Kirby Misperton Lane

Homely and cosy traditionally refurbished beamed dining pub in small village, good
cooking including fresh local fish and game, home-baked bread, Marstons-related ales,
open fire, friendly hard-working young couple; piped music, small public bar with darts
and TV; a few roadside picnic-sets (water for dogs – nice walks), open all day Sun, closed
Tues lunchtime and Mon. *Recommended by Chris Paxton*

GREAT OUSEBURN SE4461   YO26 9RF

Crown
Off B6265 SE of Boroughbridge

Nicely refurbished and welcoming, enjoyable food from pubby to more restaurary dishes,
good choice of well kept ales, back dining extension; garden with terrace tables, open all
day weekends, closed Mon lunchtime, Tues. *Recommended by Alison and Pete, David Brown,*
Ed and Anna Fraser

GREWELTHORPE SE2376   HG4 3BS

Crown
Back road NW of Ripon

Comfortable two-room Dales bar, decent good value food, Marstons-related ales, log fires,
separate back dining room; picnic-sets out in front, pleasant small village, good walks
nearby including Hackfall Wood. *Recommended by Janet and Peter Race*

GUISELEY SE1941   LS20 8AH

Coopers
Otley Road

Light and modern Market Town Taverns café-bar with good food from lunchtime
sandwiches through pastas and pies to evening paella and steaks, eight real ales including
Black Sheep and Timothy Taylors Landlord, jazz and blues nights in upstairs
function/dining room, open all day. *Recommended by the Didler*

HALIFAX SE1026   HX3 7AY

Stump Cross Inn
Kell Lane, Stump Cross

Smart dining pub, airy and modern, with enjoyable reasonably priced food, pleasant
helpful staff, well kept Copper Dragon Golden Pippin, good coffee; attractive terrace.
Recommended by Pat and Tony Martin

HALIFAX SE0924   HX1 2LX
Three Pigeons
Sun Fold, South Parade; off Church Street

Carefully restored, four-room 1930s pub (Grade II listed), art deco fittings, ceiling
painting in octagonal main area, original flooring, panelling and tiled fireplaces with log
fires, up to six well kept Ossett ales and local guests, friendly chatty staff; tables outside,
handy for Eureka! Museum and Shay Stadium, open all day Fri-Sun, from 3pm other days.
Recommended by Pat and Tony Martin

HARDROW SD8691   DL8 3LZ
☆ Green Dragon
Village signed off A684

Friendly traditional Dales pub dating from the 13th c and full of character; stripped
stone, antique settles on flagstones, lots of bric-a-brac, low-beamed snug with log fire in
old iron range, another in big main bar, four well kept ales including one brewed for them
by Yorkshire Dales, enjoyable generous food, small neat restaurant, annual brass band
competition; children and dogs welcome, bedrooms, next to Hardraw Force – England's
highest single-drop waterfall. *Recommended by Mr and Mrs Maurice Thompson, Peter Salmon,
Steve Short, Claes Mauroy*

HAROME SE6482   YO62 5JE
☆ Star
High Street; village signed S of A170, E of Helmsley

Restaurant-with-rooms (need to book for both well in advance) in pretty 14th-c thatched
building, but bar does have informal feel, bowed beam-and-plank ceiling, plenty of bric-a-
brac, interesting furniture including 'Mousey' Thompson pieces, log fire, well polished
tiled kitchen range, daily papers, Black Sheep and Wold Top, 18 wines by the glass, home-
made fruit liqueurs, snacks served in cocktail bar, popular coffee loft in the eaves,
inventive ambitious modern cooking (not cheap); piped music; children welcome, seats
on sheltered front terrace, more in garden, stylish bedrooms and suites, Pheasant Hotel
nearby under same ownership as is Corner Shop opposite and Pern's delicatessen in
Helmsley, open all day Sun, closed Mon lunchtime. *Recommended by Noel Thomas,
Christine Vallely, David Thornton, Pat and Stewart Gordon, Walter and Susan Rinaldi-Butcher and others*

HARROGATE SE3155   HG1 1BJ
Coach & Horses
West Park

Very friendly bustling pub with speciality pies and other enjoyable reasonably priced food,
several good Yorkshire ales, obliging service, nice interior with booth seating; open all
day. *Recommended by D W Stokes, Eric Larkham, the Didler, Pete Coxon, Adrian Johnson, Tim and
Sue Halstead and others*

HARROGATE SE3157   HG1 4DH
Gardeners Arms
*Bilton Lane (off A59 either in Bilton itself or on outskirts towards Harrogate – via
Bilton Hall Drive)*

Stone-built 17th-c house converted into friendly down-to-earth local, tiny bar and three
small rooms, flagstone floors, panelling, old prints, big fire in stone fireplace, very cheap
Sam Smiths OBB, decent bar lunches (not Tues), dominoes; children welcome,
surrounding streamside garden with play area, lovely peaceful setting near Nidd Gorge.
Recommended by the Didler, Alan and Shirley Sawden

HARROGATE SE2955   HG1 2RS
☆ Hales
Crescent Road

Classic Victorian décor in gas-lit 18th-c welcoming local close to Pump Rooms, leather
seats in alcoves, stuffed birds, comfortable saloon and tiny snug, seven real ales including

Daleside, simple good value lunchtime food including Sun roast; can get lively on weekend evenings. *Recommended by Eric Larkham, Greta and Christopher Wells, Michael Butler, David and Ruth Shillitoe*

HARROGATE SE2955   HG1 2SZ

☆ ## Old Bell
Royal Parade

Thriving Market Town Taverns pub with eight mainly Yorkshire beers from a handsome counter, lots of bottled continental beers, impressive choice of wines by the glass, friendly helpful staff, lunchtime snacks including sandwiches (interesting choice of breads), more elaborate evening meals upstairs, newspapers, panelling, old sweet shop ads and breweriana, no music or machines; no children; open all day. *Recommended by Eric Larkham, the Didler, Tod and Dawn Hannula, Roger and Donna Huggins*

HARTHILL SK4980   S26 7YH

Beehive
Union Street

Two-bar village pub opposite attractive church, chef/landlord doing a wide range of enjoyable generous food including proper pies and Sun lunch, friendly service, three or four well kept ales including Timothy Taylors Landlord, good choice of wines, malts and soft drinks, fresh flowers, games room with pool; piped music can be loud; children welcome till 9pm if eating, picnic-sets in attractive garden, walks nearby, closed Mon. *Recommended by JJW, CMW, Rebecca Walker, Derek and Sylvia Stephenson and others*

HEADINGLEY SE2736   LS6 2UE

Arcadia
Arndale Centre

Bustling small bank conversion, good choice of changing Yorkshire ales kept well, lots of continental bottled beers, knowledgeable staff, bar food; a Market Town Tavern, open all day. *Recommended by Peter Smith and Judith Brown, Daniel Lezcano*

HEBDEN BRIDGE SD9827   HX7 6LU

Stubbings Wharf
1 mile W

Warm and friendly pub in good spot by Rochdale Canal with adjacent moorings, enjoyable food (all day weekends) from sandwiches to good value Sun lunch, wide range of ales including local microbrews, usually three real ciders; open all day; dogs welcome. *Recommended by Dave Sumpter, Jon Moody, Andy and Jill Kassube*

HEBDEN BRIDGE SD9927   HX7 8EX

☆ ## White Lion
Bridge Gate

Solid stone-built inn with welcoming comfortable bar and country-style-furnished bare-boards back area with coal fire, reasonably priced generous home-cooked food all day (just lunchtime Sun), fish specialities, well kept Timothy Taylors Landlord and a guest beer, good friendly service; disabled facilities, attractive secluded riverside garden, ten comfortable bedrooms. *Recommended by Martin Smith, Ian and Nita Cooper*

HELMSLEY SE6183   YO62 5BH

Feathers
Market Place

Substantial stone inn with sensibly priced generous all-day bar food from sandwiches up, popular Sun lunch, well kept Black Sheep and Tetleys, good friendly service, several rooms with comfortable seats, oak and walnut tables, flagstones or tartan carpet, nice prints, huge inglenook log fire, heavy medieval beams, panelled corridors; children in eating area, tables in attractive back garden, clean comfortable bedrooms, open all day. *Recommended by Philip and Jan Medcalf, Ben and Ruth Levy*

HEPWORTH SE1606   HD9 1TE
Butchers Arms
Off A616 SE of Holmfirth; Towngate

Refurbished dark-beamed country dining pub with very good enterprising food (not cheap and emphasis on local ingredients) from Le Manoir-trained chef/owner, efficient pleasant service, Black Sheep and Timothy Taylors, traditional flagstone/bare-boards interior enhanced with contemporary décor, large log fire; outside decked seating area, open all day. *Recommended by David and Cathrine Whiting, John Holt, Oliver Richardson*

HETTON SD9658   BD23 6LT
☆ Angel
Off B6265 Skipton—Grassington

Busy dining pub with three neatly kept timbered and panelled rooms mainly set for the good imaginative food (all day Sun), friendly helpful staff, main bar with farmhouse range in stone fireplace, well kept Black Sheep, Dark Horse and a guest, 20 wines by the glass, lots of nooks and alcoves, country-kitchen and smart dining chairs, plush seats, all sorts of tables, Ronald Searle wine-snob cartoons, older engravings and photographs, log fires; children welcome, smart furniture on two covered terraces, nice bedrooms, closed Jan. *Recommended by Margaret and Jeff Graham, Ian Malone, James Stretton, Karen Eliot, Bruce and Sharon Eden, WAH and others*

HIGH BENTHAM SD6769   LA2 7HE
Coach House
Main Street

Centrally placed 17th-c coaching inn, low beams, alcoves, nooks and crannies, enjoyable good value food including OAP lunch deal, Robinsons ales; bedrooms. *Recommended by Karen Eliot*

HOLMFIRTH SD1408   HD9 2DN
Nook
Victoria Square/South Lane

Tucked-away basic 18th-c stone pub brewing its own good ales alongside Timothy Taylors and other guests, home-made pubby food all day and adjoining tapas bar, low beams, flagstones and big open fire, some live music; heated streamside terrace, open all day. *Recommended by the Didler*

HOLYWELL GREEN SE0919   HX4 9BS
Rock
Broad Carr Lane; handy for M62 junction 24

Smart comfortable hotel/restaurant rather than pub, very popular for its good food (all day Sun) including well priced set menu, friendly efficient service, small bar area serving Timothy Taylors Landlord, Churchill-themed restaurant; children welcome, 27 bedrooms, good breakfast. *Recommended by Gordon and Margaret Ormondroyd and others*

HORBURY SE2918   WF4 6LP
Boons
Queen Street

Lively, chatty and comfortably unpretentious flagstoned local, Clarks, John Smiths, Timothy Taylors Landlord and up to four quickly changing guests, no food, Rugby League memorabilia, warm fire, back tap room with pool; TV, no children; courtyard tables, open all day Fri-Sun. *Recommended by Michael Butler, the Didler*

HORBURY SE2917   WF4 5AR
Bulls Head
Southfield Lane

Large well divided pub deservedly popular for food, smart attentive staff, Black Sheep and Tetleys, lots of wines by the glass, panelling and wood floors, relaxing linked rooms including library, snug and more formal restaurant; front picnic-sets. *Recommended by Michael Butler*

HORSEHOUSE SE0481 DL8 4TS
Thwaite Arms
Coverdale Road, Middleham—Kettlewell

Early 19th-c former farm building in wonderful village setting near beautiful little church, lots of paths to nearby villages and moors, great drive along Coverdale; bargain simple home-cooked food including fine Sun roast (only a few tables in pretty homely dining room, so worth booking), well kept Theakstons Best, farm cider, genial landlord, good coal fire in cosy snug, bigger plainer locals' bar; children welcome, fell views from charming garden, two bedrooms. *Recommended by Susan and Neil McLean*

HOVINGHAM SE6675 YO62 4LA
☆ # Worsley Arms
High Street

Smart inn in pretty village handy for Castle Howard, good food in friendly and welcoming back bar and separate restaurant (different menu), Hambleton ales, several malts, good wines and coffee, friendly attentive staff, lots of Yorkshire cricketer photographs especially from 1930/40s; attractive gardens with tables by stream, 19 pleasant bedrooms, some in cottages across the green. *Recommended by Michael Butler, George Atkinson*

HUBBERHOLME SD9278 BD23 5JE
☆ # George
Dubbs Lane

Small beautifully placed ancient Dales inn with River Wharfe fishing rights, heavy beams, flagstones and stripped stone, quick simple enjoyable food, three well kept ales including Black Sheep and Copper Dragon, good log fire, perpetual candle on bar; no dogs, outside lavatories; children allowed in dining area, terrace, seven comfortable bedrooms, closed Mon. *Recommended by David and Sue Atkinson, Dr Kevan Tucker, Peter Dearing*

HUDDERSFIELD SE1416 HD1 4BP
Grove
Spring Grove Street

Lots of exotic bottled beers, well kept Timothy Taylors, Thornbridge and 16 interesting changing guest ales at sensible prices, 120 malt whiskies and 60 vodkas, no food but choice of snacks from dried crickets to biltong, traditional irish music Thurs evening, art gallery; children and dogs welcome, back terrace, open all day. *Recommended by the Didler, Andy and Jill Kassube*

HUDDERSFIELD SE1416 HD1 1JF
☆ # Head of Steam
St Georges Square

Railway memorabilia, model trains, cars, buses and planes for sale, friendly staff, long bar with up to eight changing ales, lots of bottled beers, farm ciders and perry, fruit wines, black leather easy chairs and sofas, hot coal fire, good value enjoyable back buffet, some live jazz and blues nights; unobtrusive piped music, can be very busy; open all day. *Recommended by Andy Lickfold, Chris Flynn, Wendy Jones, the Didler, David Hoult, Peter Smith and Judith Brown, Ian and Helen Stafford and others*

HUDDERSFIELD SE1520 HD2 1PX
High Park
Bradley Road, Bradley

Neatly kept modern dining pub, attractively done and keeping plenty of room for drinking and chatting, Greene King ales, wide choice of good value pub food including OAP and other deals, quick friendly service; children welcome, disabled facilities, outside seating, open all day. *Recommended by Gordon and Margaret Ormondroyd*

HUDDERSFIELD SE1416   HD1 1JF
Kings Head
Station, St Georges Square

Handsome Victorian station building housing friendly well run pub, large open-plan room
with original tiled floor, two smaller rooms off, Dark Star, Pictish, Timothy Taylors
Landlord and six guests, good sandwiches and cobs, live afternoon/evening music (Sun,
Thurs), Jimi Hendrix pub sign; disabled access via Platform 1, open all day. *Recommended by
Andy Lickfold, Chris Flynn, Wendy Jones, the Didler*

HUDDERSFIELD SE1119   HD2 2EA
Nags Head
New Hey Road, Ainley Top; handy for M62 junction 24, by A643

Comfortably refurbished and quite busy, good choice of enjoyable food at fair prices
including OAP deals, well kept Courage Directors and three other beers, friendly chatty
staff; open all day. *Recommended by Gordon and Margaret Ormondroyd*

HUDDERSFIELD SE1416   HD1 3EB
Rat & Ratchet
Chapel Hill

Flagstoned local with Fullers, Fernandes, Ossett and lots of guest beers, farm ciders,
cheap lunchtime food (not Sun-Tues), friendly staff, more comfortable seating up steps,
brewery memorabilia and music posters; open all day. *Recommended by the Didler*

HUDDERSFIELD SE1417   HD1 5AY
Sportsman
St Johns Road

Same owners as the West Riding Licensed Refreshment Rooms at Dewsbury, Timothy
Taylors and six changing guests, regular beer festivals, good value lunchtime bar snacks,
comfortable lounge and two cosy side rooms; handy for the station, open all day.
Recommended by Andy and Jill Kassube, the Didler

HUDDERSFIELD SE1415   HD1 3PJ
Star
Albert Street, Lockwood

Unpretentious friendly local with up to 12 competitively priced changing ales, such as
Empire, Mallinsons and Pictish, particularly well kept by enthusiastic landlady,
continental beers, farm cider, beer festivals in back marquee (food then), bric-a-brac and
customers' paintings, open fire; closed Mon, and lunchtimes Tues-Thurs, open all day
weekends. *Recommended by the Didler, Andy and Jill Kassube*

HULL TA0929   HU1 3TG
Hop & Vine
Albion Street

Small pub with three real ales, bottled belgian beers, farm ciders and perries, friendly
licensees, good sandwiches and bargain basic specials all day, cellar bar; closed Sun, Mon.
Recommended by the Didler

HULL TA1028   HU1 1JG
☆ Olde White Harte
Passage off Silver Street

Ancient pub with Civil War history, carved heavy beams, attractive stained glass, two big
inglenooks with frieze of delft tiles, Caledonian Deuchars IPA, Theakstons Old Peculier
and guests from copper-topped counter, 80 or so malt whiskies, bargain pubby food;
children welcome in upstairs restaurant, dogs in bar, heated courtyard, open all day.
Recommended by the Didler

HULL TA0929   HU2 0PA
Whalebone
Wincolmlee

Friendly local brewing its own ales, also Copper Dragon, Timothy Taylors Landlord and a guest, two real ciders and perry, bar food, old-fashioned décor; open all day. *Recommended by the Didler*

HUTTON-LE-HOLE SE7089   YO62 6UA
Crown
The Green

Spotless pub overlooking pretty village green with wandering sheep in classic coach-trip country, generous unfussy food (all day Sun) from sandwiches up, Black Sheep and Theakstons, cheerful efficient service, opened-up bar with varnished woodwork and whisky-water jugs, dining area; children and dogs welcome, near Folk Museum, handy for Farndale walks. *Recommended by Dr and Mrs R G J Telfer*

ILKLEY SE1048   LS29 0BE
Riverside
Nesfield Road

Friendly family run hotel in a good position by River Wharfe, cosy with nice open fire, well kept Copper Dragon, Ilkley, Tetleys and Timothy Taylors Landlord, good home-cooking all day (till early evening in winter); handy for start of Dales Way, 13 bedrooms, open from 10am. *Recommended by the Didler*

KEIGHLEY SE0941   BD20 5LY
Airedale Heifer
Bradford Road, Sandbeds (B6265 towards Bingley)

Stone-built pub with spreading series of rooms, enjoyable reasonably priced food, well kept ales including Timothy Taylors Landlord, friendly staff, open fire; children welcome, tables out in front and behind, open all day. *Recommended by Trevor and Sylvia Millum*

KEIGHLEY SE0641   BD21 5HX
Boltmakers Arms
East Parade

Small open-plan split-level characterful local, friendly and bustling, with full Timothy Taylors range and a guest kept well, keen prices, limited food, nice brewing pictures, coal fire; sports TV; short walk from Worth Valley Railway, open all day. *Recommended by Bruce Bird, the Didler, Neil Whitehead, Victoria Anderson, Allan Wolf*

KEIGHLEY SE0541   BD21 2LQ
Brown Cow
Cross Leeds Street

Extensively refurbished local, popular and friendly, with good licensee keeping Timothy Taylors ales and guests in top condition; open from 4pm Mon-Sat, all day Sun. *Recommended by Bruce Bird, the Didler*

KEIGHLEY SE0641   BD21 5JE
Cricketers Arms
Coney Lane

Moorhouses and five guests, farm cider, good value bottled beers, downstairs bar open Fri, Sat for live music; sports TV; open all day. *Recommended by the Didler*

KETTLESING SE2257   HG3 2LB

☆ Queens Head
Village signposted off A59 W of Harrogate

Welcoming stone pub with good value food popular with older diners; L-shaped carpeted main bar with lots of close-set cushioned dining chairs and tables, open fires, little heraldic shields on walls, 19th-c song sheet covers and lithographs of Queen Victoria, delft shelf of blue and white china, smaller bar on left with built-in red banquettes and cricketing prints, life-size portrait of Elizabeth I in lobby, Black Sheep, Roosters and Theakstons ales, good service; piped radio; children welcome, seats in neatly kept suntrap back garden, benches in front by the lane, seven bedrooms, open all day Sun. *Recommended by Peter Hacker, Margaret and Peter Staples, Adrian and Dawn Collinge, Simon Le Fort, B and M Kendall, Michael Butler and others*

KETTLEWELL SD9672   BD23 5QX

Blue Bell
Middle Lane

Roomy knocked-through 17th-c coaching inn, Copper Dragon ales kept well, home-made food all day using local ingredients, low beams and snug simple furnishings, old country photographs, woodburner, restaurant, newspapers; TV, free wi-fi, Sun quiz; children welcome, shaded picnic-sets on cobbles facing a River Wharfe bridge, six annexe bedrooms. *Recommended by D W Stokes, John and Helen Rushton*

KETTLEWELL SD9672   BD23 5QZ

☆ Racehorses
B6160 N of Skipton

Comfortable, civilised and friendly two-bar pub with dining area, generous good value food from substantial lunchtime rolls through pub favourites to local game, popular early evening bargains Sun-Thurs, well kept Timothy Taylors and Tetleys, good log fire; children welcome, dogs in bars, front and back terrace seating, well placed for Wharfedale walks, parking can be difficult, 13 good bedrooms, open all day. *Recommended by Bruce and Sharon Eden, Lois Dyer, John and Helen Rushton, B and M Kendall*

KIRKBY FLEETHAM SE2894   DL7 0SH

☆ Black Horse
Lumley Lane

Nicely refurbished old village pub with some contemporary touches but keeping a pubby atmosphere, good food including reasonably priced Sun lunch, well kept Black Sheep, John Smiths, Theakstons and a guest, good choice of wines by the glass, restaurant, darts; children welcome, tables in garden, quoits, three good bedrooms. *Recommended by Richard Cole, Bill Adie, Jane Taylor and David Dutton, Michael Doswell, John and Eleanor Holdsworth*

KIRKBY MALHAM SD8960   BD23 4BS

Victoria
Village centre

Understated Victorian décor in small simple rooms, good pub food including cheap Sun carvery, well kept ales such as Timothy Taylors and Tetleys, good wine choice, friendly staff, nice log fire, separate restaurant (not always in use); children welcome, lovely village with interesting church, good value bedrooms. *Recommended by John Withnell, Meg and Colin Hamilton*

KIRKBYMOORSIDE SE6986   YO62 6AA

George & Dragon
Market Place

17th-c coaching inn, front bar with beams, panelling, tubs seats around wooden tables on carpet or stripped wood, log fire, Copper Dragon, Greene King and a guest, several malt whiskies, bar food including early-bird menu, afternoon teas, also a snug, bistro and more formal restaurant; piped music; children welcome, seats and heaters on front and back terraces, bedrooms, Weds market day, open all day. *Recommended by Margaret Dickinson, Ed and Anna Fraser*

KNARESBOROUGH SE3556   HG5 8AL
☆ Blind Jacks
Market Place

Simply done multi-floor tavern in 18th-c building (pub since 1990s), old-fashioned traditional character with low beams, bare brick and floorboards, cast-iron-framed tables, pews and stools, brewery mirrors, etc, nine well kept ales including own Village Brewer (made by Hambleton), seven continental draught beers, friendly helpful staff, limited food (cheese and pâté), two small downstairs rooms, quieter upstairs; well behaved children allowed away from bar, dogs welcome, open all day Fri-Sun, closed Mon-Thurs till 4pm; shop next door sells all sorts of rare bottled beers. *Recommended by the Didler, Tim and Ann Newell, B and M Kendall, Adrian Johnson*

LANGTHWAITE NY0002   DL11 6EN
☆ Charles Bathurst
Arkengarthdale, a mile N towards Tan Hill

Busy country inn (worth checking no corporate events/weddings on your visit) with a strong emphasis on dining and bedrooms, but pubby feel in long bar; scrubbed pine tables and country chairs on stripped floors, snug alcoves, open fire, some bar stools by counter, Black Sheep, Theakstons and Timothy Taylors, several wines by the glass from list with helpful notes, popular often interesting food, dining room with views of Scar House, Robert 'the Mouseman' Thompson furniture, several other dining areas; piped music, TV, pool, darts and other games; children welcome, lovely walks from door and views over village and Arkengarthdale, smart bedrooms (best not above dining room), open all day. *Recommended by Pat and Stewart Gordon, John and Sylvia Harrop, Bruce and Sharon Eden*

LASTINGHAM SE7290   YO62 6TL
☆ Blacksmiths Arms
Off A170 W of Pickering

Popular old-fashioned beamed pub opposite beautiful Saxon church in an attractive village, log fire in open range, traditional furnishings, Theakstons and other regional ales, several wines by the glass, good food including impressive seafood platter, friendly prompt service, darts, board games; piped music – live music second Sun of month; children and walkers welcome, seats in back garden, nice bedrooms, open all day in summer. *Recommended by Brian Brooks, Dr and Mrs R G J Telfer, Michael Butler, Ed and Anna Fraser, W M Hogg*

LEALHOLM NZ7607   YO21 2AJ
Board
Off A171 W of Whitby

In a wonderful moorland village spot by wide pool of River Esk, old-fashioned stripped-stone bars, big log fire, welcoming licensees and chatty friendly staff, four changing ales, real ciders, over 60 malts, bar snacks (own pickled eggs) and good seasonal food in restaurant including home-reared meats; some live music, darts; children, dogs and muddy boots welcome, secluded riverside garden with decking, five bedrooms, self-catering cottage, open all day Sat, may be closed weekday lunchtimes in winter. *Recommended by Liz Partridge, Mike and Mary Strigenz, Mo and David Trudgill*

LEEDS SE3033   LS10 1JQ
Adelphi
Hunslet Road

Refurbished but keeping handsome mahogany screens, panelling, tiling, cut and etched glass and impressive stairway, Leeds, Timothy Taylors Landlord and guests, foreign draught beers, decent all-day food including fixed-price weekday menu, friendly service, upstairs room, live music, comedy nights and other events. *Recommended by the Didler, Paul Bromley*

LEEDS SE3033   LS1 5DL

Brewery Tap
New Station Street

Tied to Leeds Brewery, their ales and guests kept well, good value food, neat, friendly, efficient staff; piped music; open all day. *Recommended by Bruce Bird, the Didler, Peter Smith and Judith Brown*

LEEDS SE2932   LS11 5WD

Cross Keys
Water Lane

Designer bar with flagstone floors, stripped brick, original tiling, metal and timbers, good choice of Yorkshire ales and imported bottled beers, friendly knowledgeable staff, enjoyable good value interesting food, good Sun roasts, upstairs room; children welcome, tables under big parasols in sheltered courtyard, barbecues, open all day. *Recommended by Stu Mac, the Didler*

LEEDS SE3131   LS10 2QB

Garden Gate
Whitfield Place, Hunslet

Impressive early Edwardian pub (Grade II* listed) now owned by Leeds Brewery, their well kept ales served from a rare curved ceramic counter, a wealth of other period features in rooms off central drinking corridor including intricate glass and woodwork, art nouveau tiling, moulded ceilings and mosaic floors, hearty pub food (not Tues evening); tables out in front, open all day weekends. *Recommended by the Didler*

LEEDS SE2932   LS11 5PL

☆ ## Grove
Back Row, Holbeck

Unspoilt 1930s-feel local overshadowed by towering office blocks, friendly long-serving landlord, tables and stools in main bar with marble floor, panelling and original fireplace, large back room (some live music in in here) and snug off drinking corridor, good choice of well kept ales including Caledonian Deuchars IPA, Weston's cider, good live acoustic music; open all day. *Recommended by Barrie Pepper, the Didler*

LEEDS SE2932   LS11 5QN

Midnight Bell
Water Lane

Friendly tap for Leeds Brewery, their full range and guests, enjoyable home-made food, flagstones and light contemporary décor; waterside tables outside. *Recommended by the Didler, Tim and Sue Halstead*

LEEDS SE2236   LS2 7DJ

Palace
Kirkgate

Pleasantly uncitified, with stripped boards and polished panelling, unusual lighting from electric candelabra to mock street-lamps, lots of old prints, friendly helpful staff, good value lunchtime food till 7pm from sandwiches up including popular Sun roasts in dining area, fine changing choice of ales, may be bargain wine offers; games end with pool, TV, piped music; tables out in front and in small heated back courtyard, open all day. *Recommended by the Didler, Joe Green*

LEEDS SE3033   LS2 7NU

Templar
Templar Street

Tiled pub with fine panelling, stained glass and some unusual booths, well kept Tetleys and guest beers, popular with older locals; open all day. *Recommended by the Didler*

LEEDS SE3033   LS1 3DL

☆ Victoria
Great George Street

Opulent early Victorian pub with grand, cut and etched mirrors, impressive globe lamps
extending from majestic bar, carved beams, leather-seat booths with working snob-
screens, smaller rooms off, changing ales such as Cottage, Leeds, Timothy Taylors and
Tetleys, friendly efficient service even when busy, reasonably priced food 12-6pm from
sandwiches and light dishes up in separate room with serving hatch; open all day.
Recommended by the Didler, Andy Lickfold

LEEDS SE3033   LS1 6HB

☆ Whitelocks
Turks Head Yard, off Briggate

Classic Victorian pub (unspoilt but some signs of wear) with long narrow old-fashioned
bar, tiled counter, grand mirrors, mahogany and glass screens, heavy copper-topped tables
and green leather, well kept Caledonian Deuchars IPA, John Smiths, Theakstons Best and
Old Peculier and fine range of guests, good generous all-day food (not Sun evening),
friendly hard-working young staff; crowded at lunchtime; children in restaurant and top
bar, tables in narrow courtyard, open all day. *Recommended by Eric Ruff, Greta and Christopher
Wells, Dr Kevan Tucker, Bruce Bird, the Didler, Michael Butler and others*

LEYBURN SE1190   DL8 5AS
Black Swan
Market Place

Attractive old creeper-clad hotel with chatty locals in the cheerful open-plan bar,
entertaining landlord, good service, decent range of food including popular Sun carvery,
well kept Black Sheep and other ales, good wines by the glass; no credit cards; children
and dogs welcome, good disabled access, tables on cobbled terrace, seven bedrooms, open
all day. *Recommended by Andy Lickfold, the Didler, Ed and Anna Fraser*

LEYBURN SE1190   DL8 5BW
Bolton Arms
Market Place

Substantial stone-built inn at top of the market place, varied choice of well priced home-
made food including good Sun carvery, ales such as Black Sheep, good mix of customers;
bedrooms. *Recommended by R C Vincent, Mr and Mrs Ian King*

LEYBURN SE1190   DL8 5AS
Golden Lion
Market Place

Comfortable panelled and bay-windowed hotel bar, two light and airy rooms with log-
effect gas fire in eating area, varied good value generous food, well kept Black Sheep,
decent coffee, friendly efficient service, paintings for sale, evening restaurant; very busy
on Fri market day; dogs allowed, tables out in front, good value bedrooms, open all day.
Recommended by Gordon Briggs, Ed and Anna Fraser

LINTHWAITE SE1014   HD7 5SG
☆ Sair
Lane Top, Hoyle Ing, off A62

Old-fashioned four-room pub brewing its own good value Linfit beers, pews and chairs on
rough flagstones or wood floors, log-burning ranges, dominoes, cribbage and shove-
ha'penny, vintage rock juke box; no food or credit cards; dogs welcome, children till 8pm,
plenty of tables out in front with fine Colne Valley views, restored Huddersfield Narrow
Canal nearby, open all day weekends, from 5pm weekdays. *Recommended by John Fiander,
the Didler*

LINTON IN CRAVEN SD9962   BD23 5HJ
☆ Fountaine
Off B6265 Skipton—Grassington

Neatly kept pub in a charming village (parking not easy at peak times), beams in low ceilings, log fires (one in beautifully carved heavy wooden fireplace), attractive built-in cushioned wall benches and stools, plenty of prints, tasty well priced bar food, a beer named for the pub plus Dark Horse, John Smiths, Tetleys and guests; piped music, darts; children welcome, dogs in bar, teak benches and tables under parasols on terrace, pretty hanging baskets, fine surrounding walks, open all day. *Recommended by Lynda and Trevor Smith, Margaret and Peter Staples, Dr Phil Putwain, Jeremy King, Peter Salmon and others*

LITTON SD9074   BD23 5QJ
Queens Arms
Off B6160 N of Grassington

Beautifully placed Dales pub, main bar with coal fire, rough stone walls, beam-and-plank ceiling, stools around cast-iron-framed tables on stone floor, dining room with old photographs, own-brewed Litton ales and guests, hearty food; children and dogs welcome, two-level garden, plenty of good surrounding walks, bedrooms, camping, open all day weekends, closed Mon. *Recommended by Claes Mauroy*

LOCKTON SE8488   YO18 7NQ
☆ Fox & Rabbit
A169 N of Pickering

Attractive neatly kept roadside pub with a warm inviting atmosphere, good choice of generous well presented food (sandwiches too), quick cheerful service, well kept Black Sheep and Cropton ales, decent coffee, beams, panelling and some exposed stonework, plush banquettes, fresh flowers, brasses, hunting prints and old local photographs, big log fire, busy locals' bar with pool, good views from comfortable restaurant; tables outside and in sun lounge, nice spot on moors' edge, bedrooms. *Recommended by Pamela Thorne, A and N Hooper, George Atkinson*

LOW BRADFIELD SK2691   S6 6HW
☆ Plough
New Road

Popular pub with very good value home-made food (not Mon or Tues evenings), well kept and priced local Bradfield and guest beers, cheery efficient service, spotless inside with big inglenook log fire, restaurant; children welcome, picnic-sets in attractive garden, lovely scenery and local walks. *Recommended by Peter F Marshall*

LOW BRADLEY SE0048   BD20 9DE
Slaters Arms
Crag Lane, off A629 S of Skipton

Well kept ales such as Black Sheep, Timothy Taylors and Wells & Youngs, belgian beers, good sensibly priced food, real fires. *Recommended by John and Eleanor Holdsworth*

LOW ROW SD9898   DL11 6PF
☆ Punch Bowl
B6270 Reeth—Muker

Under same ownership as Charles Bathurst at Langthwaite, fresh, light and almost scandinavian in style, with friendly helpful staff, interesting food (menu on huge mirror), popular Sun carvery (best to book), several good wines by the glass, well kept Black Sheep, log fire, leather armchairs, sturdy tables and chairs; no dogs inside; children welcome, great Swaledale views from terrace, 11 comfortable bedrooms, good breakfast, open all day in summer. *Recommended by Bruce and Sharon Eden, Robin M Corlett, Walter and Susan Rinaldi-Butcher*

MALHAM SD9062   BD23 4DA
Buck
Off A65 NW of Skipton

Superbly set creeper-clad stone inn popular with walkers, enjoyable traditional food, six
ales including Timothy Taylors Landlord and Theakstons Old Peculier, log fire in panelled
lounge, big basic hikers' bar, dining room; children and dogs welcome, picnic-sets in small
heated yard, picture-book village, many good walks from the door, 12 clean bedrooms.
Recommended by Chris and Jeanne Downing

MALHAM SD9062   BD23 4DB
Lister Arms
Off A65 NW of Skipton

Friendly creeper-covered stone-built inn tied to Thwaites, their ales kept well, lots of
bottled imports, good value enjoyable food including lunchtime sandwiches, roaring fire;
pool and games machines; children and dogs welcome, seats out overlooking a small
green, more in back garden, lovely spot by river, good walking country, comfortable clean
bedrooms, open all day. *Recommended by Chris and Jeanne Downing, Barry Collett, Peter Salmon*

MANFIELD NZ2213   DL2 2RF
Crown
Vicars Lane

Traditional unpretentious village local, friendly and welcoming, with eight interesting
regularly changing ales, enjoyable simple home-made food, two bars and games room with
pool; dogs welcome (pub dog is called Leah), garden, good walks nearby. *Recommended by
Mr and Mrs Maurice Thompson, Julian Pigg, Brian Jones, D G Collinson*

MARSDEN SE0612   HD7 6EZ
New Inn
Manchester Road

Brightly modernised well run 18th-c coaching inn, open-plan interior with stripped-wood
floors, fresh flowers on bar, open fires, good choice of enjoyable evening food from
regularly changing menu (all day weekends), well kept ales, friendly attentive service,
restaurant; children and dogs welcome, tables in garden, attractive countryside nearby,
six bedrooms (named after famous local characters), closed till 5pm weekdays, open all
day weekends. *Recommended by Gill and Malcolm Stott*

MARSDEN SE0411   HD7 6BR
☆ ## Riverhead Brewery Tap
Peel Street, next to Co-op; just off A62 Huddersfield—Oldham

Owned by Ossett with up to ten well kept ales including Riverhead range (microbrewey
visible from bar), good value food from sandwiches to interesting specials in airy upstairs
beamed dining room with stripped tables and open kitchen; unobtrusive piped music;
dogs welcome, wheelchair access, riverside tables, open all day. *Recommended by Gill and
Malcolm Stott*

MARTON CUM GRAFTON SE4263   YO51 9QY
Olde Punch Bowl
Signed off A1 3 miles N of A59

Clean welcoming old pub under newish management, half a dozen well kept ales, good
reasonably priced food (not Mon, Tues lunchtimes) from interesting snacks up, good
friendly service, roomy heavy-beamed open-plan bar, real fires, restaurant; children and
dogs have been welcome, disabled facilities, picnic-sets in pleasant garden, open all day
Fri-Sun. *Recommended by Allan Westbury, Gordon and Margaret Ormondroyd*

If you stay overnight in an inn or hotel, they are allowed to serve you an
alcoholic drink at any hour of the day or night.

MASHAM SE2281   HG4 4YD
Black Bull in Paradise
Theakstons Visitor Centre, off Church Street; signed from market place

Converted outhouse of some character attached to Theakstons Visitor Centre; high-vaulted roof and galleried area, thick stone walls hung with portraits of the Theakston family and old photographs of the brewery and Masham itself, traditional furnishings on flagstones, winter open fire and full range of Theakstons ales from six handpumps; restricted hours, brewery tours. *Recommended by Adrian and Dawn Collinge, Hunter and Christine Wright*

MASHAM SE2281   HG4 4EN
☆ Black Sheep Brewery
Wellgarth, Crosshills

Unusual décor in this big warehouse room alongside brewery, more bistro than pub with a lively atmosphere and good mix of customers, well kept Black Sheep range and several wines by the glass, enjoyable reasonably priced food, friendly staff, tables with cheery patterned cloths and brightly cushioned green café chairs, pubbier tables by bar, lots of bare wood, some rough stonework, green-painted steel girders and pillars, free-standing partitions and big plants, glass wall with view into the brewing exhibition centre; piped music; children welcome, picnic-sets out on grass, brewery tours and shop, open all day Thurs-Sat, till 4.30pm Mon-Weds and Sun. *Recommended by Janet and Peter Race, WW, John and Eleanor Holdsworth, Ian and Helen Stafford and others*

MASHAM SE2381   HG4 4HR
Bruce Arms
Morton Row

Friendly local by the side of the market square, Black Sheep and Theakstons, authentic inexpensive indian food (evenings), pubby furniture on patterned carpet, some exposed stonework, hunting prints; TV, free juke box, karaoke; garden picnic-sets, nice Dales views. *Recommended by Mike and Jayne Bastin*

MASHAM SE2280   HG4 4EF
Kings Head
Market Place

Handsome 18th-c stone inn (Chef & Brewer), two modernised linked bars with stone fireplaces, well kept Black Sheep and Theakstons, good wine choice, enjoyable standard food served by friendly helpful staff, part-panelled restaurant; piped music, TV; children welcome, tables out at front and in sunny courtyard behind, 27 bedrooms, open all day. *Recommended by Peter and Anne Hollindale, Mike and Jayne Bastin, Janet and Peter Race, Ed and Anna Fraser*

MASHAM SE2281   HG4 4EN
White Bear
Wellgarth, Crosshills; signed off A6108 opposite turn into town

Comfortable stone-built beamed pub, small public bar with full range of Theakstons ales kept well, larger lounge with coal fire, food from sandwiches up (not Sun evening), decent wines by the glass, pleasant efficient staff, restaurant extension; piped music; children and dogs welcome, terrace tables, 14 bedrooms, open all day. *Recommended by Adrian and Dawn Collinge, the Didler, Dennis Jones, Ed and Anna Fraser*

MENSTON SE1744   LS29 6EB
Fox
Bradford Road (A65/A6038)

Contemporary M&B dining pub in a former coaching inn, good choice of enjoyable fairly priced food, friendly staff, Black Sheep, Timothy Taylors Landlord and a guest such as Adnams, big fireplace, flagstones and polished boards in one part; piped music; two terraces looking beyond car park to cricket field. *Recommended by D M Jack, John and Eleanor Holdsworth*

MIDDLEHAM SE1287 DL8 4NP
Black Swan
Market Place

Popular old inn by the castle, heavy-beamed bar with built-in high-backed settles, big stone fireplace, well kept ales including Theakstons and Black Sheep, bistro-style food, small restaurant; piped music, TV; children welcome, dogs in bar, tables on cobbles outside and in back garden, good walking country, eight bedrooms (can be noisy), good breakfast, open all day. *Recommended by Simon Le Fort, Michael Butler*

MIDDLEHAM SE1287 DL8 4PE
☆ **White Swan**
Market Place

Extended coaching inn opposite cobbled market town square, beamed and flagstoned entrance bar with built-in window pew and pubby furniture, open woodburner, well kept Theakstons ales, several wines by the glass and malt whiskies, enjoyable bistro-style food, friendly efficient staff, modern spacious dining room, large fireplace and small area with contemporary leather seats and sofa, more dining space in back room; piped music; children welcome, comfortable bedrooms. *Recommended by Dennis Jones, Ed and Anna Fraser*

MIDHOPESTONES SK2399 S36 4GW
Mustard Pot
Mortimer Road, S off A616

Cosy and friendly characterful 17th-c country local, three small rooms, flagstones, stripped stone and pine, assorted chairs, tables and settles, two log fires, Black Sheep and Timothy Taylors Landlord, enjoyable home-made food all day including Sun carvery, weekend restaurant; piped music; no dogs; children welcome, seats out front and back, three bedrooms, open all day, closed Mon. *Recommended by Carl Rahn Griffith*

MILLINGTON SE8351 YO42 1TX
Gait
Main Street

Friendly 16th-c beamed village pub, good straightforward food, happy staff, five well kept ales including York, nice mix of old and newer furnishings, large map of Yorkshire on ceiling, big inglenook log fire; children welcome, garden picnic-sets, appealing village in good Wolds walking country, closed Mon-Thurs lunchtimes, open all day Sun. *Recommended by Christopher Turner, Roger and Anne Newbury*

MIRFIELD SE2017 WF14 8EE
Hare & Hounds
Liley Lane (B6118 2 miles S)

Popular smartly done Vintage Inn, open-plan interior with several distinct areas, good choice of reasonably priced food all day, well kept Black Sheep and Leeds, cheerful helpful staff; tables outside with good Pennine views. *Recommended by Gordon and Margaret Ormondroyd, Michael Butler*

MIRFIELD SE2019 WF14 9JJ
Yorkshire Puddin'
Dunbottle Lane

Modernised and extended with emphasis on low-priced food including bargain OAP menu and Sun carvery, real ales; Tues quiz; children welcome, terrace picnic-sets, open all day. *Recommended by John and Eleanor Holdsworth*

MUKER SD9097 DL11 6QG
☆ **Farmers Arms**
B6270 W of Reeth

New owners for this small unpretentious walkers' pub in a beautiful valley village, warm fire, friendly staff and locals, well kept Black Sheep, John Smiths and Theakstons, wines, teas and coffees, enjoyable straightforward good value food including lunchtime sandwiches, simple modern pine furniture, flagstones and panelling, darts and dominoes; children and dogs welcome, hill views from terrace tables, stream across the road, open all day. *Recommended by Lawrence Pearse, the Didler, Arthur Pickering*

MYTHOLMROYD SD9922
HX7 5TA
Hinchcliffe Arms
Off B6138 S at Cragg Vale

Spotless old stone-built pub with enjoyable food including a good value set menu, well kept real ales, friendly staff, open fires; attractive setting near village church on road that leads only to a reservoir, popular with walkers. *Recommended by Mr and Mrs P R Thomas*

NEWLAY SE2346
LS13 1EQ
Abbey
Bridge 221, Leeds & Liverpool Canal

Six or so well kept ales, enjoyable generously served food including deals, friendly cat called Smudge. *Recommended by Alan and Shirley Sawden*

NEWTON UNDER ROSEBERRY NZ5613
TS9 6QR
Kings Head
The Green, off A173

Nicely converted 17th-c cottage row in an attractive village below Roseberry Topping (known locally as the Cleveland Matterhorn), emphasis on a wide choice of enjoyable well priced food in large restaurant area, good service, real ales including Theakstons; disabled facilities, terrace with water feature, eight bedrooms, good breakfast. *Recommended by Ed and Anna Fraser*

NEWTON-ON-OUSE SE5160
YO30 2BN
Blacksmiths Arms
Cherry Tree Avenue, S off Moor Lane

Attractive welcoming village pub, comfortable interior with big fireplace, lots of pump clips and other bits and pieces, well kept Jennings and Ringwood, wide-ranging menu. *Recommended by Roger and Lesley Everett*

NORLAND SE0521
HX6 3RP
Moorcock
Moor Bottom Lane

Simply refurbished L-shaped bar and beamed restaurant, wide choice of enjoyable generous food including good value Sun lunch, children's helpings too, Timothy Taylors and Thwaites, friendly hard-working staff. *Recommended by Pat and Tony Martin*

NORTHALLERTON SE3794
DL6 1DP
Tithe Bar
Friarage Street

Market Town Tavern with half a dozen good, mainly Yorkshire ales changing quickly, plenty of continental beers, friendly staff, tasty food lunchtime and early evening, three traditional bar areas with tables and chairs, settle and armchairs, bare boards and brewery posters, upstairs evening brasserie; open all day. *Recommended by Mr and Mrs Maurice Thompson, Adrian Johnson, Tony and Wendy Hobden, Ed and Anna Fraser*

NORWOOD GREEN SE1326
HX3 8QG
☆ Old White Beare
Signed off A641 in Wyke, or off A58 Halifax—Leeds just W of Wyke; Village Street

Nicely renovated and extended old pub named after ship whose timbers it incorporates, well kept Copper Dragon and Timothy Taylors, traditional good value home-made food all day including sandwiches and set deals, friendly service, bar with steps up to dining area, small character snug, imposing galleried flagstoned barn restaurant; children and dogs welcome, front terrace, back garden, Calderdale Way and Brontë Way pass the door, open all day. *Recommended by John and Eleanor Holdsworth, Gordon and Margaret Ormondroyd, Clive Flynn*

OAKWORTH SE0138   BD22 0RX
Grouse
Harehills, Oldfield; 2 miles towards Colne

Comfortable old Timothy Taylors pub, well altered and extended, their ales kept well, enjoyable food all day from baguettes up including weekday set deal (12-5pm), friendly staff; undisturbed hamlet in fine moorland surroundings, picnic-sets on terrace with good Pennine views. *Recommended by John and Eleanor Holdsworth*

OSMOTHERLEY SE4597   DL6 3AA
☆ ## Golden Lion
The Green, West End; off A19 N of Thirsk

Busy attractive old stone pub with friendly welcome, Timothy Taylors and three guests, around 50 malt whiskies, roomy beamed bar on left with old pews and a few decorations, similarly unpretentious well worn-in eating area on right, weekend dining room, well liked pubby food and good service; piped music; children welcome, dogs in bar, seats in covered courtyard, benches out front looking across the village green, 44-mile Lyke Wake walk starts here and Coast to Coast walk nearby, bedrooms, closed Mon and Tues lunchtimes, otherwise open all day. *Recommended by Brian Brooks, John and Eleanor Holdsworth, J F M and M West, Marlene and Jim Godfrey, Ed and Anna Fraser, Mrs J P Cleall*

OSSETT SE2719   WF5 8ND
☆ ## Brewers Pride
Low Mill Road/Healey Lane (long cul-de-sac by railway sidings, off B6128)

Friendly basic local with Bob's Brewing Comany's White Lion (brewed at back of pub), Rudgate Ruby Mild and several guests such as Ossett, cosy front rooms and flagstoned bar, open fires, brewery memorabilia, good well priced food (not Sun), new dining extension, small games room, live music first Sun of month; well behaved children welcome, big back garden, near Calder & Hebble Canal, open all day. *Recommended by Michael Butler, the Didler*

OSSETT SE2719   WF5 8JS
Tap
The Green

Basic décor with flagstones and open fire, pleasant relaxed atmosphere, Ossett ales and guests (usually Fullers London Pride), decent wines by the glass, friendly service and locals, photos of other Ossett pubs; open all day Thurs-Sun. *Recommended by the Didler, Michael Butler*

OTLEY SE2045   LS29 6BE
Chevin
West Chevin Road, off A660

Well maintained pub largely rebuilt after a fire, young enthusiastic staff, good home-made food including some inventive choices, Greene King Old Speckled Hen and Timothy Taylors Landlord; children welcome, garden with splendid Wharfedale views, open all day. *Recommended by D W Stokes*

OTLEY SE1945   LS21 3DT
Fleece
Westgate (A659)

Stone-built pub reopened after major refurbishment, full range of Wharfebank ales and three changing guests, good choice of enjoyable food; open all day. *Recommended by the Didler*

There are report forms at the back of the book.

OTLEY SE2045   LS21 1AD

Junction
Bondgate (A660)

Welcoming family-run beamed pub, single smallish bar with tiled floor, wall benches and fire, 11 well kept ales (cheaper Mon) including Caledonian Deuchars IPA, Timothy Taylors Landlord, Tetleys and Theakstons, a real cider, over 60 malts, no food but you can bring your own (good bakery nearby), live music Tues and eclectic DJ night Sun; children (till 9pm) and dogs welcome, covered smokers' area at back, open all day. *Recommended by Paul Rowe, the Didler*

OVERTON SE2516   WF4 4RF

Black Swan
Off A642 Wakefield—Huddersfield; Green Lane

Traditional local, two cosy knocked-together low-beamed rooms full of brasses and bric-a-brac, well kept John Smiths, popular Thurs quiz night. *Recommended by Michael Butler*

OXENHOPE SE0434   BD22 9SN

☆ Dog & Gun
Off B6141 towards Denholme

Beautifully placed roomy 17th-c moorland pub, smartly extended and comfortable, with good varied food from sandwiches to lots of fish and Sun roasts (worth booking then), thriving atmosphere, cheerful landlord and attentive staff, full Timothy Taylors range kept well, good choice of malts, beamery, copper, brasses, plates and jugs, big log fire each end, padded settles and stools, glass-covered well in one dining area, wonderful views; five bedrooms in adjoining hotel. *Recommended by Pat and Tony Martin, Gordon and Margaret Ormondroyd and others*

PICKHILL SE3483   YO7 4JG

☆ Nags Head
Masham turn-off from A1, and village signed off B6267 in Ainderby Quernhow

Well run dining pub with friendly landlord and staff, tables all laid for eating, but tap room (lots of ties, jugs, coach horns and ale-yards) serves Black Sheep, Theakstons and a guest ale, smarter lounge bar with green plush banquettes on matching carpet, pictures for sale, open fire, library-themed restaurant with good popular food (all day weekends); TV, piped music; well behaved children till 7.30pm (after that in dining room), seats on front verandah, boules and quoits pitch, nine-hole putting green, comfortable bedrooms, handy for an A1 break, open all day. *Recommended by Jon Clarke, Ian Malone, Don Mitchell, J F M and M West and others*

POOL SE2546   LS21 2PS

Hunters
A658 towards Harrogate

Split-level country pub with well kept Tetleys, Theakstons and lots of changing microsbrews (tasting-notes on board), farm cider, helpful staff, simple lunchtime food from sandwiches to good Sun roasts, balcony for warm weather, open fires, pool, dominoes, table skittles; open all day. *Recommended by the Didler*

POOL SE2445   LS21 1LH

White Hart
Just off A658 S of Harrogate, A659 E of Otley

Light and airy M&B dining pub (bigger inside than it looks), well liked italian-based food all day including sharing plates, pizzas and more restauranty dishes, fixed-price menu too, friendly young staff, good choice of wines by the glass, Greene King and Timothy Taylors, stylishly simple bistro eating areas, armchairs and sofas on bar's flagstones and bare boards; plenty of tables outside. *Recommended by Gordon and Margaret Ormondroyd, John and Eleanor Holdsworth, Michael Butler, Robert Turnham, Jeremy King and others*

POTTO NZ4703   DL6 3HQ
Dog & Gun
Cooper Lane

Tucked-away modern bar/restaurant/hotel, clean contemporary décor, enjoyable food (not Sun evening) from shortish menu including some interesting choices, well kept Captain Cook ales (brewed at sister pub, the White Swan at Stokesley) and guests, friendly attentive staff; tables under parasols on front decking, five bedrooms, open all day. *Recommended by David and Sue Smith*

RAMSGILL SE1171   HG3 5RL
☆ Yorke Arms
Nidderdale

Upmarket 18th-c hotel (not a pub), small smart bar with some heavy Jacobean furniture and log fires, Black Sheep Best, a fine wine list, good choice of spirits and fresh juices, Michelin-starred restaurant; piped music, no under-12s; seats outside (snack menu), comfortable bedrooms, good quiet moorland and reservoir walks. *Recommended by Robert Wivell*

REDMIRE SE0491   DL8 4EA
Bolton Arms
Hargill Lane

Nicely refurbished village pub under friendly new licensees, good food, well kept Black Sheep, Wensleydale and a guest, comfortable carpeted bar, attractive dining room; disabled facilities, small garden, handy for Wensleydale Railway and Bolton Castle, good walks, three courtyard bedrooms. *Recommended by Michael Tack, David Field*

RIBBLEHEAD SD7678   LA6 3AS
Station Inn
B6255 Ingleton—Hawes

Great spot up on the moors by Ribblehead Viaduct (Settle–Carlisle trains), friendly licensees doing varied food from snacks up, log fire, real ales, low-priced wine and coffee, simple public bar with darts and pool, dining room with viaduct mural (the bar has relevant photographs, some you can buy); piped music, TV; children welcome, muddy boots in bar, picnic-sets outside, five bedrooms (some sharing bath), bunkhouse, open all day. *Recommended by Ann and Tony Bennett-Hughes, R C Vincent*

RIPON SE3171   HG4 1LQ
☆ One-Eyed Rat
Allhallowgate

Friendly little bare-boards pub with numerous well kept real ales (occasional festivals), farm cider, lots of bottled beers and country wines, long narrow bar with warming fire, cigarette cards, framed beer mats, bank notes and old pictures, no food but may have free black pudding, pool; children welcome, pleasant outside area, open all day Sat, closed weekday lunchtimes. *Recommended by Alan Thwaite, Nick and Alison Dowson, Tim and Ann Newell*

RIPON SE3170   HG4 1QW
Water Rat
Bondgate Green, off B6265

Small pub on two levels, prettily set by a footbridge over River Skell, with good choice of well kept ales such as Adnams and York, several wines by the glass, reliable straightforward food including sandwiches, friendly service, conservatory; charming view of cathedral, ducks and weir from the riverside terrace. *Recommended by Janet and Peter Race, Chris and Jeanne Downing*

Virtually all pubs in the *Good Pub Guide* sell wine by the glass. We mention wines
if they are a cut above the average.

RISHWORTH SE0316   HX6 4QU

 Old Bore

Oldham Road (A672)

Comfortable and quirkily stylish country dining pub, good interesting seasonal food, all home-made including breads and ice-cream, not cheap but some deals, good choice of wines by the glass, Timothy Taylors and guests, friendly helpful staff, beams and standing timbers, plenty of bric-a-brac and old prints, mixed furnishings, woodburners; outside picnic-sets, closes 8pm Sun evening. *Recommended by Andy and Jill Kassube, Pat and Tony Martin, Gordon and Margaret Ormondroyd*

RISHWORTH SE0216   HX6 4RH

Turnpike

Opposite Booth Wood Reservoir, near M62 junction 22

Restored 19th-c country inn well placed for motorway, spacious modern interior keeping original features, friendly efficient staff, good choice of enjoyable food all day (till 7pm Sun) including good value set menu (Mon-Thurs) and popular Sun lunch; children welcome, fine view of reservoir and surrounding moorland, six bedrooms, open all day. *Recommended by Gordon and Margaret Ormondroyd*

ROBIN HOOD'S BAY NZ9504   YO22 4SJ

Bay Hotel

The Dock, Bay Town

Friendly old village inn at end of the 191-mile Coast to Coast walk, fine sea views from cosy picture-window upstairs bar (Wainwright bar downstairs open too, if busy), ales such as Caledonian Deuchars IPA, Courage Directors, John Smiths and Theakstons, good value home-made food in bar and separate dining area, young staff coping well, log fires; piped music; lots of tables outside, cosy bedrooms, steep road down and no parking at bottom. open all day. *Recommended by the Didler, Chris and Jeanne Downing, George Atkinson*

ROBIN HOOD'S BAY NZ9505   YO22 4SE

 Laurel

Bay Bank; village signed off A171 S of Whitby

Charming welcoming little pub at the heart of an especially pretty unspoilt fishing village, beamed neatly kept main bar with old local photographs, Victorian prints and brasses, and lager bottles from all over the world, warm open fire, Adnams and Theakstons, you can buy sandwiches from the Old Bakery Tearooms and eat them in the pub, darts and board games; piped music; children in snug bar only, dogs welcome, pretty hanging baskets and window boxes, self-contained apartment for two, open all day (from 2pm Mon-Thurs in winter). *Recommended by Eric Ruff, the Didler*

SALTBURN-BY-THE-SEA NZ6621   TS12 1HF

Ship

A174 towards Whitby

Beautiful setting among beached fishing boats, sea views from nautical-style black-beamed bars and a big dining lounge, wide range of inexpensive generous food including fresh fish, Tetleys and good choice of wines by the glass, friendly helpful service, restaurant, family room; busy at holiday times; tables outside, open all day in summer. *Recommended by Julie Halliday*

SANCTON SE9039   YO43 4QP

Star

King Street (A1034 S of Market Weighton)

Neatly modernised and recently extended village dining pub, competently cooked food (local produce including own vegetables), extensive wine list, well kept ales such as Black Sheep, good friendly service; lovely surrounding countryside, open all day Sun, closed Mon. *Recommended by Marlene and Jim Godfrey, Jonathan Laverack, Eileen and David Webster*

SAWDON TA9484   YO13 9DY

Anvil
Main Street

Pretty high-raftered former smithy with good locally sourced food from chef/landlord, well kept Black Sheep and guests, good range of wines, friendly attentive staff and immaculate housekeeping, feature smith's hearth and woodburner, lower-ceilinged second bar leading through to small neat dining room; two self-catering cottages, closed Mon, Tues. *Recommended by Keith and Margaret Kettell, Peter Burton, Steve Crosley, Matthew James*

SCARBOROUGH TA0488   YO11 1QW
Leeds Arms
St Marys Street

Proper traditional pub, interesting and friendly, with lots of fishing and RNLI memorabilia, well kept ales, great atmosphere, no food or music. *Recommended by Alan Burns*

SCAWTON SE5483   YO7 2HG
☆ Hare
Off A170 Thirsk—Helmsley

Attractive popular dining pub in a quiet spot, good carefully cooked well presented food including plenty of fish and a good vegetarian choice, enthusiastic hospitable landlord and friendly staff, good wines by the glass, three well kept ales including Black Sheep and Timothy Taylors, stripped-pine tables, heavy beams and some flagstones, old-fashioned range and woodburner, William Morris wallpaper, appealing prints and old books; children welcome, wrought-iron garden furniture, open all day in summer, closed Mon. *Recommended by Brian and Pat Wardrobe, John and Verna Aspinall, Ed and Anna Fraser, Ben and Ruth Levy*

SETTLE SD8163   BD24 0HB
☆ Golden Lion
B6480 (main road through town), off A65 bypass

Warm friendly old-fashioned atmosphere in a market-town inn with grand staircase sweeping down into baronial-style high-beamed hall bar, lovely log fire, comfortably worn settles, plush seats, brass, prints and plates on dark panelling, enjoyable good value food (all day weekends) including interesting specials, well kept Thwaites, decent wines by the glass, good-humoured helpful staff, splendid dining room; public bar with darts, pool, games machines and TV; children in eating area, 12 good-sized comfortable bedrooms, hearty breakfast, open all day. *Recommended by Neil and Anita Christopher, Peter Salmon, Clive Flynn, Tony and Maggie Harwood*

SHEFFIELD SK3487   S3 7QL
Bath
Victoria Street, off Glossop Road

Two small colourfully restored bare-boards rooms with friendly staff, well kept Abbeydale, Acorn, Tetleys and guests from a central servery, luchtime bar food (not Sat), nice woodwork, tiles and glass, live jazz/blues Sun (usually), irish music Mon; open all day, closed Sun lunchtime. *Recommended by the Didler*

SHEFFIELD SK3687   S3 8SA

☆ Fat Cat
23 Alma Street

Deservedly busy town local with good own-brewed ales and changing guests, draught and bottled belgian beers, Weston's cider and country wines, low-priced mainly vegetarian bar food (not Sun evening), friendly staff, two small downstairs rooms with coal fires, simple wooden tables and cushioned seats, brewery-related prints, jugs, bottles and advertising mirrors, upstairs room with sports TV; children welcome away from main bar, dogs allowed, picnic-sets in fairylit back courtyard, brewery visitor centre (you can book tours on 0114 249 4804), open all day. *Recommended by Marian and Andrew Ruston, John and Sharon Hancock, DC, the Didler, Ian and Helen Stafford, Mike and Eleanor Anderson and others*

SHEFFIELD SK3687   S3 8AT
Gardeners Rest
Neepsend Lane

Welcoming beer-enthusiast landlord serving his own good Sheffield ales from a light wood counter, also several changing guests tapped from the cask, farm cider and continental beers, no food, old brewery memorabilia, changing local artwork, daily papers, games including bar billiards, live music, popular Sun quiz; children welcome (till 9pm) and well behaved dogs, disabled facilities, back conservatory and tables out overlooking River Don, open all day Thurs-Sun, from 3pm other days. *Recommended by Simon Wigglesworth-Baker, the Didler*

SHEFFIELD SK3588   S3 8GG
Harlequin
Nursery Street

Welcoming open-plan corner pub owned by nearby Brew Company, their well kept ales and a great selection of changing guests, also bottled imports and real ciders/perries, straightforward cheap lunchtime food including Sun roasts, beer festivals, regular live music, Weds quiz; dogs welcome, children till 7pm, outside seating, open all day. *Recommended by the Didler, Peter Monk*

SHEFFIELD SK3687   S6 2UB
☆ Hillsborough
Langsett Road/Wood Street; by Primrose View tram stop

Chatty and friendly pub in a hotel, eight beers including own microbrews and quickly changing guests, good wine and soft drinks' choice, generous good value food including Sun roasts, daily papers, open fire, bare-boards bar, lounge, views to ski slope from attractive back conservatory and terrace tables; silent TV; children and dogs welcome, six good value bedrooms, covered parking, open all day. *Recommended by JJW, CMW, the Didler*

SHEFFIELD SK4086   S3 8RY
☆ Kelham Island Tavern
Kelham Island

Busy backstreet local with up to 12 competitively priced ales including a mild and stout/porter, real ciders, knowledgeable helpful staff, traditional pubby furnishings, some nice artwork on yellow walls, perhaps Puss Cat the ginger pub cat, cheap well liked bar food (not Sun), live folk music Sun evening; children and dogs welcome, plenty of seats and tables in unusual flower-filled back courtyard with woodburner for chilly evenings, award-winning front window boxes, open all day. *Recommended by Simon Wigglesworth-Baker, the Didler, Tony Hobden, Matthew Lidbury*

SHEFFIELD SK3290   S6 2GA
☆ New Barrack
601 Penistone Road, Hillsborough

Lively and friendly pub with 11 changing ales, lots of bottled belgian beers and 28 malt whiskies, tasty good value bar food (Fri, Sat light suppers till midnight), comfortable front lounge with log fire and upholstered seats on old pine floors, tap room with another fire, back room for small functions, daily papers, regular events including a chess club, live weekend music and comedy nights; TV; children till 9pm, dogs welcome, award-winning small walled garden, difficult local parking, open all day. *Recommended by JJW, CMW, the Didler, Matthew Lidbury*

SHEFFIELD SK3186   S10 3GD
Ranmoor
Fulwood Road

Comfortable open-plan Victorian local with good value home cooking (not Sun, Mon), Abbeydale and guest ales, piano (often played); pleasant garden, open all day. *Recommended by the Didler*

SHEFFIELD SK3389   S6 2LN
Rawson Spring
Langsett Road

Popular airy Wetherspoons in former swimming baths, their usual value, well kept changing ales, impressive décor with unusual skylights. *Recommended by the Didler*

SHEFFIELD SK3185   S10 3QA
Rising Sun
Fulwood Road

Friendly drinkers' pub with up to 14 ales including full Abbeydale range (many more during summer beer festival), bottled beers, decent food, large lounge with games and reference books; dogs welcome, nice back garden, open all day. *Recommended by the Didler, Mr and Mrs Alesbrook*

SHEFFIELD SK3687   S1 2BS
Rutland Arms
Brown Street/Arundel Lane

Comfortable one-room corner pub with handsome façade, Jennings Cumberland and a great range of changing guests, real cider, food all day till 8pm (not Sun); tables in compact garden, handy for the Crucible and station, bedrooms. *Recommended by the Didler*

SHEFFIELD SK3585   S2 3AA
Sheaf View
Gleadless Road, Heeley Bottom

Wide range of local and other changing ales, farm cider, spotless unusually shaped bar, pleasant staff; very busy on match days; disabled facilities, tables outside, open all day weekends, closed Mon lunchtime. *Recommended by the Didler*

SHEFFIELD SK3586   S1 2BP
Sheffield Tap
Station, Platform 1B

Busy station bar in restored Victorian refreshment room, popular for its huge choice of world beers on tap and in bottles, also five Thornbridge ales and half a dozen guests, knowledgeable helpful staff may offer tasters, snacky food, tiled interior with vaulted roof; open all day. *Recommended by Ian and Helen Stafford, the Didler, Mike and Eleanor Anderson, Adam Gordon, Terry Barlow and others*

SHEFFIELD SK3487   S3 7HG
University Arms
Brook Hill

Former university staff club, comfortable and relaxed, with well kept Thornbridge and changing guests, decent food (not Sat evening), unspoilt interior with old woodwork and alcove seating, back conservatory and small garden, some live music; open all day, closed Sun. *Recommended by the Didler*

SHEFFIELD SK3687   S3 7EQ
☆ Wellington
Henry Street; Shalesmoor tram stop right outside

Unpretentious relaxed pub with up to ten changing beers including own bargain Little Ale Cart brews, bottled imports, real cider, coal fire in lounge, photographs of old Sheffield, daily papers and pub games, friendly staff; tables out behind, open all day with afternoon break on Sun. *Recommended by the Didler*

SHELLEY SE2112   HD8 8LR
☆ Three Acres
Roydhouse (not signed); from B6116 towards Skelmanthorpe, turn left in Shelley (signposted Flockton, Elmley, Elmley Moor), go up lane for 2 miles towards radio mast

Civilised former coaching inn with all emphasis now on hotel and dining side; roomy lounge with leather chesterfields, old prints and so forth, tankards hanging from main beam, Copper Dragon, 40 malt whiskies and up to 17 wines by the glass from serious (not cheap) list, several formal dining rooms, wide choice of often interesting expensive food from lunchtime sandwiches up, good service; conferences, weddings and events; children welcome, fine moorland setting and lovely views, smart well equipped bedrooms. *Recommended by Andy and Jill Kassube, Gordon and Margaret Ormondroyd*

SHEPLEY SE1809   HD8 8AP

☆ **Farmers Boy**
Junction of A629 and A635, from village centre by Black Bull

Good if pricey food (some from own smokery) in comfortably modern barn restaurant at the back, friendly efficient service, welcoming cottage-conversion beamed bar, well kept ales such as Black Sheep, Copper Dragon and Tetleys; terrace, open all day. *Recommended by David and Cathrine Whiting, Stu Mac, Matthew Lidbury*

SHIPLEY SE1437   BD18 3JN
Fannys Ale House
Saltaire Road

Cosy and friendly bare-boards alehouse on two floors, gas lighting, log fire and woodburner, brewery memorabilia, up to ten well kept ales including Timothy Taylors and Theakstons, bottled beers and farm ciders, new back extension; can be crowded on weekend evenings; dogs welcome, open all day, closed Mon lunchtime. *Recommended by James Stretton, the Didler, Neil Whitehead, Victoria Anderson, David Bishop, C Cooper*

SINNINGTON SE7485   YO62 6SQ

☆ **Fox & Hounds**
Off A170 W of Pickering

Popular neat 18th-c coaching inn, carpeted beamed bar with woodburner, various pictures and old artefacts, comfortable seats, good imaginative food, particularly friendly and helpful staff, well kept Black Sheep and Copper Dragon, several wines by the glass, a few rare whiskies, lounge and smart separate evening restaurant; piped music; children and dogs welcome, picnic-sets in front, more in garden, pretty village, comfortable bedrooms. *Recommended by Marian and Andrew Ruston, Pat and Stewart Gordon, M S Catling, Leslie and Barbara Owen, Martin Clerk and others*

SKIPTON SD9851   BD23 1JE

☆ **Narrow Boat**
Victoria Street; pub signed down alley off Coach Street

Lively extended pub down cobbled alley, eight real ales, draught and bottled continental beers, farm cider and perry, church pews, dining chairs and stools around wooden tables, old brewery posters, mirrors decorated with beer advertisements, upstairs gallery area with interesting canal mural, decent reasonably priced bar food (not Sun evening), folk club Mon evening; children allowed if eating, dogs welcome, picnic-sets under front colonnade; Leeds & Liverpool Canal nearby, open all day. *Recommended by Dennis Jones, the Didler, Steve Nye*

SKIPTON SD9851   BD23 1HY
Woolly Sheep
Sheep Street

Big bustling pub with full Timothy Taylors range, prompt friendly enthusiastic service, two beamed bars off flagstoned passage, exposed brickwork, stone fireplace, lots of sheep prints and bric-a-brac, daily papers, attractive and comfortable raised lunchtime dining area, good value food (plenty for children); unobtrusive piped music; spacious pretty garden, six good value bedrooms, good breakfast. *Recommended by Stuart Paulley*

SLEDMERE SE9364 YO25 3XQ

☆ **Triton**

B1252/B1253 junction, NW of Great Driffield

Handsome old inn by Sledmere House, open-plan bar with old-fashioned atmosphere, dark wooden furniture on red patterned carpet, 15 clocks ranging from a grandfather to a cuckoo, lots of willow pattern plates, all manner of paintings and pictures, open fire, John Smiths, Timothy Taylors, Tetleys and a guest, 50 different gins, honest bar food (only take bookings in separate restaurant); children welcome till 8pm, bedrooms, open all day Sun till 9pm, closed Mon lunchtime in winter. *Recommended by WW, Gerard Dyson, Pete Coxon, Ed and Anna Fraser*

SNAINTON TA9182 YO13 9PL

Coachman

Pickering Road W (A170)

More restaurant-with-rooms but also a small bar serving Wold Top ales, good well presented food in smart white-tableclothed dining room, friendly service, comfortable lounge with squashy sofas; well tended gardens, smokers' shelter at front, three bedrooms, good breakfast. *Recommended by Ian Malone, Peter Burton*

SNAITH SE6422 DN14 9JS

Brewers Arms

Pontefract Road

Converted mill brewing its own good range of distinctive beers, fairly priced home-made food from shortish menu, friendly staff, open-plan bar and conservatory-style dining area, old well, open fireplace; children welcome in eating areas. *Recommended by Ross Gibbins, John and Eleanor Holdsworth, Pat and Stewart Gordon*

SNAPE SE2684 DL8 2TB

☆ **Castle Arms**

Off B6268 Masham—Bedale

Neat homely pub in pretty village, flagstoned bar with open fire, horsebrasses on beams, straightforward pubby furniture, Banks's, Jennings and Marstons, well liked bar food, dining room (also flagstoned) with another fire and plenty of dark tables and chairs; children and dogs welcome, picnic-sets out at front and in courtyard, fine walks in the Yorkshire Dales and on North York Moors, bedrooms. *Recommended by Tim and Sue Halstead*

SOUTH DALTON SE9645 HU17 7PN

☆ **Pipe & Glass**

West End; brown sign to pub off B1248 NW of Beverley

Charmingly tucked-away village dining pub with very good inventive food (not Sun evening) cooked by young landlord; small bar area with beams, traditional pubby furniture, old prints, bow windows and log fire, Black Sheep and guests, several wines by the glass, 50 malt whiskies, contemporary area beyond with leather chesterfields leading to a stylish restaurant overlooking Dalton Park, serious cookbooks on shelves and framed big-name restaurant menus, attentive staff, piped music; children welcome, seats and tables on quiet lawn with picnic-sets on front terrace, ancient yew tree, luxury bedroom suites, open all day, closed Mon (except bank holidays) and two weeks in Jan. *Recommended by G Jennings, Richard Cole, Robert Wivell*

SOWERBY BRIDGE HX6 3AB

Jubilee Refreshment Rooms

Sowerby Bridge Station

Refurbished station building run by two railway-enthusiast brothers, up to five real ales, bottled continental beers, simple food including breakfast and good home-made cakes, railway memorabilia, old enamel signs, art deco ceiling lamps and feature jeweller's clock; open all day from 9.30am (12 Sun). *Recommended by Pat and Tony Martin*

SOWERBY BRIDGE SE0623   HX6 2BD

Shepherds Rest

On A58 Halifax to Sowerby Bridge

Friendly two-room Ossett pub, their full range and guests, no food; suntrap terrace, open all day Fri-Sun, from 3pm other days. *Recommended by Pat and Tony Martin*

SOWERBY BRIDGE SE0523   HX6 2QG

Works

Hollins Mill Lane, off A58

Big airy two-room bare-boards pub in converted joinery workshop, seating from pews to comfortable sofas, eight real ales and a couple of ciders, good bargain home-made food from pies and casseroles to vegetarian choices, Weds curry night, Sun brunch (10-3pm), poetry readings and live music in backyard (covered in poor weather), comedy night in upstairs room; children and dogs welcome, disabled facilities, open all day. *Recommended by Pat and Tony Martin*

STAMFORD BRIDGE SE7055   YO41 1AX

 ## Three Cups

A166 W of town

Clean and spacious Vintage Inn family dining pub in cosy, timbered, country style, enjoyable good value food all day from regularly changing menu, plenty of wines by the glass, real ales, friendly helpful staff, two blazing fires, glass-topped well; children welcome, disabled access, play area behind, bedrooms. *Recommended by Pat and Graham Williamson*

STANBURY SE0037   BD22 0HW

Old Silent

Hob Lane

Neatly rebuilt moorland dining pub near Ponden Reservoir, friendly atmosphere, good reasonably priced fresh food including specials, real ales such as Timothy Taylors, attentive helpful service, character linked rooms with beams, flagstones, mullioned windows and open fires, games room, restaurant and conservatory; children welcome, bedrooms. *Recommended by John and Eleanor Holdsworth*

STILLINGTON SE5867   YO61 1JU

☆ Bay Tree

Main Street; leave York on outer ring road (A1237) to Scarborough, first exit on left signposted B1363 to Helmsley

Cottagey pub in pretty village's main street, contemporary bar areas with civilised chatty atmosphere, comfortable cushioned wall seats and leather/bamboo tub chairs around mix of tables, church candles and lanterns, fresh flowers, basketwork and attractive prints on cream or brick walls, central gas-effect coal fire, good bistro-style food including sandwiches, Copper Dragon, fair-priced wines, friendly helpful staff, steps up to cosy dining area, larger conservatory-style back restaurant; piped music; seats in garden and picnic-sets at front under parasols, closed Mon. *Recommended by anon*

STOKESLEY NZ5208   TS9 5BL

☆ White Swan

West End

Good Captain Cook ales brewed in attractive flower-clad pub, L-shaped bar with three relaxing seating areas, log fire, lots of brass on elegant dark panelling, lovely bar counter carving, assorted memorabilia and unusual clock, good lunchtime ploughman's (Weds-Sat), live music, beer festivals; no children; open all day. *Recommended by the Didler*

Half pints: by law, a pub should not charge more for half a pint than half the price of a full pint, unless it shows that half-pint price on its price list.

SUTTON UPON DERWENT SE7047   YO41 4BN
☆ St Vincent Arms
Main Street (B1228 SE of York)

Enjoyable consistently cheerful pub with Fullers and up to seven guests, 14 wines by the glass, good popular bar food (more elaborate evening meals), bustling parlour-style front bar with panelling, traditional high-backed settles, windsor chairs, cushioned bow-window seat and gas-effect coal fire, another lounge and separate dining room open off here; children welcome, dogs in bar, garden tables, handy for Yorkshire Air Museum. *Recommended by G Dobson, Stanley and Annie Matthews, David and Ruth Hollands, Kay and Alistair Butler, Pat and Tony Martin, Roger and Anne Newbury and others*

SUTTON-UNDER-WHITESTONECLIFFE SE4983   YO7 2PR
Whitestonecliffe Inn
A170 E of Thirsk

Well located beamed roadside pub with wide choice of good value food from sandwiches up in bar and restaurant, ales such as Black Sheep, John Smiths and Tetleys in good condition, interesting 17th-c stone bar, log fire, friendly staff, pool room; children welcome, six self-catering cottages. *Recommended by Michael Butler, Stanley and Annie Matthews*

TAN HILL NY8906   DL11 6ED
Tan Hill Inn
Arkengarthdale Road Reeth—Brough, at junction Keld/West Stonesdale Road

Basic old pub in wonderful bleak setting on Pennine Way – Britain's highest, full of bric-a-brac and interesting photographs, simple sturdy furniture, flagstones, ever-burning big log fire (with prized stone side seats), chatty atmosphere, five real ales including one for the pub by Dent, good cheap pubby food, family room, live music weekends, Swaledale sheep show here last Thurs in May; can get overcrowded, often snowbound; children, dogs and even the pub's ducks welcome, seven bedrooms, bunkrooms and camping, open all day; still for sale as we went to press but operating as usual. *Recommended by Claes Mauroy*

TERRINGTON SE6770   YO60 6PP
☆ Bay Horse
W of Malton

Friendly landlord at 17th-c pub with cosy log-fire lounge bar, own Storyteller ales and a guest like Wylam, several wines by the glass, over 30 whiskies, shortish choice of good value home-made pub food including good set Sun lunch (best to book), refurbished dining area, conservatory with old farm tools, traditional games in public bar; children and dogs welcome, garden tables, unspoilt village, may be closed lunchtimes Mon-Weds in winter, open all day Thurs-Sun. *Recommended by Christopher Turner, Pat and Tony Martin*

THIRSK SE4282   YO7 1LL
Golden Fleece
Market Place

Comfortable bustling old coaching inn with enjoyable generous bar food, local real ales, friendly competent service, restaurant, view across market place from bay windows; 23 bedrooms, good breakfast. *Recommended by Janet and Peter Race*

THORNTON SE0933   BD13 3QL
☆ Ring o' Bells
Hill Top Road, off B6145 W of Bradford

19th-c moortop dining pub very popular for its reliably good food including early evening deals, themed and gourmet evenings too, well kept ales from Black Sheep, Courage and Saltaire, panelled bar/dining area with photographs of old Thornton, elegant more modern restaurant with paintings from local artist, pleasant conservatory lounge; no dogs; children welcome, wide views towards Shipley and Bingley. *Recommended by Stanley and Annie Matthews, Keith Moss*

THORNTON SE0832 BD13 3SJ

White Horse

Well Heads

Deceptively large country pub popular for its wide choice of good value generous food and five well kept Timothy Taylors ales, pleasant helpful staff, four separate areas, two with log fires; upstairs lavatories (disabled ones on ground level), also disabled space in car park. *Recommended by Andrew Bosi, Pat and Tony Martin*

THORNTON IN LONSDALE SD6873 LA6 3PB

Marton Arms

Off A65 just NW of Ingleton

Good choice of beers such as Black Sheep, Coniston Bluebird and Sharps Doom Bar, 280 whiskies, friendly helpful staff, standard food, beamed bar with stripped-pine tables and chairs, pews and built-in seats in airy main part, flagstoned public bar with darts and piped music, log fires; picnic-sets on front terrace and at back, great walking country, 13th-c church opposite, comfortable bedrooms, good breakfast. *Recommended by Ian Herdman, Mike and Shelley Woodroffe, David Heath*

THORNTON-LE-CLAY SE6865 YO60 7TG

☆ ## White Swan

Off A64 York—Malton; Low Street

Comfortable and welcoming early 19th-c family-run dining pub, good generous fairly traditional food including daily roasts and children's meals, John Smiths and a guest, decent wines, reasonable prices, beams and brasses, board games and toys; disabled access, neat grounds with terrace tables, duck pond, herb and vegetable gardens, orchard, two summerhouses, donkey paddock, attractive countryside near Castle Howard, closed all day Mon. *Recommended by Paul Tutill, Matthew Tritton- Hughes, Michael Page, Harry Gordon-Finlayson, Mr and Mrs R W Haste, Mr and Mrs R J Oliver*

THRESHFIELD SD9863 BD23 5HB

Old Hall Inn

B6160/B6265 just outside Grassington

Popular place with three old-world linked rooms including smart candlelit dining room, well kept John Smiths, Timothy Taylors and Theakstons, helpful friendly staff, enjoyable food, nice coffee, log fires, high beam-and-plank ceiling, cushioned wall pews, tall well blacked kitchen range; children in eating area, neat garden. *Recommended by John and Eleanor Holdsworth, Bruce and Sharon Eden, Greta and Christopher Wells*

THUNDER BRIDGE SE1811 HD8 0PX

Woodman

Off A629 Huddersfield—Sheffield

Stone-built village pub with two roomy spotless bars, low beams and heavy wooden tables, smart fresh décor, good welcoming service, popular reasonably priced food, well kept Timothy Taylors and Tetleys, upstairs restaurant; tables outside, 12 good bedrooms in adjoining cottages. *Recommended by John and Eleanor Holdsworth, Matthew Lidbury, Gordon and Margaret Ormondroyd*

TICKTON TA0742 HU17 9SH

New Inn

Just off A1035 NE of Beverley

Friendly, efficiently run country pub and restaurant, good up-to-date well presented food all day (including sandwiches) using local produce in modern simply decorated dining area (closed Sun evening, Mon), traditional log-fire locals' bar (closed Mon lunchtime) with well kept Black Sheep and Tetleys, Sun quiz night; farm shop in car park. *Recommended by Marlene and Jim Godfrey*

TIMBLE SE1852   LS21 2NN
Timble
Off Otley—Blubberhouses moors road

Well restored 18th-c stone-built village inn, popular food from pub favourites up (not Sun evening, Mon, Tues – booking advised), real ales; good bedrooms. *Recommended by John and Eleanor Holdsworth*

TOCKWITH SE4652   YO26 7PY
Spotted Ox
Westfield Road, off B1224

Welcoming traditional beamed village local, three areas off central bar, well kept ales, including Tetleys, carefully served the old-fashioned way, good choice of enjoyable sensibly priced home-made food, attentive staff, relaxed atmosphere, interesting local history; open all day Fri-Sun. *Recommended by Les and Sandra Brown*

TONG SE2230   BD4 0RR
Greyhound
Tong Lane

Traditional stone-built, low-beamed and flagstoned local by the village cricket field, distinctive areas including small dining room, enjoyable good value local food, Black Sheep, Greene King Abbot and Tetleys, many wines by the glass, good service; tables outside. *Recommended by Michael Butler, Frank Dowsland*

TOPCLIFFE SE4076   YO7 3RW
Angel
Off A1, take A168 to Thirsk, after 3 miles follow signs for Topcliffe; Long Street

Big bustling place with well kept Camerons ales, enjoyable pubby food, separately themed areas including softly lit stripped-stone faux-irish bar, also billiards room and two dining rooms; piped music, no credit cards; tables outside, bedrooms. *Recommended by William and Ann Reid, Ed and Anna Fraser*

TOTLEY SK3080   S17 3AZ
Cricket
Signed from A621; Penny Lane

Tucked-away stone-built pub opposite rustic cricket field, much focus on dining but still a friendly local atmosphere, pews, mixed chairs and pine tables on bare boards and flagstones, good-quality blackboard food (all day weekends) from sandwiches and pubby staples to some interesting imaginative cooking, friendly service, Thornbridge ales, log fires, good Peak District views, local artwork for sale; children and dogs welcome, tables outside, open all day. *Recommended by W K Wood, Matthew Lidbury*

WAKEFIELD SE3320   WF1 1DL
Bull & Fairhouse
George Street

Welcoming chatty 19th-c pub (was O'Donoghues), well kept Bobs White Lion, Great Heck Golden Bull and four other changing ales (beer festivals), bare-boards bar with comfortable rooms off, open fire, no food, live music weekends, quiz Thurs; children welcome till 8pm, dogs on leads, open all day Sat, Sun, from 5pm other days. *Recommended by the Didler*

WAKEFIELD SE3320   WF1 1UA
Fernandes Brewery Tap
Avison Yard, Kirkgate

Owned by Ossett but still brewing Fernandes ales in the cellar, interesting guest beers, bottled imports, farm ciders, newish ground-floor bar with flagstones, bare brick and panelling, original raftered top-floor bar with unusual breweriana; closed Mon-Thurs lunchtime, open all day Fri-Sun with some lunchtime food. *Recommended by the Didler*

WAKEFIELD SE3220   WF1 1EL
Harrys Bar
Westgate

Cheery, well run one-room local, Bobs, Leeds, Ossett and guests, free buffet early Fri
evening, stripped-brick walls, open fire; small back garden, open all day Sun, closed
lunchtime other days. *Recommended by the Didler*

WALTON SE4447   LS23 7DQ
Fox & Hounds
Hall Park Road, off back road Wetherby—Tadcaster

Popular dining pub with enjoyable food from good sandwiches up (should book Sun
lunch), well kept John Smiths and a guest such as Black Sheep or Caledonian Deuchars
IPA, good friendly service, thriving atmosphere. *Recommended by Greta and Christopher Wells,
Pat and Graham Williamson, Les and Sandra Brown*

WEST TANFIELD SE2678   HG4 5JJ
Bruce Arms
Main Street (A6108 N of Ripon)

Comfortable and welcoming under new licensees, good affordable freshly made food, well
kept Black Sheep and Copper Dragon, friendly service, flagstones and log fires; two
bedrooms, good breakfast, closed Sun evening, Mon. *Recommended by Philip Silvester, Guy,
I M Harbinger, Helen Tilford*

WEST TANFIELD SE2678   HG4 5JQ
Bull
Church Street (A6108 N of Ripon)

Open-plan with slightly raised dining area to the left and flagstoned bar on right, popular
blackboard food (all day Sat, not Sun evening) from lunchtime sandwiches up, well kept
Theakstons and guests, decent wines, brisk pleasant service; piped music; children
allowed away from bar, tables on terraces in attractive garden sloping steeply to River Ure
and its old bridge, five bedrooms, open all day weekends, closed Tues. *Recommended by Earl
and Chris Pick, Dennis Jones, Tim and Sue Halstead*

WESTOW SE7565   YO60 7NE
Blacksmiths Inn
Off A64 York—Malton; Main Street

18th-c inn doing well under current friendly landlord; attractive beamed bar, woodburner
in big inglenook, good choice of beers and well liked pub food, darts and dominoes,
restaurant; picnic-sets on side terrace, separate bedroom block. *Recommended by
Christopher Turner*

WHITBY NZ9011   YO22 4DE
☆ Duke of York
Church Street, Harbour East Side

Busy pub in fine harbourside position, handy for famous 199 steps leading up to abbey;
comfortable beamed lounge bar with fishing memorabilia, Black Sheep, Caledonian and
three guests, decent wines and several malt whiskies, straightforward bar food all day;
piped music, TV, games machine; children welcome, bedrooms overlooking water, no
nearby parking. *Recommended by the Didler, Roger and Ann King, Pete Coxon, Adrian Johnson*

WHITBY NZ8911   YO21 1DH
Station Inn
New Quay Road

Friendly three-room bare-boards drinkers' pub, wide range of well kept changing ales,
farm cider, good wines by the glass, traditional games; piped music – live music Weds;
open all day. *Recommended by the Didler, Tony and Wendy Hobden*

WHIXLEY SE4457   YO26 8AG

Anchor
New Road, E of village (first left turn heading N from Green Hamerton on B6265)

Family-friendly pub with traditional generous food including bargain lunchtime carvery particularly popular with OAPs, friendly young staff, John Smiths and Tetleys, straightforward main eating extension, original core with some character and coal fire in the small lounge. *Recommended by Mrs Joy Griffiths, Pete Coxon*

WIGHILL SE4746   LS24 8BQ

White Swan
Main Street

Updated village pub with enjoyable food from local suppliers including Yorkshire tapas and seasonal game, pub favourites too, ales such as Black Sheep, Timothy Taylors Landlord and a house brew from Moorhouses, pub shop; quiz (first Sun of month); tables outside. *Recommended by anon*

YORK SE5951   YO1 6LN

Ackhorne
St Martins Lane, Micklegate

Proper unspoilt pub under new management, friendly and welcoming, with good choice of changing ales and ciders, simple food, beams, bare boards, panelling, stained glass, leather wall seats, old range and open fire, Civil War prints, bottles and jugs, carpeted snug, traditional games; suntrap back terrace, smokers' shelter, open all day. *Recommended by the Didler, Pete Coxon*

YORK SE5952   YO30 7BH

Bay Horse
Marygate

Large mock-Tudor pub with comfortably refurbished open-plan interior, six well kept changing ales (beer festivals), tea/coffee, fresh food from sandwiches up; piped music, TV; seats out in front, four bedrooms. *Recommended by the Didler*

YORK SE6051   YO1 7PR

☆ Black Swan
Peaseholme Green (inner ring road)

Striking timbered and jettied Tudor building, compact panelled front bar, crooked-floored central hall with fine period staircase, black-beamed back bar with vast inglenook, good choice of real ales, decent wines, good value pubby food from sandwiches up; piped music; children welcome, useful car park, bedrooms, open all day. *Recommended by the Didler, Pete Coxon*

YORK SE6051   YO1 9TF

☆ Blue Bell
Fossgate

Delightfully old-fashioned little Edwardian pub, very friendly and chatty, with well kept Black Sheep, Roosters, Timothy Taylors Landlord and three guests, a mild always available too, good value lunchtime sandwiches (not Sun), daily papers, tiny tiled-floor front bar with roaring fire, panelled ceiling, stained glass, bar pots and decanters, corridor to small back room, hatch service, lamps and candles, pub games; soft piped music; no children; dogs welcome, open all day. *Recommended by Eric Ruff, Eric Larkham, Greta and Christopher Wells, the Didler, Pete Coxon and others*

YORK SE5951   YO1 6JX

☆ Brigantes
Micklegate

Comfortably traditional Market Town Taverns bar/bistro, eight well kept mainly Yorkshire ales, good range of bottled beers, good wines and coffee, enjoyable unpretentious brasserie food all day including snacks and sandwiches, friendly helpful staff, simple pleasant décor, upstairs dining room; open all day. *Recommended by Brian and Janet Ainscough, Eric Larkham, the Didler, Pete Coxon and others*

YORK SE6051   YO1 6DU
Golden Ball
Cromwell Road/Bishophill

Unspoilt and buoyant 1950s local feel in this friendly and well preserved four-room Edwardian corner pub, enjoyable straightforward weekday lunchtime food, six well kept changing ales, Sept beer festival, bar billiards, cards and dominoes; TV, can be lively evenings, live music Thurs; lovely small walled garden, open all day Fri-Sun. *Recommended by the Didler, Richard Marvell*

YORK SE6052   YO1 7LG
Golden Slipper
Goodramgate

Dating from the 15th c with an unpretentious bar and three comfortably old-fashioned small rooms, one lined with books, cheerful efficient staff, good cheap plain lunchtime food from sandwiches up including an OAP special, John Smiths and up to three other beers; TV; tables in back courtyard. *Recommended by Pete Coxon, Eric Larkham*

YORK SE6052   YO1 7HP
Guy Fawkes
High Petergate

Friendly pub in splendid spot next to the Minster, dark panelled interior with small bar to the left and two sizeable rooms to right, good real ale choice, decent food including bargain Sun lunch; bedrooms. *Recommended by Dr Kevan Tucker, Eric Larkham, Dave Webster, Sue Holland, the Didler*

YORK SE6052   YO1 7EH
Lamb & Lion
High Petergate

Sparse furnishings and low lighting including candles giving a spartan Georgian feel, friendly helpful service, four well kept ales including Black Sheep and one brewed for the pub locally, enjoyable simple bar food plus a more elaborate evening set menu (Tues-Sat), no food Sun evening, compact rooms off dark corridors; steep steps up to small attractive garden below city wall and looking up to the Minster, 12 bedrooms, open all day.
Recommended by Eric Larkham, Richard Marvell

YORK SE6051   YO1 8BN
☆ ## Last Drop
Colliergate

Basic traditional York Brewery pub, their own beers and one or two well kept guests, samples offered by friendly knowledgeable young staff, decent wines and country wines, nice fresh good value food (12-4pm) including sandwiches and shared platters, big windows, bare boards, barrel tables and comfortable seats (some up a few steps); no children, can get very busy at lunchtime, may ask to keep a credit card while you eat, attic lavatories; tables out behind, open all day. *Recommended by Dennis Jones, Rob and Catherine Dunster, Eric Larkham, the Didler, Derek and Sylvia Stephenson and others*

YORK SE6051   YO1 8AA
Lendal Cellars
Lendal

Split-level ale house in broad-vaulted 17th-c cellars, stripped brickwork, stone floor, linked rooms and alcoves, good choice of changing ales and wines by the glass, foreign bottled beers, farm cider, decent coffee, enjoyable generous pub food all day, friendly helpful staff; piped music; no dogs; children allowed if eating, open all day. *Recommended by Edward Pearce, Jeremy King, the Didler*

YORK SE5951   YO1 6HU

☆ **Maltings**

Tanners Moat/Wellington Row, below Lendal Bridge

Lively friendly city pub by the river, cheerful landlord, well kept Black Sheep and half a dozen quickly changing interesting guests, several continental beers, 13 ciders, country wines, generous standard bar food (not evenings), old doors for bar front and ceiling, fine collection of railway signs and amusing notices, old chocolate dispensing machine, cigarette and tobacco advertisements, cough and chest remedies and even a lavatory pan in one corner, day's papers framed in gents'; games machine, no credit cards, difficult nearby parking; children allowed mealtimes only, dogs welcome, handy for Rail Museum and station, open all day. *Recommended by Dennis Jones, Eric Larkham, Andy Lickfold, Tim and Ann Newell, Andy and Jill Kassube, the Didler and others*

YORK SE5952   YO30 7BH

Minster Inn

Marygate

Multi-roomed Edwardian local, bric-a-brac and dark old settles, fires and woodburners, corridor to distinctive back room, friendly staff, well kept changing Marstons-related ales, sandwiches, table games; children welcome, tables out behind. *Recommended by Dr Kevan Tucker, Eric Larkham, the Didler*

YORK SE6052   YO1 7LF

Old White Swan

Goodramgate

Bustling spacious pub with Victorian, Georgian and Tudor-themed bars, popular lunchtime food including nine types of sausage, Black Sheep and several other well kept ales, good whisky choice, central glass-covered courtyard good for families; piped and frequent live music, big-screen sports TV, games machines, Mon quiz; open all day. *Recommended by Jeremy King, Derek and Sylvia Stephenson, Pete Coxon*

YORK SE6051   YO1 9PT

Phoenix

George Street

Friendly, well restored little pub next to the city walls, proper front public bar and comfortable back horseshoe-shaped lounge, fresh flowers and candles, four well kept Yorkshire ales, good wines, simple food, popular live jazz Sun evening; beer garden, handy for Barbican, open all day. *Recommended by Rick Howell, Stewart Morris, David Gamston, Pat and Tony Martin, Jon Fulton*

YORK SE6051   YO1 8AN

Punch Bowl

Stonegate

Bustling old black and white fronted pub, friendly helpful service, wide range of generous bargain food all day, small panelled rooms off corridor, TV in beamed one on left of food servery, well kept ales such as Black Sheep Leeds, John Smiths and Thornbridge, good wine choice; piped music, games machines, regular quiz nights; open all day. *Recommended by Jeremy King, Edna Jones, Eric Larkham, Mrs Edna M Jones, Pete Coxon*

YORK SE6151   YO10 3WP

Rook & Gaskill

Lawrence Street

Traditional Castle Rock pub with up to a dozen ales including guests like York, enjoyable food (not Sun), dark wood tables, banquettes, chairs and high stools, conservatory; open all day. *Recommended by Eric Larkham, the Didler, Pete Coxon*

Every entry includes a postcode for use in Sat Nav devices.

YORK SE6052   YO1 7LS
Snickleway
Goodramgate

Interesting little open-plan pub behind big shop-front window, lots of antiques, copper and brass, cosy fires, five well kept ales such as Brains Rev James, John Smiths and Timothy Taylors Landlord, some lunchtime food including good doorstep sandwiches, prompt friendly service. *Recommended by T Gott, Gerard Dyson, D Walkden*

YORK SE6051   YO23 1JH
Swan
Bishopgate Street, Clementhorpe

Unspoilt 1930s pub (Grade II listed), hatch service to lobby for two small rooms off main bar, several changing ales and ciders, friendly knowledgeable staff may offer tasters; busy with young people at weekends; small pleasant walled garden, near city walls, closed weekday lunchtimes, open all day weekends. *Recommended by the Didler, James Hibbins*

YORK SE6052   YO31 7PB
☆ Tap & Spile
Monkgate

Friendly open-plan late-Victorian pub with Roosters and other mainly northern ales, farm cider, decent choice of wines by the glass including country ones, bookshelves, games in raised back area, cheap straightforward lunchtime bar food (not Mon); children in eating area, garden and heated terrace, closed Mon lunchtimes otherwise open all day.
Recommended by the Didler, Eric Larkham, Pete Coxon

YORK SE6052   YO1 7EN
☆ Three Legged Mare
High Petergate

Bustling light and airy modern café-bar with York Brewery's full range and guests kept well (12 handpumps), plenty of belgian beers, quick friendly young staff, interesting sandwiches and some basic lunchtime hot food, low prices, back conservatory; no children; disabled facilities (other lavatories down spiral stairs), back garden with replica gallows after which pub is named, open all day till midnight (11pm Sun). *Recommended by Eric Larkham, Richard Marvell, Pete Coxon, Barry Webber*

YORK SE5951   YO1 6JT
☆ York Brewery Tap
Toft Green, Micklegate

Members only for York Brewery's upstairs lounge (annual fee £3 unless you live in Yorkshire or go on brewery tour), their own full cask range in top condition, also bottled beers, nice clubby atmosphere with friendly staff happy to talk about the beers, lots of breweriana and view of brewing plant, comfortable sofas and armchairs, magazines and daily papers, brewery shop; no food; children allowed, open all day except Sun evening. *Recommended by the Didler, Pete Coxon, Ian and Nita Cooper, Eric Larkham*

YORK SE6052   YO1 8AS
Yorkshire Terrier
Stonegate

York Brewery shop: behind this, a smallish well worn-in bar with their full beer range and guests, tasting trays of four one-third pints, interesting bottled beers, winter mulled wine, dining room upstairs (where the lavatories are – there's a stair lift) allowing children, limited range of food including bargain 'curry and pint' Weds evening, small conservatory; handy for the Minster, open all day. *Recommended by Eric Larkham, Andy Lickfold, the Didler, Pete Coxon, Derek and Sylvia Stephenson and others*

ALSO WORTH A VISIT IN CHESHIRE

Besides the region's top pubs, we recommend the following. Do tell us
what you think of them: **feedback@goodguides.com**

ALPRAHAM SJ5759   CW6 9JA
Travellers Rest
A51 Nantwich—Chester

Unspoilt four-room country local in same friendly family for three generations, well kept
Tetleys, Weetwood and a guest, low prices, leatherette, wicker and Formica, some flock
wallpaper, fine old brewery mirrors, darts and dominoes, back bowling green; no
machines, piped music or food (apart from crisps/nuts), closed weekday lunchtimes.
Recommended by the Didler, Dave Webster, Sue Holland

ANDERTON SJ6475   CW9 6AG
Stanley Arms
Just NW of Northwich; Old Road

Busy friendly local by Trent & Mersey Canal overlooking amazing restored Anderton boat
lift, wide choice of good value, well presented pubby food from sandwiches up, well kept
ales including Greene King, John Smiths and Tetleys, nice family dining area; tables on
decked terrace, play area, overnight mooring. *Recommended by Tom and Jill Jones, Ben Williams*

BARTHOMLEY SJ7752   CW2 5PG
☆ ## White Lion
M6 junction 16, B5078 N towards Alsager, then Barthomley signed on left

Charming 17th-c thatched tavern with wide mix of customers, good value straightforward
tasty food (lunchtime only), five real ales, friendly timeless main bar with latticed
windows, heavy low beams, moulded black panelling, prints on walls and blazing open
fire, steps up to room with another fire, more panelling and a high-backed winged settle;
children allowed away from bar, dogs welcome, seats out on cobbles overlooking
attractive village and the early 15th-c red sandstone church, open all day. *Recommended by
the Didler, Mr and Mrs P R Thomas, Edward Mirzoeff, Dr and Mrs A K Clarke, Edward Leetham,
Dave Webster, Sue Holland and others*

BARTON SJ4454   SY14 7HU
☆ ## Cock o' Barton
Barton Road (A534 E of Farndon)

Stylish and witty contemporary décor and furnishings in spreading bright and open skylit
bar, good enterprising up-to-date food, good choice of wines by the glass, Moorhouses
Pride of Pendle and Stonehouse Station, plenty of neat courteous staff; unobtrusive piped
music; tables in sunken heated inner courtyard with artful canopies and modern water
feature, picnic-sets on back lawn, open all day, closed Mon. *Recommended by Jonny Kershaw,
Tony Husband, Bradley Beazley*

BICKERTON SJ5254   SY14 8BE
Bickerton Poacher
A534 E of junction with A41

Rambling 17th-c poacher-themed pub, linked beamed rooms with open fires, glass-
covered well, copper-mining memorabilia and talkative parrot, good choice of enjoyable
reasonably priced food including carvery (Sat evening, Sun), cheerful attentive staff, up
to four well kept ales including Wells & Youngs Bombardier, selection of wines, skittle
alley; sheltered partly covered courtyard, play area, bedrooms, adjoining campsite.
Recommended by Alan and Eve Harding, Edward Leetham

BOLLINGTON SJ9377 · SK10 5JT
Vale
Adlington Road

Friendly refurbished 19th-c village pub under same ownership as nearby Bollington
Brewery, several of their ales and local guests, good range of well priced food including
some imaginative dishes, young efficient staff; nice outside area behind looking over
cricket pitch, near Middlewood Way and Macclesfield Canal, open all day weekends.
Recommended by Andy and Jill Kassube, Brian and Anna Marsden, the Didler, Ludo McGurk, Malcolm and
Pauline Pelliatt

CHESTER SJ4065 · CH1 1RU
☆ Bear & Billet
Lower Bridge Street

Handsome 17th-c timbered Okells pub with four changing guest ales, belgian and
american imports and a nice range of wines by the glass, reasonably priced home-made
pubby food, interesting features and some attractive furnishings in friendly and
comfortable open-plan bar with fire, sitting and dining rooms upstairs; sports TVs;
pleasant courtyard, open all day. *Recommended by the Didler, Paul Humphreys*

CHESTER SJ4065 · CH1 1RU
Brewery Tap
Lower Bridge Street

Tap for Spitting Feathers Brewery in interesting Jacobean building with 18th-c brick
façade, steps up to hall-like bar serving their well kept ales plus guests (mainly local) and
real cider, good home-made food all day using local suppliers. *Recommended by*
Edward Leetham, Rosalyn Thomas, Dave Webster, Sue Holland, Anton

CHESTER SJ4066 · CH1 2HQ
Coach House
Northgate Street

Refurbished 19th-c coaching inn by town hall and cathedral, comfortable lounge with
central bar, Shepherd Neame, Spitting Feathers and Thwaites, decent choice of food from
semi-open kitchen including good fish and chips, prompt friendly service; nine bedrooms.
Recommended by Gerry and Rosemary Dobson, Eileen McCarthy

CHESTER SJ4066 · CH1 1LQ
Olde Boot
Eastgate Row N

Good value in lovely 17th-c Rows building, heavy beams, dark woodwork, oak flooring,
flagstones, some exposed Tudor wattle and daub, old kitchen range in lounge beyond, old-
fashioned settles and oak panelling in upper area popular with families, standard food,
bargain Sam Smiths OB kept well, good cheerful service, bustling atmosphere; piped
music. *Recommended by Tom and Jill Jones, Eric Larkham, the Didler, George Atkinson, Joe Green*

CHESTER SJ4066 · CH1 4EZ
Telfords Warehouse
Tower Wharf, behind Northgate Street near railway

Well kept interesting ales in large converted canal building, generous fresh up-to-date
food including good sandwich menu, efficient staff, bare brick and boards, high-pitched
ceiling, big wall of windows overlooking water, massive iron winding gear in bar, some old
enamel signs, steps to heavy-beamed area with sofas, artwork and restaurant; late-night
live music, bouncers on door; tables out by water, open all day. *Recommended by the Didler,*
Andy and Jill Kassube

If you have to cancel a reservation for a bedroom or restaurant, please telephone or
write to warn them. You may lose your deposit if you've paid one.

CHESTER SJ4166
Union Vaults
Francis Street/Egerton Street

CH1 3ND

Friendly old-fashioned street-corner local, well kept Caledonian Deuchars IPA and two changing guests, three separate dining areas, old local photographs, back games room; piped music, sports TV; good outside seating for smokers, open all day. *Recommended by the Didler, Dave Webster, Sue Holland*

CHRISTLETON SJ4465
Cheshire Cat
Whitchurch Road

CH3 6AE

Large canalside Vintage Inn in restored early 19th-c building, popular good value food all day including weekday lunch deal, well kept ales such as Black Sheep, Cains and Purity, attentive cheerful service; garden, 14 bedrooms, open all day. *Recommended by Alan and Eve Harding*

CHRISTLETON SJ4565
Plough
Plough Lane

CH3 7PT

Popular 18th-c country local with three linked areas, ales such as Caledonian Deuchars IPA and Theakstons, enjoyable home-made local food (not Sun), friendly staff; garden with play area, nice setting. *Recommended by the Didler, Alan Hardy*

CHURCH LAWTON SJ8255
Red Bull
Congleton Road S (A34), by Trent & Mersey Canal

ST7 3AJ

Welcoming three-room pub by Trent & Mersey Canal, good value home-made food, well kept Robinsons and guest ales, beams and open fire, old photographs of canal barges, upstairs lounge and eating area; no credit cards; outside grassy area by the lock, walkers welcome (on Cheshire Ring path). *Recommended by Peter and Vivienne Shilston*

COMBERBACH SJ6477
☆ # Spinner & Bergamot
Warrington Road

CW9 6AY

Comfortable 18th-c beamed village pub (named after two racehorses) with two-room carpeted lounge, good home-made bar and restaurant food (12-7.30 Sun) including fresh fish, well kept Robinsons ales, good wines, log fires, hunting prints, toby jugs and brasses, daily papers, pitched-ceiling timber dining extension, simple tiled-floor public bar; unobtrusive piped music, service pleasant but can be slow; dogs welcome, picnic-sets on sloping lawn, lots of flowers, small verandah, bowling green, open all day. *Recommended by Mark Sowery, Simon J Barber, Dr and Mrs D Scott, Mike Moss and others*

CONGLETON SJ8663
Beartown Tap
Willow Street (A54)

CW12 1RL

Friendly tap for small nearby Beartown Brewery, their interesting beers well priced and perhaps a guest microbrew, farm cider, bottled belgian beers, bare boards in down-to-earth bar and two light airy rooms off, no food, games or music; upstairs lavatories; open all day Fri-Sun. *Recommended by the Didler*

CONGLETON SJ8659
Horseshoe
Fence Lane, Newbold Astbury, between A34 and A527 S

CW12 3NL

Former farmhouse in peaceful countryside, three small carpeted rooms with decorative plates, copper and brass and other knick-knacks (some on delft shelves), mix of seating including plush banquettes and iron-base tables, well kept Robinsons, enjoyable good value pub food, friendly staff and locals, log fire; children welcome, rustic garden furniture, play area with tractor, good walks. *Recommended by Dr D J and Mrs S C Walker*

DISLEY SJ9784   SK12 2AE
Rams Head
A6

Large M&B dining pub doing enjoyable food all day including fixed-price menu and children's meals, well kept Bass, Timothy Taylors Landlord and Thwaites Lancaster Bomber, good choice of wines by the glass, prompt friendly service, unusual gothic-arched interior, lots of different areas, some with open fires; big enclosed garden behind, open all day. *Recommended by Murtagh David, Gerry and Rosemary Dobson*

FADDILEY SJ5852   CW5 8JE
☆ Thatch
A534 Wrexham—Nantwich

Attractive, thatched, low-beamed and timbered dining pub carefully extended from medieval core, open fires, raised room to right of bar, back barn-style dining room (children allowed here), friendly helpful service, relaxing atmosphere, ales including Greene King Old Speckled Hen, Timothy Taylors Landlord and Wells & Youngs Bombardier, enjoyable food including children's helpings; soft piped music, silent games machine; charming country garden, landlords listed on outside plaque, open all day. *Recommended by R L Borthwick*

FIVECROSSES SJ5276   WA6 6SL
Travellers Rest
B5152 Frodsham—Kingsley

Well run and focus on food since 2011 refurbishment (booking advised), well kept beers; superb views across Weaver Valley. *Recommended by Linda Carter*

FRODSHAM SJ5277   WA6 6BS
Bulls Head
Bellemonte Road, Overton – off B5152 at Parish Church sign; M56 junction 12 not far

Cheerful relaxed local with good choice of well kept ales, enjoyable food including good specials and popular Sun lunch, attentive service, sensible prices, darts and dominoes. *Recommended by Sue and Alex Crooks, Linda Carter*

FRODSHAM SJ5177   WA6 6PN
Helter Skelter
Church Street

Well kept Weetwood BB and seven changing guests from long counter on right, imported beers too, good selection of wines, freshly made imaginative food from sandwiches up in bar and upstairs restaurant, friendly efficient service, airy and comfortable, with tall stools, leaning-post seating, window tables and raised back area, real fire; open all day. *Recommended by Stephen H Johnston, Darren and Clare Jones*

FRODSHAM SJ5177   WA6 6UL
Netherton Hall
A56 towards Helsby

Large converted town-edge farmhouse with emphasis on good food, competent service, real ales and good choice of wines by the glass; nice setting. *Recommended by Gill and Keith Croxton*

FULLERS MOOR SJ4954   CH3 9JH
Sandstone
A534

Refurbished dining pub, light and airy, with wide choice of enjoyable good value fresh food from sandwiches and lunchtime snacks up, well kept local ales, friendly staff, modern décor, woodburner, dining conservatory, Tues quiz; children welcome, spacious garden with lovely views, handy for Sandstone Trail, open all day weekends. *Recommended by R L Borthwick, John and Susan Hacking*

GAWSWORTH SJ8869   SK11 9RJ
☆ **Harrington Arms**
Church Lane

Rustic 17th-c farm pub, well run and now doing food, Robinsons Hatters Mild, Unicorn
and a guest ale, two small gently updated rooms (children allowed in one), bare boards
and panelling, fine carved oak bar counter; sunny benches on small front cobbled terrace.
Recommended by the Didler

GRAPPENHALL SJ6386   WA4 3EP
☆ **Parr Arms**
Near M6 junction 20 – A50 towards Warrington, left after 1.5 miles; Church Lane

Charming solidly traditional black-beamed pub in picture-postcard setting with picnic-
sets out on cobbles by the church, more tables on canopied back deck, well kept
Robinsons ales, friendly personal service, decent food from sandwiches up, daily papers,
central bar serving lounge and smaller public bar (both comfortable), open fire; open all
day Fri-Sun. *Recommended by Andy West*

HENBURY SJ8873   SK10 3LH
Cock
Chelford Road

Well kept Robinsons ales, short choice of enjoyable fairly simple food, friendly staff.
Recommended by Ben Williams

HUXLEY SJ5061   CH3 9BG
☆ **Farmers Arms**
Off A51 SE of Chester

Long low white building with bar and separate restaurant, small cosy rooms with bric-a-
brac and open fires, good food (not Sun evening) including speciality steaks and
lunchtime/early evening set deals, good choice of beers, over 90 wines (own wine shop),
friendly staff and locals, nice relaxed atmosphere; children welcome, attractive garden
area with gazebo, hanging baskets and wisteria, open all day weekends, closed Mon
lunchtime. *Recommended by Ann and Tony Bennett-Hughes, Simon Ely*

LANGLEY SJ9471   SK11 0NE
☆ **Leather's Smithy**
Off A523 S of Macclesfield, OS Sheet 118 map reference 952715

Isolated stone-built pub up in fine walking country next to reservoir, four well kept ales
including Black Sheep and Wells & Youngs Bombardier, lots of whiskies, enjoyable food
from sandwiches and bloomers up, good welcoming service, beams and log fire, flagstoned
bar, carpeted dining areas, interesting local prints and photographs; unobtrusive piped
music, no dogs; picnic-sets in garden behind and on grass opposite, open all day
weekends. *Recommended by Malcolm and Pauline Pellatt*

LITTLE BOLLINGTON SJ7387   WA14 4TJ
Swan With Two Nicks
*2 miles from M56 junction 7 – A56 towards Lymm, then first right at Stamford Arms
into Park Lane; use A556 to get back on to M56 westbound*

Extended village pub full of beams, brass, copper and bric-a-brac, some antique settles,
log fire, welcoming helpful service, good choice of enjoyable food from filling baguettes up
including popular Sun lunch (best to book), several good local ales including one brewed
for the pub, decent wines and coffee; children and dogs welcome, tables outside,
attractive hamlet by Dunham Massey (NT) deer park, walks by Bridgewater Canal, open
all day. *Recommended by Peter Webb*

All *Guide* inspections are anonymous. Anyone claiming to be a *Good Pub Guide*
inspector is a fraud. Please let us know.

LITTLE BUDWORTH SJ5965   CW6 9BY
Red Lion
Vicarage Lane

Traditional beamed local in unspoilt spot, hospitable licensees serving well kept Robinsons and good helpings of sensibly priced pub food, long bar with ladder-back chairs and stools around dark wood tables, patterned carpets, nice fire; a couple of picnic-sets out in front, more seats in garden, country walks. *Recommended by Roger and Anne Newbury, John Andrew*

LOWER PEOVER SJ7474   WA16 9PZ
☆ Bells of Peover
Just off B5081; The Cobbles

Lovely old refurbished building in a charming spot, panelling, beams, open fires and antiques, three well kept Robinsons ales, good food from sandwiches up, dining room; piped music, children till 8pm, disabled facilities, terrace tables, big side lawn with trees, rose pergolas and little stream, on quiet cobbled lane with fine black and white 14th-c church, open all day. *Recommended by Mrs P J Carroll, Donna Somerset*

LYMM SJ7087   WA13 0SW
Barn Owl
Agden Wharf, Warrington Lane (just off B5159 E)

Comfortably extended building in picturesque setting by Bridgewater Canal, good value fresh food all day including OAP bargains, Marstons and guest beers, decent wines by the glass, friendly atmosphere, pleasant service even when busy; disabled facilities, may be canal trips, moorings, open all day. *Recommended by Ben Williams*

LYMM SJ6886   WA13 0AP
Church Green
Higher Lane

Chef/landlord doing good seasonal food (some of it quite pricey) in refurbished bar and restaurant, Caledonian Deuchars IPA and Greene King Old Speckled Hen; piped music; children welcome, disabled facilities, heated side terrace, open all day. *Recommended by W K Wood*

MACCLESFIELD SJ9272   SK11 7JW
Railway View
Byrons Lane (off A523)

Pair of 1700 knocked-through cottages under new owners, attractive snug corners, up to eight well kept changing ales (cheaper Mon evening), good value food, friendly service, remarkably shaped gents'; back terrace overlooking railway, open all day weekends. *Recommended by the Didler*

MACCLESFIELD SJ9173   SK11 6LH
Waters Green Tavern
Waters Green, opposite station

Seven quickly changing and interesting largely northern ales in roomy L-shaped open-plan local, good value home-made lunchtime food (not Sun), friendly staff and locals, back pool room. *Recommended by the Didler, David Crook*

MARBURY SJ5645   SY13 4LS
Swan
NNE of Whitchurch; OS Sheet 117 map reference 562457

Reopened under new management; good range of food from traditional things up, three real ales including Caledonian Deuchars IPA and local Woodlands, roomy partly panelled lounge with upholstered banquettes and copper-canopied log fire, cottagey dining room with another inglenook; piped and occasional live music; children and dogs welcome, picnic-sets in big back garden with vegetable patch, attractive village with lakeside church, not far from the Llangollen Canal (Bridges 23/24). *Recommended by anon*

MIDDLEWICH SJ7066   CW10 9DN
Big Lock
Webbs Lane

Sizeable 19th-c canalside pub on two floors, good value food including deals, mainstream ales; tables out by the water, good for boat watching. *Recommended by Ben Williams*

NANTWICH SJ6452   CW5 5ED
 ## Black Lion
Welsh Row

Old black and white building smartened up but keeping beams, timbered brickwork and an open fire, good food from short but interesting menu, three Weetwood ales and three regularly changing guests, upstairs rooms with old wooden tables and sumptuous leather sofas on undulating floors; open all day. *Recommended by Edward Leetham, Dave Webster, Sue Holland*

NANTWICH SJ6551   CW5 7EA
Globe
Audlem Road

Full range of well kept Woodlands ales and a guest, ten wines by the glass, regularly changing good value food all day using local produce, lunchtime deals, friendly helpful staff, comfortable open-plan layout keeping distinct areas, local artwork, newspapers and magazines, occasional live music; garden tables. *Recommended by David Webster*

NANTWICH SJ6552   CW5 5RP
Vine
Hospital Street

Dates from the 17th c, sympathetically modernised and stretching far back with old prints, books and dimly lit quiet corners, well kept Hydes and a guest, friendly staff and locals, lunchtime sandwiches, baguettes, wraps, baked potatoes and simple hot dishes, raised seating areas; unobtrusive piped music and TV; children welcome, small outside area behind, open all day. *Recommended by Charles and Pauline Stride, Edward Leetham*

NESTON SJ2976   CH64 0TB
☆ ## Harp
Quayside, SW of Little Neston; keep on along track at end of Marshlands Road

Tucked-away two-room country local, well kept Holts and up to five interesting guests, some good malt whiskies, good value unfussy home-made lunchtime food (not weekends), woodburner in pretty fireplace, pale quarry tiles and simple furnishings, hatch servery in one room; children allowed in lounge, dogs welcome, garden behind, picnic-sets up on front grassy bank facing Dee marshes and Wales, glorious sunsets with wild calls of wading birds, open all day. *Recommended by Roger and Anne Newbury, Maurice and Gill McMahon, Andy and Jill Kassube, Don Bryan, MLR*

OLLERTON SJ7776   WA16 8RH
☆ ## Dun Cow
Chelford Road; outskirts of Knutsford towards Macclesfield

Attractive well run Robinsons country pub, emphasis on good food but room for drinkers too, modern décor, cosy alcoves, two fine log fires, dominoes; children welcome, good disabled access, seats in nice outside area, open all day Sat, closed Sun evening and Mon. *Recommended by David Heath, P J and R D Greaves, Andrew Jackson*

We say if we know a pub allows dogs.

PARKGATE SJ2778   CH64 6RN

Boathouse
Village signed off A540

Popular black and white timbered pub with attractively refurbished linked rooms, good food including fresh fish, cheerful attentive staff, well kept changing ales including local Brimstage, good choice of wines by the glass, big conservatory with great views to Wales over silted Dee estuary (RSPB reserve). *Recommended by Maurice and Gill McMahon, Pat and Tony Hinkins, Clive Watkin*

PLUMLEY SJ7275   WA16 9RX

Golden Pheasant
Plumley Moor Lane (off A556 by The Smoker)

Civilised well extended pub, locally sourced food including Sun carvery, Lees ales, comfortable lounge areas, roomy restaurant and conservatory, friendly efficient staff; children welcome, spacious gardens including play area and bowling green, bedrooms. *Recommended by Malcolm and Pauline Pellatt*

PRESTBURY SJ8976   SK10 4DG

☆ Legh Arms
A538, village centre

Smart beamed hotel with divided up bar and lounge areas, Robinsons ales, decent wines, bar food (all day weekends) and more elaborate restaurant choices, soft furnishings, ladder-back chairs around solid dark tables, brocaded bucket seats, stylish french prints and italian engravings, staffordshire dogs on mantelpiece, cosy panelled back part with comfy narrow offshoot, coal fire, daily papers; piped music; children and dogs welcome, seats on heated terrace, bedrooms, open all day. *Recommended by Pam and John Smith*

SHOCKLACH SJ4349   SY14 7BL

☆ Bull
Off B5069 W of Malpas

Welcoming and comfortable, with exhilarating mix of some contemporary furnishings and artwork with much more traditional features, beams, open fire and mixed furniture on stone and wood floors, nice range of interesting fresh food from changing menu, good choice of wines and of well kept local ales (summer beer festival), friendly informal service, conservatory; teak tables under cocktail parasols on back terrace, garden; open all day at least Fri-Sun, closed Mon. *Recommended by Alun Jones*

STOAK SJ4273   CH2 4HW

Bunbury Arms
Little Stanney Lane; a mile from M53 junction 10, A5117 W then first left

Big but cosy beamed lounge with antique furniture, pictures and books, small snug, wide choice of enjoyable food (all day Sun) from sandwiches to interesting specials including fresh fish, good changing ales, extensive wine list, jovial landlord and friendly staff, open fires, board games; can get busy; garden tables (some motorway noise), short walk for Shropshire Union Canal users from Bridge 136 or 138, handy for Cheshire Oaks shopping outlet, open all day. *Recommended by Jack Spratt, Janet McClure*

SWETTENHAM SJ7967   CW12 2LF

☆ Swettenham Arms
Off A54 Congleton—Holmes Chapel or A535 Chelford—Holmes Chapel

Attractive gently upmarket country pub in pretty setting by a lavender plot and the scenic Quinta arboretum, good popular food from sandwiches and pubby things to more imaginative dishes in an immaculate line of individually furnished rooms, early evening deals too, several well kept ales such as Moorhouses and Sharps Doom Bar, good wine choice, friendly service, log fires, some live jazz; children welcome, picnic-sets on quiet side lawn, open all day weekends. *Recommended by Malcolm and Pauline Pellatt, Brian and Anna Marsden*

WARMINGHAM SJ7161   CW11 3QN

Bears Paw

School Lane

Attractive 19th-c inn with well liked food served in bar or restaurant, good choice of local ales and of wines by the glass, quick friendly service; good spot by the river and ancient church in a picturesque village, seats in front garden, 17 good bedrooms. *Recommended by Rachel Hine, Andrew Williams, William and Ann Reid*

WILLINGTON SJ5367   CW6 0NH

☆ **Boot**

Boothsdale, off A54 at Kelsall

Attractive hillside dining pub in a row of converted cottages, views over Cheshire plain to Wales, popular food from pub staples to daily specials (they may ask to keep a credit card while you run a tab), Greene King and local Weetwood ales, decent wines, 30 malt whiskies, friendly staff, small opened-up unpretentiously furnished room areas, lots of original features, woodburner, extension with french windows overlooking garden, pub cats, dog and donkey; well behaved children welcome (no pushchairs), picnic-sets in front on raised suntrap terrace, open all day. *Recommended by Roger and Anne Newbury, Brian and Anna Marsden, Grahame and Myra Williams*

WINCLE SJ9665   SK11 0QE

☆ **Ship**

Village signposted off A54 Congleton—Buxton

16th-c stone-built country pub under friendly new licensees, bare-boards bar leading to carpeted dining room, old stables area with flagstones, beams, woodburner and open fire, good fresh food from daily-changing varied menu, up to five Lees ales, 11 wines by the glass, good attentive service; children and dogs welcome, tables in small well kept side garden, good Dane Valley walks. *Recommended by Malc Newton, Al M*

WRENBURY SJ5947   CW5 8HG

Dusty Miller

Cholmondeley Road; village signed from A530 Nantwich—Whitchurch

New landlord for well converted corn mill with fine canal views from gravel terrace and series of tall glazed arches in bar, spacious modern feel with comfortable mix of seats, oak settle and refectory table in quarry-tiled part by counter, old lift hoist under rafters, Robinsons beers tapped from the cask, bar food has been liked, restaurant; piped music; children and dogs welcome, open all day. *Recommended by Mike Proctor*

ALSO WORTH A VISIT IN CUMBRIA

Besides the region's top pubs, we recommend the following. Do tell us
what you think of them: **feedback@goodguides.com**

AMBLESIDE NY4008   LA22 9LQ

☆ **Kirkstone Pass Inn**

A592 N of Troutbeck

Lakeland's highest pub, in grand scenery, hiker-friendly décor of flagstones, stripped
stone and dark beams and furniture, lots of old photographs and bric-a-brac, open fires,
good value food all day from 9.30am, changing ales such as Hesket Newmarket Kirkstone
Pass and Tirril Old Faithful, hot drinks, daily papers, games and books; soft piped music,
they may try to keep your credit card while you eat; well behaved children and dogs
welcome, tables outside with incredible views to Windermere, camping field next door,
three bedrooms, open all day. *Recommended by Robin Constable*

AMBLESIDE NY3703   LA22 0EP

☆ **Wateredge Inn**

Borrans Road

Lovely spot with sizeable garden running down to edge of Windermere (own moorings),
lots of tables here, same splendid view through big windows in much-modernised bar
(originally two 17th-c cottages), prompt cheerful staff, ales from Barngates, Theakstons,
Tirril and local Watermill, several wines by the glass, wide choice of enjoyable food till
8.30pm, cosy beamed area down steps with fireside sofa; piped music, can get very busy;
children welcome, dogs in bar, 22 comfortable bedrooms, open all day. *Recommended by Hugh
Roberts, Margaret and Jeff Graham, Mr and Mrs D J Nash, Ian and Deborah Carrington, Margaret Dickinson*

APPLEBY NY6819   CA16 6UN

☆ **Royal Oak**

B6542/Bongate

Attractive old beamed and timbered coaching inn, popular bar food (all day Sun), well
kept ales such as Black Sheep, Hawkshead and Jennings, friendly efficient young staff, log
fire in panelled bar, armchair lounge with carved settle, traditional snug, nicely
refurbished dining room; piped music; children and dogs welcome, terrace tables, good-
sized bedrooms, nice breakfast, open all day. *Recommended by Maurice and Gill McMahon,
Ivan and Margaret Scott, Claes Mauroy*

ARMATHWAITE NY5046   CA4 9PB

☆ **Dukes Head**

Off A6 S of Carlisle; right at T junction

Genuine friendly welcome for all at this traditional family-run Eden Valley inn;
comfortable properly old-fashioned lounge with settles and little armchairs around oak
and mahogany tables, antique hunting and other prints, brass and copper powder-flasks
above open fire, ales such as Black Sheep and Jennings, Weston's cider, may be home-
made lemonade and ginger beer, enjoyable bar food including daily specials, public bar
with table skittles and TV; children and dogs welcome, seats on heated area outside, more
on back lawn, boules, bedrooms, open all day. *Recommended by Roger and Anne Newbury, Alan
Thwaite, Dr A M Rankin, Helen Cradock, A J Barker, Archibald Rankin*

ARMATHWAITE NY5045   CA4 9PY

☆ **Fox & Pheasant**

E of village, over bridge

Friendly licensees and locals in attractive spotless coaching inn, lovely River Eden views,
well kept Robinsons ales, decent wines by the glass, sensibly short choice of good fresh
reasonably priced food, inglenook log fire in main beamed and flagstoned bar, another in

second bar, charming small dining room; picnic-sets outside, comfortable bedrooms.
Recommended by Brad Oud

ASKHAM NY5123   CA10 2PF
Punch Bowl
4.5 miles from M6 junction 40

Attractive 18th-c village inn reopened under new management, spacious beamed main
bar, locals' bar, snug lounge and dining room, open fires, traditional food including early-
bird deals (not at Sun lunchtime), ales such as Adnams, Cumberland, Hawkshead, Copper
Dragon and Greene King; picnic-sets out in front, on edge of green opposite Askham Hall,
bedrooms being refurbished. *Recommended by anon*

ASKHAM NY5123   CA10 2PF
Queens Head
Lower Green; off A6 or B5320 S of Penrith

Traditional 17th-c beamed pub under new enthusiastic local licensees, enjoyable good
value home-made food all day, well kept beers, open fires; tables out at front and in
pleasant garden, four bedrooms. *Recommended by Colin and Sue Wilkinson, Rosemary and
Mike Fielder*

BAMPTON NY5118   CA10 2RQ
Mardale
Village signposted off A6 in Shap; in Bampton turn left over bridge by Post Office

Pretty village pub under newish management, several opened-up rooms decorated in
contemporary style, chunky modern country tables and chairs on big flagstones, a few
rugs, one or two big Lakeland prints and some rustic bygones, log fire and woodburner,
four local ales including one brewed for the pub, fairly traditional food; well behaved
children and dogs welcome, good walks from the door, four bedrooms, open all day.
Recommended by Pam and John Smith, David and Katharine Cooke

BEETHAM SD4979   LA7 7AL
☆ Wheatsheaf
Village (and inn) signed off A6 S of Milnthorpe

Striking 17th-c coaching inn with handsome timbered cornerpiece, opened-up front
lounge bar, lots of exposed beams and joists, main bar (behind on right) with open fire,
two upstairs weekend dining rooms, good often interesting food, three changing regional
ales and several wines by the glass, friendly accommodating staff; soft piped music;
children welcome, pretty 14th-c church opposite, quiet village with surrounding walks,
bedrooms, open all day. *Recommended by Dennis Jones, Noel Grundy, William and Ann Reid, Stephen
Funnell, Simon Le Fort, Francesca Salvini*

BOOT NY1701   CA19 1TG
☆ Boot Inn
aka Burnmoor; signed just off the Wrynose/Hardknott Pass road

Comfortable beamed pub with ever-burning fire, Black Sheep, Jennings and a guest ale
(June beer festival), decent wines and malt whiskies, good friendly staff, realistically
priced home-made local food from sandwiches up, restaurant and dining conservatory;
games room with pool and TV; children and dogs welcome, sheltered front lawn with play
area, lovely surroundings and walks, nine bedrooms, open all day. *Recommended by
Adrian Johnson, Mr and Mrs D J Nash, Mike and Eleanor Anderson, Ludo McGurk*

BOOT NY1701   CA19 1TG
☆ Brook House
Handy for Eskdale railway terminus

Good views and walks, friendly family service, wide choice of good sensibly priced country
cooking including some interesting dishes and unusual sandwiches, great whisky
selection, well kept ales such as Barngates, Cumbrian and Hesket Newmarket, decent

wines, Weston's farm cider, log fires, relaxed and comfortable raftered bar with woodburner and stuffed animals, smaller plush snug, peaceful separate restaurant; tables on flagstoned terrace, seven good value bedrooms, good breakfast (for nearby campers too), mountain weather reports, excellent drying room, open all day. *Recommended by John and Sylvia Harrop, Alison Ball, Ian Walton, Neil Whitehead, Victoria Anderson, the Didler, Kay and Alistair Butler, Pam and John Smith and others*

BOOT NY1901   CA19 1TH
Woolpack
Bleabeck, mid-way between Boot and Hardknott Pass

Last pub before the notorious Hardknott Pass; refurbished and welcoming, main walkers' bar with big woodburner, snug and restaurant, enjoyable home-made locally sourced food all day, up to eight well kept ales including Woolpackers (still brewed for the pub by previous landlord), Thatcher's cider, good choice of malts, June beer festival; children and dogs welcome, mountain-view garden, play area, seven bedrooms. *Recommended by Alan Hill, Neil Whitehead, Victoria Anderson, Mike and Eleanor Anderson*

BOUTH SD3285   LA12 8JB
☆ ## White Hart
Village signed off A590 near Haverthwaite

Cheerful bustling old inn with Lakeland feel, six changing ales, 25 malt whiskies, popular generously served food (all day Sun) using local beef and lamb, good friendly service, sloping ceilings and floors, old local photographs, farm tools, stuffed animals, collection of long-stemmed clay pipes, two woodburners; piped music; children welcome and dogs (not at mealtimes), seats outside, fine surrounding walks, five comfortable bedrooms, open all day. *Recommended by Dennis Jones, Alison Ball, Ian Walton, Peter Smith and Judith Brown, Lucien Perring*

BOWNESS-ON-WINDERMERE SD4096   LA23 3BY
Albert
Queens Square

Refurbished Robinsons inn keeping traditional feel, their ales and guests kept well, good choice of food all day; children welcome, terrace tables, six comfortable bedrooms. *Recommended by John and Helen Rushton, Dr E Scarth and Miss A Pocock*

BOWNESS-ON-WINDERMERE SD4096   LA23 3DH
☆ ## Hole in t' Wall
Lowside

Bustling unchanging pub – the town's oldest and packed in high season; split-level rooms, beams, stripped stone and flagstones, country knick-knacks and old pictures, fine log fire under vast slate mantelpiece, upper room with attractive plasterwork, Robinsons ales, decent traditional food (not Sun evening), friendly staff; piped music; children welcome, sheltered picnic-sets in small flagstoned and heated front courtyard, open all day. *Recommended by Dennis Jones, Dr Kevan Tucker, John and Helen Rushton, Kurt Woods*

BRAITHWAITE NY2323   CA12 5SY
Royal Oak
B5292 at top of village

Bustling local atmosphere, four well kept Jennings ales, reasonable choice of food including children's helpings, prompt helpful service, well worn-in flagstoned bar; piped music, Sky TV; dogs welcome except mealtimes, open all day. *Recommended by Mr and Mrs D J Nash, John and Angie Millar*

BRIGSTEER SD4889   LA8 8AN
☆ ## Wheatsheaf
Off Brigsteer Brow

Attractive relaxed dining pub with good well priced food from interesting sandwiches (nice breads baked here) to local trout, steaks and game, stylishly simple contemporary décor, cheerful attentive staff, real ale such as Langdale, good choice of wines by the glass, sofas and dining tables in entrance bar, further two-room dining area; well reproduced nostalgic piped music; picnic-sets on pretty little terrace across the quiet lane, attractive village, bedrooms. *Recommended by anon*

BROUGHTON-IN-FURNESS SD2187   LA20 6HY
Manor Arms
The Square

Fine choice of interesting well priced changing ales in this open-plan drinkers' pub a quiet sloping square, flagstones and nice bow-window seat in well worn front bar, coal fire in big stone fireplace, chiming clocks, old photographs, limited food (rolls and soup), two pool tables; stairs down to lavatories; children allowed, bedrooms, open all day. *Recommended by David and Sue Smith*

BUTTERMERE NY1716   CA13 9XA
Fish
B5289 SE of Buttermere

Spacious, light and airy former coaching inn on NT property between Buttermere and Crummock Water, fine views, Jennings ales and guests, wide range of good value food, friendly helpful staff; suntrap terrace attracting greedy sparrows and finches, popular with walkers and anglers, bedrooms. *Recommended by the Didler, John Wooll*

CARLETON NY5329   CA11 8TP
☆ Cross Keys
A686, off A66 roundabout at Penrith

Under same management as Highland Drove at Great Salkeld; modernised beamed main bar with straightforward furniture on light boards, pictures on bare stone walls, steps down to small area and up again to airy vaulted-ceiling restaurant with doors to verandah, well liked food including steaks and grills, Theakstons Black Bull, Tirril 1823 and a guest, good choice of wines by the glass, two further rooms with games machine, pool, juke box and TV; piped music; children and dogs welcome, fell views from garden, open all day weekends. *Recommended by Phil Bryant, Richard J Holloway, Michael Doswell, Rosemary and Mike Fielder and others*

CARLISLE NY4056   CA3 8RF
Kings Head
Pedestrianised Fisher Street

Heavy beams, lots of old local prints, drawings and black and white photographs, friendly bustling atmosphere, generous bargain pub lunches, good range of mainly cumbrian beers including Yates, raised dining area; piped music, TV; interesting historical plaque outside, partly covered courtyard, open all day. *Recommended by Eric Larkham, Derek and Sylvia Stephenson, the Didler, Robert Turnham, Barbarrick, Meg and Colin Hamilton and others*

CARTMEL SD3778   LA11 6QB
☆ Kings Arms
The Square

This previously well liked pub has recently reopened after refurbishment – news please. *Recommended by anon*

CARTMEL SD3778   LA11 6QB
Royal Oak
The Square

Low-beamed flagstoned local with cosy nooks and big log fire, ornaments and brasses, enjoyable good value bar food including specials, well kept Coniston Bluebird, Timothy Taylors Landlord and two changing local guests (Aug beer festival), decent wines, welcoming helpful staff; piped music and sports TV, autographed sporting memorabilia in gents'; dogs welcome, nice big riverside garden with summer bar, four bedrooms, open all day. *Recommended by Ben Williams, Phil Hollowood, Adrian Johnson*

CASTERTON SD6379   LA6 2RX

☆ Pheasant
A683

Traditional 18th-c inn with neat beamed rooms, straightforward pubby furniture, coal-effect gas fire, Dent, Greene King and Theakstons, several malt whiskies, restaurant, board games; piped music; children welcome, seats under cocktail parasols by road, more in pleasant garden, near church with pre-Raphaelite stained glass and paintings, bedrooms. *Recommended by Pat and Stewart Gordon, Mr and Mrs Ian King*

CHAPEL STILE NY3205   LA22 9JH

Wainwrights
B5343

White-rendered former farmhouse, up to eight real ales, plenty of wines by the glass, enjoyable quickly served food from pubby things up including sandwiches and baguettes, roomy new-feeling bar welcoming walkers and dogs, slate floor and fire, other spreading carpeted areas with beams, some half-panelling, cushioned settles and mix of dining chairs around wooden tables, old kitchen range; piped music, TV and games machines; children welcome, terrace picnic-sets, fine views, open all day in summer. *Recommended by John Woodward, John and Helen Rushton, Michael Doswell, Ewan and Moira McCall, Mr and Mrs Maurice Thompson*

COCKERMOUTH NY1230   CA13 9PJ

☆ Bitter End
Kirkgate, by cinema

Liked for its eight own-brewed ales and lots of bottled beers in three interesting bars – each with a different atmosphere from quietly chatty to sporty (décor reflecting this with unusual pictures of old Cockermouth to up-to-date sporting memorabilia), also framed beer mats, various bottles, jugs and books, log fire, good choice of traditional food; piped music; no dogs; children welcome, public car park round the back, open all day Sat in summer. *Recommended by Adrian Johnson, Geoff and Linda Payne, Pat and Stewart Gordon, the Didler, Helen, J Chilver and others*

CONISTON SD3097   LA21 8DU

☆ Black Bull
Yewdale Road (A593)

Own-brewed Coniston beers remain a draw to this bustling old inn; back area (liked by walkers and their dogs) with slate flagstones, carpeted front part more comfortable with open fire and Donald Campbell memorabilia, bar food served all day, residents' lounge with 'big toe' of Old Man of Coniston (large piece of stone in the wall), restaurant; children welcome, plenty of seats in former coachyard, bedrooms, open all day from 8am (parking not easy at peak times). *Recommended by Mr and Mrs D J Nash, Michael Butler, Mike Gorton, Rob and Catherine Dunster*

CONISTON SD3098   LA21 8HQ

☆ Sun
Signed left off A593 at the bridge

16th-c inn in terrific setting below dramatic fells, interesting Donald Campbell and other Lakeland photographs in extended old-fashioned bar with beams, flagstones, log-fire range, cask seats and old settles, well kept Black Sheep, Coniston Bluebird, Copper Dragon, Hawkshead and four local guests, several wines by the glass, wide choice of food all day, big conservatory restaurant off carpeted lounge, more seating in large refurbished upstairs room with suspended rowing boat; well behaved children and dogs welcome, great views from front terrace, big tree-sheltered garden, eight comfortable bedrooms, hearty breakfast, open all day. *Recommended by Luke Bosman, Mr and Mrs J Hilton, E Ling, Brian Fairey, Mike Gorton*

CROOK SD4695   LA8 8LA
Sun
B5284 Kendal—Bowness

Good bustling atmosphere in low-beamed bar with two dining areas off, good generous traditional food (all day weekends), reasonable prices, prompt cheerful service, Fullers London Pride and John Smiths, good value wines, roaring log fire. *Recommended by G Jennings, Martin Smith, Hugh Roberts*

☆ **CROSTHWAITE** SD4491   LA8 8HR
Punch Bowl
Village signed off A5074 SE of Windermere

Civilised, stylish and well run dining pub, raftered and hop-hung public bar, stools by the slate-topped counter, eye-catching rugs on slate floor, Barngates, Ulverston and a guest, lots of wines by the glass including champagne, a dozen malt whiskies, two linked carpeted and beamed rooms with country pine furnishings, attractive prints, dresser with china and glass, log fire and woodburner, light and airy oak-floored restaurant, good if pricey food, friendly helpful staff; children welcome, dogs in bar, seats on stepped hillside terrace overlooking lovely Lyth Valley, nine well equipped bedrooms, open all day. *Recommended by D M Heath, Michael Harrison, David Thornton, Bill Adie, Rob and Catherine Dunster G Jennings, and others*

DACRE NY4526   CA11 0HL
Horse & Farrier
Between A66 and A592 SW of Penrith

Pleasant 18th-c village pub with well priced home-made food (not Sun evening) from sandwiches up, well kept Jennings, unsmart front room with big old-fashioned range and nice beam-and-plank ceiling, more modern dining extension down steps on the left, darts and dominoes; children and dogs welcome, post office, pretty village, closed Mon lunchtime. *Recommended by Brian Abbott, Noel Grundy, Natalie Wittering, Comus and Sarah Elliott*

DEAN NY0725   CA14 4TJ
Royal Yew
Just off A5086 S of Cockermouth

Busy modernised village local in a nice spot, good range of enjoyable food from sandwiches up, well kept ales such as Bitter End and Jennings, good choice of wines by the glass, cheerful service. *Recommended by Richard and Tanya Smith*

DENT SD7086   LA10 5QL
George & Dragon
Main Street

Two-bar corner pub owned by Dent with seven of their well kept beers (including a real lager) and Weston's cider, some dark panelling, partitioned tables and open fire, food from light meals up, prompt friendly service, comfortable back restaurant, games room with pool; sports TV; children, walkers and dogs welcome, ten bedrooms, lovely village, open all day. *Recommended by Brian and Anna Marsden, Dr Kevan Tucker, J C Burgis*

DOCKRAY NY3921   CA11 0JY
Royal
A5091, off A66 or A592 W of Penrith

Former coaching inn with bright open-plan bar including walkers' part with stripped settles on flagstones, Black Sheep, Jennings and a guest, good food here from sandwiches up or in more formal restaurant, good friendly service; piped music; children welcome, dogs in bar, picnic-sets in large peaceful garden, great setting, ten comfortable bedrooms, open all day. *Recommended by James Morrell, Comus and Sarah Elliott*

You can send reports directly to us at **feedback@goodguides.com**

ESKDALE GREEN NY1200   CA19 1TD

☆ **Bower House**

0.5 miles W of Eskdale Green

Civilised old-fashioned stone-built inn extended around a beamed and alcoved core, good
fires, well kept local ales, good choice of interesting food in bar and biggish restaurant
including home-made black pudding, friendly relaxed atmosphere; nicely tended
sheltered garden by cricket field, charming spot with great walks, bedrooms, open all day.
Recommended by Tina and David Woods-Taylor, Paul J Robinshaw

FAUGH NY5054   CA8 9EG

String of Horses

S of village, on left as you go down hill

Welcoming 17th-c coaching inn with cosy communicating beamed rooms, log fires,
panelling and some interesting carved furniture, tasty well prepared food, Theakstons
Bitter and another ale, restaurant; children welcome, sheltered terrace, comfortable
bedrooms, good breakfast. *Recommended by Les and Sandra Brown*

FOXFIELD SD2085   LA20 6BX

☆ **Prince of Wales**

Opposite station

Cheery bare-boards pub with half a dozen good changing ales including bargain beers
brewed here and at their associated Tigertops Brewery, bottled imports, farm cider,
enjoyable home-made food including lots of unusual pasties, hot coal fire, bar billiards
and other pub games, daily papers and beer-related reading matter; children very
welcome, games for them too, reasonably priced bedrooms, open all day Fri-Sun, from
mid-afternoon weekdays. *Recommended by the Didler, Clifford Walker*

GOSFORTH NY0703   CA20 1AZ

Gosforth Hall

Off A595 and unclassified road to Wasdale

Jacobean building with interesting history, beamed carpeted bar (popular with locals)
with fine plaster coat-of-arms above woodburner, lounge/reception area with huge
fireplace, ales such as Hawkshead, Keswick and Yates, enjoyable food including good
range of pies, restaurant; TV; back garden with boules, nine bedrooms, self-catering lodge.
Recommended by Mr and Mrs Maurice Thompson, Pam and John Smith

GREAT CORBY NY4854   CA4 8LR

Queen

Centre of village

Friendly extended pub with well kept local ales including Cumberland Corby brewed in
the village, enjoyable locally sourced food from a short menu, spacious beamed bar with
two log fires, airy mediterranean-themed lounge with own terrace, two dining rooms (one
upstairs); children welcome, tables out at front overlooking green. *Recommended by Marylou*

GREYSTOKE NY4430   CA11 0TP

Boot & Shoe

By village green, off B5288

Cosy two-bar pub by the green in pretty 'Tarzan' village; low ceilings, exposed brickwork
and dark wood, good generous reasonably priced food including popular theme nights,
well kept Black Sheep and local microbrews, bustling friendly atmosphere; sports TV; on
national cycle route, bedrooms. *Recommended by Phil Bryant, Maurice and Gill McMahon,
D A Warren*

'Children welcome' means the pub says it lets children inside without any special
restriction; some may impose an evening time limit earlier than 9pm –
please tell us if you find this.

HALE SD5078   LA7 7BH
Kings Arms
A6 S of Beetham

Traditional place doing good generous pubby food (all day weekends) including good Sun roasts, friendly landlord and attentive uniformed staff, real ales, plenty of brass, china and hunting prints, two open fires, restaurant section. *Recommended by Mr and Mrs Ian King*

HAWKSHEAD NY3501   LA22 0NG
☆ Drunken Duck
Barngates; the hamlet is signposted from B5286 Hawkshead—Ambleside, opposite the Outgate Inn; or it may be quicker to take the first right from B5286, after the wooded caravan site; OS Sheet 90 map reference 350013

Civilised inn with more informal feel during the day when popular with walkers – get there early for a seat; small smart bar with beams and oak boards, stools by slate-topped counter, leather club chairs, photographs, coaching and hunting pictures, own good Barngates ales, continental draught beers, 17 wines by the glass from fine list, good bar food from sandwiches up, more elaborate and pricey evening choice, three restaurant areas; children welcome, dogs in bar, tables and benches out on grass with spectacular fell views, profusion of spring and summer bulbs, good bedrooms, open all day.
Recommended by Chris Johnson, Brian Dawes, David and Sue Atkinson, Janet and Peter Race, Mike and Sue Loseby, Marianne and Peter Stevens and others

HESKET NEWMARKET NY3438   CA7 8JG
☆ Old Crown
Village signed off B5299 in Caldbeck

Straightforward cooperative-owned local in an attractive village, good own-brewed Hesket Newmarket beers (can book tours – £10 including meal); small friendly bar with bric-a-brac, mountaineering kit and pictures, log fire, dining room and garden room, simple bar food; pool, juke box and board games; children and dogs welcome, closed Mon-Thurs lunchtimes (open Weds and Thurs lunchtimes in school holidays). *Recommended by Maurice and Gill McMahon, John and Anne Mackinnon, Howard Bowen*

HIGH NEWTON SD4082   LA11 6JH
Crown
Just off A590 Lindale—Newby Bridge, towards Cartmel Fell

Refurbished 18th-c coaching inn, enjoyable food from well filled sandwiches to good value Sun lunch, changing ales and decent wines by the glass, beamed and flagstoned bar with log fire in stone fireplace, restaurant, trad jazz first Mon of month; children and dogs welcome, beer garden, seven bedrooms, open all day weekends. *Recommended by Michele Pearson*

KENDAL SD5192   LA9 4TN
Globe
Market Place

Compact town pub with carpeted beamed split-level bar, good new landlord and friendly staff, well kept Thwaites, enjoyable locally sourced food including Sun roasts, separate dining room upstairs. *Recommended by John and Helen Rushton*

KESWICK NY2623   CA12 5BT
☆ Dog & Gun
Lake Road; off top end of Market Square

Unpretentious town pub liked by locals and their dogs, homely bar with low beams and timbers, partly slate, part wood, part carpeted flooring, fine collection of striking mountain photographs, brass and brewery artefacts, half a dozen ales, all-day pubby food including popular goulash, log fires; children welcome if eating before 9pm, open all day.
Recommended by John Luckes, Bill Adie, Chris and Jo Parsons, Geoff and Linda Payne, J Buckby, Brendon Skinner and others

KIRKBY LONSDALE SD6178   LA6 2BD
Orange Tree
Fairbank

Family-run inn acting as tap for Kirkby Lonsdale brewery, well kept guest beers too and good choice of wines, beams, sporting pictures, old range, enjoyable food in back dining room including a lunchtime bargain special; pool, darts, piped music; children and dogs welcome, comfortable bedrooms (some next door). *Recommended by David Baldwin, the Didler, Andy and Jill Kassube*

KIRKBY LONSDALE SD6278   LA6 2AH
Snooty Fox
Main Street (B6254)

Rambling partly panelled 17th-c coaching inn, beams, country furniture, two open fires, dining annexe, four real ales, generous good quality traditional food, reasonable prices, cheerful attentive young staff; piped music, sports TV and machines; children and dogs welcome, garden tables, bedrooms, open all day. *Recommended by JCW*

KIRKBY LONSDALE SD6178   LA6 2AU
 ## Sun
Market Street (B6254)

Friendly 17th-c inn striking a good balance between pub and restaurant; unusual-looking building with upper floors supported by three sturdy pillars above the pavement, attractive rambling beamed bar with flagstones and stripped-oak boards, pews, armchairs and cosy window seats, big landscapes and country pictures on cream walls, two log fires, comfortable back lounge and modern dining room, good contemporary food (booking advised), well kept Kirkby Lonsdale, Timothy Taylors and Thwaites, good service; piped music; children and dogs welcome, bedrooms, open all day from 9am, closed Mon till 3pm. *Recommended by Chris and Meredith Owen, G and P Vago, Stu Mac, Michael Doswell, Malcolm and Pauline Pellatt, John and Eileen Mennear and others*

KIRKBY STEPHEN NY7808   CA17 4QN
Kings Arms
A685 corner of High Street and Market Square

Former 17th-c posting inn with oak-panelled bar, well kept ales from Copper Dragon, Dent, Greene King and Kirkby Lonsdale, range of malt whiskies, decent food, restaurant; popular with walkers, tables in walled garden, nine bedrooms. *Recommended by Clive Gibson*

LANGDALE NY2906   LA22 9JU
Stickle Barn
By car park for Stickle Ghyll

Lovely views from this roomy and busy walkers'/climbers' bar (boots welcome), three or four changing ales such as Barngates, decent good value food including packed lunches, quick friendly service, mountaineering photographs; piped music (live on Sat), TV, games machines; big terrace with inner verandah, bunkhouse, open all day. *Recommended by Chris Johnson, Jane and Alan Bush*

LEVENS SD4885   LA8 8PN
Hare & Hounds
Off A590

Welcoming smartened-up village pub handy for Sizergh Castle, well kept ales including Black Sheep, friendly efficient service, good home-made pub food, partly panelled low-beamed lounge bar, front tap room with coal fire, pool room down steps, restaurant; children welcome, good views from terrace. *Recommended by Mr and Mrs Richard Osborne*

Half pints: by law, a pub should not charge more for half a pint than half the price of a full pint, unless it shows that half-pint price on its price list.

LORTON NY1526   CA13 9UW

☆ **Wheatsheaf**

B5289 Buttermere—Cockermouth

Friendly local atmosphere in neatly furnished bar with two log fires, affable hard-working landlord, Jennings and regular changing guests, several good value wines, good home-made food (all day Sun) from sandwiches to fresh fish (Thurs, Fri evening), smallish restaurant; children welcome, dogs on leads, tables out behind, campsite, open all day weekends, closed Mon lunchtime and weekday lunchtimes in winter. *Recommended by Sylvia and Tony Birbeck, Edward Mirzoeff, Geoff and Linda Payne, Pat and Stewart Gordon, Julian Cox*

LUPTON SO5581   LA6 1PJ

☆ **Plough**

A65, near M6 junction 36

Large refurbished slate-roofed pub with lots of spreading open-plan bar rooms, rugs on wood floors, beams and grey walls throughout, stools by granite-topped counter, ales such as Hawkshead, Jennings, Kirkby Lonsdale and Wychwood Hobgoblin, good interesting modern food, area to the left with logs stacked by open stone fireplace, some nice oval tables and rush-seated chairs, hunting prints and *Punch* cartoons, two further areas with station clock above woodburner, dark wood tables and leather sofa, fresh flowers and daily papers, large carpeted dining room, friendly chatty staff; picnic-sets to one side behind white picket fence, more in back garden. *Recommended by Margaret Dickinson, Dr Kevan Tucker, Christopher Mobbs, David Heath, Pat and Graham Williamson and others*

MELMERBY NY6137   CA10 1HF

Shepherds

A686 Penrith—Alston

Friendly split-level country pub with comfortable heavy-beamed dining room off flagstoned bar, spacious end room with woodburner, hearty helpings of tasty food served promptly, well kept local ales, good wine and whisky choice, games area with darts and pool; children welcome, terrace tables. *Recommended by Kevin and Rose Lemin*

NENTHEAD NY7843   CA9 3PF

Miners Arms

A689

Friendly early 18th-c village pub, good freshly made food from pub standards and wood-fired pizzas to interesting specials, reasonable prices, well kept changing ales, stripped-stone lounge, partly panelled flagstoned public bar, view from big dining conservatory; pool, TV; children welcome, picnic-sets out in front, two bedrooms, Sept leek show, handy for Pennine Way and cycle path, open all day. *Recommended by Mr and Mrs Maurice Thompson, Averell Kingston*

NETHER WASDALE NY1204   CA20 1ET

☆ **Strands**

SW of Wast Water

Lovely spot below the remote high fells around Wast Water, brews its own Strands ales (lots of varieties), popular good value food, good-sized well cared-for high-beamed main bar with woodburner and relaxed friendly atmosphere, smaller public bar with pool, separate dining room, pleasant staff; piped music may obtrude; children and dogs welcome, neat garden with terrace and belvedere, 14 bedrooms, open all day. *Recommended by Mr and Mrs Maurice Thompson, Pam and John Smith, Ludo McGurk*

PENRITH NY5130   CA11 7XD

Lowther Arms

Queen Street

Comfortable and welcoming local in handsome 17th-c building, long bar with beams, bare boards and flagstones, log fire and mix of traditional furniture in various alcoves and recesses, reasonably priced food, several real ales, friendly service. *Recommended by Rosemary and Mike Fielder*

PENRUDDOCK NY4227   CA11 0QU
☆ Herdwick
Off A66 Penrith—Keswick

Attractively cottagey and sympathetically renovated 18th-c inn, warm welcoming atmosphere, well kept Jennings, Marstons and summer guests from unusual curved bar, decent wines, friendly efficient service, enjoyable sensibly priced food from lunchtime sandwiches up, good open fire, stripped stone and white paintwork, nice dining room with upper gallery, games room with pool and darts; children in eating areas, five good value bedrooms. *Recommended by S D and J L Cooke, Comus and Sarah Elliott, Maurice and Gill McMahon, Phil Bryant, Dr and Mrs S G Barber, Mr and Mrs Maurice Thompson*

ROSTHWAITE NY2514   CA12 5XB
Scafell
B5289 S of Keswick

Hotel's big plain slate-floored back bar useful for walkers, weather forecast board, four well kept ales such as Black Sheep and Theakstons, blazing log fire, enjoyable food from sandwiches up, afternoon teas, also, an appealing cocktail bar/sun lounge and dining room, friendly helpful staff; piped music, pool; children and dogs welcome, tables out overlooking beck, bedrooms. *Recommended by Sylvia and Tony Birbeck, Simon Watkins, Lawrence R Cotter, Mr and Mrs Maurice Thompson*

RYDAL NY3606   LA22 9LR
Glen Rothay Hotel
A591 Ambleside—Grasmere

Attractive small 17th-c hotel with enjoyable pubby food from sandwiches up in back bar, well kept changing local ales, helpful friendly staff, banquettes and stools, lots of badger pictures, fireside armchairs in beamed lounge bar, restaurant; walkers and dogs welcome, tables in pretty garden, boats for residents on nearby Rydal Water, eight comfortable bedrooms. *Recommended by Andy and Jill Kassube, Mr and Mrs Maurice Thompson*

SANDFORD NY7316   CA16 6NR
☆ Sandford Arms
Village and pub signposted just off A66 W of Brough

Neat former 18th-c farmhouse in peaceful village, enjoyable food (all day weekends Apr-Oct) from chef/landlord, L-shaped carpeted main bar with stripped beams and stonework, collection of Royal Doulton character jugs and some Dickens ware, ales from Black Sheep, Lancaster and Tirril, comfortable raised and balustraded eating area, more formal dining room and second flagstoned bar, log fire; piped music; children and dogs welcome, seats in front garden and covered courtyard, bedrooms, closed Tues. *Recommended by C J Beresford-Jones, M and GR*

SANTON BRIDGE NY1101   CA19 1UX
☆ Bridge Inn
Off A595 at Holmrook or Gosforth

Charming riverside spot with fell views, beamed and timbered bar bustling with locals, log fire, some booths around stripped-pine tables, Jennings and guest ales, enjoyable traditional food including Sun carvery, family dining room, italian-style bistro, friendly helpful staff, small reception hall with log fire and daily papers; piped music, games machine; dogs welcome in bar, seats outside by quiet road, plenty of walks, 16 bedrooms, open all day. *Recommended by Susan and Nigel Brookes*

SATTERTHWAITE SD3392   LA12 8LN
☆ Eagles Head
S edge of village

Pretty and prettily placed on the edge of beautiful Grizedale Forest, low black beams, comfortable traditional furnishings, big log fire, lots of local photographs and maps, welcoming and obliging landlord, good fairly priced generous pubby food (not Mon) including notable filled rolls, wider evening choice, well kept local ales including Barngates and one brewed for the pub; children welcome, picnic-sets in attractive tree-shaded courtyard garden with pergola, comfortable bedrooms, open all day on summer weekends, closed Mon and Tues lunchtimes. *Recommended by Roger and Kathy Elkin*

SEATHWAITE SD2295   LA20 6ED

☆ **Newfield Inn**

Duddon Valley, near Ulpha (ie not Seathwaite in Borrowdale)

Genuinely friendly 16th-c cottage despite weekend and holiday popularity; local atmosphere in slate-floored bar, wooden tables and chairs, interesting pictures, Jennings and quickly changing guests, straightforward food all day, comfortable side room, games room; no credit cards; children and dogs welcome, tables in nice garden with hill views, play area, good walks, self-catering flats, open all day. *Recommended by John Luckes, E Ling, Alan Hill*

SEDBERGH SD6592   LA10 5BN

Dalesman

Main Street

Three linked modernised rooms, good freshly made seasonal food from sandwiches up, well kept ales including Tetleys and one brewed for the pub, stripped stone and beams, central woodburner; piped music; children welcome, picnic-sets out in front, bedrooms, open all day. *Recommended by John and Helen Rushton*

SEDBERGH SD6592   LA10 5BZ

☆ **Red Lion**

Finkle Street (A683)

Cheerful beamed local, down to earth and comfortable, with good value generous food (meat from next-door butcher), well kept Jennings, good coal fire; sports TV, can get very busy at weekends, no dogs. *Recommended by John and Helen Rushton*

SHAP NY5614   CA10 3PW

☆ **Greyhound**

A6, S end, handy for M6 junction 39

Good value former coaching inn, quickly served enjoyable food in open-plan bar with sofas and armchairs as well as dining tables, more choice in two restaurants, several well kept ales such as Dent, Keswick and Timothy Taylors Landlord, good house wines, daily papers, cheerful bustle and friendly helpful young staff; TV, unobtrusive piped music; dogs welcome, picnic-sets under canopy on flagstoned back terrace, ten comfortable bedrooms, good breakfast, open all day. *Recommended by John Wymer, Andy West, Christine and Neil Townend*

STONETHWAITE NY2513   CA12 5XG

☆ **Langstrath**

Off B5289 S of Derwent Water

Neat, simple bar (pubbiest at lunchtime) with welcoming fire in the big stone fireplace, traditional furniture, several walking cartoons and attractive Lakeland mountain photographs, Black Sheep and Jennings ales, 25 malt whiskies, decent bar food including some interesting dishes, residents' lounge in small left room (original 16th-c cottage), restaurant with fine views; piped music; children over 7 welcome, picnic-sets under big sycamore, fine surrounding walks – in heart of Borrowdale and en route for Cumbrian Way and Coast to Coast Walk, bedrooms, closed Mon, plus Tues and Weds in winter and part of Dec and Jan, otherwise open all day. *Recommended by Simon Watkins, Alison Ball, Ian Walton, Peter Smith and Judith Brown, Mr and Mrs Maurice Thompson*

The letters and figures after the name of each town are its Ordnance Survey map reference. 'Using the *Guide*' explains how it helps you find a pub, in road atlases or on large-scale maps as well as in our own maps.

TROUTBECK NY4103   LA23 1PL
Mortal Man
A592 N of Windermere; Upper Road

Refurbished beamed and partly panelled bar with cosy room off, log fires, Black Sheep, Coniston, Timothy Taylors Landlord and a beer brewed for them by Hawkshead, several wines by the glass, generally well liked food in bar and picture-window restaurant, young willing staff; children and dogs welcome, great views from sunny garden, lovely village, bedrooms, open all day. *Recommended by Dave Traynor, Ian and Rose Lock, Mr and Mrs Richard Osborne*

TROUTBECK NY4028   CA11 0SG
Sportsman
B5288, just off A66 – the 'other' Troutbeck, near Penrith

Small welcoming bar and large dining area with great views, enjoyable standard food, well kept Jennings ales and an interesting guest, good wine choice; children welcome, pretty back terrace overlooking valley, open all day. *Recommended by E Clark*

TROUTBECK NY4103   LA23 1HH
Sun
A591 N of Windermere

Well refurbished hotel with enjoyable reasonably priced food including lunchtime sandwiches, Hawkshead and Jennings ales; 12 bedrooms, open all day Fri-Sun, from 3pm Mon-Thurs (all day in school holidays). *Recommended by V and E A Bolton*

TROUTBECK NY3827   CA11 0SJ
Troutbeck Inn
A5091/A66

Refurbished old railway hotel with bar, lounge and restaurant, good food, real ales, efficient friendly service; children and dogs welcome, seven bedrooms, self-catering cottages in former stables. *Recommended by E Clark*

ULDALE NY2436   CA7 1HA
Snooty Fox
Village signed off B5299 W of Caldbeck

Comfortable well run two-bar village inn with good-quality food using local ingredients, well kept changing ales, friendly attentive staff; bedrooms. *Recommended by Dr Nigel Bowles*

ULVERSTON SD2878   LA12 7BA
☆ ## Farmers Arms
Market Place

Convivial attractively modernised town pub, front bar with comfortable sofas, contemporary wicker chairs, original fireplace, daily newspapers, quickly changing real ales, a dozen wines by the glass, interesting fairly priced food, second bar leading to big raftered dining area (children here only); unobtrusive piped music; seats on attractive heated front terrace, lots of colourful tubs and hanging baskets, Thurs market day (pub busy then), three cottages to rent, open all day from 9am. *Recommended by Chris Clark*

WHITEHAVEN NX9718   CA28 7LL
Vagabond
Marlborough Street

Old-fashioned town-centre pub with bare boards and oak settles, lots of american memorabilia – Jack Kerouac posters, car number plates etc, good basic low-priced food, well kept Jennings, friendly helpful staff. *Recommended by Susan and Nigel Brookes*

ALSO WORTH A VISIT IN
GREATER MANCHESTER, LANCASHIRE
& MERSEYSIDE

Besides the region's top pubs, we recommend the following. Do tell us
what you think of them: **feedback@goodguides.com**

ALTRINCHAM SJ7689   WA14 5NT
Railway Inn
153 Manchester Road (A56), Broadheath

Early Victorian with lounge, bar, games room (darts and dominoes), snug and dining
room, church pews, well kept bargain Holts Bitter and Mild, friendly landlady and chatty
locals; back terrace, open all day (Sun 3-7pm). *Recommended by the Didler*

APPLEY BRIDGE SD5210   WN6 9DY
Dicconson Arms
B5375 (Appley Lane North)/A5209, handy for M6 junction 27

Well run and civilised, with good nicely presented food (all day Sun), friendly attentive
service, two well kept ales in uncluttered bar area with clubby chairs, dining room
beyond, pine floors, woodburner; some seats outside. *Recommended by Jeremy King,*
Mr and Mrs I Templeton, Norma and Noel Thomas

AUGHTON SD3905   L39 6SA
Stanley Arms
St Michael Road

Spacious and spotless cottagey pub behind medieval church, wide choice of changing
ales, reasonably priced home-made food from sandwiches to daily specials, helpful
service; picnic-sets in garden with smokers' shelter, open all day. *Recommended by*
Peter Hacker

BARLEY SD8240   BB12 9JX
Pendle
Barley Lane

Friendly 1930s pub in shadow of Pendle Hill, three cosy rooms, two open fires, simple
substantial pub food (all day weekends), well kept local ales, conservatory; garden, lovely
village and good walking country, bedrooms, open all day. *Recommended by Len Beattie,*
Dr Kevan Tucker

BARNSTON SJ2783   CH61 1BW
☆ ## Fox & Hounds
3 miles from M53 junction 3: A552 towards Woodchurch, then left on A551

Spotless well run pub with cheerful welcome, six real ales including Theakstons, 60 malt
whiskies, good value traditional lunchtime food, roomy carpeted bay-windowed lounge with
built-in banquettes and plush-cushioned captain's chairs around solid tables, old local
prints and collection of police and other headgear, charming old quarry-tiled corner with
antique range, copper kettles, built-in pine kitchen cupboards, enamel food bins and
earthenware, small locals' bar (worth a look for its highly traditional layout and collection
of horsebrasses and metal ashtrays), snug where children allowed; dogs welcome in bar,
picnic-sets under cocktail parasols and colourful hanging baskets in back yard, open all
day. *Recommended by Tony Nolan, John and Helen Rushton, Maurice and Gill McMahon, Clive Watkin*

BARROW SD7337   BB7 9AQ
☆ Eagle
Village signed off A59; Clitheroe Road (A671 N of Whalley)

Stylish dining pub with modern light leather chairs, sofas and big low tables in bar, brasserie-style dining room with busy open kitchen and cabinet displaying their 35-day dry-aged steaks, good food (all day Sun) including sandwiches, excellent home-made sausages and imaginative main choices, five real ales, good wines, young uniformed staff, back area with chandeliers and big mirrors, clubby panelled piano bar; children welcome, tables outside overlooking big car park, open all day. *Recommended by John and Eleanor Holdsworth, Steve Whalley, Mr and Mrs John Taylor*

BAY HORSE SD4952   LA2 0HR
☆ Bay Horse
1.2 miles from M6 junction 33: A6 southwards, then off on left

Civilised redecorated country dining pub – a useful motorway stop; cosily pubby bar with good log fire, cushioned wall banquettes, fresh flowers, Black Sheep and Hawkshead, 15 wines by the glass, smarter restaurant with cosy corners, another log fire and carefully presented innovative food; children welcome, tables in garden, bedrooms, closed Mon. *Recommended by Adrian Johnson, Karen Eliot, Dave Braisted, David and Katharine Cooke, Dr Kevan Tucker, Mr and Mrs J E Fisher and others*

BEBINGTON SJ3385   CH62 1BQ
Travellers Rest
B5151, not far from M53 junction 4; New Ferry Road, Higher Bebington

Friendly semi-rural pub with several areas around central bar, good value food all day from lunchtime sandwiches and snacks to more substantial evening meals (till 7pm), up to eight well kept real ales including some from small breweries, efficient staff, alcoves, beams, brasses etc; no children; open all day. *Recommended by MLR*

BELMONT SD6715   BL7 8AB
☆ Black Dog
Church Street (A675)

Nicely set Holts pub with their usual good value food (all day Fri-Sun, not Tues evening), bargain beers, friendly prompt staff, cheery small-roomed traditional core, coal fires, picture-window extension; children welcome, seats outside with moorland views above village, attractive part-covered smokers' area, good walks, decent well priced bedrooms (breakfast from 9am), open all day. *Recommended by Peter Heaton, Simon Le Fort, Yvonne and Mike Meadley, the Didler, Norma and Noel Thomas and others*

BIRKENHEAD SJ3389   CH41 5DQ
Gallaghers
Chester Street

Friendly 19th-c place uniquely combining barbershop at back with traditional pub at front, local real ales including a house beer appropriately named Half Cut, interesting books, ship pictures and military memorabilia. *Recommended by Colin Ebbrell*

BIRKENHEAD SJ3289   CH41 6JN
Stork
Price Street

Welcoming early Victorian pub with tiled façade, four well restored civilised rooms around island bar, polished mosaic floor, old photographs, several well kept changing ales, bargain basic food weekday lunchtime and early evening; open all day. *Recommended by the Didler*

BLACKO SD8641 · BB9 6LS
Rising Sun
A682 towards Gisburn

Welcoming traditional village pub with good Moorhouses ales, enjoyable well priced pubby food, tiled entry, open fires in three rooms off main bar; tables out on front terrace, open all day weekends. *Recommended by Dr Kevan Tucker*

☆ BLACKSTONE EDGE SD9617 · OL15 0LG
White House
A58 Ripponden—Littleborough, just W of B6138

Beautifully placed moorland dining pub with remote views, emphasis on good value hearty food from sandwiches up (all day Sun), prompt service, well kept Theakstons Best and changing regional guests, belgian bottled beers, cheerful atmosphere, carpeted main bar with hot fire, other areas off, most tables used for food; children welcome.
Recommended by Gordon and Margaret Ormondroyd, Clive Flynn

BOLTON SD7112 · BL1 7AN
Brewery Tap
Belmont Road

Simply refurbished tap for Bank Top (their first pub), well kept guest ales too, no food.
Recommended by Ben Williams

BOLTON SD7109 · BL1 2JU
Howcroft
Pool Street

Friendly local serving as tap for good Bank Top ales, guests including Timothy Taylors Landlord, enjoyable good value pubby lunches, screened-off rooms around central servery with fine glass and woodwork, cosy snug, open fires, conservatory, pub games; crown bowling green, open all day. *Recommended by the Didler*

BOLTON SD6809 · BL1 5AG
Victoria
Markland Hill

Extensively refurbished and extended inn known locally as Fannys, decent food, beer and wine; open all day. *Recommended by W K Wood*

BOLTON SD6913 · BL1 7BT
Wilton Arms
Belmont Road, Horrocks Fold

Friendly low-beamed roadside pub, consistently good well priced fresh food, well kept ales such as Bank Top Flat Cap and Coniston Bluebird, open fires; garden overlooking valley, Pennine walks, open all day. *Recommended by W K Wood, Rob and Gill Wood*

BOLTON BY BOWLAND SD7849 · BB7 4NW
Coach & Horses
Main Street

Refurbished stone-built beamed pub/restaurant with bar and two dining areas, good interesting food from open sandwiches up at reasonable prices, bargain Weds evening set menu, changing ales such as Bowland, Copper Dragon and Moorhouses, good choice of wines, friendly helpful staff, log fires; children welcome, tables out at back, lovely streamside village with interesting church, bedrooms. *Recommended by Neil and Jacqui Victor-Corrie, Mary Hill*

The letters and figures after the name of each town are its Ordnance Survey map reference. 'Using the *Guide*' explains how it helps you find a pub, in road atlases or on large-scale maps as well as in our own maps.

BROUGHTON SD4838   PR4 0BJ
☆ **Plough at Eaves**
*A6 N through Broughton, first left into Station Lane under a mile after traffic lights,
then left after 1.5 miles*

Pleasantly unpretentious old country tavern with two beamed homely bars, Thwaites ales,
straightforward food (all day Sun), lattice windows and traditional furnishings, old guns
over woodburner in one room, Royal Doulton figurines above log fire in dining bar with
conservatory; quiet piped music, games machine; children welcome, front terrace and
spacious side/back garden, well equipped play area, open all day weekends (till 1am Sat),
closed Mon (except bank holidays). *Recommended by Dr and Mrs A K Clarke*

BURNLEY SD8432   BB11 1UH
Bridge
Bank Parade

Open-plan town-centre pub with well kept Hydes Original, several other changing ales
(hundreds each year), continental beers on tap and many dozen by the bottle, farm
ciders, bargain lunchtime food, friendly atmosphere and good young staff, simple chairs
and tables on left, small snug and leather sofas on right; open all day (till 1am Fri, Sat),
closed Mon, Tues. *Recommended by Dr Kevan Tucker*

BURY SD8313   BL9 0EY
Trackside
East Lancashire Railway Station, Bolton Street

Welcoming busy station bar by East Lancashire steam railway, bright, airy and clean with
eight changing ales, bottled imports, farm cider and great range of whiskies, enjoyable
home-made food (not Mon, Tues), fine display of beer labels on ceiling; children welcome
till 7.30, platform tables, open all day. *Recommended by the Didler, Don Bryan, Ben Williams*

CARNFORTH SD5173   LA6 1JH
Longlands
Tewitfield, about 2 miles N; A6070, off A6

Bustling family-run village inn with good local beer range, friendly helpful staff, good
interesting food in bar and restaurant (worth booking), live music Mon; bedrooms, self-
catering cottages. *Recommended by Tony and Maggie Harwood, Becky Mason*

CHEADLE HULME SJ8785   SK8 7EG
Church Inn
Ravenoak Road (A5149 SE)

Bustling friendly local, smart and genuinely old, with good fresh mediterranean-
influenced food (all day Sun) in restaurant and (ordered from small hatch) in bar,
pleasant waitresses, four well kept Robinsons, coal fire; open all day. *Recommended by
Stuart Paulley, Andy and Jill Kassube*

CHIPPING SD6141   PR3 2TH
☆ **Dog & Partridge**
Hesketh Lane; crossroads Chipping—Longridge with Inglewhite—Clitheroe

Comfortable old-fashioned and much altered 16th-c dining pub in grand countryside,
enjoyable food (all day Sun) served by friendly staff, Tetleys ales, beams, exposed stone
walls and good log fire, small armchairs around close-set tables in main lounge, smart
casual dress for evening restaurant; children welcome, open all day Sun, closed Mon.
Recommended by anon

If a service charge is mentioned prominently on a menu or accommodation terms, you must
pay it if service was satisfactory. If service is really bad, you are legally entitled to
refuse to pay some or all of the service charge as compensation for not getting
the service you might reasonably have expected.

CHORLEY SD5817 · PR6 9HA
Yew Tree
Dill Hall Brow, Heath Charnock – out past Limbrick towards the reservoirs

Attractive tucked-away restaurant pub with good food from open kitchen (all day Sun – best to book at weekends), lunchtime sandwiches too, helpful friendly staff; children welcome, picnic-sets out on decked area, closed Mon. *Recommended by Simon Stott*

CHORLTON CUM HARDY SJ8193 · M21 9HS
Horse & Jockey
Chorlton Green

Refurbished low-beamed pub with mock-Tudor façade, own-brewed Bootleg ales and guests, knowledgeable chatty staff, all-day bar food, more restauranty things in high-ceilinged evening/weekend dining room (part of former Victorian brewery), good mix of customers from mothers with prams to the local history society; dogs allowed in tap room, picnic-sets on front terrace looking across to green, open all day. *Recommended by Pete Yearsley, Malcolm and Pauline Pelliatt*

CONDER GREEN SD4655 · LA2 0BD
Thurnham Mill Hotel
Signed off A588 just S

Converted early 19th-c stone-built mill, comfortable beamed and flagstoned bar with good reasonably priced food, Everards and other ales, lots of whiskies, friendly helpful staff, log fires, restaurant overlooking Lancaster Canal lock; children welcome, tables out on terrace, fenced play area, 15 comfortable bedrooms, good breakfast, open all day. *Recommended by Margaret Dickinson*

CROSBY SJ3100 · L23 7XY
Crows Nest
Victoria Road, Great Crosby

Unspoilt character roadside local with cosy bar, snug and Victorian-style lounge, all neatly looked after by welcoming landlady, well kept Cains, Theakstons and guests; tables outside, open all day. *Recommended by the Didler, Brian Conrad*

DENSHAW SD9710 · OL3 5SN
Printers Arms
Oldham Road

Above Oldham in shadow of Saddlesworth Moor, modernised interior with small log-fire bar and three other rooms, popular competitively priced food including OAP midweek deals, a beer brewed for them by Bazens and Timothy Taylors Golden Best, several wines by the glass, friendly efficient young staff. *Recommended by Michael Butler, Stuart Paulley*

DENSHAW SD9711 · OL3 5UN
☆ ## Rams Head
2 miles from M62 junction 2; A672 towards Oldham, pub N of village

Sweeping moorland views from inviting dining pub with four thick-walled traditional little rooms, tasty food (all day Sun) including seasonal game and plenty of seafood, well kept Black Sheep and Timothy Taylors, good attentive service, beam-and-plank ceilings, panelling, oak settles and built-in benches, log fires, tea room and adjacent delicatessen selling locally sourced meat and other produce; soft piped music; children welcome (not Sat evening), open all day Sun, closed Mon (except bank holidays). *Recommended by Gordon and Margaret Ormondroyd, Dr Kevan Tucker, Gill and Malcolm Stott, Clive Flynn, Brian and Anna Marsden and others*

Half pints: by law, a pub should not charge more for half a pint than half the price of a full pint, unless it shows that half-pint price on its price list.

DENTON SJ9395   M34 3FF

Lowes Arms
Hyde Road (A57)

For now no longer brewing their own LAB ales but serving good local Hornbeam and Phoenix, jovial landlord and helpful friendly staff, wide choice of good bargain food including offers, bar with games, restaurant; tables outside, smoking shelter, open all day weekends. *Recommended by Dennis Jones, Stuart Paulley and others*

☆ DOWNHAM SD7844   BB7 4BJ

Assheton Arms
Off A59 NE of Clitheroe, via Chatburn

Neatly kept 18th-c pub in lovely village location with Pendle Hill view, cosy low-beamed L-shaped bar with pews, big oak tables and massive stone fireplace, good range of food (all day Sun) including seafood menu, quick service, lots of wines by the glass, two real ales; piped music; children and dogs welcome, picnic-sets outside, open all day weekends. *Recommended by C A Bryson*

DUNHAM TOWN SJ7288   WA14 5RP

Rope & Anchor
Paddock Lane, Dunham Massey

Popular recently refurbished dining pub, good food, first-rate service, well kept Holts, garden room for families. *Recommended by Hilary Forrest, David Heath, David M Smith*

ECCLES SJ7798   M30 0LS

Albert Edward
Church Street

Popular cheery local with main bar and three other rooms, flagstones and old tiles, fire, old local photographs, bargain Sam Smiths; small back terrace, open all day. *Recommended by the Didler*

ECCLES SJ7598   M30 7HD

Grapes
Liverpool Road, Peel Green; A57 0.5 miles from M63 junction 2

Handsome brawny Edwardian local with superb etched glass, wall tiling and mosaic floor, lots of mahogany, eye-catching staircase, well kept bargain Holts and maybe a guest beer, good service, fairly quiet roomy lounge areas (children welcome till 7pm), pool in classic billiards room, vault with Manchester darts, drinking corridor; tables outside, open all day. *Recommended by the Didler*

ECCLES SJ7798   M30 0BP

Lamb
Regent Street (A57)

Full-blooded Edwardian three-room local, splendid etched windows, fine woodwork and furnishings, extravagantly tiled stairway, trophies in display case, bargain Holts and lunchtime sandwiches, full-size snooker table in original billiards room, friendly atmosphere with many older regulars; open all day. *Recommended by the Didler*

ECCLES SJ7798   M30 0EN

Royal Oak
Barton Lane

Large old-fashioned Edwardian corner pub, several busy rooms off corridor, handsome tilework, mosaic floors and fittings, well kept cheap Holts, good licensees, pool; children allowed daytime in back lounge (may be organ sing-alongs), open all day from 9.30am. *Recommended by the Didler*

ECCLES SJ7698   M30 0QN
Stanley Arms
Eliza Ann Street/Liverpool Road (A57), Patricroft

Unspoilt mid-Victorian corner local with bargain Holts, popular front bar, hatch serving
lobby and corridor to small back rooms, one with cast-iron range, lunchtime cobs, friendly
licensees; open all day. *Recommended by the Didler*

EUXTON SD5318   PR7 6EG
Travellers Rest
Dawbers Lane (A581 W)

Refurbished old dining pub (most here to eat) with good varied range of popular food
including daily specials, well organised staff, real ales; dogs welcome in part of back bar,
nice side garden. *Recommended by Margaret Dickinson, Sandie and Andrew Geddes*

FENCE SD8338   BB12 9QG
Old Sparrow Hawk
Wheatley Lane Road

Big rambling black and white timbered pub, good selection of real ales, enjoyable popular
food, good service. *Recommended by Guy Vowles, Ken and Lynda Taylor, Dr Kevan Tucker*

FRECKLETON SD4328   PR4 1HA
Ship
Towards Naze Lane industrial estate, then right into Bunker Street

Old pub with roomy main bar, big windows overlooking water meadows, good choice of
enjoyable generous well priced pubby food (all day weekends), attentive service, half a
dozen well kept ales, games area with TV, upstairs restaurant; children allowed, disabled
facilities, tables out behind, open all day. *Recommended by E A Eaves*

GARSTANG SD4945   PR3 1PA
☆ ## Th'Owd Tithebarn
Off Church Street

Large barn with flagstoned terrace overlooking Lancaster Canal marina, Victorian
country life theme with long refectory table, old kitchen range, masses of farm tools,
stuffed animals and birds, flagstones and high rafters, generous simple food all day from
filled baguettes up, Black Sheep and York ales, good value wine by the glass, quieter
parlour welcoming children; piped music; open all day summer. *Recommended by
Dr Kevan Tucker, Francesca Salvini*

GOOSNARGH SD5636   PR3 2AU
☆ ## Stags Head
Whittingham Lane (B5269)

Lots of separate mainly old-world areas rambling around central servery, plenty of nice
features including proper old-fashioned radiators, open fires too, good value interesting
home-made food from local produce (even their own pork scratchings), children's
helpings, good service, well kept changing ales, popular restaurant; piped and some live
music; dogs welcome, tables out in pleasant pergola and on lawn, closed Tues otherwise
open all day. *Recommended by Margaret Dickinson, Denise L Painter*

GREAT HARWOOD SD7332   BB6 7BA
Royal
Station Road

Substantial Victorian pub with good changing range of beers from small breweries, tap
for nearby Red Rose brewery, good soft drinks choice (own sarsaparilla), great selection
of bottled beers, enjoyable wholesome food, simple traditional fittings, friendly
atmosphere, pub games including pool and darts; big-screen TV, live music Fri; partly
covered terrace, three bedrooms, closed lunchtime Mon-Thurs, open all day Fri-Sun.
Recommended by the Didler

GRINDLETON SD7545   BB7 4QR
☆ Duke of York
Off A59 NE of Clitheroe, either via Chatburn, or off A671 in W Bradford; Brow Top

Welcoming chef/landlord and neat helpful staff in comfortable and civilised dining pub,
good imaginative well presented food including set deals, good wines, Black Sheep Best
and Thwaites Original, various areas including one with open fire, views over Ribble Valley
to Pendle Hill; tables on raised decking and in garden behind, closed Mon. *Recommended by
John and Sylvia Harrop, Michael Ellis, Peter and Josie Fawcett, Steve Whalley*

HAWKSHAW SD7515   BL8 4JS
Red Lion
Ramsbottom Road

Refurbished pub/hotel now owned by Lees, their ales, enjoyable good value food; children
welcome, bedrooms, quiet spot by River Irwell. *Recommended by Ben Williams, Norma and
Noel Thomas, John and Sylvia Harrop*

HESKIN GREEN SD5315   PR7 5NP
☆ Farmers Arms
Wood Lane (B5250, N of M6 junction 27)

Popular family-run country pub, good choice of well priced home-made food in two-level
dining area, cheerful helpful staff, Black Sheep, Jennings, Prospect and Timothy Taylors
Landlord, heavy black beams, sparkling brasses, china and stuffed animals, darts in
public bar; piped and some live music, Sky TV, Thurs quiz; picnic-sets in big colourful
garden, play area, more tables front and side, good value bedrooms, open all day
weekends. *Recommended by Margaret Dickinson, Norma and Noel Thomas*

HEST BANK SD4766   LA2 6DN
☆ Hest Bank Inn
Hest Bank Lane; off A6 just N of Lancaster

Good choice of enjoyable food in picturesque three-bar coaching inn, nice setting close to
Morecambe Bay, well kept ales, decent wines, friendly helpful young staff, separate
restaurant area with pleasant conservatory; children welcome, plenty of tables out by
Lancaster Canal, open all day. *Recommended by Tony and Maggie Harwood*

HURST GREEN SD6837   BB7 9QJ
☆ Shireburn Arms
Whalley Road (B6243 Clitheroe—Goosnargh)

Quiet comfortable 17th-c hotel with peaceful Ribble Valley views from big light and airy
restaurant and lovely neatly kept garden with attractive terrace and wendy house,
friendly helpful staff, decent reasonably priced food from sandwiches and snacks (9-5)
through pubby favourites to restaurant dishes, Bowland Hen Harrier and Theakstons
Best, daily papers, armchairs, sofas and log fire in beamed lounge bar with linked dining
area; faint piped music; pretty Tolkien walk from here, comfortable bedrooms.
Recommended by anon

HYDE SJ9495   SK14 2BJ
Cheshire Ring
Manchester Road (A57, between M67 junctions 2 and 3)

Welcoming pub tied to Beartown brewery, their good value ales kept well, guest beers and
imports on tap, farm ciders and perries, good house wines, nice home-made pies and
curries; piped and some live music; open all day weekends, from 4pm Mon and Tues, 1pm
Weds-Fri. *Recommended by Dennis Jones, the Didler and others*

Though we don't usually mention it in the text, most pubs now provide
coffee or tea – so it's always worth asking.

HYDE SJ9493   SK14 5EZ

Joshua Bradley
Stockport Road, Gee Cross

Former mansion handsomely converted to pub/restaurant keeping panelling, moulded ceilings and imposing fireplaces, good range of well priced pubby food, three well kept Hydes ales and a guest, friendly efficient staff; heated terrace, play area. *Recommended by Dennis Jones*

HYDE SJ9595   SK14 2NN

Sportsman
Mottram Road

Bright cheerful Victorian local, Pennine ales and lots of changing guests (frequent beer festivals), welcoming licensees, bargain bar food, upstairs cuban restaurant, bare boards and open fires, pub games, full-size snooker table upstairs; children and dogs welcome. *Recommended by Dennis Jones, the Didler and others*

IRBY SJ2586   CH49 3NT

Irby Mill
Mill Lane, off Greasby Road

Converted miller's cottage (original windmill demolished 1898) doing well under present management, eight well kept ales, good choice of wines by the glass, popular reasonably priced food all day (till 6pm Sun) from generous sandwiches up, friendly service, two low-beamed traditional flagstoned rooms and comfortable carpeted lounge, log fire, interesting old photographs and history; tables on terraces and side grass, open all day. *Recommended by David Duff, Tony Tollitt, Clive Watkin and others*

LANCASTER SD4761   LA1 1PP

☆ Borough
Dalton Square

Popular city-centre pub, stylishly civilised, with chandeliers, dark leather sofas and armchairs, antique tables and lamps, chunky candles, high stools and elbow tables, good variety of ales including locals such as Bowland, Hawkshead, Lancaster and Thwaites, lots of bottled beers, big dining room with central tables and booths along one side, enjoyable all-day food with emphasis on local suppliers, good value two course lunch (not Sun), snacks from deli counter, jams and local produce for sale; comedy last Sun of month, poker Mon night; children welcome, dogs in bar, lovely tree-sheltered garden. *Recommended by Karen Eliot, Mike Horgan, Di Wright, Colin Woodward*

LANCASTER SD4761   LA1 1SU

☆ Water Witch
Parking in Aldcliffe Road behind Royal Lancaster Infirmary, off A6

Attractive conversion of 18th-c canalside barge-horse stabling, flagstones, stripped stone, rafters and pitch-pine panelling, seven well kept ales (third-of-a-pint glasses available) from mirrored bar, enjoyable food all day including specials, prompt pleasant service, upstairs restaurant; children in eating areas, tables outside. *Recommended by Brian and Anna Marsden*

LEIGH SJ6599   WN7 4DB

Waterside
Twist Lane

Civilised pub in tall converted 19th-c warehouses by Bridgewater Canal, handy for indoor and outdoor markets, wide choice of enjoyable bargain food all day including OAP and other deals, Greene King ales, good friendly service, chatty lunchtime atmosphere; live music or disco Thurs-Sat; children welcome, disabled access and facilities, plenty of waterside tables, ducks and swans, open all day. *Recommended by Ben Williams*

LITTLE ECCLESTON SD4240   PR3 0YP

☆ Cartford

Cartford Lane, off A586 Garstang—Blackpool, by toll bridge

Prettily placed 17th-c coaching inn on river banks, unusual four-level layout combining traditional and contemporary elements, oak beams, light wood floors, log fire, changing real ales and speciality bottled beers, Weston's cider, food generally well liked, french owners and friendly young staff, restaurant; TV; children welcome, tables in garden looking out over River Wyre (crossed by toll bridge), the Trough of Bowland and Beacon Fell, bedrooms, open all day, closed Mon lunchtime. *Recommended by Nik Maguire, Phil and Helen Holt, P M Dodd*

LIVERPOOL SJ3489   L1 8DQ

☆ Baltic Fleet

Wapping, near Albert Dock

Unusual bow-fronted pub, easy convivial local atmosphere, wide range of interesting beers including own good Wapping brews, several wines by the glass, enjoyable straightforward well priced food (not Sat lunchtime) including traditional scouse, weekend breakfasts, bare boards, big arched windows, simple mix of furnishings, nautical paraphernalia, newspapers, upstairs lounge; piped music, TV; children welcome in eating areas, dogs in bar, back terrace, open all day. *Recommended by Tony and Wendy Hobden, Eric Larkham, Rob and Catherine Dunster, the Didler, Peter Smith and Judith Brown, Andy and Jill Kassube and others*

LIVERPOOL SJ3589   L7 7EB

Belvedere

Sugnall Street

Unspoilt Victorian pub with friendly chatty bar, original fittings including etched glass, coal fires, four changing ales, good pizzas, darts and other games; open all day. *Recommended by the Didler*

LIVERPOOL SJ3588   L8 5XJ

☆ Brewery Tap

Cains Brewery, Stanhope Street

Victorian pub with full Cains range at reasonable prices, guest beers, friendly efficient staff, good value food weekday lunchtimes, nicely understated clean décor, wooden floors, plush raised side snug, interesting old prints and breweriana, handsome bar, gas fire, daily papers; sports TV, no dogs; children till 8pm, disabled access, brewery tours, open all day. *Recommended by Eric Larkham, the Didler, Claes Mauroy*

LIVERPOOL SJ3589   L1 9BB

Cracke

Rice Street

Friendly unsmart local popular with students, Liverpool Organic, Thwaites, and several guests, farm cider, sandwiches till 6pm, small unspoilt bar with bare boards and bench seats, snug and bigger back room with unusual Beatles diorama, lots of posters for local events; juke box, sports TV; picnic-sets in sizeable back garden, open all day. *Recommended by the Didler*

LIVERPOOL SJ3589   L1 2SP

☆ Dispensary

Renshaw Street

Small busy central pub with up to ten well kept ales including Cains and other local brews, bottled imports, no food, polished panelling, wonderful etched windows, bare boards, comfortable raised back bar with coal fire, Victorian medical artefacts; piped music, silent TVs; open all day. *Recommended by Tony and Wendy Hobden, Eric Larkham, Maurice and Gill McMahon, the Didler, Andy and Jill Kassube and others*

LIVERPOOL SJ3490   L1 1HF

☆ Doctor Duncan

St Johns Lane

Friendly Victorian pub with several rooms including impressive back area with pillared and vaulted tiled ceiling, full Cains range and guest beers well kept, belgian beers on tap, enjoyable good value food, pleasant helpful service, daily papers; may be piped music, can get lively in evenings and busy weekends; family room, open all day. *Recommended by Eric Larkham, the Didler, Claes Mauroy*

LIVERPOOL SJ3590   L1 9BH

Everyman Bistro

Hope Street, below Everyman Theatre

Busy low-ceilinged clattery basement, spotless with long wooden tables on tiled floor, four well kept ales, side room with good reasonably priced home-made food, friendly service; closed Sun, otherwise open all day. *Recommended by the Didler*

LIVERPOOL SJ3589   L1 9AS

Fly in the Loaf

Hardman Street

Former bakery with smart gleaming bar serving Okells and up to seven ales from smaller brewers, foreign beers too, simple low-priced home-made food (not Mon), friendly service, long room with panelling, some raised sections, even a pulpit; piped music, sports TV, upstairs lavatories, open all day, till midnight weekends. *Recommended by Eric Larkham, Rachel Platonov, Nigel Schaay, the Didler, Jeremy King, Claes Mauroy*

LIVERPOOL SJ3490   L1 1HW

Globe

Cases Street, opposite station

Chatty traditional little local in busy shopping area (can get packed), friendly staff, good selection of well kept ales, lunchtime filled cobs, sloping floor, quieter cosy back room, prints of old Liverpool; 60s piped music; open all day. *Recommended by the Didler*

LIVERPOOL SJ3490   L2 2AW

Hole In Ye Wall

Off Dale Street

Well restored 18th-c pub, thriving local atmosphere in high-beamed panelled bar, seven changing ales (fed by gravity from upstairs – no cellar as pub is on Quaker burial site), sandwiches and basic food till 5pm, free chip butties Sun when there's a traditional sing-along, friendly staff, plenty of woodwork, stained glass, old Liverpool photographs, coal-effect gas fire in unusual brass-canopied fireplace; no dogs; children allowed till 5pm, open all day. *Recommended by the Didler, Claes Mauroy*

LIVERPOOL SJ3490   L2 2BP

Lion

Moorfields, off Tithebarn Street

Beautifully preserved ornate Victorian tavern, great changing beer choice, over 80 malt whiskies, friendly landlord interested in pub's history, good value lunchtime food including splendid cheese and pie specialities, sparkling etched glass and serving hatches in central bar, unusual wallpaper and matching curtains, big mirrors, panelling and tilework, two small back lounges one with fine glass dome, coal fire; silent fruit machine; open all day. *Recommended by the Didler, Andy and Jill Kassube, Claes Mauroy*

If you have to cancel a reservation for a bedroom or restaurant, please telephone or write to warn them. You may lose your deposit if you've paid one.

LIVERPOOL SJ3489   L1 5AG
Monro
Duke Street

Stylish gastropub, popular comfortable and well run, with good choice of interesting food including vegetarian menu, early evening deals (not Sun), well kept Marstons and guests from small bar, fast friendly service; courtyard tables, open all day till late. *Recommended by the Didler, Peter Smith and Judith Brown*

LIVERPOOL SJ3589   L8 7LY
Peter Kavanaghs
Egerton Street, off Catherine Street

Shuttered Victorian pub with interesting décor in several small rooms including old-world murals, stained glass and lots of bric-a-brac (bicycle hanging from ceiling), piano, wooden settles and real fires, well kept Cains, Greene King, Wychwood and guests, friendly licensees happy to show you around including cellars, popular with locals and students; open all day. *Recommended by Eric Larkham, the Didler, Claes Mauroy*

LIVERPOOL SJ3490   L1 1EB
Richmond
Williamson Street

Popular small corner pub in pedestrianised area, nice old interior and fittings including original Bass mirror, Bass, Black Sheep Cains, Caledonian Deuchars IPA, Timothy Taylors Landlord and changing guests, over 50 malts; sports TV; tables out in front, open all day from 10am. *Recommended by the Didler*

LIVERPOOL SJ3589   L1 2SX
Roscoe Head
Roscoe Street

Unassuming old local with cosy bar, snug and two other spotless unspoilt little rooms, friendly long-serving landlady, well kept Jennings, Tetleys and four guests, inexpensive home-made lunches (not weekends), interesting memorabilia, traditional games including cribbage, quiz Tues and Thurs; open all day till midnight. *Recommended by Eric Larkham, the Didler, Sean Brophy, Andy and Jill Kassube, Claes Mauroy*

LIVERPOOL SJ3490   L2 2JH
Ship & Mitre
Dale Street

Friendly local with fine art deco exterior and ship-like interior, popular with university people, up to 12 changing unusual ales (many beer festivals), over 70 bottled continental beers, farm ciders, good value basic food (all day Fri-Sun), upstairs function room with original 1930s décor; well behaved children till 7pm, dogs welcome, open all day. *Recommended by Eric Larkham, the Didler, Andy and Jill Kassube*

LIVERPOOL SJ3589   L1 4DQ
Swan
Wood Street

Neon sign for this busy unsmart three-floor pub, bare boards and dim lighting, up to eight beers including good value Hydes, bottled belgian beers, Weston's cider, good value cobs and weekday lunches, friendly staff; loud juke box draws younger crowd, silent fruit machine; open all day (till 2am Thurs-Sat). *Recommended by the Didler, Jeremy King*

LIVERPOOL SJ3490   L2 2EZ
☆ Thomas Rigbys
Dale Street

Spacious beamed and panelled Victorian pub with mosaic flooring, old tiles and etched glass, Okells and five changing guests, lots of bottled imports, impressively long bar, steps up to main area, table service from attentive staff, reasonably priced hearty home-made

food (such as scouse) all day till 7pm; disabled access, seats in big courtyard, open all day.
Recommended by the Didler, Frank Blanchard, Matt Haycox, David Crook and others

LIVERPOOL SJ3197   L22 8QR
Volunteer
East Street

Classic friendly old local with superb etched glass and wood panelling, busy bar,
comfortable lounge (table service here), well kept Black Sheep, Tetley and guests,
newspapers; open all day. *Recommended by the Didler*

LIVERPOOL SJ3490   L2 6PT
White Star
Rainford Gardens, off Matthew Street

Lively traditional local dating to the 18th c, cosy bar, lots of woodwork, boxing
photographs, White Star shipping line and Beatles memorabilia (they used to rehearse in
back room), well kept ales including Bass, Bowland and Caledonian Deuchars IPA, basic
lunchtime food, friendly staff; sports TVs; open all day. *Recommended by the Didler, Andy and Jill
Kassube, Claes Mauroy*

LONGRIDGE SD6137   PR3 2YJ
Corporation Arms
Lower Road (B6243)

Comfortably refurbished 18th-c pub next to reservoir, wide range of largely traditional
food all day, small helpings available, three or four well kept changing ales such as
Bowland and Brysons, lots of malt whiskies, good atmosphere in three small linked rooms
and restaurant; good bed and breakfast, open all day. *Recommended by Andy and
Jill Kassube, Ron Neville*

☆ LYDGATE SD9704   OL4 4JJ
White Hart
*Stockport Road; Lydgate not marked on some maps and not the one near Todmorden;
take A669 Oldham—Saddleworth, right at brow of hill to A6050 after almost 2.5 miles*

Smart up-to-date dining pub overlooking Pennine moors, mix of locals in bar or simpler
end rooms and diners in elegant brasserie with smartly dressed staff, high quality (not
cheap) food, Lees, Timothy Taylors and a guest beer, 16 wines by the glass, old beams and
exposed stonework contrasting with deep red or purple walls and modern artwork, open
fires, newspapers; TV in lounge; children welcome, dogs in bar, picnic-sets on back lawn
making most of position, bedrooms, open all day. *Recommended by Brian and Anna Marsden,
P J and R D Greaves, David and Cathrine Whiting, Gill and Malcolm Stott, Ed and Anna Fraser*

LYDIATE SD3604   L31 4HD
Scotch Piper
Southport Road; A4157

Medieval thatched pub, well worn-in, with heavy low beams, flagstones, thick stone walls
and dogs sprawled in front of roaring fires, Banks's and a guest from tiny counter in main
room, corridor to middle room with darts and back snug, no food; bikers' night Weds,
outside lavatories; big garden, open all day weekends. *Recommended by the Didler,
Mike Leadbetter*

MANCHESTER SJ8498   M4 4BR
Angel
Angel Street, off Rochdale Road

Good value home-made food from pub standards to more upscale dishes, eight well kept
changing ales including Bobs, bottled beers, farm cider and perry, bare boards bar with
piano, smaller upstairs restaurant with log fire, and paintings by local artist; children and
dogs welcome, back beer garden, open all day, closed Sun. *Recommended by
Chris Johnson, the Didler*

MANCHESTER SJ8398   M2 6HQ
Ape & Apple
John Dalton Street

Big no-frills open-plan pub, well kept bargain Holts, hearty bar food (Weds curry night), comfortable seats in bare-boards bar with lots of old prints and posters, armchairs in upstairs lounge, friendly atmosphere; piped music, TV area, games machines, Thurs quiz; beer garden, bedrooms, open all day, closes 9pm Sun. *Recommended by the Didler, Dr and Mrs A K Clarke*

MANCHESTER SJ8498   M4 5JN
Bar Fringe
Swan Street

Long bare-boards bar specialising in continental beers, also five changing ales from small local breweries and farm cider, friendly staff, basic snacks till 4pm (no food at weekends), daily papers, shelves of empty beer bottles, cartoons, posters, motorcycle hung above door, rock juke box; no children or dogs; tables out behind, open all day, till late Sat, Sun. *Recommended by Jeremy King, Chris Johnson, the Didler*

MANCHESTER SJ8397   M1 5LE
☆ ## Britons Protection
Great Bridgewater Street, corner of Lower Mosley Street

Lively unpretentious city pub with five well kept ales, 235 malt whiskies and cheap lunchtime snacks including range of pies, unspoilt little rooms including two cosy inner lounges with hatch service, attractive brass, solidly comfortable furnishings, tiled murals of 1819 Peterloo Massacre (took place nearby), massive bar counter with heated footrails, coal-effect gas fire, may have storytelling, silent film shows and acoustic music; gets very busy lunchtime and weekends; tables in back garden, open all day. *Recommended by Simon Greenwood, Dr and Mrs A K Clarke, Jeremy King, the Didler, Dennis Jones and others*

MANCHESTER SJ8498   M4 1LE
Castle
Oldham Street, about 200 yards from Piccadilly, on right

Refurbished 17th-c pub well run by former *Coronation Street* actor, simple traditional front bar, small snug, full Robinsons range from fine bank of handpumps, games in back room, nice tilework outside, live music; open all day. *Recommended by the Didler*

MANCHESTER SJ8497   M1 4GX
Circus
Portland Street

Traditional little bare-boards local with particularly well kept Tetleys from minute corridor bar (or may be table service), friendly landlord and staff, walls covered with photos of regulars and local celebrities, football memorabilia, leatherette banquettes in panelled back room; often looks closed but normally open all day (you may have to knock), can get very busy. *Recommended by the Didler, Mike and Eleanor Anderson*

MANCHESTER SJ8398   M2 4BQ
City Arms
Kennedy Street, off St Peters Square

Well kept Tetleys and five quickly changing guests, belgian bottled beers, occasional beer festivals, busy for bargain bar lunches, quick friendly service, coal fires, bare boards and banquettes, prints, panelling and masses of pump clips, handsome tiled façade and corridor; piped music, TV, games machine; wheelchair access but steps down to back lounge, open all day. *Recommended by the Didler, Dennis Jones, Dean Johnson, Jamie Price*

We accept no free drinks or meals and inspections are anonymous.

MANCHESTER SD8104 M45 6TB
Coach & Horses
Old Bury Road, Whitefield; A665 near Besses o' the Barn Station

Thriving early 19th-c Holts pub with traditional bar and lounge, their well kept ales at bargain prices, table service, darts and cards; open all day. *Recommended by the Didler*

MANCHESTER SJ8298 M5 4PF
Crescent
Crescent (A6) – opposite Salford University

Three areas off central servery with eight changing ales (regular beer festivals), many continental bottled beers and real cider, friendly licensees and young staff, buoyant local atmosphere (popular with university), low-priced home-made food including good breakfast and Weds curry night, bare boards and open fire, plenty of character, pool room, juke box; small enclosed terrace, open all day. *Recommended by Ben Williams, the Didler*

MANCHESTER SJ8397 M3 4LZ
 ## Dukes 92
Castle Street, below the bottom end of Deansgate

Imaginatively converted spacious stable block by Rochdale Canal, bare whitewashed walls, old and modern furnishings including comfortable chaises-longues and deep armchairs, spiral staircase to stylish gallery bar with canal views, well kept Moorhouses ales, decent wines and wide choice of spirits from handsome granite-topped counter, pubby food including excellent range of over three dozen cheeses and pâtés, pizzas only mid-afternoon onwards, grill menu in restaurant; piped music; children welcome till 8.30pm, waterside tables on big terrace, open all day. *Recommended by Jeremy King, Andy and Jill Kassube, Tracey and Stephen Groves*

MANCHESTER SJ8399 M3 1EU
Dutton
Park Street, Strangeways

Welcoming old-fashioned corner local near prison, three unusually shaped cosy rooms, Hydes from central servery, lots of bric-a-brac; open all day. *Recommended by the Didler*

MANCHESTER SJ8398 M3 5FP
Egerton Arms
Gore Street, Salford; A6 by station

Well cared-for character local with chandeliers, art nouveau lamps, attractive prints and dark varnished tables, well kept low-priced Holts and guests, friendly service, small room with pool and TV; piped music, silent fruit machines; open all day. *Recommended by the Didler*

MANCHESTER SJ8491 M20 6RQ
Fletcher Moss
William Street

Popular traditional local with well kept Hydes (always a mild) and interesting guests, friendly knowledgeable staff, lunchtime pies, small comfortable rooms, modern conservatory; outside seating area with smokers' shelter, open all day. *Recommended by Craig Stott*

MANCHESTER SJ8497 M1 4QX
Grey Horse
Portland Street, near Piccadilly

Small traditional one-bar Hydes local, their Bitter and Mild kept well, some unusual malt whiskies, friendly licensees, panelled servery with colourful gantry, lots of prints, photographs and plates; piped 60s/70s music, small TV, net curtains; can bring good sandwiches from next door, open all day. *Recommended by the Didler*

MANCHESTER SJ8498   M4 4AA
Hare & Hounds
Shudehill, behind Arndale

Old-fashioned 18th-c local with long narrow bar linking front snug and comfortable back lounge, notable tilework, panelling and stained glass, cheap Holts beer, friendly staff; piped music, TV; open all day. *Recommended by Jeremy King, the Didler, Douglas Wren*

MANCHESTER SJ8398   M3 6AN
Kings Arms
Bloom Street, Salford

Plain tables, bare boards and flagstones contrasting with opulent maroon/purple décor and stained glass, Bazens and changing guests, no food; juke box, music, poetry or theatre nights upstairs, knitting in snug Mon evening; children welcome till 7pm, open all day, closed Sun. *Recommended by the Didler*

MANCHESTER SJ8397   M3 4LY
Knott Fringe
Deansgate

Friendly modern glass-fronted café-bar under railway arch by Castlefield heritage site; Marble organic ales and guests, lots of continental imports, good value all-day food with emphasis on greek dishes, upstairs smokers' balcony overlooking Rochdale Canal; open all day. *Recommended by Chris Johnson, the Didler, Dr and Mrs A K Clarke, Andy and Jill Kassube*

MANCHESTER SJ8497   M1 7DB
Lass o' Gowrie
36 Charles Street; off Oxford Street at BBC

Unspoilt tiled Victorian sidestreet local, welcoming big-windowed long bar with cosy room off, stripped brickwork, nine well kept ales including Greene King, Wadworths and a good house beer (Betty's Bitter) brewed by Outstanding, bargain food (good home-made pies), friendly service; terrace overlooking river, open all day. *Recommended by the Didler*

MANCHESTER SJ8499   M4 4HY
☆ Marble Arch
Rochdale Road (A664), Ancoats; corner of Gould Street, just E of Victoria Station

Cheery own-brew pub with fine Victorian interior, magnificently restored lightly barrel-vaulted high ceiling, extensive marble and tiling, look out for sloping mosaic floor and frieze advertising various spirits, rustic furniture, their own five beers plus guests (brewery visible from windows in back dining room – tours by arrangement), sandwiches and simple bar food; piped music, juke box and Laurel and Hardy Preservation Society meetings third Weds of month showing old films; children welcome, small garden, open all day (till midnight Fri, Sat). *Recommended by Chris Johnson, the Didler, Andy and Jill Kassube, Ben Williams, Pat and Tony Martin*

MANCHESTER SJ8398   M3 5EJ
Mark Addy
Stanley Street, off New Bailey Street, Salford

Unusual converted waiting rooms for boat passengers, barrel-vaulted red sandstone bays with wide glassed-in brick arches, cast-iron pillars and flagstones, views over river, enjoyable food including signature cheese and pâté board, four real ales, lots of wines by the glass, brisk friendly service; piped music, sports TV facing bar; flower-filled waterside courtyard. *Recommended by Dennis Jones*

MANCHESTER SJ8492   M20 2WS
Metropolitan
Lapwing Lane, Didsbury

Large gabled dining pub (former railway hotel) with good imaginative food, well kept Caledonian Deuchars IPA, Timothy Taylors Landlord and Wells & Youngs Bombardier, extensive wine list, efficient service, numerous airy rooms, impressive period décor, open fires; tables out on decking. *Recommended by Malcolm and Pauline Pellatt*

MANCHESTER SJ8298   M3 6DB
New Oxford
Bexley Square, Salford

Up to 16 well kept ales including Mallinsons and Moorhouses (regular beer festivals), good range of imported beers, farm cider, friendly staff, light and airy café-style feel in small front bar and back room, coal fire, good value basic food till 6pm; nice terrace, open all day. *Recommended by Ben Williams, the Didler*

MANCHESTER SJ8397   M1 4BH
Paramount
Oxford Street

Well run Wetherspoons with their usual good value, particularly friendly service, beer festivals. *Recommended by Ben Williams*

MANCHESTER SJ8397   M1 5JQ

☆ Peveril of the Peak
Great Bridgewater Street

Vivid art nouveau external tilework, three sturdily furnished bare-boards rooms, interesting pictures, lots of mahogany, mirrors and stained or frosted glass, log fire, very welcoming family service, changing mainstream ales from central servery, cheap basic lunchtime food (not Sun), busy lunchtime but friendly and homely evenings; TV; children welcome, pavement tables, closed weekend lunchtimes, open all day Fri. *Recommended by the Didler*

MANCHESTER SJ8397   M1 5JG
☆ Rain Bar
Great Bridgewater Street

Bare boards and lots of woodwork in former umbrella works, well kept Lees ales, plenty of wines by the glass, generous good value pubby food all day, friendly efficient staff, relaxed atmosphere, nooks and corners, coal fire in small snug, large upstairs bar/function room; Weds quiz, piped music may be loud, can be busy with young crowd in evenings; good back terrace overlooking spruced-up Rochdale Canal, handy for Bridgwater Hall, open all day. *Recommended by Jeremy King, the Didler, Dr and Mrs A K Clarke*

MANCHESTER SJ8398   M2 1HN
Sams Chop House
Back Pool Fold, Chapel Walks

Small pleasant dining pub, offshoot from Mr Thomas Chop House, with thriving atmosphere, huge helpings of good plain english food, well kept beers, good wine choice, formal waiters, original Victorian décor, live music Mon night. *Recommended by Ian Leadbetter*

MANCHESTER SJ8398   M3 1SW
☆ Sinclairs
Cathedral Gates, off Exchange Square

Charming low-beamed and timbered 18th-c Sam Smiths pub (rebuilt here in redevelopment), all-day food including fresh oysters, no real ale (keg beers), brisk friendly service, bustling atmosphere, quieter upstairs bar with snugs and Jacobean fireplace; tables out in Shambles Square (plastic glasses), open all day. *Recommended by Ben Williams, the Didler*

Most pubs with any outside space now have some kind of smokers' shelter. There are regulations about these – for instance, they have to be substantially open to the outside air. The best have heating and lighting and are really quite comfortable.

MANCHESTER SJ8498   M4 5JZ
Smithfield
Swan Street

Clean bright refurbishment by welcoming new owners, one long room with eight
interesting ales including Phoenix and a house beer brewed by Facers, plenty of bottled
beers too, enjoyable food; good value bedrooms in nearby building, open all day.
Recommended by Chris Johnson, the Didler

MANCHESTER SJ8284   M4 1PW
Unicorn
Church Street

Friendly and relaxed four-room pub, well kept Bass and Copper Dragon from island bar,
oak panelling, lovely snug; open all day, Sun till 7pm. *Recommended by the Didler*

MARPLE SJ9389   SK6 7EJ
Hare & Hounds
Dooley Lane (A627 W)

Popular dining pub above River Goyt, modern layout and décor, some imaginative food
including good mezze, well kept Hydes ales from stainless servery, good service; sports TV,
no dogs; well behaved children welcome, open all day. *Recommended by Dennis Jones*

MARPLE SJ9588   SK6 7AY
Ring o' Bells
Church Lane; by Macclesfield Canal, Bridge 2

Popular old-fashioned local with newish licensees, canal and other local memorabilia in
four linked rooms, well kept Robinsons ales, decent food at reasonable prices, darts and
quiz nights; canalside garden, own narrowboat, open all day. *Recommended by David Hoult,
Dennis Jones*

MARPLE BRIDGE SJ9889   SK6 5LW
Hare & Hounds
*Mill Brow: from end of Town Street in centre turn left up Hollins Lane and keep on
uphill*

Comfortable and civilised stone-built country pub in lovely spot, smallish and can get
crowded, good interesting local food (not Mon, Tues) from short menu, well kept
Robinsons, log fires; garden behind. *Recommended by David Hoult, Gary Wilkinson*

MELLOR SJ9888   SK6 5PP
☆ ## Devonshire Arms
*This is the Mellor near Marple, S of Manchester; heading out of Marple on the A626
towards Glossop, Mellor is the next road after the B6102, signposted off on the right at
Marple Bridge; Longhurst Lane*

Cheerful, unpretentious and cosy, front bar with old leather-seated settles and open fire,
two small back rooms with Victorian fireplaces, well kept Robinsons ales, reliable pubby
food; children welcome, garden with waterfall tumbling into fish pond crossed by
japanese bridge, large pergola, play area on small tree-sheltered lawn; new licensee took
over in spring 2011. *Recommended by David Hoult*

MELLOR SD6530   BB2 7JR
☆ ## Millstone
The Mellor near Blackburn; Mellor Lane

Restauranty stone-built village dining pub, smart and well run, panelled bar with
comfortable lounge one side, modern dining extension the other, good food from all-day
bar meals to enterprising cooking and popular substantial Sun lunch, obliging friendly
staff, well kept Thwaites, good choice of wines by the glass, big log fire, mementoes of
former landlord and England cricketer Big Jim Smith; good bedrooms and breakfast, open
all day. *Recommended by Andy and Jill Kassube, P M Dodd*

MORECAMBE SD4264   LA4 4BZ
Midland Grand Plaza
Marine Road W

Classic art deco hotel in splendid seafront position, comfortable if unorthodox
contemporary furnishings in spacious seaview Rotunda Bar, rather pricey but enjoyable
food from interesting lancashire tapas to restaurant meals, good service; children
welcome, 44 bedrooms, open all day. *Recommended by Mr and Mrs John Taylor, Peter and
Eleanor Kenyon*

MORECAMBE SD4364   LA4 5BZ
Palatine
The Crescent

Comfortable seafront pub, enjoyable reasonably priced wholesome food, four Lancaster
ales and guests, friendly helpful staff, leather armchairs and some high tables with stools,
upstairs sea-view dining lounge. *Recommended by Pat and Tony Martin, Rev Mike Peatman*

NEWTON SD6950   BB7 3DY
Parkers Arms
B6478 7 miles N of Clitheroe

Friendly welcome from chatty landlord, good locally sourced food (suppliers listed)
from lunchtime sandwiches up, you can eat in bar or restaurant, four real ales including
Bowland, good range of wines, nice coffee and afternoon tea, log fires; children welcome,
garden with lovely views, four bedrooms, pretty spot. *Recommended by R L Borthwick,
Steve Whalley*

PRESTON SD5329   PR1 2EJ
Black Horse
Friargate

Friendly unspoilt pub in pedestrianised street, good Robinsons ales, inexpensive
lunchtime food, unusual ornate curved and mosaic-tiled Victorian main bar, panelling,
stained glass and old local photographs, two quiet cosy snugs, mirrored back area,
upstairs 1920s-style bar, good juke box; no children, open all day from 10.30am, closed
Sun evening. *Recommended by the Didler, Barbarrick*

RABY SJ3179   CH63 4JH
☆ ## Wheatsheaf
*Raby Mere Road, The Green; from A540 heading S from Heswall, turn left into Upper
Raby Road, village about a mile further*

Up to nine real ales in pretty thatched black and white pub, simply furnished rambling
rooms with homely feel, cosy central bar and nice snug formed by antique settles around
fine old fireplace, small coal fire in more spacious room, reasonably priced bar food (not
Sun or Mon evenings), à la carte menu in large restaurant (Tues-Sat evenings) in former
cowshed leading to conservatory (piped music); children welcome, dogs in bar, picnic-sets
on terrace and in pleasant back garden, open all day. *Recommended by MLR, Clive Watkin,
Maurice and Gill McMahon, Roger and Anne Newbury*

RADCLIFFE SD7608   M26 3WY
Sparking Clog
Radcliffe Moor Road

Bright and clean with welcoming friendly staff, wide choice of good value enjoyable food,
three Marstons ales. *Recommended by Ben Williams*

RAINFORD SD4898   WA11 7QT
Bottle & Glass
St Helens Road

Spacious but cosy Chef & Brewer popular with families, generous tasty food all day,
reasonable prices, good friendly staff; tables outside. *Recommended by Adrian and Dawn Collinge*

RAMSBOTTOM SD8017   BL0 0HH

☆ **Fishermans Retreat**

Twine Valley Park/Fishery signed off A56 N of Bury at Shuttleworth; Bye Road

Remote yet busy pub/restaurant, generous food all day using produce from surrounding
estate and trout lakes (they can arrange fishing), also have own land where they raise
cattle, mountain-lodge-feel bar with beams and bare-stone walls, four well kept ales, over
500 malt whiskies (some sold in shop), good wine list, small dining room, helpful friendly
staff; children welcome, a few picnic-sets with lovely valley views, closed Mon, otherwise
open all day. *Recommended by John and Helen Rushton, Brian and Anna Marsden, David Schofield,
Simon Bessell, Stuart and Sarah Barrie*

RIBCHESTER SD6535   PR3 3ZP

Ribchester Arms

B6245

Enjoyable generous food from bar snacks to imaginative specials and Sun roasts,
welcoming staff, comfortable bar and two pleasant dining rooms; children welcome,
bedrooms, tables outside with plenty of space. *Recommended by Hilary Forrest*

RILEY GREEN SD6225   PR5 0SL

☆ **Royal Oak**

A675/A6061

Cosy low-beamed three-room former coaching inn, good generous home cooking including
notable steaks and game, four well kept Thwaites ales from long back bar, friendly
efficient service, ancient stripped stone, open fires, seats from high-backed settles to red
plush armchairs on carpet, lots of nooks and crannies, soft lighting, impressive woodwork,
fresh flowers, interesting model steam engines and plenty of bric-a-brac, two comfortable
dining rooms; can get packed at weekends; tables outside, short walk from Leeds &
Liverpool Canal, footpath to Hoghton Tower, open all day Sun. *Recommended by
Eric Ruff, Yvonne and Mike Meadley, Margaret Dickinson, Norma and Noel Thomas, Mrs Cooper*

RIMINGTON SD8045   BB7 4DS

Black Bull

Rimington Lane

French-themed inn/restaurant, small red-walled bar with mixed furniture and open fire,
large smart dining room, top-notch french country cooking, attentive service, two well
kept ales including one brewed for them, good choice of wines by the glass, decent coffee,
back function room; good local walks, five bedrooms. *Recommended by Yvonne and
Mike Meadley, Peter and Liz Smalley, Margaret Dickinson, Dr Kevan Tucker, John and Eleanor Holdsworth*

ROCHDALE SD8913   OL12 0NU

Baum

Toad Lane

Old-fashioned charm, great choice of changing ales, lots of bottled beers, food from tapas
and good sandwiches to home-made casseroles etc, bare boards, old advertisements,
conservatory; garden tables, handy for Co-op Museum (reopening in 2012 after
refurbishment), open all day. *Recommended by Ken and Lynda Taylor, Henry Paulinski*

SAWLEY SD7746   BB7 4NH

☆ **Spread Eagle**

Village signed just off A59 NE of Clitheroe

Well run carefully updated dining pub by River Ribble and near substantial 12th-c abbey
ruins; low ceilings and cosy sectioning, cottagey windows, pleasing mix of nice old and
quirky modern furniture, open fire, more formal dining areas, Theakstons, Thwaites,
Timothy Taylors and a guest ale, good food (all day Sun till 7.30pm) from sandwiches up,
afternoon teas, friendly helpful service; piped music; children welcome, handy for Forest
of Bowland walks, open all day. *Recommended by R L Borthwick, Steve Whalley, Dr Kevan Tucker,
Brian and Anna Marsden and others*

SLAIDBURN SD7152 BB7 3EP

☆ **Hark to Bounty**

B6478 N of Clitheroe

Attractive old stone-built pub with homely linked rooms, some gentle refurbishment, wide choice of enjoyable fresh food from sandwiches and light dishes up, friendly hard-working young staff, four real ales, decent wines and whiskies, comfortable chairs by open fire, games room one end, restaurant the other; pleasant back garden, charming Forest of Bowland village, good walks, nine bedrooms, open all day. *Recommended by Yvonne and Mike Meadley, Michael Lamm, Norma and Noel Thomas*

SOUTHPORT SD3316 PR9 0QE

Guest House

Union Street

Old-fashioned no-frills town pub with three rambling rooms, friendly atmosphere, up to ten well kept ales, simple lunchtime food; pleasant garden. *Recommended by David Martin, David Rainey*

SOUTHPORT SD3317 PR8 1RH

Sir Henry Segrave

Lord Street

Well placed comfortable Wetherspoons, good choice of food all day, well kept cheap beer, efficient service even when busy; open from 7am till late. *Recommended by George Atkinson, Ben Williams*

STALYBRIDGE SJ9598 SK15 1RF

☆ **Station Buffet**

The Station, Rassbottom Street

Eight quickly changing ales, foreign bottled beers and farm cider in classic Victorian station buffet bar, cheap basic meals (including all day breakfast and pots of tea), cheerful and bustling with period advertisements, station photographs and other railway memorabilia on wood panelled and red walls, newspapers and magazines, cards and board games, newish conservatory, an extension into what was ladies' waiting room and part of station-master's quarters featuring original ornate ceilings and Victorian-style wallpaper; no credit cards; children till 8pm, dogs welcome, picnic-sets on sunny Platform One by the Manchester to Huddersfield line, open all day. *Recommended by Dennis Jones, the Didler, Chris Flynn, Wendy Jones, John Fiander and others*

STALYBRIDGE SJ9896 SK15 2SU

Waggon & Horses

Mottram Road

Popular family-run pub/restaurant with good choice of enjoyable generously served food, Robinsons ales, wines by the glass, Thurs quiz; children welcome. *Recommended by JCW*

STALYBRIDGE SJ9698 SK15 2AG

White House

Water Street

Traditionally refurbished beamed Hydes pub, their ales and guests kept well, friendly welcoming staff. *Recommended by Daniel Davies*

STANDISH SD5711 WN1 2XF

Crown

Not far from M6 junction 27; Platt Lane

Refurbished traditional country pub with comfortable panelled bar, impressive range of ales kept in top condition by enthusiastic landlord (regular festivals), several bottled continental beers, enjoyable food all day including grills priced and chosen by weight from chiller, good value fixed-price menu, airy dining extension and pleasant conservatory; children allowed away from bar, comfortable clean bedrooms. *Recommended by Andy Witcomb, Bill Worthington*

STOCKPORT SJ8990   SK1 2LX

☆ **Arden Arms**

Millgate Street/Corporation Street, opposite pay & display car park

Cheerful Victorian pub in handsome dark brick building, several well preserved high-ceilinged rooms off island bar (one tiny old-fashioned snug accessed through servery), good reasonably priced daytime food, half a dozen well kept Robinsons ales, friendly efficient service, tiling and panelling, two coal fires; piped pop music may obtrude; tables in sheltered courtyard with much-used smokers' shelter, open all day. *Recommended by Dennis Jones, the Didler, Mr and Mrs Butler and others*

STOCKPORT SJ8989   SK2 6NU

Blossoms

Buxton Road (A6)

Bustling main-road Victorian local, Robinsons ales including Old Tom from bar-top cask, nice home-made pies weekday lunchtimes, three rooms off corridor including attractive back lounge with handsome fireplace, pool room; open all day weekends. *Recommended by the Didler*

STOCKPORT SJ8990   SK4 1AR

Crown

Heaton Lane, Heaton Norris

Partly open-plan Victorian pub popular for its 16 well kept changing ales, also bottled beers and real cider, three cosy lounge areas off bar, spotless stylish décor, wholesome bargain lunches, darts; frequent live music; tables in cobbled courtyard, huge viaduct above. *Recommended by Chris Morris, Dennis Jones, the Didler*

STOCKPORT SJ8991   SK4 1TY

Navigation

Manchester Road (B6167, former A626)

Friendly pub refurbished under new licensees, well kept Beartown ales and a guest, farm ciders, good pies; open all day. *Recommended by the Didler, Simon Bessell*

STOCKPORT SJ8890   SK4 2NA

Nursery

Green Lane, Heaton Norris; off A6

Popular 1930s pub on narrow cobbled lane (E end of N part of Green Lane), enjoyable straightforward lunchtime food from kitchen servery on right, friendly efficient service, well kept Hydes, big bays of banquettes in panelled stained-glass front lounge, brocaded wall banquettes in back one; children welcome if eating, immaculate bowling green behind, open all day weekends. *Recommended by the Didler*

STOCKPORT SJ8990   SK1 1JT

Queens Head

Little Underbank (can be reached by steps from St Petersgate)

Splendid Victorian restoration, long and narrow, with charming separate snug and back dining area, rare brass cordials fountain, double bank of spirits taps and old spirit lamps, old posters and adverts, reasonably priced lunchtime snacks, bargain Sam Smiths, daily papers, good friendly bustle, bench seating and bare boards; famous tiny gents' upstairs; open all day, till 7pm Sun. *Recommended by the Didler*

STOCKPORT SJ8990   SK1 2BZ

Railway

Avenue Street (just off M63 junction 13, via A560)

Bright and airy L-shaped bar with up to 15 real ales (always a mild), lots of foreign beers, farm cider, no food, friendly staff, old Stockport and railway photographs, bar billiards, tables out behind; open all day. *Recommended by Dennis Jones, the Didler*

STOCKPORT SJ8990 SK1 3AY

☆ ## Red Bull
Middle Hillgate

Steps up to friendly well run local, impressive beamed and flagstoned bar with dark panelling, substantial settles and seats, open fires, lots of pictures, mirrors and brassware, traditional island servery with well kept Robinsons ales, good value home-cooked bar lunches (not Sun); has expanded into adjoining building, open all day except Sun afternoon. *Recommended by the Didler*

STOCKPORT SJ8990 SK1 1RY

Swan With Two Necks
Princes Street

Traditional welcoming local with comfortable panelled bar, back lounge with skylighting and drinking corridor, bargain pub lunches from sandwiches up, teas with home-made scones, Robinsons ales; open all day (till 6pm Sun). *Recommended by the Didler, M J Winterton*

STRINES SJ9686 SK6 7GE

Sportsmans Arms
B6101 Marple—New Mills

Pleasant well kept roadside local with panoramic Goyt Valley view from picture-window lounge bar, good ever-changing ale range, enjoyable well priced home-made food including specials board, small separate bar; children welcome, tables out on side decking, heated smokers' shelter, open all day weekends. *Recommended by David Hoult, Frank Blanchard*

TODMORDEN SD9125 OL14 8JF

Staff of Life
A646

Revitalised roadside pub in steep wooded valley, five ales including Timothy Taylors and Moorhouses, traditional food using local ingredients, bargain lunch (Mon-Fri), beams, flagstones and exposed stonework, woodburner; children welcome if eating, dogs in bar, two new bedrooms. *Recommended by Geoff Boswell*

TYLDESLEY SD6902 M29 8DG

Mort Arms
Elliott Street

Bargain Holts ales in two-room 1930s pub, etched glass and polished panelling, comfortable lounge with old local photographs, friendly staff and regulars, darts and dominoes; nice back terrace, open all day. *Recommended by the Didler*

WEST KIRBY SJ2186 CH48 4EE

White Lion
Grange Road (A540)

Interesting 17th-c sandstone building, friendly proper pub with several small beamed areas on different levels, four well kept ales including a couple of local brews, good value simple bar lunches, coal stove; no children even in attractive secluded back garden up steep stone steps, open all day. *Recommended by Clive Watkin, Calvin Morton, MLR*

WHALLEY SD7336 BB7 9SN

☆ ## Swan
King Street

Good value food, well kept ales such as Timothy Taylors Landlord and Bowland Hunters Moon and Hen Harrier, decent choice of wines by the glass and quick friendly service in large cheery bar with colourful blinds and some modern artwork, quieter room off with leather sofas and armchairs; unobtrusive piped music, games machine, Weds quiz night; disabled access, picnic-sets on back terrace and grass strip by car park, bedrooms, open all day. *Recommended by Yvonne and Mike Meadley*

WHEELTON SD6021   PR6 8HD
☆ **Dressers Arms**
Briers Brow; off A674, 2.1 miles from M61 junction 8

Traditional pub in converted cottage, eight real ales including own brew, several malt
whiskies, pubby food (all day weekends), snug low-beamed rooms with simple furnishings
on patterned carpets, handsome woodburner, newspapers and magazines, restaurant;
piped music, juke box, pool, games machine, TV; children welcome (not in bar after
9.30pm), dogs allowed in bar, picnic-sets under large umbrella on heated front terrace,
open all day till 12.30am (1am Sat). *Recommended by Yvonne and Mike Meadley, Peter Heaton,
Maurice and Gill McMahon, Ben Williams, Norma and Noel Thomas and others*

WHEELTON SD5921   PR6 8LS
Top Lock
Copthurst Lane

Picturesque spot on Leeds & Liverpool Canal, friendly hard-working staff, canal-related
décor, nine well kept ales (beer festivals), enjoyable inexpensive food all day including
curries, prompt friendly service, upstairs dining room, good value food; picnic-sets
outside. *Recommended by Peter Heaton, Brian and Anna Marsden*

WOODFORD SJ8882   SK7 1PS
Davenport Arms
A5102 Wilmslow—Poynton

Good down-to-earth country local, well kept Robinsons ales, decent pub food, snug rooms
and open fires; children allowed, tables on front terrace and in nice back garden.
Recommended by Andrew Todd

WORSLEY SD7500   M28 2ED
Barton Arms
Stablefold; just off Barton Road (B5211, handy for M60 junction 13)

Bright clean Ember Inn, popular and friendly, with good value food, Black Sheep, Timothy
Taylors Landlord and a guest; children welcome in dining areas, open all day. *Recommended
by Ben Williams*

WORSLEY SD7201   M28 1ES
Woodside
Ellenbrook Road, just off A580

Vintage Inn with several eating areas around central bar, good choice of enjoyable food all
day, well kept Thwaites and guests, decent wines by the glass, open fires; children
welcome. *Recommended by Gerry and Rosemary Dobson*

WORSTON SD7642   BB7 1QA
Calfs Head
Village signed off A59 NW of Clitheroe

Large old stone-built coaching inn, very busy with mostly older people eating wide choice
of moderately priced food including popular Sun carvery in bar and spacious conservatory
looking towards Pendle Hill, well kept ales such as Black Sheep and Jennings, friendly
attentive service, snug with coal fire; lovely big garden with summerhouse and stream,
11 comfortable bedrooms, open all day. *Recommended by E A Eaves*

WRAY SD6067   LA2 8QN
☆ **Inn at Wray**
2 miles E of Hornby off A683 Kirkby Lonsdale—Lancaster

Family-run dining pub, snug sitting room with soft leather sofas and easy chairs, further
rooms with oriental rugs on polished boards or flagstones, open fires and woodburner,
larger end room with cabinet of home-made preserves, two elegant upstairs carpeted
dining rooms with comfortably upholstered chairs around smart tables, food from

sandwiches to restaurant-style meals, Thwaites and Tirril ales; piped music; children welcome, dogs in bar, bedrooms, open all day weekends, closed Mon. *Recommended by Chris and Meredith Owen, Dr Kevan Tucker, Maurice and Gill McMahon*

WRIGHTINGTON SD5011   WN6 9QB
Rigbye Arms
3 miles from M6 junction 27; off A5209 via Robin Hood Lane and left into High Moor Lane

17th-c inn in attractive moorland setting, welcoming and relaxed, with good value generous food (all day Sun) including some interesting specials, friendly prompt service even when busy, well kept Tetleys and guests, decent wines, several carpeted rooms, open fires; garden, bowling green, regular car club meetings, open all day Sun. *Recommended by Margaret Dickinson, Yvonne and Mike Meadley, Jack Clark*

YEALAND CONYERS SD5074   LA5 9SJ
New Inn
3 miles from M6 junction 35; village signed off A6

Ivy-covered 17th-c village pub under new management, traditionally furnished cosy beamed bar, log fire, Robinsons ales and a guest, good choice of malt whiskies, two communicating dining rooms, pubby food; piped radio; children welcome, dogs in bar, picnic-sets on sheltered lawn, smokers' shelter, usefully positioned for walks through Leighton Moss RSPB reserve and up Warton Crag, open all day. *Recommended by Don Bryan*

PUBS NEAR MOTORWAY JUNCTIONS

The number at the start of each line is the number of the junction. Detailed directions are given in the entry for each pub. To help you find the pubs quickly before you're past the junction, we give the name of the chapter where you'll find the text.

M6
17: Sandbach, Old Hall (North West) 1.2 miles
19: Plumley, Smoker (North West) 2.5 miles
36: Levens, Strickland Arms (North West) 4 miles

40: Yanwath, Gate Inn (North West) 2.25 miles; Tirril, Queens Head (North West) 3.5 miles

M62
25: Hartshead, Gray Ox (North East & Yorkshire) 3.5 miles

PUBS SERVING FOOD ALL DAY

We list here all the top pubs that have told us they plan to serve food all day, even if it's only one day of the week. The individual entries for the pubs themselves show the actual details.

THE NORTH EAST & YORKSHIRE
County Durham
Aycliffe, County
Blanchland, Lord Crewe Arms
Carterway Heads, Manor House Inn
Greta Bridge, Morritt Arms

Northumberland
Weldon Bridge, Anglers Arms

Yorkshire
Blakey Ridge, Lion
Bradfield, Strines Inn
Broughton, Bull
Elslack, Tempest Arms
Grinton, Bridge Inn
Halifax, Shibden Mill
Hartshead, Gray Ox
Ledsham, Chequers
Long Preston, Maypole
Widdop, Pack Horse

THE NORTH WEST
Cheshire
Aldford, Grosvenor Arms
Astbury, Egerton Arms
Aston, Bhurtpore
Bickley Moss, Cholmondeley Arms
Bunbury, Dysart Arms
Burleydam, Combermere Arms
Burwardsley, Pheasant
Chester, Mill, Old Harkers Arms
Cotebrook, Fox & Barrel
Eaton, Plough
Lach Dennis, Duke of Portland
Macclesfield, Sutton Hall
Marton, Davenport Arms
Mobberley, Roebuck
Peover Heath, Dog
Plumley, Smoker
Tarporley, Rising Sun

Cumbria
Cartmel Fell, Masons Arms
Elterwater, Britannia
Ings, Watermill
Levens, Strickland Arms
Ravenstonedale, Black Swan
Threlkeld, Horse & Farrier

Lancashire
Bashall Eaves, Red Pump
Bispham Green, Eagle & Child
Great Mitton, Three Fishes
Longridge, Derby Arms
Nether Burrow, Highwayman
Pleasington, Clog & Billycock
Uppermill, Church Inn
Waddington, Lower Buck
Wheatley Lane, Sparrowhawk

Merseyside
Liverpool, Philharmonic Dining Rooms

Maps

Map A: Cleveland, County Durham,
        Northumberland, Tyne & Wear
        & Yorkshire

Map B: Cumbria

Map C: Cheshire, Cumbria, Greater
        Manchester, Lancashire, Merseyside
        & Yorkshire

Map D: Yorkshire

Map A

BERWICKSHIRE

BERWICK-UPON-TWEED

PEEBLES

GALASHIELS

Innerleithen

Melrose

KELSO

COLDSTREAM

Seahous

SELKIRKSHIRE

NT

Kirk Yetholm

WOOLER

JEDBURGH

HAWICK

ROXBURGHSHIRE

ALNWICK

Weldon Bridge

DUMFRIESSHIRE

Stannersburn

NORTHUMBERLAND

MORPETH

B

Wark

Barrasford

Anick

M74

Haltwhistle

Haydon Bridge

NEWCASTLE UPON TYNE

BRAMPTON

HEXHAM

CORBRIDGE

GATESHEAD

CARLISLE

Talkin

Hedley on the Hill

CONSETT

NY

Blanchland

Carterway Heads

M6

ALSTON

Durham

DURHAM

Great Salkeld

BISHOP AUCKLAND

Mungrisdale

PENRITH

A1

Threlkeld

Yanwath

Clifton

Romaldkirk

Aycliffe

KESWICK

Tirril

BARNARD CASTLE

DARLINGTON

CUMBRIA

Greta Bridge

SCOTCH CORNER

Langdale

Elterwater

Moul

Ambleside

Troutbeck

Ravenstonedale

Little

Ings

Langdale

Staveley

Grinton

NORT

Torver

Near Sawrey

Winster

KENDAL

Downholme

Constable Burton

Cartmel Fell

Bowland Bridge

Levens

SEDBERGH

Leyburn

East Witton

Witherslack

SD

C

Thornton Watla

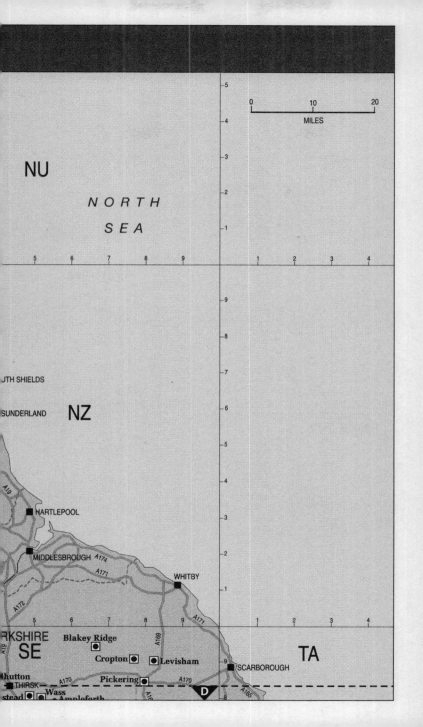

Map B

GIGHA

A83

NR

CAMPBELTOWN

A841

A R R A N

A841

BRODICK

ARDROSSAN

A8

KILMAR

A78

FIRTH OF
CLYDE

AYR

A77

A

GIRVAN

AYRSHIRE

A77

A714

NW

NEWTON STEWAR

A75

STRANRAER

WIGTOV

WIGTOWNSHIP

A747

Isle of Man

A3

A4

A2

A3

A5

DOUGLAS

0   10   20
MILES

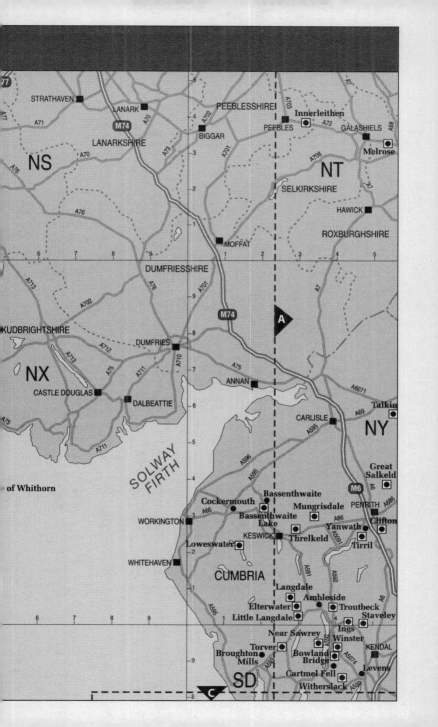

Map C

Ulverston • Nether Burrowe
Tunstall

A590
M6 A685
BARROW-IN-FURNESS
LANCASTER
LANCASHIRE
SD

Long Pres

A65

0 10 20
MILES

Whitewell
A588
A6
Wadding
A586
Bashall Eaves
Great Mitton
A59

BLACKPOOL
M55
Longridge
Wiswell
BLACKBURN
A584 PRESTON
Lytham
Pleasington M65
BURN

A59
A581
A575
A676
SOUTHPORT
Bispham Green
A5209
M61
GREATER
MANCHEST
M58
WIGAN
A560
M6
M6

MERSEYSIDE
BIRKENHEAD
Liverpool
M62
M56
WARRINGTON
RHYL
RUNCORN
M53
Mobbe
Colwyn Bay
ELLESMERE
PORT
CHESHIRE
Chelf
CONWY
A55
Llanelian
-yn-Rhos
M56
NORTHWICH
Plumley
Pec
Ty'n-y-groes
A540
Lach Dennis
He
A541
A54
DENBIGH CLWYD
Chester
Cotebrook
M6
A525
Mold
Tarporley
SH
A470
Llanferres
A494
Aldford
Bunbury
Sandba
RUTHIN
Burwardsley
A49
Spurstow
A5
BETWS-Y-COED
Gresford
A534
CREWE
WREXHAM
NANTWICH
A528 A525
Bickley Moss
GWYNEDD
SJ
Aston
Wein
Llangollen A5 Overton Bridge
Burleydam
BALA
WHITCHURCH
A41
A483
A49
MARKET DRAYT
OSWESTRY
A495
A5
A528
SHROPSHIRE NEWPO
A5
DOLGELLAU
A494
A458
A53
Chetwynd Aston
A495 POWYS
Shrewsbury
TELFORD

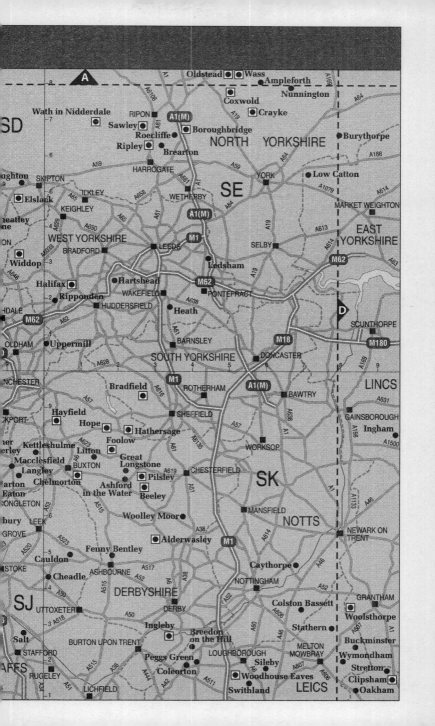

Map D

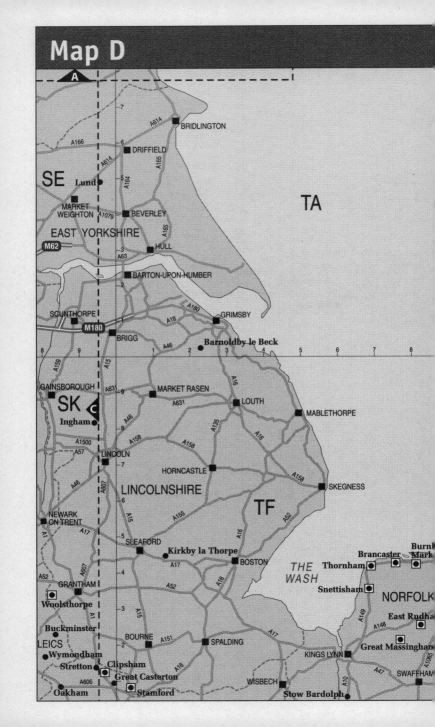

A

BRIDLINGTON
DRIFFIELD
SE Lund
MARKET WEIGHTON
BEVERLEY
EAST YORKSHIRE
M62
HULL
BARTON-UPON-HUMBER
SCUNTHORPE
M180
GRIMSBY
BRIGG
Barnoldby le Beck
GAINSBOROUGH
MARKET RASEN
SK
Ingham
LOUTH
MABLETHORPE
LINCOLN
HORNCASTLE
LINCOLNSHIRE
SKEGNESS
NEWARK ON TRENT
TF
SLEAFORD
Kirkby la Thorpe
BOSTON
Brancaster
Burn
Mark
GRANTHAM
THE WASH
Thornham
Woolsthorpe
Snettisham
NORFOLK
Buckminster
East Rudha
LEICS
Wymondham
BOURNE
SPALDING
Great Massinghan
Stretton
Clipsham
KINGS LYNN
Great Casterton
SWAFFHAM
Oakham
Stamford
WISBECH
Stow Bardolph

TA

SK

TF

Report Forms

We need to know about pubs in this edition, pubs worthy of inclusion and ones that should not be included. Sometimes pubs are dropped simply because very few readers have written to us about them. You can use the cut-out forms on the following pages, email us at **feedback@goodguides.com** or write to us and we'll gladly send you more forms:

The Good Pub Guide
FREEPOST TN1569
WADHURST
East Sussex TN5 7BR

Though we try to answer all letters, please understand if there's a delay (particularly in summer, our busiest period). We'll assume we can print your name or initials as a recommender unless you tell us otherwise.

FULL ENTRY OR OTHER GOOD PUBS?

Please try to gauge whether a pub should be a top pub with a full entry or whether it should be in the Also Worth a Visit section (and tick the relevant box). Full entries need qualities that would make it worth other readers' while to travel some distance to them. If a pub is an entirely new recommendation, the Also Worth a Visit section may be the best place for it to start its career in the *Guide* – to encourage other readers to report on it.

The more detail you can put into your description of a pub, the better. Any information on how good the landlord or landlady is, what it looks like inside, what you like about the atmosphere and character, the quality and type of food, whether the real ale is well kept and which real ales are available, whether bedrooms are available, and how big/attractive the garden is. Other things that help (if possible) include prices for food and bedrooms, food service and opening hours, and if children or dogs are welcome.

If the food or accommodation are outstanding, tick the **FOOD AWARD** or the **STAY AWARD** box.

If you're in a position to gauge a pub's suitability or otherwise for **disabled people**, do please tell us about that.

If you can, give the full address or directions for any pub not yet in the *Guide* – best of all please give us its post code. If we can't find a pub's post code, we don't include it in the *Guide*.

I have been to the following pubs in *The Good Pub Guide 2012* in the last few months, found them as described, and confirm that they deserve continued inclusion:

Continued overleaf

PLEASE GIVE YOUR NAME AND ADDRESS ON THE BACK OF THIS FORM

Pubs visited continued...

Your own name and address *(block capitals please)*

Postcode

Please return to
The Good Pub Guide,
FREEPOST TN1569,
WADHURST,
East Sussex
TN5 7BR

IF YOU PREFER, YOU CAN SEND US REPORTS
BY EMAIL:
feedback@goodguides.com

I have been to the following pubs in *The Good Pub Guide 2012* in the last few months, found them as described, and confirm that they deserve continued inclusion:

Continued overleaf

PLEASE GIVE YOUR NAME AND ADDRESS ON THE BACK OF THIS FORM

Pubs visited continued...

Your own name and address *(block capitals please)*

Postcode

Please return to
The Good Pub Guide,
FREEPOST TN1569,
WADHURST,
East Sussex
TN5 7BR

IF YOU PREFER, YOU CAN SEND US REPORTS
BY EMAIL:
feedback@goodguides.com

I have been to the following pubs in *The Good Pub Guide 2012* in the last few months, found them as described, and confirm that they deserve continued inclusion:

Continued overleaf

PLEASE GIVE YOUR NAME AND ADDRESS ON THE BACK OF THIS FORM

Pubs visited continued...

Your own name and address *(block capitals please)*

Postcode

Please return to
The Good Pub Guide,
FREEPOST TN1569,
WADHURST,
East Sussex
TN5 7BR

IF YOU PREFER, YOU CAN SEND US REPORTS
BY EMAIL:
feedback@goodguides.com

I have been to the following pubs in *The Good Pub Guide 2012* in the last few months, found them as described, and confirm that they deserve continued inclusion:

Continued overleaf

PLEASE GIVE YOUR NAME AND ADDRESS ON THE BACK OF THIS FORM

Pubs visited continued...

Your own name and address *(block capitals please)*

Postcode

Please return to
The Good Pub Guide,
FREEPOST TN1569,
WADHURST,
East Sussex
TN5 7BR

IF YOU PREFER, YOU CAN SEND US REPORTS
BY EMAIL:
feedback@goodguides.com